20th CENTURY AMERICAN FOREIGN POLICY

Security and Self-Interest

RONALD J. CARIDI
Trenton State College

PRENTICE-HALL, INC., *Englewood Cliffs, New Jersey*

Library of Congress Cataloging in Publication Data

CARIDI, RONALD J
   20th century American foreign policy.

   Includes bibliographical references.
    1. United States—Foreign relations—20th century.
I. Title.
E744.C355 1974   327.73   73-21526
ISBN 0-13-934935-9
ISBN 0-13-934927-8 (pbk.)

For
Teresa and Charles

Printed in the United States of America

10 9 8 7 6 5 4 3 2 1

PRENTICE-HALL INTERNATIONAL, INC., *London*
PRENTICE-HALL OF AUSTRALIA, PTY. LTD., *Sydney*
PRENTICE-HALL OF CANADA, LTD., *Toronto*
PRENTICE-HALL OF INDIA PRIVATE LIMITED, *New Delhi*
PRENTICE-HALL OF JAPAN, INC., *Tokyo*

ACKNOWLEDGMENTS

Acknowledgment is made to publishers and individuals for permission to reprint the following:

CHAPTER TWO

Excerpt from *The Aftermath* by Winston Churchill is used with the permission of Charles Scribner's Sons. Copyright 1929 Charles Scribner's Sons. It is also reproduced by permission of The Hamlyn Publishing Group Limited.

Excerpt from *Letters and Friendships of Sir Cecil Spring Rice*, edited by Stephen L. Gwynn, is used with the permission of Houghton Mifflin Company and with the permission of Constable and Company Ltd.

CHAPTER THREE

Excerpt from *The Proud Tower* by Barbara W. Tuchman. (Copyright © 1962, 1963, 1965 Barbara W. Tuchman. Copyright © 1966 by Macmillian Publishing Co., Inc.) It is also reproduced by permission of Hamish Hamilton Ltd., London.

33500

CHAPTER FOUR

Excerpt from *The Second World War: Their Finest Hour* by Winston Churchill is used with the permission of Houghton Mifflin Company and with the permission of Cassell & Co. Ltd.

Excerpt from *Memoirs of Cordell Hull* (Copyright 1948 by Cordell Hull) by permission of the Macmillan Publishing Co., Inc.

CHAPTER FIVE

Excerpt from *The Second World War: The Grand Alliance* by Winston Churchill is used with the permission of Houghton Mifflin Company and with the permission of Cassell & Co. Ltd.

Excerpt from *Churchill: Taken from the Diaries of Lord Moran* by Lord Moran is used with the permission of Houghton Mifflin Company and with the permission of Nutley Publications Ltd. and Lord Moran.

Excerpt from "Origins of the Cold War," by Arthur Schlesinger, Jr., *Foreign Affairs* (October 1967) is used with the permission of *Foreign Affairs* and Mr. Schlesinger.

Excerpt from Edward R. Stettinius, Jr., *Roosevelt and the Russians: The Yalta Conference*. Copyright 1949 by The Stettinius Fund, Inc. Reprinted by permission of Doubleday & Company, Inc.

CHAPTER SIX

Excerpts from *The Korean War and American Politics* by Ronald J. Caridi by permission of The University of Pennsylvania Press.

Excerpt from Henry A. Kissinger, *Nuclear Weapons and Foreign Policy*, (New York: Harper & Row, for the Council on Foreign Relations, 1957).

Excerpt from "Reminiscences," by General of the Army Douglas MacArthur, McGraw-Hill Book Co., © 1964 Time Inc. Reprinted with permission.

CHAPTER SEVEN

Excerpt from *Intervention and Revolution* by Richard J. Barnet by permission of The New American Library.

Excerpt from *Eisenhower: Captive Hero* by Marquis Childs is used with the permission of Harcourt Brace Jovanovich, Inc. and with the permission of Brandt and Brandt.

Excerpt from John Foster Dulles, "A Policy of Boldness," LIFE Magazine, © 1952 Time Inc.

Excerpt from *Full Circle* by Sir Anthony Eden is used with the permission of Houghton Mifflin Company and with the permission of Cassell & Co. Ltd.
Excerpt from *The Arrogance of Power* by J. William Fulbright. © Copyright, 1966, by J. William Fulbright and reproduced with the permission of Random House, Inc.
Excerpts from *Lyndon B. Johnson and the World* by Philip Geyelin used with the permission of the Pall Mall Press.
Excerpt from "James Reston Column" of March 6, 1968. © 1968 by The New York Times Company. Reprinted by permission.
Excerpt from *With Kennedy* by Pierre Salinger. Copyright © by Pierre Salinger. Reprinted by permission of Doubleday and Company, Inc.
Excerpts from *A Thousand Days* by Arthur Schlesinger, Jr. is used with the permission of Houghton Mifflin Company and with the permission of Andre Deutsch Ltd.
Excerpt from *Dominican Diary* by Tad Szulc. © 1965 by the Delacorte Press.

CHAPTER EIGHT

Excerpts from *The White House Years: Mandate for Change, 1953–1956* by Dwight D. Eisenhower. Copyright © 1963 by Dwight D. Eisenhower. Excerpts from *The White House Years: Waging Peace, 1956–1962* by Dwight D. Eisenhower. Copyright © 1965 by Dwight D. Eisenhower. Reprinted by permission of Doubleday & Company, Inc. and William Heinemann Ltd. Publishers.
Excerpt from *To Move A Nation* by Roger Hilsman. Copyright © 1964, 1967 by Roger Hilsman. Reprinted by permission of Doubleday & Company, Inc. and the Robert Lantz-Candida Donadio Literary Agency Inc.
Excerpt from Gabriel Kolko, "A War from Time to Time," March 6, 1973. © 1973 by The New York Times Company. Reprinted by permission.

CONTENTS

PREFACE

The fearful threat of nuclear war in the post-1945 era, and the disenchantment with United States involvement in the Indochina War, have led increasing numbers of historians to examine more critically the fundamental assumptions of American foreign policy. This re-evaluation, which began about 1960, has resulted in hundreds of "revisionist" monographs and articles challenging traditional interpretations of American diplomacy. These critiques have not been limited to the past few decades or even to the twentieth century. Rather, the handiwork of American policymakers from the colonial era to the present has been scrutinized by a cluster of doubtful, and at times cynically hostile, scholars.

These historians have been vigorously criticized for ignoring many of the generally accepted tenets of their craft; their work has been, perhaps too often, both strident and highly subjective. But for all of their shortcomings, the "revisionists" have made a meaningful contribution to the study of American history by forcing the discipline to rethink conventional wisdoms, and by providing alternative interpretations of past events. Equally important, these "New Left" scholars have suggested a theoretical framework for the consideration of contemporary issues.

I stress the revisionist critique at the outset not because this is a revisionist text. It is, rather, a text that reflects many of the alternative interpretations offered by historians dissatisfied with traditional explanations of the course of American foreign relations. The aggressively expansionist and counter-revolutionary characteristics of American diplomacy are given considerable space. To my knowledge, this is the first general text of twentieth century American foreign policy which places considerable emphasis on the work of the revisionists. It has been written in an attempt to offer the college student and the general reader a spectrum of approaches to the American diplomatic experience.

A number of libraries were helpful to me in the preparation of this study: the Rockefeller Library at Brown University, the Firestone Library at Princeton University, and the New York University Library. The Trenton State College Library staff provided valuable assistance; I am particularly grateful to Louise Fradkin of the Reference Department.

I am indebted to Adrienne Neufeld of Prentice-Hall for her creative assistance, and for her patience.

Several friends were very generous in helping me prepare the manuscript for publication: Larry Collins, Paul DuBois, Stella Evans, Karl Gottesman, Marta Kaufmann, Lillian Kessin, Kenneth Kessin, Marilyn Long, and Harriet Nelson. Without Carol Rushton's encouragement, the manuscript would not have been completed.

The University of Pennsylvania Press' cooperation in permitting me to utilize portions of my *The Korean War and American Politics* is very much appreciated.

Finally, I am most pleased to dedicate this book to my mother, Teresa Oliva, and to my brother, Charles.

Ronald J. Caridi

One

AMERICA
AS WORLD POWER

The drive for territorial and economic expansion has been a dominant theme of the American experience. The descendants and followers of those who settled Jamestown, Plymouth, and Massachusetts Bay were adventurous pragmatists whose acquisitiveness drove them beyond their legitimate boundaries and gained them an empire. The new nation wrested the Mississippi boundary from England and grasped at the opportunity to acquire Louisiana; it had the temerity to issue the Monroe Doctrine and the ruthlessness to instigate the Mexican War. Toward the close of the nineteenth century this drive became flagrantly imperialistic as the maturing nation succeeded in extending its influence from the Caribbean to China, with implications envisioned by only an astute few.

A GREAT NATIONAL ABERRATION?

There are two general approaches to nineteenth-century American imperialism. In its more narrow conception, imperialism has been viewed as the denial of one nation's sovereignty by another nation; in

1

its broader definition, control of another people's resources, trade, and markets, even if such control does not bring with it the total loss of territorial integrity and national sovereignty, is seen as imperialistic. In this chapter, the concept is utilized in its broader sense.

Some "New Left" historians, such as William Appleman Williams, have insisted that if the concepts of expansionism and imperialism are enlarged to include the economic sphere, the nation has been imperialistic from its very inception.[1] Preferring the term "colonialism" to imperialism, Walter La Feber suggests that "the United States did not set out on an expansionist path in the late 1890s in a sudden, spur-of-the-moment fashion. The overseas empire that Americans controlled in 1900 was not a break in their history, but a natural culmination. . . . Americans neither acquired this empire during a temporary absence of mind nor had the empire forced upon them." [2] Another commentator, Richard Van Alstyne, has observed that "The early colonies were no sooner established in the seventeenth century than expansionist impulses began to register in each of them. Imperial patterns took shape, and before the middle of the eighteenth century the concept of an empire that would take in the whole continent was fully formed." [3]

The three studies of American foreign policy cited here were all published during the past decade and indicate a growing tendency among American historians to attack the long-held notion that the tragic events which occurred at the close of the nineteenth century represented a temporary departure from the isolationist, anti-imperialist tradition of the nation. The contention that the United States was imperialistic from its very inception represents a sharp and fundamental break from the conventional wisdom, which has taught that prior to 1890 the nation had consistently disavowed foreign entanglements, to say nothing of outright imperialism. This view has been most closely identified with Yale historian Samuel Flagg Bemis. In the fifth edition (1965) of his *A Diplomatic History of the United States*, Bemis concludes that the issue of "outright and undisguised imperialism" was not only "the most important question in foreign policy which the nation had been called upon to decide since its independence," it was also an "absolutely new question . . . to be decided promptly in the fever-time of exuberant war feeling. . . . Looking back on those years

---

[1] See William Appleman Williams, *The Tragedy of American Diplomacy* (New York: Dell Publishing Co., 1962), pp. 18–50, and Williams, *The Roots of the Modern American Empire: A Study of the Growth and Shaping of Social Consciousness in a Marketplace Society* (New York: Random House, Inc., 1969). This is not to suggest that Williams was the first to offer this perspective.

[2] Walter La Feber, *The New Empire: An Interpretation of American Expansion, 1860–1898* (Ithaca, N.Y.: Cornell University Press, 1963), Preface.

[3] Richard W. Van Alstyne, *The Rising American Empire* (Chicago: Quadrangle, 1960), p. v.

of adolescent irresponsibility we can now see the acquisition of the Philippines, the climax of American expansion, as a great national aberration." [4] In perhaps the most popular of all American diplomatic history texts, Thomas A. Bailey asserts that in its emergence as a "great" power in the years surrounding 1898 the United States evidenced its "new-found willingness . . . to forsake isolationist traditions." [5]

The durability of the "New Left" challenge to such a reading of American foreign policy remains to be seen. And even if one accepts the validity of the new revisionist critique it must still be acknowledged that the final 20 years of the last century did constitute a departure if the sweep of the imperialist drive is taken into account. The thrust was felt in Hawaii, Samoa, Cuba, Puerto Rico, the Philippines, Panama, and China; moreover, for the first time in their history, Americans were successful in their quest for territory not contiguous to continental United States (Alaska represents an understandable exception to this generalization). Even more important, for the first time the nation acquired land heavily inhabited by people which it considered civilized (the Indian territory was neither heavily populated nor looked upon as being under civilized control). Finally, and most tragic of all, the headlong expansion of the period ignored the historic principle of self-determination—the Declaration of Independence had insisted that governments derive "their just powers from the consent of the governed."

To some extent, this accelerated expansionist thrust was the result of a rational, carefully conceived design by certain highly influential individuals within and without official government circles, men who were consciously expansionist and whose goals were sharply defined. For some of these proponents of expansion, national security was of greatest importance. They sought control of a future interoceanic canal, of potential supply stations (e.g., Samoa, Hawaii, and the Philippines) for the "new navy," and of strategically positioned enclaves of American power and influence. American dominance over vital world water highways was an abiding passion of this group. These concerns have long been considered "rational" in the face of accelerated British, French, German, and Japanese attempts to gain hegemony over much of Asia. They have also been defended as

---

[4] Samuel Flagg Bemis, *A Diplomatic History of the American People*, 5th ed. (New York: Holt, Rinehart and Winston, 1965), pp. 468, 475. Also see Bemis, "American Foreign Policy and the Blessings of Liberty," reprinted in *American Foreign Policy and the Blessings of Liberty and Other Essays* (New Haven, Conn.: Yale University Press, 1962), esp. p. 7.

[5] Thomas A. Bailey, *A Diplomatic History of the American People*, 7th ed. (New York: Appleton-Century-Crofts, 1964), p. 483.

legitimate in terms of the greatly expanded naval program which had been inaugurated in the early 1880s, when the Congress authorized large expenditures for coastal fortifications and the construction of steel warships. By 1900 the nation's projected fleet consisted of 15 cruisers and six battleships, with three of the battleships planned to be the world's most heavily armed and armored warships. It was anticipated that the completion of this naval building program would give the United States a navy equal to Germany's and more powerful than Austria-Hungary's and Italy's.[6]

The limitations of the traditional, more narrow definition of American imperialism become readily apparent in considering the economic motivations of expansionism. The Civil War had provided an enormous thrust for the American industrial machine, and within two decades of the close of the war the United States was well on its way toward achieving major industrial status. The need for markets overseas—if not colonies—seemed obvious to many. With China greatly weakened as a result of the Sino-Japanese War of 1894–95, and with a fundamental realignment of power in the Far East in the offing, it is little wonder that influential men in government and industry feared European hegemony over the potentially vast Asian market.

Such economic considerations were brought into sharp focus by the depression which followed the Panic of 1893 and which lasted, with fluctuations, until the very turn of the century. So intense was this crisis that by 1894 unemployment approached 20 percent, remained above 12 percent through 1898, and was over 6 percent in the last year of the century. Until 1898, real earnings were cut an average of 15 percent, and the drop in farm income was as severe.[7] In the past 100 years, only the Great Depression of the 1930s has been more catastrophic. The Japanese defeat of China, occurring just two years after the Panic, reinforced the determination of those who viewed overseas markets and trading partners as central to the continuance of a healthy, viable economy. The two, security and a strong economy, were often seen as inseparable. Yet since the 1936 publication of Julius Pratt's *Expansionists of 1898* historians have had to adjust this economic argument in light of Pratt's thesis that "American business had been either opposed or indifferent to the expansionist philosophy which had arisen since 1890." It was only with the onset of

---

[6] Ernest R. May, *Imperial Democracy: The Emergence of America as a Great Power* (New York: Harcourt Brace Jovanovich, 1961), p. 7.

[7] For statistics, see William Appleman Williams, *The Roots of the Modern American Empire*, p. 358.

war that a large section of the business community "converted to the belief that a program of territorial expansion would serve its purposes." [8] But so-called New Left historians have tended, despite Pratt, to return to an earlier interpretation by broadening the concept of empire to include more than overt "territorial expansion."

The economic depression had other, less obvious, influences. The anxiety which it produced, the frustration of expectations unfulfilled, contributed to the restlessness and the pugnacity of the times. Theodore Roosevelt wrote in *The Winning of the West* (1889–96) that the removal of the Indians by what amounted to a race war on the North American continent was not only justified, but represented the culmination of centuries of German and English conquest of much of the unsettled portions of the world. It has recently been demonstrated that Roosevelt's aggressiveness was shared by a large portion of the public who were hit hardest by the depression.[9]

In addition to considerations of national security and economics, there were less tangible, more subtle motivations, not the least of which was a species of jingoism which taught that if the nation was indeed great, it must prove it in a sort of primitive, Darwinian struggle. Charles Darwin's *On the Origin of Species* (1859) and *Descent of Man* (1871) were of central importance because popularizers of "natural selection" utilized the theory to justify a latter-day Manifest Destiny. Darwin had reported on the evolutionary process as it affected a select group of animals, but those seeking to defend their belief in the superiority of the Anglo-Saxon found his work most adaptable. Hence propagandists such as the popular lecturer John Fiske argued that while violence was not to be condoned, conflict (military or industrial) between superior and backward nations was inevitable; the would-be oppressor was thus handed a "scientific" justification for his aggressiveness.[10]

Ideology also played its role in the acceleration of American expansionism. While some avowed their primary concern to be the transmission of republicanism and democracy to backward nations, others were more involved with spreading Christianity (or, more specifically, Protestantism) abroad. The American Home Missionary Society, which published the Reverend Josiah Strong's *Our Country: Its Possible Future and Its Present Crisis*, was a potent force. Strong was a Congregationalist minister who, it has recently been shown, was

[8] Julius Pratt, *Expansionists of 1898* (Baltimore: The Johns Hopkins University Press, 1936), p. 233.

[9] See Williams, *The Roots of the Modern American Empire,* Chap. 15.

[10] John Fiske, *Outlines of Cosmic Philosophy* (London: Macmillan, 1874).

centrally interested in "world evangelization" by individuals rather than by conquering nations. Nevertheless, his celebration of the full-flowering of the Anglo-Saxons was useful to expansionists, especially his prediction that "this powerful race will move down upon Mexico, down upon Central and South America, out upon the islands of the sea, over upon Africa and beyond. And can anyone doubt that the result of this competition of races will be the 'survival of the fittest'?" [11] Given the prevailing Protestant attitude toward Catholicism, expansionist missionaries had an unparalleled opportunity in the Philippines, where they could both expound their conception of Christianity and undermine the role of the Catholic Church.

It is also possible to establish a direct link between the close of the frontier and American imperialism. In his tradition-shattering address to the American Historical Association in 1893, the historian Frederick Jackson Turner celebrated, although not without reservation, the enormous influence the persistent surge westward had had on American development. His "The Significance of the Frontier in American History" theorized that "the existence of an area of free land, its continuous recession, and the advance of American settlement westward explain American development." This concept of the immense and beneficial influence of the push westward not only revolutionized American historiography but doubtless encouraged those who easily ignored Turner's remarks on the detrimental effects of the frontier experience (e.g., the lawlessness and anti-intellectualism of the American), and concentrated solely on the positive consequences of the march to the Pacific. For those who defended imperialism for bringing American institutions to less developed nations, there was comfort in Turner's observation that American democracy "came stark and strong and full of life out of the American forest, and it gained new strength each time it touched a new frontier."

Turner was not an imperialist, and neither was Darwin; but like Darwin's work, Turner's thesis was conveniently adjusted to fit the current ideology. Williams argues that more than anyone else, the agriculturalists distorted the earlier definition of territorial and economic expansion:

> Given their strong traditional commitment to the marketplace conception of reality, and the experience they could so easily interpret as confirming that conception of the world, American agriculturalists

[11] Dorothea R. Muller, "Josiah Strong and American Nationalism: A Reevaluation," *Journal of American History*, LIII, No. 3 (Dec. 1966), 487–503. Josiah Strong, *Our Country: Its Possible Future and Its Present Crisis* (Cambridge, Mass.: Harvard University Press, 1963), p. 214. Originally published by The Baker and Taylor Company, New York, 1885.

moved from a continental to an overseas imperial outlook with relatively little intellectual difficulty or emotional shock.[12]

Unable to accept the economic interpretation and unconvinced by other explanations for the rise of pugnacious expansionism at the turn of the century, Richard Hofstadter has stressed less "rational" motivations. In a group of essays discussing certain "paranoid" tendencies in American politics, Hofstadter argued that the imperialist drive in the 1890s is best understood within the context of the "psychic crisis" of that decade. This climate of crisis and anxiety had been generated, in good measure, by the depression, which not only convulsed the economic system but also gave rise to a political movement—Populism—which seemed to threaten the entire social order. The public's recognition that enormous concentrations of economic power were undermining one of the most basic dogmas of the American credo, freedom of opportunity, deepened the sense of crisis. The symbolic closing of the frontier was yet another sign that the decade was witnessing a fundamental change in the nation's operative assumptions. One of the symptoms of the resultant unrest, Hofstadter claimed, was a seemingly irrational aggression which expressed itself as expansionism.[13]

American imperialism in the late nineteenth century was prompted by a hard core of individuals within and without the government whose cause was immeasurably aided by the economic depression, the crisis in Cuba, and the prevailing domestic anxiety. Given this general climate, the imperialists were soon able to secure a wide and often enthusiastic following because they seemed to fill a need, either economic, psychological, or otherwise. Their message was most tempting: Strong asserted that the Anglo-Saxon's commission was to bring democracy and Christianity to the mass of humanity, while Fiske argued that the obvious intellectual and moral superiority of the Anglo-Saxon destined that race to world supremacy. Professor John W. Burgess of Columbia University told his classes that the race from which Americans had descended was "intrusted, in the general economy of history, with the mission of conducting the political civilization of the modern world." [14] His student, Theodore Roosevelt, wrote in "The Strenuous Life" (1899) that "If we stand idly by, if we seek merely swollen, slothful ease and ignoble peace, if we shrink from the hard contests where men must win at hazard of their lives and at

---

[13] Richard Hofstadter, *The Paranoid Style in American Politics and Other Essays* (New York: Knopf, 1965), pp. 148–51.
[14] Quoted in Pratt, *Expansionists of 1898*, p. 8.
[12] Williams, *The Roots of the Modern American Empire*, p. 271.

the risk of all they hold dear, then the bolder and stronger peoples will pass us by, and will win for themselves the domination of the world." [15] That same year Senator Albert J. Beveridge announced on the Senate floor that God had made the English-speaking and Teutonic peoples adept in government so that they might "administer government among savages and senile peoples." [16]

But without a receptive public, the urging of this core group would have been without effect. As noted above, the depression did much to influence the public mood, and while there have been attempts to document the hostility or at least the indifference of American businessmen to expansion before 1898,[17] the economic interpretation has proven exceedingly hardy.[18] It is quite clear that the depression had a profound impact on the thinking of those who had previously viewed adjustments in the monetary system (e.g., free silver, gold standard) as the best way of solving the nation's economic ills. The rapid expansion of the American industrial plant after the Civil War had not been an unmixed blessing. The rememdy for overproduction and its consequences was increasingly seen to be the expansion of American trade to underdeveloped regions. This concept, together with imperialist thrusts by England, France, Germany, and Japan in Asia and Latin America, lent a note of urgency to the argument that the nation's economic problems could be cured only by opening new frontiers for American producers. In Asia, the consequences of Japan's 1895 victory over China compounded this sense of urgency, for it seemed obvious that one or more nations would quickly fill the power vacuum in Asia.[19]

Thus to deal with nineteenth-century American imperialism is to deal with its economic and territorial definitions. In some instances this imperialism took the form of outright acquisition of territory: Hawaii, the Philippines, Puerto Rico; at other times it became manifest in de facto control: Panama and Cuba. But either way, it was the result of pride, concern over prestige, and barefaced aggression. It was also the product of seemingly legitimate fears regarding the nation's security. And it was, perhaps more than anything else, the logical consequence of an economic theory about America's place in the world marketplace.

[15] See Theodore Roosevelt, *The Works of Theodore Roosevelt*, National Edition (New York: Scribner's, 1926), XIII, p. 331.

[16] Quoted in Claude Bowers, *Beveridge and the Progressive Era* (Cambridge, Mass.: Houghton Mifflin, 1932), p. 121.

[17] See Pratt, *Expansionists of 1898*.

[18] An early, and extremely influential, economic interpretation is J. A. Hobson, *Imperialism: A Study*, rev. ed. (London: Allen and Unwin, 1938).

[19] See Thomas J. McCormick, *China Market: America's Quest for Informal Empire, 1893–1901* (Chicago: Quadrangle, 1967), Chap. 2.

THE NEGATIVE SIDE OF A GREAT ISSUE

The critics of this wave of highly charged nationalism were also to be heard, and although their crusade was to end in defeat, the next century would learn to respect their views and to greatly regret their failure. The anti-imperialists were of widely divergent political backgrounds—both Gold and Bryan Democrats, New England Conscience Republicans, and independents—who were united on only one basic issue, rejection of the territorial expansion of the United States. They organized late (the Anti-Imperialist League was not founded until November of 1898) and they neither sought nor were able to control a major political party. Intellectuals, reformers, millionaires, ex-Presidents, and literary figures were all represented in this uncommonly heterogeneous group. Democratic anti-imperialists included ex-President Grover Cleveland, William Jennings Bryan, former Speaker of the House Champ Clark, and Senator Ben Tillman. From the Republican side came former President Benjamin Harrison, Senator George F. Hoar, House Speaker Thomas B. Reed, and former Secretary of State John Sherman. Reformers such as Carl Schurz, E. L. Godkin (founder of the *Nation*), Charles Francis Adams, Jr., Henry Demarest Lloyd, and Jane Addams swelled the ranks. A number of university presidents, such as Stanford's David Starr Jordan and Harvard's Charles W. Eliot were outspoken opponents of expansion. The Social Darwinist William Graham Sumner was one of the intellectuals who was active, together with William James, Charles Eliot Norton, and Thorstein Veblen. The labor leader Samuel Gompers and the steel magnate Andrew Carnegie found a common denominator in the movement. Most of the leading literary figures of the late nineteenth century were represented: Mark Twain, William Dean Howells, Edgar Lee Masters, Hamlin Garland, and Ambrose Bierce among them.[20]

Less influenced by what Hofstadter has termed the "psychic crisis" of the late nineteenth century, the crusade's most prominent members were alike in that they were old, high principled, and conservative in their insistence that both the spirit and the letter of the Constitution must not be violated.[21] They strongly believed that an

[20] Perhaps the most complex member of the group in terms of motivation was Bryan. See Paul W. Glad, *The Trumpet Soundeth: William Jennings Bryan and His Democracy* (Lincoln: University of Nebraska Press, 1960), Chap. 4. Also Paolo E. Coletta, *William Jennings Bryan: Political Evangelist, 1860–1908* (Lincoln: University of Nebraska Press, 1964).

[21] See Fred H. Harrington, "The Anti-Imperialist Movement in the United States, 1898–1900," *Mississippi Valley Historical Review*, XXII (Sept. 1935), pp. 217, 218(n).

expansionist policy which denied to the conquered the doctrine of rule by the consent of the governed acted against one of the most basic guarantees of the Constitution. They sought to preserve the old order by preventing the United States from embarking on an adventure that appeared to them to shatter precedent and to set the nation on an uncharted, dangerous course. While appreciating the economic advantages of overseas markets, the anti-imperialists asserted that colonialism was not the only method of gaining new trading partners. Cheap, attractive goods, rather than economic spheres of influence, would win an international market for surplus American production.

In the anti-imperialist view, the United States' safety was imperiled rather than made more secure by an overseas empire which went beyond the protective shield of the nation's most imposing defenses: the Atlantic and Pacific Oceans. The great cost of conquering and uplifting these far-flung colonies was a further concern. The immorality of subjugating an unwilling people provided a common principle for the movement.[22]

There has been considerable controversy over the alleged racism of the anti-imperialists, for critics have charged them with classifying peoples and nations as civilized, uncivilized, superior, and inferior; the high percentage of Southerners in the movement has not gone unnoticed.[23] It is certainly true that, like the expansionists, they did utilize such characterizations; but it is also true, as a leading student of anti-imperialism has pointed out, that few were immune to the "prevailing racism" of the late nineteenth century, and if the anti-imperialists were guilty, so was their society.[24]

Scores of anti-imperialist leagues and societies sprang up throughout the United States at the end of the century, from Boston to Detroit to Los Angeles. In 1899 the national organization, the Anti-Imperialist League, boasted a membership of 30,000, along with more than half a million "contributors." [25] But even by the League's own count, these numbers, though impressive, were insufficient to stem the jingoist tide. The movement failed in large part because of the very diverse composition of the group and because, fraught with internal contradictions, it was unable to present convincing arguments to counter the emotional appeal of the expansionists. The political power wielded by the imperialists proved another insuperable barrier

---

[22] *Ibid.,* p. 211.

[23] See Christopher Lasch, "The Anti-Imperialists, the Philippines, and the Inequality of Man," *Journal of Southern History,* XXIV (Aug. 1958), pp. 319–31.

[24] Robert L. Beisner, *Twelve Against Empire* (New York: McGraw-Hill, 1968), p. 233.

[25] See Harrington, "The Anti-Imperialist Movement . . . ," *Mississippi Valley Historical Review,* p. 223.

to success. Had the Democratic party presented a united political front against the forces of expansion, the anti-imperialists might have had some influence. But given the party's divisiveness over this issue, and its pro-war stance in 1898, a potential political counterweight could not be utilized. The decision of many of the most influential anti-imperialists to remain aloof from the national party system went far toward neutralizing the movement's effectiveness. And although the debate over territorial expansion had raged for years, the actual annexation of Hawaii, the Philippines, and Puerto Rico was accomplished with such stunning swiftness as to disarm the opponents.

Perhaps most important of all, the anti-imperialists, on the negative side of a great emotional issue, were at a tremendous disadvantage. While their opponents dramatically promised that an empire would affect the destiny and the very survival of the nation, the anti-imperialists appeared to be merely old, conservative proponents of the established order. The decade of the 1890s had, for the most part, witnessed economic failure, widespread uncertainty, and a basic reevaluation of the very assumptions governing American society. The jingoist call for a revitalized nation through overseas adventure (territorial or economic) was a welcome relief from the strains of a troubled decade. It had the appeal of a fresh promise for a new century, and William James was correct in concluding that to oppose this force was "to blow cold upon the hot excitement." [26]

SAMOA

Those who linked economic necessity or racial superiority with expansionism eventually prevailed in the policy-making centers of the nation. Their victory came at a time when the United States was seeking a broadly based expansion of its trade with the Far East, particularly in the South Pacific. A group of 14 islands midway between Australia and Hawaii, Samoa was viewed by post-Civil War expansionists as an ideal way station for an accelerated commerce with the Pacific. The near perfect harbor of Pago Pago on the island of Tutuila offered a particular attraction, while obvious German and British designs provided a keen sense of urgency.

Although American whalers and some warships had used the harbor of Pago Pago, by the close of the Civil War the islands were under the influence of British and German traders, with the Germans predominating. By 1868 the American-owned Polynesian Land

[26] Quoted in Beisner, *Twelve Against Empire*, p. 228.

Company had been formed, and it proceeded to gain control over a large portion of land on two of the largest islands. The next step, of course, was to have the United States acquire the territory in order to secure these interests. Two years after the company was formed, an American steamship line connecting San Francisco and Australia was established and it attempted to use Pago Pago as a coaling station. Although this attempt was unsuccessful, interest in the islands was aroused and the commander of the American Pacific fleet sent Commander Richard W. Meade to the area to explore its potential. Favorably impressed, Meade and the chief of Pago Pago reached an agreement in 1872 by which the United States was granted exclusive use of that harbor for naval operations. However, later that same year the Senate refused to ratify the treaty.

Undaunted, American interests on the islands, fearing a German or British seizure, convinced the Samoan chiefs to send a representative to the United States to request annexation! Once again the Senate refused to cooperate, but the Samoan representative, M. K. Le Mamea, and Secretary of State William M. Evarts did conclude a treaty of friendship which established a quasi-protectorate over the islands. Thus while the expansionists had been thwarted in their bid for formal annexation of the islands, they had accomplished their major objective: a strong foothold for the United States in the area so as to protect and enlarge economic interests there. In return the United States committed itself, however vaguely, to the use of its good offices in conflicts between Samoa and other nations. It all seemed harmless enough, but the implications in terms of the nation's future involvement in the Far East were considerable.

Understandably, both Germany and Britain sought and obtained treaties from the Samoan government the following year, assuring them control over naval stations. At the request of the island's rulers, the three powers established a joint protectorate over Samoa. This led to an uneasy truce between the three colonizers until 1884, when Germany appeared determined to seize control. An 1887 conference in Washington failed to settle the dispute since the United States refused to accede to Germany's contention that her economic position on the islands entitled her to political control. Germany then switched tactics and declared war on the Samoan king, removed him from the islands, and set up a government dominated by Germans. When Samoan rebels attacked a group of its sailors, Germany burned and shelled the rebel-controlled area, which included land owned by American nationals. President Cleveland then precipitated a full-scale debate over expansionism in Asia by referring the matter to Congress, which appropriated $500,000 to protect American life and property in Samoa and $100,000 for harbor improvements at Pago Pago.

British and American warships were by this time facing the German fleet in Samoa, but just as this tinderbox was about to explode, disaster arrived in the form of a hurricane which destroyed virtually all of the foreign warships in the area. Unwilling to undertake further risk, the three powers met in Berlin in 1889 and signed a treaty establishing tripartite control over the islands; lip service was paid to Samoan independence.[27]

American ratification of this treaty followed an intense debate between those who were loathe to see the nation disavow its tradition of non-entangling alliances and those who were unwilling to witness German domination of Samoa by default.[28] A bloody civil war in 1899, pitting German-supported natives against islanders assisted by the United States and Great Britain, failed to win a majority of Americans over to the anti-imperialist position. And so despite the 1889 treaty's recognition of the independence of the Samoan government, the civil war led to the partition of the islands into German and American Samoa. The United States took the island of Tutuila, which contains Pago Pago, along with some lesser islands; the Germans acquired the rest. Britain received the Tonga Islands from Germany, along with certain concessions in West Africa. In thus dividing the spoils, the objectives of the Polynesian Land Company were finally realized. Even President Cleveland's strong opposition to the continued occupation of the islands during his second term of office[29] did not lead to withdrawal; with McKinley in power the rationale of working for the eventual independence of the islands was dropped. Yet it was not until February of 1929 that the Congress, by joint resolution, formally declared the islands to be possessions of the United States.

THE HAWAIIAN PEAR

The chain of events leading to the annexation of American Samoa closely parallels the course of American control over Hawaii. Broadly

[27] *Public Statutes at Large of the United States* (Washington, D.C.: Government Printing Office), XXVI, pp. 1497–1507.

[28] For samples from the debate, see Richard E. Welch, Jr., *Imperialists vs. Anti-Imperialists: The Debate Over Expansionism in the 1890's* (Itasca, Ill.: F. E. Peacock, 1972), pp. 32–35.

[29] For Cleveland's opposition, see his Annual Message of 1894, reprinted in James D. Richardson, ed., *A Compilation of the Messages and Papers of the Presidents, 1789–1897* (Washington, D.C.: Government Printing Office, 1896–99), IX, p. 532.

speaking, American economic interests in both cases called for American absorption, and the American government at first refused the call. But the fear of losing the area to a foreign power, heightened by the disruptions resulting from a civil war or rebellion, led to annexation. In both cases the imperialists were opposed by President Cleveland and then found a willing ally in the McKinley Administration.

American interest in the Hawaiian Islands dates from about the close of the eighteenth century. Pacific traders took advantage of Hawaii's location between Asia and the western rim of North America and used it as a resting place, supply base, and area of trade (particularly in sandalwood, which was then traded in China). These commercial groups were soon followed by New England whalers. But it was the New England missionaries who had the first major impact on the islands. They arrived in the 1820s under the auspices of the American Board of Commissioners for Foreign Missions and successfully influenced the ruling family; if the population was not formally converted to Christianity, it did acquiesce at least to the new faith. But the influence went far beyond religion, and in a short while Americans had gained considerable cultural and political sway over the islands. An American consul was designated in 1823, and less than 20 years later, in 1842, the Tyler Administration warned that it would not permit another power to gain control over any portion of the islands. Tyler's intentions were clearly to keep the area open to American trade, and while he noted that the Hawaiian government "should be respected, and all its rights strictly and conscientiously regarded," the emphasis of his message was on Washington's commercial interests there:

> [Hawaii's] near approach to [the American] continent, and the intercourse which American vessels have with it . . . could not but create dissatisfaction on the part of the United States at any attempt by another power, should such attempt be threatened or feared, to take possession of the islands, colonize them, and subvert the native Government.[30]

The acquisition of territory along the Pacific Ocean after the war with Mexico was understandably accompanied by an increased interest in Hawaii. This concern over the eventual disposition of the islands was heightened in 1849 when the French succeeded, although only temporarily, in gaining control of Honolulu. For a while

---

[30] *Papers Relating to the Foreign Relations of the United States, 1894* (Washington, D.C.: United States Government Printing Office), Appendix II, pp. 39–41.

Congress was occupied with debates over annexation, and the Pierce Administration actually formulated plans for annexation. The Senate was offered an agreement which had been negotiated with the Hawaiian government, but the major stumbling block proved to be the provision granting the islands immediate statehood.

Frustrated in its ambitious plans for Hawaii, the Pierce Administration next attempted a commercial treaty, which was defeated by American sugar interests keenly aware that a favorable trade relationship would enable Hawaiian sugar to be imported and sold at competitive prices. A second unsuccessful attempt to secure such a treaty was made in 1867; in 1875, however, the plan met with success. By agreeing not to yield any of its territory to another power, the Hawaiian kingdom received in return the right to export sugar and other products to the United States duty free. The result was a windfall for the planters on the islands; determined to retain this favorable status with the United States, they devoted themselves to strengthening political ties, with annexation the ultimate goal. These attempts by the planters were encouraged by the American government in the 1880s. In a letter to the American minister in Hawaii, Secretary of State James G. Blaine wrote: "The Hawaiian Islands cannot be joined to the Asiatic system. If they drift from their independent station it must be toward assimilation and identification with the American system, to which they belong by the operation of natural laws, and must belong by the operation of political necessity. . . ." [31]

The letter was extraordinary in its blend of surface concern for the independence of the islands and an absolute determination to place American interest in the area above the rights of the sovereign government there. By 1887 these commercial ties were strengthened by granting to the United States exclusive rights for a naval station at Pearl River Harbor. With white Hawaiians in control of the economic life of the nation, the native rulers struggled manfully to retain the islands' sovereignty. Two years after the Pearl River Harbor agreement, Secretary of State Blaine attempted to move the Hawaiians one step closer to his goal of "assimilation and identification with the American system" by seeking Hawaiian acceptance of a treaty which would have made the islands an American protectorate. The native leaders, understandably apprehensive, refused to sign under pressure.

Given the political implications of American economic involvement in Hawaii, it is not surprising that a tariff, the McKinley Tariff of 1890, proved to be the catalyst in the assimilation process. That

[31] *Papers Relating to the Foreign Relations of the United States, 1881*, p. 638.

tariff removed the duty paid by nations importing sugar into the United States, thus giving to all sugar-producing areas the same advantage previously enjoyed by Hawaii. Even more disastrous for the sugar economy there was the bounty of two cents per pound which was paid to American sugar producers. The consequences of the sugar section of the McKinley Tariff were as swift as they were predictable: Hawaii was plunged into a severe economic depression. Adding to the turmoil was the ascension a few months later of the politically astute Princess Liliuokalani to the throne. Long an opponent of white economic and political domination of the islands, "Queen Lil" attempted in January of 1893 to rescind the existing constitution by royal order and to substitute in its place one which vested considerable political power in the hands of the natives.

Although they had sought the closest possible ties with the United States, the American planters had opposed annexation because they feared American laws would restrict their supply of Oriental labor.[32] But the McKinley Tariff had hurt them badly, and Queen Lil seemed to be taking her "Hawaii for the Hawaiians" slogan seriously. Her proposed constitution was far from democratic, but it did threaten the existing order by calling for rule by royal decree. At this time John L. Stevens, an avid supporter of Blaine's annexation plans for Hawaii, was minister to the islands and the whites solicited his aid. A revolution against the Queen was quickly organized, and under the pretext of protecting American life and property, Stevens ordered 150 men from a cruiser in Honolulu harbor, the U.S.S. *Boston*, to take positions in the port city. It was a move clearly calculated to intimidate the Queen, as was Stevens' unauthorized recognition of the revolutionary government the day after the outbreak of fighting. The show of force, coupled with the obvious, if unstated, involvement of the United States government, led the Queen to abdicate her powers. It is interesting to note that she did not surrender to the leaders of the revolution but rather to the United States, specifically mentioning that she had yielded "to the superior force of the United States." [33]

The revolution lasted all of three days, and on February 1, 1893, Minister Stevens declared Hawaii to be a protectorate of the United States, raised the American flag over the government buildings in Honolulu, and wrote Secretary of State Foster that "The Hawaiian pear is now fully ripe, and this is the golden hour for the United States to pluck it." To encourage action by the State Department the

[32] See William A. Russ, Jr., "The Role of Sugar in Hawaiian Annexation," *Pacific Historical Review*, Vol. XII (1943).

[33] Quoted in William A. Russ, Jr., *The Hawaiian Revolution* (Selingsgrove, Pa.: Susquehanna University Press, 1959), pp. 95–96.

minister warned, "If annexation does not take place promptly . . . these people, by their necessities, might be forced towards becoming a British colony." [34] The previous November Stevens had also used the threat of a British seizure to spur American action by writing to Foster that "so long as the islands retain their own independent government there remains the possibility that England or the Canadian Dominion might secure one of the Hawaiian harbors for a coaling station. Annexation excludes all dangers of this kind." However, in a recent study of America's Hawaiian policy, Merze Tate was unable to find any convincing evidence of British intent to absorb the islands into the Empire.[35]

The move for annexation gathered momentum as a commission of five whites (four Americans and an Englishman) arrived in San Francisco representing the government established by the Committee of Safety, which had proclaimed the revolution. A treaty with the United States, which called for territorial status for Hawaii, was quickly signed by Foster and presented to the Senate; the treaty was not acted upon, however, because in two weeks Harrison was to be replaced by the Democrat Grover Cleveland.

It was Cleveland who put the brakes on the annexation movement, although a good deal of the credit must go to his Secretary of State, Walter Q. Gresham. The treaty was immediately withdrawn from the Senate and James H. Blout, a former congressman from Georgia, was sent to Hawaii to investigate the course of the revolution and to recommend further action. Once in Hawaii, Blout declared Stevens' protectorate void and removed the American flag from the government buildings. Blout also reported the extent of Stevens' involvement in the "revolution":

> The earnest appeals to the American minister for military protection by the officers of that Government, after it had been recognized, show the utter absurdity of the claim that it was established by a successful revolution of the people of the Islands. . . . a majority of the people . . . earnestly desire that the government of their choice shall be restored and its independence respected.[36]

On the strength of Blout's report and Gresham's recommendation, Cleveland replaced Stevens and ordered the new minister to help restore the Queen to her throne if she would grant amnesty to those

---

[34] *Papers Relating to the Foreign Relations of the United States, 1894*, Appendix II, p. 402.

[35] *Ibid.*, p. 195. See Merze Tate, *Hawaii: Reciprocity or Annexation* (East Lansing, Mich.: Michigan State University Press, 1968), pp. 102–04.

[36] See Gresham's Oct. 18, 1893, letter to Cleveland in *Papers Relating to the Foreign Relations of the United States, 1894*, Appendix II, p. 463.

engaged in the revolution. She at first refused, then thought the better of it and agreed to Cleveland's formula. Cleveland's task was greatly complicated by the refusal of Sanford B. Dole, president of the provisional government, to yield control. It had by this time become clear that Dole and his group would not step down without a show of force, and Congress was unwilling to spill American blood to restore a monarchy. Dole's next move was to establish the Republic of Hawaii on, appropriately enough, July 4, 1894; the very constitution of the new republic authorized its president to seek a union with the United States. The Cleveland Administration promptly recognized the Republic of Hawaii, but the imperialists knew that they would have to wait out Cleveland's term before securing annexation.

The election of 1896 was one of the more interesting in American history in that it pitted the conservative former Congressman and Ohio Governor, William McKinley, against the flamboyant William Jennings Bryan who, at 36, stampeded the Democratic convention by dramatically calling for an end to the gold standard. ("You shall not press down upon the brow of labor this crown of thorns," Bryan stormed, "you shall not crucify mankind upon a cross of gold.") Large business interests led by Ohio industrialist Mark Hanna backed McKinley in a campaign that cost the Republican party in excess of $15 million. McKinley was not himself an imperialist,[37] but many of his backers were; predictably, the 1896 Republican platform contained a strong interventionist plank (vis-à-vis Cuba). It is doubtful, however, that the 1896 election represented a mandate for imperialistic policies. The flood tide of popular sentiment for expansion did not occur until a year and a half later, and it was only after Dewey's victory at Manila that the idea of retaining overseas colonies really gripped the public imagination. The election might more accurately be viewed as a mandate for the new industrialism (and its attendant philosophies) over the populist, agrarian view. Agriculture, declining in importance since the Civil War, could not overcome the power of the new industrial order.[38]

The Republican party's overt support in 1896 of American control of the Hawaiian Islands ended the last hope of the anti-imperialists, even though the new President himself was only "at the last moment" converted to annexation.[39] Furthermore, the call for Hawaii

---

[37] Two students of this question claim that McKinley became more expansionist after the war broke out. See John A. S. Grenville and George B. Young, *Politics, Strategy and American Diplomacy* (New Haven, Conn.: Yale University Press, 1966), p. 286.

[38] See Stanley L. Jones, *The Presidential Election of 1896* (Madison, Wis.: University of Wisconsin Press, 1964), Chap. 23.

[39] May, *Imperial Democracy*, p. 243.

was considerably strengthened by the threat of a Japanese takeover of the islands. By the time McKinley took office the Japanese comprised about one-fourth of the population of Hawaii and the home government was understandably aroused by official discriminatory policies against its nationals, particularly the refusal to allow them to vote. When 122 Japanese immigrants were denied admittance to the islands, their government formally protested and sent a warship to Honolulu. President McKinley and Secretary of State John Sherman then used the Japanese threat in the same way that Stevens had used the threat of a British takeover. In June of 1897 McKinley signed and reluctantly sent to the Senate a treaty calling for the annexation of Hawaii as a territory of the United States. He did not press the issue at this time, and even assured opponents of the measure that it would not pass. Ratification was blocked by "sugar men" and political and ideological opponents of annexation. This coalition was strong enough to forestall ratification until July of 1898 when the Senate was bypassed and the territory was admitted by joint resolution of the entire Congress during the Spanish-American War. It was Dewey's victory at Manila that was the turning point, and only after Congressional expansionists demonstrated (through a petition) that they had sufficient votes to annex Hawaii even without the President's support, did McKinley cave in. The joint resolution passed the House by a 209–16 margin, and the Senate by 42–21. With few exceptions, such as the New York *Evening Post*, the press was jubilant. Even religious and business journals, which in 1893 had opposed a similar scheme, were now enthusiastically favorable.[40]

WAR WITH SPAIN

The most blatant example of American imperialism and the rise of the New Manifest Destiny was the Spanish-American War. By the 1820s a series of revolts by her North American colonies had left Spain with only the islands of Cuba and Puerto Rico, and her authority in those two outposts in the Caribbean was threatened by a failure to reform the governmental structure there. Cuba had tempted American statesmen throughout the nineteenth century, and Secretary of State John Quincy Adams perhaps best summed up American designs when he wrote to the American delegation in Madrid:

> there are laws of political, as well as of physical gravitation; and if an apple, severed by the tempest from its native tree, cannot choose but fall

[40] *Ibid.*

to the ground, Cuba, forcibly disjoined from its own unnatural connection with Spain, and incapable of self-support, can gravitate only towards the North American Union, which, by the same law of nature, cannot cast her off from its bosom.[41]

Adams may have kept his metaphor fairly consistent, but he was clearly in error in thinking that Cuba would naturally gravitate toward the United States. It took a war, followed by stern threats of military occupation, to bring Cuba within the American sphere of influence.

The closest the United States dared move toward Cuba in the years prior to the Civil War was the issuance of the ill-advised Ostend Manifesto. Briefly put, during the Pierce Administration Secretary of State William L. Marcy instructed the American Minister to Spain, Pierre Soule, to offer a maximum of $130 million for Cuba. Failing this, Soule was to attempt to convince Spain to grant the island its independence; but as Marcy suspected, "the pride of Spain revolt[ed] at the proposition to sell the island of Cuba to a foreign power." [42] Soule was then instructed to meet with James Buchanan, minister to England, and John Mason, minister to France, and the three were to advise Marcy on the Cuba question. Their meeting resulted in the signing of the so-called Ostend Manifesto in October of 1854. The trio recommended that the United States first offer Spain $120 million for the "Ever Faithful Isle," and should Spain refuse once again to sell, America would then "neither . . . count the cost nor regard the odds which Spain might enlist against us." [43] In other words, the United States would forcibly wrest the island from the Spanish.

It should be noted that the "manifesto" was actually a secret message to the Secretary of State from the three ministers; it gained considerable notoriety when its contents became known to antislavery forces who saw Cuba as a breeding ground for the further expansion of "the peculiar institution." They vigorously attacked the manifesto as a plot to add more slave territory to the Union and this reaction, coupled with a setback for the Pierce Administration in the Congressional elections of 1854, led Marcy to curtail all attempts to acquire Cuba.

Meanwhile, Spain's corrupt and autocratic rule continued unabated in Cuba, accompanied by intermittent periods of revolt on the island. A Ten Years' War began toward the close of 1868 when a

[41] Ruhl F. Bartlett, ed., *The Record of American Diplomacy: Documents and Readings in the History of American Foreign Relations*, 4th ed., (New York: Knopf, 1964), p. 233.
[42] *Ibid.*, p. 240.
[43] *Ibid.*, p. 242.

rebellious faction declared Cuba to be independent and established a provisional government. Unable to rule the island effectively, Spain was at least able to thwart its self-proclaimed independence and for years the Spanish authorities and the Cubans participated in a virtual bloodbath. President Grant and his Secretary of State, Hamilton Fish, attempted to mediate the differences, but these overtures also failed. Fish met with at least partial success when in November of 1875 he informed the Spanish government that if a resolution to the fighting were not forthcoming, other governments would be forced to intervene. A copy of the communique was sent to England and several other European powers, and Spain took heart from Fish's warning:

> In the absence of any prospect of a termination of the war, or of any change in the manner in which it has been conducted on either side, [President Grant] feels that the time is at hand when it may be the duty of other Governments to intervene, solely with a view of bringing to an end a disastrous and destructive conflict, and of restoring peace in the island of Cuba.[44]

In 1878 the Spanish government offered the insurgents some concessions and, as usual, promised reforms; an uneasy truce resulted. Spain did end the practice of slavery in Cuba, but this did little to alleviate the plight of the vast majority on the island. Politically Cuba remained under Spain's autocratic military rule, and economically she was brought to the verge of ruin by high taxes and a commercial policy which not only prevented islanders from trading with such neighbors as the United States, but also taxed exports to the mother country (in seeming violation of the mercantilist theory).

The McKinley Tariff of 1894, which offered a bounty to the producers of domestic sugar, caused much suffering in Cuba. This tariff, coupled with the general depression of 1893, made the economic plight of the "Pearl of the Antilles" most acute. The pressure added by continual political restraints led to still another revolt in February of 1895. Once again a provisional republican government was established, and the insurgents gained wide control of the eastern portion of the island. Americans were directly involved in this latest revolt since Cuban exiles had established revolutionary committees to raise money, men, and moral support in the United States. The sensationalism of the American press, particularly Hearst's New York *Journal* and Pulitzer's New York *World*, played into the hands of these self-styled propagandists.[45] These journals and their imitators tended to exagger-

---

[44] *Ibid.*, p. 371.
[45] Joseph E. Wisan, *The Cuban Crisis as Reflected in the New York Press, 1895–1898* (New York: Columbia University Press, 1934), stresses the role of journalists such as Pulitzer and Hearst, but

ate the Spanish atrocities without taking sufficient note of the brutal conduct of the revolutionaries. The "scorched earth" policy was a favorite of the insurgents, who reasoned that if they could devastate the island the Spanish would be happy to yield. In so doing a considerable amount of American property was destroyed by those who calculated that the American government would intervene to save the assets of its nationals. It was also hoped that news such as the steamer *Alliance*'s having been fired upon by a Spanish gunboat would precipitate American intervention.

Exaggerated and often one-sided accounts of atrocities, interference with American shipping, the open sympathy of a portion of the press, and the propaganda of the revolutionary junta all caused the Administration to yearn for peace on the island.

A year after the outbreak of the revolution the Spanish government had made little progress in pacifying its colony and so it sent General Valeriano Weyler to Cuba. Weyler was forceful but ruthless, and his appointment led to a further deterioration of relations between Spain and the United States. For example, the General concluded that civilian support for the revolution was so widespread that it prevented the effective operation of his army. As a result he instituted a policy whereby Cubans were placed in barbed-wire reconcentration camps where they died by the thousands. Most of these civilians were women and children who daily perished from malnutrition, disease, and inadequate sanitation. Weyler was dubbed the "Butcher" by an outraged and at times hysterical American public which failed to take sufficient note of the atrocities of the roving guerrilla bands that Weyler hoped to control. Hearst's *Journal* wrote of "Weyler the brute, the devastator of haciendas, the destroyer of families, and the outrager of women. . . . Pitiless, cold, an exterminator of men. . . . There is nothing to prevent his carnal, animal brain from running riot with itself in inventing tortures and infamies of bloody debauchery." [46]

Once again it was the task of the beleaguered Cleveland to deal with the rising demand for American intervention. In June of 1895 he issued a proclamation of neutrality which simply recognized that the rebellion existed. Dissatisfied, the Congress by joint resolution in April of 1896 voted to recognize Cuban belligerency and urged that the United States attempt to mediate. Although Cleveland was opposed to any inroads upon America's neutral stance, he did authorize Secretary of State Richard Olney to offer to "co-operate with Spain in the

---

subsequent research has tended to downgrade their importance by noting that the New York press' influence was limited.

[46] *New York Journal*, Feb. 23, 1896, p. 27.

immediate pacification of the island on such a plan as, leaving Spain her rights of sovereignty, shall yet secure to the people of the island all such rights and powers of local self-government as they can reasonably ask." [47] Spain refused this offer just as the Republican party was planning to use expansionist sentiment in the country to wrest control of the White House from the ruling Democratic party.

About a year after McKinley's election a new and far more liberal government was installed in Spain, and this government offered some concessions to the insurgents. The hated Weyler was recalled, home rule was promised, and considerable political freedom was granted. But the opportunity for reconciliation had been lost, and the Cuban revolutionaries demanded a complete break. At the same time, Spanish loyalists in Cuba protested the removal of Weyler and rioted in Havana when they heard the peace terms of the new liberal regime in Madrid. Unfortunately, the United States government then decided to send a battleship to Havana to protect American lives and property and to underscore its determination to take strong action if the unrest continued.

The indiscretion of sending the *Maine* to Havana was matched by the diplomatic bumbling of the Spanish minister in Washington, Dupuy de Lôme. The infamous "de Lôme Letter" was written to a friend in Cuba, stolen by one of the revolutionaries—who undoubtedly accomplished more by that one act than he could have in a lifetime in the field—and published by Hearst's *Journal* on February 9. The letter described President McKinley as "weak and a bidder for the admiration of the crowd . . . a would-be politician who tries to leave a door open behind himself while keeping on good terms with the jingoes of his party." [48] The American public rose in self-righteous indignation and de Lôme offered his resignation before Madrid had the opportunity to demand it.

American tempers were still frayed from the de Lôme incident when, on February 15, 1898, an explosion ripped through the *Maine*, sending her to the bottom of Havana harbor. The tragedy provided a field day for the so-called yellow journals, with Hearst's paper insisting that intervention must follow if the nation was to retain its honor. Imperialists such as Assistant Secretary of the Navy Theodore Roosevelt bellowed that the sinking of the *Maine* was obviously a Spanish plot without considering that Madrid had little, if anything, to gain from the affair and had an enormous amount to lose by precipitating America's active intervention. Despite the ensuing

[47] Bartlett, *The Record of American Diplomacy*, p. 374.
[48] *Papers Relating to the Foreign Relations of the United States, 1898,* p. 1007.

uproar, the expansionists failed to win a declaration of war; rather the
Congress unanimously voted to expend $50 million for war prepara-
tions. The war fever gained strength when on March 28 a naval board
of inquiry investigating the *Maine* tragedy concluded that an explosion
from a submarine mine had sunk the battleship. The report did not
accuse Spain of setting the mine—in fact, to this day the question
remains an open one. Flying in the face of logic, the American people
concluded that Madrid was responsible. That the Cuban insurgents
had everything to gain by American intervention seems not to have
been seriously considered by most at the time.

The reaction to the de Lôme Letter and the *Maine* incident did
not obscure the impact of the continued reports of atrocities on the
island. Perhaps the most famous of these accounts was offered by
Senator Redfield Proctor of Vermont after he returned from a private
inspection tour of Cuba. A month after the sinking of the *Maine*,
Proctor reported to the Senate the plight of those who were victims of
the reconcentration policy:

> Torn from their homes, with foul earth, foul air, foul water, and foul
> food or none, what wonder that one-half have died and that one-quar-
> ter of the living are so diseased that they cannot be saved? . . . Little
> children are still walking about with arms and chest terribly emaciated,
> eyes swollen, and abdomen bloated to three times the natural size. . . .
> I was told by one of our consuls that they have been found dead about
> the markets in the morning, where they had crawled, hoping to get
> some stray bits of food from the early hucksters.[49]

The nation's mood was not difficult to judge and McKinley
recognized that he would have to move quickly if peace was to be
preserved. The American Minister to Spain, Stewart L. Woodford,
was instructed to attempt to gain Spanish acceptance of an armistice
until October 1; revocation of the reconcentration order; and, if
possible, agreement to permit the President to act as final arbiter if
peace terms were not settled by October 1. The proposal placed the
Spanish government in a precarious position. To yield nothing in the
face of American demands would almost guarantee intervention. To
yield too much would probably mean the fall of the new and liberal
government. At first Madrid hesitated and sought the aid of the
European powers, but no such aid was forthcoming. A way out of the
dilemma did present itself when the Pope offered to use his offices to
mediate between Spain and her colony. Spain then announced that
she would grant an armistice if the Pope asked for one, thereby

[49] *Congressional Record*, 55th Cong., 2nd sess., p. 2917.

allowing the government to tell its people that it had granted the armistice at the request of the Holy Father and not because of pressures from Washington. For a time it seemed as if an honorable solution had been found.

The role of the other European powers in the effort to preserve the peace is also of interest, especially the degree to which they sought to pressure Spain to come to terms with the United States. Even though the European ambassadors sent a joint note to McKinley on April 7 urging moderation, it was well known in diplomatic circles that England would not interfere with an American decision to go to war with Spain.[50] That, unfortunately, was sufficient insurance for many of the more jingoist elements in the nation.

It is difficult to assess the outcome of these enormous cross-currents of pressure had Cleveland still been in the White House. Cleveland had been able to withstand demands for the acquisition of Samoa and the Hawaiian Islands, but it is most doubtful that the pressure for the annexation of those areas even resembled the demand for war with Spain by April of 1898. Speculation aside, McKinley lost control over the nation's war fever after the *Maine* disaster.[51] The President's central political problem was that the majority of his party had adopted a decidedly expansionist stance. Looking ahead to the 1898 Congressional elections and the 1900 Presidential election, McKinley valiantly sought to preserve party unity and thereby retain the Republican majority in the Congress. In his view, the paramount task at hand was to keep Bryan and the Democrats out of the White House, for he sincerely believed that the Great Commoner's victory would result in the nation's economic ruin. McKinley did not want to intervene in Cuba and would have greatly preferred a solution in which Spain maintained sovereignty, with wide local autonomy. But as public pressure increased, particularly after the *Maine* sinking, he knew that unless he accommodated the dominant expansionist position within his party, there would follow a very serious political crisis. And so he reluctantly asked the Congress for a declaration of war.[52] McKinley's biographer suggests that while a more aggressive Chief Executive might have broken with the Congress and won the favor of the minority pacifists, "it would not have prevented war."

[50] England's strategy here had much to do with the fact that she was without a major ally in Europe and so needed America's friendship. See Charles S. Campbell, Jr., *Anglo-American Understanding, 1898–1903* (Baltimore: The Johns Hopkins University Press, 1957).

[51] See Margaret Leech, *In the Days of McKinley* (New York: Harper & Row, 1959), esp. pp. 180–85.

[52] This thesis is offered in an "interview" of Ernest R. May by a fellow historian, John A. Garraty. See Garraty, *Interpreting American History: Conversations with Historians* (New York: Macmillan, 1970), Part II, p. 79.

"The President rightly refused to abdicate his function as Commander in Chief," Leech concludes, "and leave nation, as well as party, divided and rudderless in a time of crisis." [53]

The tragedy of the Spanish-American War is compounded by Spain's capitulation to American demands regarding the reconcentration order and the armistice two days before the war message was delivered. The only demand that had not been met was for American mediation, and that was far from essential; once the armistice was in effect another country could have served as mediator. The American minister to Madrid had good reason for optimism when on April 10 he wired McKinley: "I hope that nothing will now be done to humiliate Spain, as I am satisfied that the present government is going, and is loyally ready to go, as fast and as far as it can. With your power of action sufficiently free you will win the fight on your own lines." [54] The war message had been written before Spain announced its concessions, and McKinley has been criticized for not restructuring the message to fit this new development. But it was virtually impossible for the President to make concessions since the Republican leadership had threatened to declare war without him. The only way a declaration of war could have been avoided was for Spain to have made the greatest concession, complete freedom for Cuba. And this she was not about to do.

Instead of recasting the message, the President added the following two paragraphs at the end of his appeal:

> Yesterday, and since the preparation of the foregoing message, official information was received by me that the latest decrees of the Queen Regent of Spain directs General Blanco, in order to prepare and facilitate peace, to proclaim a suspension of hostilities, the duration and details of which have not yet been communicated to me.
>
> This fact with every other pertinent consideration will, I am sure, have your just and careful attention in the solemn deliberations upon which you are about to enter. If this measure attains a successful result, then our aspirations as a Christian, peace-loving people will be realized. If it fails, it will be only another justification for our contemplated action.[55]

McKinley of course knew that the inclusion of such a statement would have no meaningful influence on the already determined Congress.

The President outlined his justification for intervention as follows:

[53] Leech, *In the Days of McKinley*, p. 185.
[54] *Papers Relating to the Foreign Relations of the United States, 1898,* p. 747.
[55] James D. Richardson, ed., *A Compilation of the Messages and Papers of the Presidents,* X, p. 67.

First. In the cause of humanity and to put an end to the barbarities, bloodshed, starvation, and horrible miseries now existing there, and which the parties to the conflict are either unable or unwilling to stop or mitigate. . . .

Second. We owe it to our citizens in Cuba to afford them that protection and indemnity for life and property which no government there can or will afford. . . .

Third. The right to intervene may be justified by the very serious injury to the commerce, trade, and business of our people, and by the wanton destruction of property and devastation of the island.

Fourth, and which is of the utmost importance. The present condition of affairs in Cuba is a constant menace to our peace and entails upon this Government an enormous expense.[56]

The war message was followed by a prolonged Senate debate, complicated by the determination of some to recognize Cuba as an independent state. Such action would have obviously constituted a serious interference with the President's prerogatives relative to the recognition of a foreign state. The attempt was beaten back and instead the Congress authorized intervention in Cuba by joint resolution. In addition, the so-called Teller Amendment, sponsored by Senator Henry M. Teller of Colorado, was passed pledging that the United States would not annex Cuba at the close of hostilities.

The Teller Amendment has satisfied some that the United States entered the war in the cause of humanity; others have seen it as a blatant piece of hypocrisy. It is difficult to support those who wish to prove American intentions were honorable, especially if the declaration of war is viewed in tandem with the series of events leading to the annexation of Puerto Rico, Guam, and the Philippines. In the past 30 years historians have come full circle in debating this point. In his classic work on the subject, the English economist J. A. Hobson wrote: "The spirit of adventure, the American 'mission of civilization,' were as forces making for Imperialism, clearly subordinate to the driving force of the economic factor. The dramatic character of the change is due to the unprecedented rapidity of the industrial revolution in the United States from the eighties onward. . . . The power of production far outstripped the actual rate of consumption, and, contrary to the older economic theory, was unable to force a corresponding increase of consumption by lowering prices." [57] The result was a search for overseas markets.

Other historians in the 1930s drew a parallel between the Cuban

56 *Ibid.*, p. 64.
57 Hobson, *Imperialism*, pp. 74–75.

intervention and the findings of Senator Gerald P. Nye that the United States had been manipulated into World War I by self-seeking bankers and industrialists who recognized the enormous profits to be made by an interventionist policy. These critics[58] insisted that the business community had been responsible for other wars, particularly the one against Spain. It was Julius W. Pratt in his *Expansionists of 1898* who refuted this assumption by arguing that businessmen did not want the war because it endangered currency stability (the Republicans at this time were challenged by Bryan's "free silver" Democrats), interrupted trade, and threatened shipping. Wall Street became "bullish" when there were signs of peace, and "bearish" when an outbreak of war seemed likely. A study of many of the publications of banking, commercial, and manufacturing interests led Pratt to conclude that businessmen were against American intervention in Cuba. It was only *after* the outbreak of hostilities that business interests acknowledged the benefits of expansion; thus, according to this interpretation, the business community did not push the United States into the war—rather it only very belatedly recognized the advantages that might accrue. It is Pratt's contention that emotional factors, rather than economic ones, motivated imperialism.[59]

This argument over how to define the business community's concern for territorial expansion has been somewhat muted by the consideration that the once reluctant businessmen soon fought for the retention of the Philippines and Hawaii, for the Americanization of the Caribbean, and for the construction of the Panama Canal. Returning to the approach first suggested by Hobson, Walter La Feber in *The New Empire* contends:

> [T]he American business community would not suddenly discover the advantage of and need for foreign markets during and after the Spanish-American War. Indeed, the American businessman's quest for these markets was one of the most striking characteristics of the national scene in the months immediately preceding the war with Spain. The results of this war provided these businessmen with new opportunities for further economic expansion. But the war did not provide the impetus for this expansion. The impetus had been provided by the impact of the industrial revolution, especially the depression that followed the panic of 1893.[60]

[58] Such as Charles A. Beard in *The Idea of National Interest* (New York: Macmillan, 1934).
[59] Pratt, *Expansionists of 1898.*
[60] La Feber, *The New Empire*, p. 379. It should be noted that the term "revisionist" is used loosely here. To some, Pratt was the true revisionist because his 1936 study challenged the existing thesis that businessmen were aggressively imperialist. Latter-day revisionists, such as La Feber, actually expanded on the economic interpretation set forth by Beard and other historians of the Progressive era—except that La Feber and others have defined the concept of "empire" more broadly.

The problem has become all the more complex since the publication in 1969 of William Appleman Williams' *The Roots of the Modern American Empire*, for this study argues that an agricultural majority, and not the more narrowly defined "commercial interests," were responsible for the acquisition of an empire. It is Williams' thesis that "the expansionist outlook that was entertained and acted upon by metropolitan American leaders during and after the 1890s was actually a crystallization in industrial form of an outlook that had been developed in agricultural terms by the agrarian majority of the country between 1860 and 1893." [61]

The war itself could have been ruled "no contest" from the very outset. The Spanish fleet was easily outclassed by the emerging American navy, which had just added four new battleships. The Spanish army and navy was ill prepared for war, and morale was as low as the line of supply was long; from the very beginning the Spanish were on the defensive.

Ironically, the most dramatic American victory was not in Cuba but in the Far East, in the Philippines. It is tempting to romanticize the role of Theodore Roosevelt (then Assistant Secretary of the Navy) in this, and other, phases of the war. Roosevelt considered Secretary of the Navy John D. Long far too conservative for his liking and so utilized his interest to secure the appointment of Commodore George Dewey as commander of the American Asiatic Squadron. On February 25, 1898, nearly two months before war had been declared, TR found himself Acting Secretary when Long went home early. The astonished Long wrote in his dairy that when he returned to his office the next day he discovered that Roosevelt had "immediately . . . launch[ed] peremptory orders: distributing ships; ordering ammunition, which there is no means to move, to places where there is no means to store it; . . . sending messages to Congress for immediate legislation, authorizing the enlistment of an unlimited number of seamen; and ordering guns from the Navy Yard at Washington to New York. . . . He has gone at things like a bull in a china shop." [62] The incident has become a legend, but too much can be made of TR's conspiratorial action since Long had two months in which to reverse the orders. McKinley's biographer is certain that Roosevelt's actions "had no actual bearing on subsequent events," except to persuade Long that "his assistant was too nervous to be entrusted with serious responsibility." [63]

[61] Williams, *The Roots of the Modern American Empire*, p. xvii.

[62] Quoted in Howard K. Beale, *Theodore Roosevelt and the Rise of America to World Power* (Baltimore: The Johns Hopkins University Press, 1956), pp. 61–62.

[63] Leech, *In the Days of McKinley*, p. 169.

When Dewey heard of the war he readied his ships and steamed into Manila Bay, where on the morning of May 1 he sank or burned the entire Spanish fleet. The War Department then decided to take possession of the Philippine capital; by mid-August the army had not only captured Manila, but had also occupied the island of Guam, whose commander at first thought the shelling to be an American salute.

The remainder of the Spanish fleet then sailed for Cuba and managed to reach Santiago harbor, where it was blockaded by the American Atlantic fleet. While the American navy guarded the entrance to Santiago Bay, 16,000 army regulars marched toward the city and by July 1 had the Spanish trapped between the outskirts of Santiago and the bay. In his attempt to escape this vise, Admiral Cervera lost all his ships—by July 16 the city was taken and the war, for all practical purposes, was over. Almost as an afterthought the American forces, flushed with victory, captured Puerto Rico, adding it to the prizes of the ten-week war. The Spanish were reduced to this pitiful condition in a predictably short period of time—their navy was destroyed and their army was under seige in Cuba and the Philippines. It is therefore not surprising that two days after the capture of Santiago, on July 18, Spain sued for peace.

GUERRILLA WARFARE

United States policies in Cuba following the capitulation of the Spanish severely strains the credibility of those who contend that Washington entered the war primarily for humanitarian reasons. It was obvious that the independence of Cuba was to be one of the conditions of peace, and it was equally obvious that the United States government could not fly in the face of the Teller Amendment by annexing the island. But other territory was involved. Puerto Rico and Guam had been captured, and Manila was in the hands of the Americans; the Teller Amendment did not apply to any of these areas. McKinley gave an early indication of his strategy when, at the end of July, the Administration outlined its terms for peace: Spanish surrender of Cuba, transfer of Puerto Rico and one of the islands in the Marianas (Guam was soon designated), and the occupation of Manila until the Philippine issue was resolved. Spain, feebly protesting this ignoble end to her once-proud empire, signed the preliminary peace terms on August 12. Formal peace negotiations began in Paris on October 1, and once again McKinley gave every indication of supporting the imperialists: a five-man commission was named, dominated by expansionist Republicans.

The major stumbling block in the negotiations was the question of the disposition of the Philippines, for it was soon decided that the islands would be retained. General Emilio Aguinaldo, exiled leader of the Filipino Katipunan underground movement against Spain,[64] met with Dewey after the spectacular American victory at Manila Bay and later insisted that he had been assured the United States had no interest in colonies; thus encouraged, Aguinaldo agreed to utilize his still potent underground force to lead another revolt against Spain. Unfortunately, the General had only Dewey's verbal assurances, which were soon supported, but again verbally, by the United States Consul General, E. Spencer Pratt. Aguinaldo was told that the Congress had ". . . made a solemn declaration disclaiming any desire to possess Cuba . . . promising to leave the country to the Cubans after having driven away the Spaniards and pacified the country. As in Cuba, so in the Philippines. Even more so, if possible; Cuba is at our door while the Philippines are 10,000 miles away!" [65]

But when Aguinaldo proclaimed an independent Philippine Republic on August 6, 1898, three months after his American-supplied forces gained substantial control over the islands, he learned that Dewey had informed Washington that the newly established government did not enjoy the support of a majority of the people and was unable to ensure domestic order. Since then, and particularly after the 1902 Senate hearings on the Philippine question, debate has raged as to the nature of Dewey's agreement with the Philippine insurgents. The Admiral steadfastly insisted that he never entered into any alliance, however informal, with Aguinaldo and certainly never established any connection between insurgent cooperation and Filipino independence. A recent history of the insurrection concludes that the two sides were operating under quite different sets of assumptions. Dewey needed native support and most probably did not think beyond the immediate necessity of defeating Spain, while the Filipinos grossly miscalculated American intentions.[66]

The group which profited most by the miscalculations of both sides and the resultant falling-out between Dewey and Aguinaldo

[64] For a fascinating study of the Katipunan movement, written by a Filipino, see Teodoro A. Agoncillo, *The Revolt of the Masses: The Story of Bonifacio and the Katipunan* (Quezon City, Philippines: University of the Philippines, 1956).

[65] Quoted in Henry F. Graff, *American Imperialism and the Philippine Insurrection* (Boston: Little, Brown, 1969), p. xi.

[66] See Leon Wolff, *Little Brown Brother: How the United States Purchased and Pacified the Philippine Islands at the Century's Turn* (Garden City, N.Y.: Doubleday, 1961), pp. 66–68.

were those who had already decided upon colonial status for the islands. McKinley shrewdly measured the political currents and supported the imperialist drive, declaring that Dewey's success had "brought us new duties and responsibilities which we must meet and discharge as becomes a great nation." He also cited, somewhat parenthetically, "the commercial opportunity to which American statesmen can not be indifferent." [67] The President toured the Midwest in early autumn and returned to Washington convinced that the American people were in favor of annexation. "We have good money, we have ample revenues, we have unquestioned national credit," he told a gathering in Hastings, Iowa, "but what we want is new markets, and as trade follows the flag it looks very much as if we were going to have new markets." [68]

In October he instructed his peace commissioners in Paris to treat the Philippines differently than Cuba (whose annexation was precluded by the Teller Amendment), for he had firmly determined to have the entire archipelago. Apologists for the President have argued that Dewey was correct in asserting that Aguinaldo was unprepared to lead his people and that the Filipinos were unfit for independence; others have claimed that Spain or Germany would have annexed the islands if the United States did not. But all of this fails to acknowledge that the American conquerer could have established a temporary protectorate over the area while readying the country for independence.

With little choice except to resume the hopeless struggle, Madrid agreed to relinquish the islands for $20,000,000—ostensibly, the sum was to reimburse Spain for a series of public improvement projects she had undertaken in her former colony.

Submission of the Treaty of Paris to the Senate unleashed one of the most bitter of all Congressional debates, a debate in which McKinley's opponents charged the President with violating the basic philosophy of the American republic. Having committed himself to annexation, the President lobbied heavily for the treaty's passage; unexpectedly, McKinley's avowed political enemy and the titular head of the Democratic party, William Jennings Bryan, came out in favor of the measure. Bryan had decided that it was preferable "to trust the American people to give independence to the Filipinos rather than to trust the accomplishment of that purpose to diplomacy with an unfriendly nation [Spain]." [69] Bryan planned to utilize the 1900

[67] Quoted in Pratt, *Expansionists of 1898*, pp. 335–36.
[68] Quoted in Leech, *In the Days of McKinley*, p. 341.
[69] Quoted in Glad, *The Trumpet Soundeth*, p. 72.

election as the great test of public support for expansion. The effect of Bryan's support of the treaty remains in question, but when it was ratified, it was by only one vote more than the requisite two-thirds.

The American public was as divided as the Senate, and the anti-imperialists, after a late start organizing, marshalled their forces and hurled verbal and written brickbats at the expansionists.[70] But only a week after ratifying the treaty, the Senate vote on a resolution calling for Philippine independence ended in a tie which was broken by a vote cast by McKinley's ardently expansionist Vice President, Theodore Roosevelt.

Two days before passage of the Treaty of Paris, Aguinaldo and his followers began a long and bitter struggle to free the archipelago from colonial, now American, rule. The resultant conflict lasted four years, cost more than $600,000,000 and slaughtered over 4,000 Americans and perhaps 20,000 Filipinos.[71] In this jungle guerrilla warfare the insurgents soon discovered that the new colonialists could be just as brutal and repressive as the Spanish had been. Civilians were murdered, native huts were burned around the heads of women, children, and the aged, and the agricultural base of the country was critically weakened by the extensive physical destruction. Concentration camps were established reminiscent of Spain's reconcentrado policies in Cuba; captives were tortured; and many civilians, as well as prisoners of war, were summarily executed. Perhaps the most shocking American atrocity was the so-called water cure, used to force captured Filipino insurgents to confess secret information. A witness of the "cure" described it at a Senate hearing:

> [O]ne of the scouts for the Americans grabbed one of the men by the head and jerked his head back, and then they took a tomato can and poured water down his throat until he could hold no more, and during this time one of the natives had a rattan whip, about as large as my finger, and he struck him on the face and on the bare back, and every time they would strike him it would raise a large welt, and some blood would come. And when this native could hold no more water, then they forced a gag into his mouth; they stood him up and tied his hands behind him; they stood him up against a post and fastened him so he could not move. Then one man, an American soldier, who was over six feet tall, and who was very strong, too, struck this native in the pit of the stomach as hard as he could strike him, just as rapidly as he could. It seemed as if he didn't tire of striking him.[72]

[70] See above, pp. 9–11.
[71] Wolff, *Little Brown Brother*, p. 360.
[72] Testimony in Richard Hofstadter, ed., *American Violence* (New York: Knopf, 1970), pp. 285–86. Also Graff, *American Imperialism and the Philippine Insurrection*, p. 81.

Mounting public and Congressional concern over the conduct and implication of the war forced expansionist Senator Henry Cabot Lodge, Chairman of the Committee on the Philippines, reluctantly to initiate a full-scaled hearing in late January, 1902. Admiral Dewey, William Howard Taft (then civil governor of the Philippine Islands and later President of the United States), and scores of military and civilian personnel involved in the insurrection were recalled from the islands to testify. Since three of the committee's members were anti-imperialist Democrats who sharply questioned all witnesses, the hearing was far from perfunctory. These, often bitter attacks on American policy, however, were of limited impact since the hearing was closed to the public and the press, leaving the American people generally unaware of the most tragic atrocities of the war.[73]

The Democratic party attempted to capitalize on the war-weariness and limited anti-imperialist sentiment of the country by including in the 1900 platform the premise "that any government not based upon the consent of the governed is a tyranny; and that to impose upon any people a government of force is to substitute the methods of imperialism for those of a republic."[74] But Bryan was once again defeated by McKinley—the return of prosperity after the economic doldrums of the early 1890s was an unbeatable issue.

The Spanish-American War has been viewed as a watershed in American history, and rightly so. The proponents of expansionism, imperialism, and colonialism had triumphed over those calling for moderation and a policy that more closely reflected basic American principles, if not practices. The United States had acquired the responsibilities of an empire 6,000 miles from its Pacific coast without realizing the commercial gains that had been anticipated. Far more important, the new territory represented a military and diplomatic liability which hampered rather than expanded the nation's ability to control its own destiny.

EXPANDING PACIFIC INFLUENCE

Less than a year after the end of the war with Spain, American economic expansionism, this time directed toward China, was again manifest in the form of the first of the so-called Open-Door Notes. American interest in the Orient had been in evidence since the end of

[73] See *Hearings Before the Senate Committee on the Philippines*, Senate Document 331, 57th Cong., 1st sess. (1902). Important sections of the testimony are in Graff, *American Imperialism and the Philippine Insurrection.*

[74] See Kirk H. Porter, *National Party Platforms* (New York: Macmillan, 1924), pp. 210–11.

the eighteenth century, but it was not until the British defeated China in the Opium War (1839–1842) that the United States saw the clear possibility of establishing trading "priviliges" in the area. The attempt by Chinese authorities to limit British commercial and political influence had led to the Opium War, but the Chinese were defeated and by the Treaty of Nanking (1842) England was awarded the island of Hong Kong and free trade with four ports (plus Canton). Further indignities were heaped upon the Chinese, such as forcing them to repay England the cost of prosecuting the war, granting England control of the duty rate, and acknowledging the right of European consuls in so-called international settlements to try cases, even those involving Chinese nationals. The following year the British negotiated a most-favored-nation treaty which gave to England and any other country having treaties with the Chinese the same privileges that any other foreign nation might enjoy in China.

The American government wasted little time in negotiating similar agreements with the now weakened China. The Tyler Administration, whose foreign relations were directed by Secretary of State Daniel Webster, sent Caleb Cushing to China to win concessions equal to those enjoyed by the British. Cushing was instructed by Webster to "signify, in decided terms and a positive manner, that the Government of the United States would find it impossible to remain on terms of friendship and regard with the Emperor, if greater privileges or commercial facilities should be allowed to the subject of any other Government than should be granted to the citizens of the United States. . . ." [75] By such a standard, the Secretary of State could not have been disappointed in Cushing's work, for by the Treaty of Wanghia (1844) the five Chinese treaty ports of Canton, Amoy, Fuchow, Ningpo, and Shanghai were opened to American trade; consuls could be appointed; and Americans could own property in the port cities. The extent of the infringement upon Chinese sovereignty can be demonstrated by the award of "extra-territoriality." Under the treaty China waived its right to try American nationals. In addition, the tariff was set at a very low rate, and could not be changed except by American consent. The treaty also contained a most-favored-nation clause.

The decade of the 1840s witnessed not only the establishment of important American trading privileges in China, but also an increased interest in the Pacific area because of the acquisition of Oregon and California. The American and British governments settled their differences over Oregon in 1846 and the United States wrested

[75] Bartlett, *The Record of American Diplomacy*, p. 260.

California and other valuable real estate from Mexico by 1848. With over a thousand miles of Pacific coastline and with several important harbor areas (particularly San Francisco Bay and the Puget Sound), it was not surprising that the following decade would experience a sharpened awareness of Pacific interests. Because favorable trade relations with China were assured for the foreseeable future, Japan became the target of considerable attention. Japan lay within the China-San Francisco axis and was therefore a convenient coaling and supply station; more importantly, it was tempting to speculate on that nation's future as a trading partner. But from at least the conclusion of the eighteenth century Japan had expressed a decided distaste for foreigners. American, British, and Russian diplomats had attempted to secure contacts and trading agreements without success, while shipwrecked sailors were often imprisoned and cruelly treated, if not killed.

American success in "opening" Japan was greatly aided by British and Russian interest in the area and by the presence of warships from those nations in Japanese harbors. Early in 1852 President Millard Fillmore appointed Commodore Matthew C. Perry special envoy to Japan, sending him to the country at the head of a naval expedition. Perry's instructions were specific regarding American aims in the area: (1) arrange for the protection of American lives and property when ships were wrecked off the Japanese islands or driven into Japanese ports during foul weather; (2) obtain permission to provision American ships on the islands; and (3) negotiate trading privileges.[76]

Perry first arrived in Japan in the summer of 1853 and, after outlining his government's position regarding trade and other matters, withdrew to China until February of the following year. The American show of naval force, the urging of Perry, the presence of foreign warships (particularly the Russian fleet which appeared off Nagasaki in August, 1853), and the rise of the commercial-urban class in Japan, all combined to pressure Japan into signing a Treaty of Peace, Amity, and Commerce in March of 1854. The treaty is more important for its implications than for its content. It provided for restricted trade at two rather isolated ports, an American consul at one of the ports, and humane treatment for shipwrecked sailors. The 1854 treaty also contained the famous most-favored-nation clause:

> It is agreed that if at any future day the government of Japan shall grant to any other nation or nations privileges and advantages which are not herein granted to the United States and the citizens thereof,

[76] *Ibid.*, p. 269.

that these same privileges and advantages shall be granted likewise to the United States and to the citizens thereof, without any consultation or delay.[77]

This document did not, however, adequately reflect the importance of the opening of Japan to the Western world, a breakthrough that soon led to a treaty of far greater magnitude.[78]

The first American consul to Japan was the New York businessman Townsend Harris who in 1858 concluded a treaty with Japan which opened several additional ports, provided for the appointment of consuls to each port, widened trade, and permitted Americans to own property in the treaty ports.[79]

The diplomatic and, more importantly, commercial advantages sought and partially secured in the Far East in the nineteenth century have traditionally been viewed as attempts to selflessly (rather than selfishly) secure the "territorial integrity" of China and Japan so as to ensure an "open-door" policy vis-à-vis international trade. But "revisionists" have been pointing out that the reason the United States adopted the Open Door policy instead of a more aggressive commercial posture was its inability to compete with its more powerful European rivals.[80] America's China Policy was not that of a strong nation attempting to retain its hegemony over a trading area but rather that of a comparatively weak nation (in the Pacific) utilizing, as it had done so often before, the realities of world power for its own advantage.

The clamor of the Western powers for commercial interests in the Far East was intensified by the territorial intrigues of the Oriental nations. Korea was of particular interest to China, Japan, and Russia during this period, and by 1876 Japan had forced Korea to sign a treaty declaring itself to be an independent state. China's claim to a special interest in the area was thereby set aside. For nearly 20 years after the signing of this treaty, tension mounted between China and Japan, leading both to station troops in Korea. An outbreak of hostilities was inevitable, and in August of 1894 Japan declared war on China, executed several spectacular land and naval victories, and forced the China giant to surrender in less than a year. Japan then exacted severe peace terms: the independence of Korea; cession of

---

[77] *Public Statutes at Large of the United States*, XI, p. 598.

[78] For Perry's own account of the mission, see Roger Pineau, ed., *The Japan Expedition, 1852–1854: The Personal Journal of Commodore Matthew C. Perry* (Washington, D.C.: Smithsonian Institution Press, 1968).

[79] *Public Statutes at Large of the United States*, XII, pp. 1051–68 for the text of the so-called Townsend Treaty.

[80] La Feber, *The New Empire*, pp. 43–44.

part of Manchuria, Formosa, and the Pescadores Islands; economic privileges; and war reparations. Alarmed by this marked increase in Japanese influence in China, three of the great powers, Russia, France, and Germany, intervened immediately after the Treaty of Shimonoseki was signed and forced Japan to return that area of Manchuria which she had claimed as a war prize.

These three powers soon demonstrated that the advantages they wished to deny to the Japanese were advantages which they sought for themselves. China was exhausted from the war, leaving Germany free to demand exclusive mining rights, coaling stations, and control over the building of railroads in that portion of China which she considered to be within her sphere of influence. Russia insisted upon similar privileges in the Port Arthur area while France solidified her control over the peninsula of Indo-China. England was placed in a most difficult position by these new demands since she had been the major trading power in China, enjoying at the height of her influence about 80 percent of the China trade. At first she hoped to maintain the Open Door policy but quickly saw that the concessions already granted to the other great powers had doomed such a policy. Britain's alternative was either to demand a sphere for herself as soon as possible or to seek the cooperation of another power—the United States was the most likely candidate—to block the spreading influence of her European rivals. In March of 1898 the British Foreign Office asked American cooperation in maintaining the Open Door, but the overture was rebuffed. The pressure of the Cuban crisis and the disinclination of the McKinley Administration to enter into an alliance with a foreign power doomed the British effort. As a result England adopted the strategy of her European competitors and established her own strong sphere of influence in China.

With the conclusion of the Spanish-American War the United States joined the ranks of the imperialist powers in the Far East. Interest in increased trade with the area, and especially with China (whose population at that time numbered approximately 400,000,000), was an understandable consequence of the nation's Pacific status. The Open Door philosophy of England now became of considerable interest to a nation eager for trade with China but without a sphere of its own. Faced with the necessity of formulating an Asian policy, McKinley's new Secretary of State, John Hay, turned to his adviser on Far Eastern affairs, William W. Rockhill, who, in turn, sought the advice of an old English friend, Alfred E. Hippisley. Hippisley was employed by China's Imperial Maritime Customs Service, and so was theoretically opposed to the system of spheres. Although he realized that economic imperialism via spheres was already deeply established, Hippisley's ties to the customs service led him to favor the retention of the Chinese treaty tariff as it applied to all foreign goods entering the ports within each sphere.[81] The concept seemed to fit very neatly into the designs of the McKinley Administration, which recognized that it would be impossible to dismantle the sphere arrangement. The President hoped to ensure free trade within each sphere without interfering with the railroad, mining, and other investment privileges of the various nations with China interests.

The United States was ready for such a concept. Since the nation had little excess capital to invest abroad in railways and mining schemes, trade was its most important consideration. The spectacular rate of American economic growth in these years provided excellent domestic investment opportunities for those Americans with surplus capital. However, in enunciating the McKinley Administration's policy, Secretary of State Hay went far beyond offering to cooperate in a free-trade arrangement in China. Instead, Hay included (in the second Open Door Note) a strong expression of American interest in the preservation of China's territorial and administrative integrity.

The first Open Door Note was sent to Germany, England, and Russia on September 6, 1899, and to France, Japan, and Italy in November. The note was a precisely worded proposal:

> First. [Each of the nations addressed] will in no way interfere with any treaty port or any vested interest within any so-called "sphere of interest" or leased territory it may have in China.
>
> Second. That the Chinese treaty tariff of the time being shall apply to all merchandise landed or shipped to all such ports as are within said "sphere of interest" (unless they be "free ports"), no matter to what nationality it may belong, and that duties so leviable shall be collected by the Chinese Government.
>
> Third. That it will levy no higher harbor dues on vessels of another nationality frequenting any port in such "sphere" than shall be levied on vessels of its own nationality, and no higher railroad charges over lines built, controlled, or operated within its "sphere" on merchandise belonging to citizens or subjects of other nationalities. . . .[82]

Hay's confident expectation of a favorable reaction to his proposal was not forthcoming. Only Italy, which did not enjoy a sphere in China, found the proposal acceptable. London replied that it would agree to the declaration regarding the treatment of foreign trade "provided that a similar declaration is made by other powers

---

[81] For a discussion of Hippisley's role in the Open Door Notes, see George Kennan, *American Diplomacy; 1900–1950* (New York: The New American Library, 1951), pp. 23–37.

[82] *Papers Relating to the Foreign Policy of the United States, 1899,* pp. 129–30.

concerned." Japan also gave assurances that "the Imperial Government will have no hesitation to give their assent to so just and fair a proposal of the United States, provided that all the other powers concerned shall accept the same." The German government replied that if "the other powers interested in the industrial development of the Chinese Empire are willing to recognize the same principles, this can only be desired by the Imperial Government." The uniformity of the replies was marred by the Russian note, which was decidedly hostile to the idea and agreed to the formula only as it applied to ports "which lie beyond the territory leased to Russia" and only "upon condition that a similar declaration shall be made by other powers having interests in China." [83] Those nations which had given qualified replies based on the acceptance of all other nations concerned were thus released from any obligation. Nevertheless, Hay acted as if the Russian response were sufficiently vague to warrant an announcement that all nations had agreed to the principles set forth in the Open Door Note!

The Open Door Note of 1899 was clearly selfish in design and execution. It was an attempt to secure trading rights for Americans in areas of China where they would have been excluded or at very least would have operated at a disadvantage. It was not an attempt to open all of China's ports to a free-trade policy; it was not an attempt to undermine the "sphere of influence" system—in fact it accepted much of that system; and it certainly was not an attempt to guarantee the territorial rights of China.

The second Open Door Note (1900) went far beyond considerations of commercial advantage and represented a dangerous and misguided attempt to insure the territorial and administrative integrity of a vast and crumbling empire. The immediate impetus for this excursion into missionary diplomacy was the so-called Boxer Rebellion of 1900. The "Boxers" were Chinese nationals, fanatic jingoes determined to launch a bloody crusade against foreign influence in China. Whites were murdered, the possessions of foreigners were destroyed, and the legations of the Western powers were beseiged. In an attempt to restore stability the European nations sent an international force of nearly 20,000 men to rescue their nationals and legations (the United States contributed 2,500 men). Hay feared that once order was restored the other participating nations, England, France, Russia, Germany, and Japan, would utilize the presence of their troops in China to expand their influence; Russia, for example, was soon to assume virtual control over all of Manchuria. In an

[83] Replies printed in *Ibid.*, pp. 131–42.

attempt to forestall this eventuality, the second Open Door Note was circulated on July 3, 1900.

The scope of this statement far exceeded the implications of the first message. Hay first outlined the reasons for American participation in the international rescue force so as to assure the other nations concerned that America's objectives were both limited and altruistic. This introduction was followed by a new principle which placed the United States in the strange position of proposing to guarantee the integrity of an empire being dismantled by powers whose collective strength far exceeded that of the United States. That is to say, Hay informed the concerned powers that

> the policy of the Government of the United States is to seek a solution [to the disorder] which may bring about permanent safety and peace to China, preserve Chinese territorial and administrative entity, protect all rights guaranteed to friendly powers by treaty and international law, and safeguard for the world the principle of equal and impartial trade with all parts of the Chinese Empire.[84]

Unwilling to risk the blunt refusal of the other powers, Hay constructed the second note so that it did not require a reply. This was most probably for the best since to do otherwise would have invited needless humiliation. It is clear that China was kept reasonably intact not because of the moral suasion of the Open Door Notes, but rather because of the imperialist powers' distrust of one another; an additional factor which permitted the Chinese Empire to enjoy some degree of territorial and administrative integrity by the opening of the twentieth century was the powers' desire to prevent open warfare over the division of the China spoils. It is therefore not surprising that historians have discounted Hay's contention that he had "accomplished a good deal in the East . . . thus far without the expense of a single commitment or promise." [85] H. Whitney Griswold's conclusion in *The Far Eastern Policy of the United States* reflects a general consensus: "Hay had not secured anything approaching an international guarantee of the open door or the 'territorial and administrative entity' of China. He had merely oriented American policy toward a more active participation in Far Eastern politics in support of those principles. In so doing he had kept pace with the expansionist forces (of which he was as much product as cause) that had propelled the United States into the conquest and annexation of the Philippines." [86]

---

[84] *Papers Relating to the Foreign Relations of the United States, 1901*, Appendix, p. 12.

[85] Quoted in Tyler Dennett, *John Hay* (New York: Dodd, Mead, 1933), p. 406.

[86] A. Whitney Griswold, *The Far Eastern Policy of the United States* (New Haven, Conn.: Yale University Press, 1962), p. 86.

In the years following the circulation of the Open Door Notes the United States entered into a series of agreements with China and Japan. Japan's success in the Russo-Japanese War, and particularly her increased control over Korea, caused the Roosevelt Administration to fear Japanese designs on the Philippines. These fears were allayed by the signing of the Taft-Katsura Agreement in 1905 (William Howard Taft was Secretary of War and Count Taro Katsura was Prime Minister of Japan). The United States acquiesced to Japan's takeover of Korea and in return Katsura "confirmed in the strongest terms the correctness of [Taft's] views [that] Japan's only interest in the Philippines would be . . . to have these islands governed by a strong and friendly nation like the United States." [87] The agreement was based upon Roosevelt's clear recognition that it would have been virtually impossible to rescue Korea from Japan.

Roosevelt helped to further solidify Japan's position in the Far East with the signing of the so-called Root-Takahira Agreement in 1908. Here the United States pledged to support the "existing status quo" in the Pacific; "to respect the territorial possessions belonging to each other [Japan and the United States] in said region"; "to preserve . . . by all pacific means at their disposal the independence and integrity of China and the principle of equal opportunity for commerce and industry of all nations in that Empire"; and "to communicate with each other in order to arrive at an understanding as to what measures they may consider . . . useful to take" should any event occur threatening the status quo.[88] While the agreement admittedly provided further guarantees for continued American control over the Philippines, it was a long step toward the dismantling of the Open Door policy. The two powers had pledged to respect the integrity of China, but also to maintain the status quo—and at that time the status quo included Japan's control over Manchuria. Once again the Roosevelt Administration recognized that: (a) the United States had little or nothing to lose by agreeing to continued Japanese control over Korea and Manchuria; and (b) the United States would set aside its avowed principles in the Far East for the protection of its own interests. Roosevelt himself wrote to Taft in 1910 that "the 'Open Door' policy, as a matter of fact, completely disappears as soon as a powerful nation determines to disregard it, and is willing to run the risk of war rather than forego its intention." [89]

[87] Bartlett, The Record of American Diplomacy, p. 414.
[88] Papers Relating to the Foreign Relations of the United States, 1908, pp. 511–12.
[89] Quoted in Griswold, The Far Eastern Policy of the United States, p. 132.

HIGHWAY OF CIVILIZATION

Another body of water, the Caribbean, occupied the attention of American policy-makers during the period of American expansionism at the turn of the century. With the "successful" resolution of the Cuban issue the United States once again became interested in an isthmian canal. Without a waterway between the oceans, passage from East Coast to West Coast involved either an arduous overland trip or a long and dangerous voyage around the tip of South America. A half-century before the war with Spain the United States had attempted to gain access to the passage between the oceans. At mid-century the successful conclusion of the Mexican-American War and the acquisition of a portion of Oregon provided the United States with obvious reasons for concern over the fate of the isthmus. The discovery of gold in California and the resultant migration west added to the pressure for American control.

In December of 1846 the United States concluded a treaty with Colombia (then called New Granada) which provided for transit rights in the Panama area in return for a pledge to maintain the neutrality of the route.[90] New Granada was most anxious to ratify such an agreement because of its fear that an imperialist power might wrest the isthmus from her. The treaty was passed by the Senate in 1848, and seven years later a 48-mile railroad connecting the two oceans was completed by the United States. A second route across the isthmus, and long considered to be the better route, was controlled by Nicaragua. Like New Granada, Nicaragua feared a British takeover of this territory and so signed an unauthorized treaty with the United States, exchanging exclusive rights over the area for guarantees of Nicaraguan sovereignty. American determination to gain hegemony over the isthmus increased when it was rumored that Mexico was about to transfer the peninsula of Yucatan to England.

The desire for American control of the isthmus, and the threat of competition from England, led Polk to issue his corollary to the Monroe Doctrine: "it should be distinctly announced to the world as our settled policy that no future European colony or dominion shall with our consent be planted or established on any part of the North American continent." [91] Polk argued (and historians have hotly denied his contention ever since) that the Monroe Doctrine opposed

[90] For the text, see Hunter Miller, ed., *Treaties and Other International Acts of the United States*, V, pp. 115–43.
[91] James D. Richardson, ed., *Messages and Papers of the Presidents*, IV, p. 399.

any transfer of territory to a foreign power, even if that transfer had the consent of the Western Hemisphere nation involved! England was obviously alarmed by this interpretation for she had important colonial interests in the Caribbean area—particularly British Honduras and Jamaica. In addition, she was the world's leading commercial power and well understood the implications of permitting another nation to control such a strategic commercial route. It is little wonder that the British seized the town of San Juan, Nicaragua, at the Atlantic side of the proposed Nicaraguan canal route and took an active interest in the Gulf of Fonseca at the Pacific end of the passageway.

Alarmed by the growing polarization of positions, and sobered by the unquestioned superiority of the British navy, the United States sought to negotiate its differences with England. To this end Henry Lytton Bulwer was sent to Washington to confer with the new Secretary of State, John M. Clayton. It was a foregone conclusion that neither party would grant exclusive rights to the other, and so the only reasonable solution was a pact pledging cooperative construction and renouncing exclusive control. Thus Article One of the 1850 Clayton-Bulwer Treaty states that the two governments declare:

> that neither the one nor the other will ever obtain or maintain for itself any exclusive control over the said Ship Canal; agreeing, that neither will ever erect or maintain any fortification commanding the same, or in the vicinity thereof, or occupy, or fortify, or colonize, or assume, or exercise any dominion over Nicaragua, Costa Rica, the Mosquito Coast, or any part of Central America.[92]

A clarifying "Declaration" was added by England, noting that the pledge regarding the occupation, fortification, and colonization of Central America did not apply to territory already controlled by England. It is difficult to understand the subsequent criticism of the treaty—particularly the contention that in violation of the Monroe Doctrine it acquiesced to continued British control over portions of Central America which had been acquired illegally—when one considers the relative strength of both parties at the time the treaty was concluded.[93]

As America's Pacific ambitions grew, increased pressure was placed on England to modify its position on the control of an interoceanic canal. At the opening of the 1880s, Garfield's Secretary of

[92] Miller, *Treaties and Other International Acts*, V, pp. 671–72.
[93] The differences between the American and British positions are outlined in the correspondence of Secretary of State James Buchanan and the British Foreign Secretary, Lord Clarendon. See Bartlett, *The Record of American Diplomacy*, pp. 253–55.

State, James G. Blaine, attempted to pressure Lord Granville, the British Foreign Secretary, to renegotiate the Clayton-Bulwer Treaty. His object was British assent to a plan for American construction and fortification of the canal. Blaine contended that the circumstances surrounding the ratification of the Treaty of 1850 no longer applied; that the strength of the British navy, coupled with Britain's refusal to allow the United States to fortify the area, placed the United States in an entirely subordinate position in the Caribbean area; and that the treaty acted against America's "rightful and long-established claim to priority on the American continent." [94]

Lord Granville rejected Blaine's overture and the British stood firm for another 20 years. But in 1900 the Congress considered a bill calling for the construction of a Nicaraguan canal in violation of the treaty with England. The timing of the measure's sponsors was perfect, for England was deeply occupied with the Boer War. Since the African adventure had not been supported by other European nations, London was seeking an accommodation with the United States. A month after the bill for the Nicaraguan canal was introduced, Secretary of State Hay and the British Ambassador to the United States, Lord Pauncefote, completed the draft of a treaty calling for American ownership and construction, but non-fortification, of an isthmian canal. Many were dissatisfied with this diplomatic half loaf, fearing that in time of war a foreign nation might not only seize the canal but also use it against the United States. The Senate then attempted to introduce a series of amendments to the proposed treaty, but these so changed the character of the original agreement that England rightly refused to give her consent. By March of 1901 hopes for an Anglo-American compromise appeared to be shattered. But proponents of the construction of an American-controlled waterway argued that the Boer War, the deterioration of England's relations with Germany, and the recent excellent record of Anglo-American relations would convince England to let the United States have its way. Finally, in November of 1901 a second Hay-Pauncefote Treaty was concluded, this time omitting reference to fortification. The implication, of course, was that the United States would own, construct, and fortify the projected canal. European instability and England's desire for sympathetic friendship had once again worked to America's advantage.

Two months before the canal treaty was concluded President McKinley was assassinated, thus snuffing out the one life which stood

[94] Blaine to James Russell Lowell, November 19, 1881, *Papers Relating to the Foreign Relations of the United States*, 1881, p. 555.

between TR (Republican boss Mark Hanna had called him "that damned cowboy") and the presidency. Armed with the new agreement, the determined Teddy had only to choose between the Panama and Nicaragua routes. There were complications in either choice. The French builder of the Suez Canal, Ferdinand de Lesseps, had been granted rights by Colombia to build a canal across the Isthmus of Panama and he had formed a private stock company to raise the requisite funds. Construction began in February of 1881. During the 1880s the de Lesseps enterprise continued its work on the canal, but with less than half of the excavation completed it was forced to a halt by internal corruption, mismanagement of funds, heat, and tropical disease. The de Lesseps effort was replaced by the New Panama Canal Company, a French firm which had obtained its rights and assets. It soon became apparent that the objective of this new group was to sell its holdings to the United States and not to complete the canal. Since Nicaragua was anxious to control any interoceanic canal built on her territory, there was considerable Congressional support for the Panama route. The Walker Commission was established to study the Panama alternative, and its first report recommended the Nicaraguan route since the New Panama Canal Company was asking $109 million for its rights. Upon hearing of the Walker Commission's recommendation, the French company dropped its price to a far more realistic $40 million.

President Roosevelt preferred the Panama route at the lower price, but the Congress, by an overwhelming vote of 308 to 2, approved the Nicaraguan plan. In a last-ditch effort to swing the final decision to its favor the New Panama Canal Company enployed a group of professional lobbyists who sought to prove that the Nicaragua area was characterized by volcanic activity. Meeting with little success at first, fate intervened in the form of a cooperative Mont Pelée, which erupted on the island of Martinique in May of 1902, killing 30,000. This eruption was followed by another on the Nicaraguan mainland; as luck would have it the Nicaraguan volcano was the very one pictured on a postage stamp of that country. One of the lobbyists, Philippe Bunau-Varilla, sent the stamp to every Senator. All of this occurred at a most opportune time since the Senate was then debating the Hepburn Bill, which instructed the President to obtain the rights for a Nicaraguan canal and appropriated funds for the construction of such a canal. The Spooner Amendment to the bill, backed by the Roosevelt Administration, authorized the President to pay $40,000,000 for the rights of the New Panama Canal Company and to begin construction of a canal in Panama unless within a "reasonable time" he was unable to secure the cooperation of the Company or of

Colombia (which then controlled Panama). In that event, a Nicaraguan canal was to be constructed.

After the volcanic eruption in Nicaragua, the Senate and then the House passed the Spooner Amendment, and the Isthmian Canal Act was finalized on June 28, 1902. There were sound engineering reasons for the Administration's support of the Panama route. The Walker Commission had determined that a Panama canal could be constructed at less expense than the proposed Nicaraguan waterway; in addition, the Panama route was shorter than the alternative. Supporters of the Panamanian route now had to deal with Colombia, and it was here that they displayed a callous disregard for the sovereignty of that hemispheric neighbor. The Colombian *chargé* in Washington, Dr. Tomas Herrán, had been sent to the United States to negotiate a canal settlement with the Administration. Herrán's position was a difficult one since to yield to American plans for Panama would be to surrender Colombia's sovereignty over the area. On the other hand, to refuse meant either losing the expected economic gains from the canal or (worse) risking an American seizure of Panama.

Secretary Hay chose to be highhanded with the Colombian *chargé*. Skillfully threatening to select the Nicaraguan route he secured Herrán's signature to a treaty giving the United States a 100-year lease on a six-mile strip across the isthmus for $10,000,000 and an annual fee of $250,000, which was not to begin until nine years after the treaty was signed. The United States Senate ratified the Hay-Herrán Treaty in March of 1903, but the Colombian Senate, ignoring Hay's threats, unanimously rejected the pact in August. Unfortunately, in protesting the treaty Colombia did not limit her objections to the agreement's obvious violations of her sovereignty. While this was of course an issue, Colombia seemed more interested in exacting a larger payment from both the United States and the New Panama Canal Company, whose rights and assets would belong to Bogotá after its franchise expired in 1910. Yet the Hay-Herrán accord did represent a naked attempt by the United States to pressure a foreign state to relinquish control over a portion of its territory. Roosevelt, disregarding these considerations, told Secretary of State Hay: "I do not think that the Bogotá lot of jack rabbits should be allowed permanently to bar one of the future highways of civilization." [95]

Several alternatives were open to Roosevelt: he could forget Colombia and turn to all-too-willing Nicaragua; he could simply

[95] Quoted in Dwight C. Miner, *The Fight for the Panama Route: The Story of the Spooner Act and the Hay-Herrán Treaty* (New York: Columbia University Press, 1940), p. 345.

conquer Panama and dig the canal; or he could encourage Panama to secede and, once independent, renegotiate the canal route. Panamanians had become increasingly restive under Colombia's rule, especially since the 1880s when dictatorial controls had markedly tightened. This discontent was deepened by Colombia's refusal to sign the treaty, which Panama hoped would bring an economic resurgence to the area. Hence a small band of Panamanian nationals, working in cooperation with the New Panama Canal Company (which had $40,000,000 to lose if the Nicaraguan route were selected) planned to secede from Colombia. The details of this plot were hatched in the most unlikely of places, New York City's Waldorf-Astoria Hotel. The extent of Roosevelt's direct involvement in these plans is still debated, but Bunau-Varilla has written that it was during this period that the President told him that the revolt would be useful to his canal plans.[96] Although at first denying any complicity, Roosevelt later wrote to a friend that Bunau-Varilla was a "very able fellow, and it was his business to find out what he thought our Government would do. I have no doubt that he was able to make a very accurate guess, and to advise his people accordingly. In fact, he would have been a very dull man had he been unable to make such a guess." [97]

The ragged force of Panamanian revolutionaries was enormously encouraged by Bunau-Varilla's cable indicating that the U.S.S. *Nashville*, one of a group of warships which had been sent to Central America in October, would arrive in Panama on November 2, 1903. The plan was to use the *Nashville* to enforce Roosevelt and Hay's startling interpretation of the 1848 treaty with Colombia pledging to protect free transit across the isthmus.[98] It had been abundantly clear at the time the 1848 treaty was ratified that Article Six, dealing with free transit, was directed against an attempt by a foreign power (at the time England was the most likely candidate) to seize and control the Panama area. The use of Article Six to hinder Colombia's ability to quell a revolt within Panama would have shocked the formulators of the agreement. Moreover, although American troops had been utilized in Panama on a number of occasions between 1848 and 1903 to protect the isthmus from uprisings in Panama, such American intervention was always accompanied by Colombian consent.

[96] See Philippe Bunau-Varilla, *Panama: The Creation, Destruction, and Resurrection* (London: Constable and Company, 1913), p. 312.

[97] Quoted in Joseph B. Bishop, *Theodore Roosevelt and His Times* (New York: Scribner's, 1920), I, p. 296. For a somewhat parallel account, see George E. Mowry, *The Era of Theodore Roosevelt and the Birth of Modern America, 1900–1912* (New York: Harper & Row, 1958), Chap. 8. But also see R. A. Friedlander, "A Reassessment of Roosevelt's Role in the Panamanian Revolution of 1903," *Western Political Quarterly*, XIV (1961), 535–43.

[98] See above, p. 43.

The day following the arrival of the *Nashville* the Panamanians revolted while American troops prevented the Colombian army from suppressing the insurrection. Worse still, three days after the revolutionaries proclaimed Panama to be an independent nation, the new state was granted de facto recognition; a week later the former lobbyist Bunau-Varilla was received as Panama's Minister to the United States. This recognition was accorded despite Colombia's offer to sign the Hay-Herrán Treaty in exchange for American cooperation in restoring Panama. The unseemly haste of these actions and the barely suppressed delight of members of the Administration infuriated Colombia. A formal protest was sent to Secretary Hay, outlining Colombia's grievances: "If there be an end and eternal and immutable principle in right, that right of Colombia has been injured by the United States by an incredible transgression of the limits set by equity and justice." [99] The protest included a proposal to submit Colombia's claims against the United States to the Arbitration Tribunal at The Hague. The Roosevelt Administration rejected the claims of Colombia in a note which piously concluded:

> The Government of the United States, in common with the whole civilized world, shares in a sentiment of sorrow over the unfortunate conditions which have long existed in the Republic of Colombia by reason of the factional and fratricidal wars which have desolated her fields, ruined her industries, and impoverished her people.[100]

A mere 15 days after the revolution the United States concluded the Hay–Bunau-Varilla Treaty with Panama. The accord was formulated along the lines of the Hay-Herrán Pact, except this time the United States asked for, and received, even wider concessions. Payment for use of the zone was $10,000,000 plus an annual rate of $250,000; the new lease was in perpetuity, rather than 100 years; the strip of land was ten miles wide, rather than six; and further limitations were placed upon Panama's sovereignty. The Panama Affair was an example of "Big Stick" diplomacy at its worst. Determined to have the canal, Roosevelt remained stubbornly disinclined to offer responsible justifications for his actions. Roosevelt was not far from the truth when he told his University of California audience in 1911, "I took the Canal Zone." [101] In a story that is possibly apocryphal, Roosevelt is said to have offered the Cabinet an extensive defense of his canal policy and then asked the new Secretary

---

[99] *Papers Relating to the Foreign Policy of the United States*, 1903, p. 287.
[100] *Ibid.*, p. 306.
[101] *New York Times*, 25 March 1911, p. 10.

of State, Elihu Root, if he had answered the charges against him. Root replied: "You certainly have, Mr. President. . . . You have shown that you were accused of seduction and you have conclusively proved that you were guilty of rape." [102]

The canal was completed in 1914. After repeated efforts by the Taft and Wilson administrations to improve relations with Colombia, a treaty was negotiated which expressed regret for America's part in the revolution and offered to pay Colombia $25,000,000. Roosevelt was outraged, and his supporters in the Senate blocked ratification until two years after his death. There is considerable support for the theory that the discovery of the extent of Colombia's oil holdings had much to do with the desire for improved relations with that country.

THE RIGHT OF INTERVENTION

The acquisition of the Panama route deepened American concern over the security and independence of the Caribbean area. The Administration feared that instability in the Caribbean would lead to foreign intervention and thereby threaten American hegemony. Roosevelt reasoned that European debtors would continue to intervene in Latin America unless America assumed some responsibility for the stability of the area. Operating under this set of assumptions he formulated what has come to be known as the Roosevelt Corollary to the Monroe Doctrine, which was outlined in his 1904 annual message to the Congress.

> All that this country desires is to see the neighboring countries stable, orderly, and prosperous. Any country whose people conduct themselves well can count upon our hearty friendship. If a nation shows that it knows how to act with reasonable efficiency and decency in social and political matters, if it keeps order and pays its obligations, it need fear no interference from the United States. Chronic wrongdoing, or an impotence which results in a general loosening of the ties of civilized society, may in America, as elsewhere, ultimately require intervention by some civilized nation, and in the Western Hemisphere the adherence of the United States to the Monroe Doctrine may force the United States, however reluctantly, in flagrant cases of such wrongdoing or impotence, to the exercise of an international police power.[103]

The corollary was clearly a distortion of Monroe's principles. The Doctrine had been designed to prevent further colonization by

---

[102] Quoted in Philip C. Jessup, *Elihu Root* (New York: Dodd, Mead, 1938), I, pp. 404–05.
[103] *Papers Relating to the Foreign Relations of the United States*, 1904, p. xli.

European states of the Western Hemisphere; Roosevelt was asserting an entirely different principle by insisting that the United States could intervene, at will, in the internal affairs of other sovereign nations of the Western Hemisphere. The Roosevelt Corollary was the logical conclusion of a series of positions taken by the United States regarding its privileges and responsibilities in the world community. It was an attitude born of misplaced zeal and misdirected force—it was not an attitude which demonstrated a decent respect for the opinions of mankind.

The drive for hegemony over Panama and the Roosevelt Administration's insistence upon its prerogatives in the Caribbean were two of many manifestations of the nation's determination to expand its influence, both economic and political, over Latin America. The phenomenal economic growth of the United States—which was the product of the mature stage of its nineteenth-century industrial revolution—accounts for much of the motivation for its aggressive moves to the south. Although the value of American goods produced in the 1870 to 1910 period rose dramatically, the United States remained a debtor nation; the tariff had been used as an instrument to control the rate of imports, but it was nevertheless necessary to expand export markets and overseas investment opportunities if a balance favorable to the United States was to be established. By 1914 a half billion dollars had been invested by American corporations in factories in Canada, Europe, and Latin America; an additional quarter billion was invested in foreign railroads, chiefly in the Caribbean area. Cuba, Puerto Rico, and Mexico, as well as Hawaii and the Philippines, provided fertile ground for additional American investments in agricultural enterprises. By 1920, exports to the Americas were valued at $2,553,000,000 as compared with the $872,000,000 of exports to Asia. The European market, however, absorbed 4.5 billion dollars worth of American goods.[104]

The determination to secure the Canal Zone, coupled with the goal of an expanded intra-American trade network, led to Washington's interference in the internal and external affairs of a number of Latin American nations under the guise of the Roosevelt Corollary and other instruments of similar intent. Thus in 1901 an understandably reluctant Cuba was given the choice of agreeing to the terms of the Platt Amendment or enduring continued American military occupation of the island. The April, 1898, Teller Amendment had disavowed any intent of annexing Cuba following the Spanish-Ameri-

[104] See Arthur C. Bining and Thomas C. Cochran, *The Rise of American Economic Life*, 4th ed. (New York: Scribner's, 1964), pp. 496, 498.

can War, and so the United States sought an alternate means of protecting its interests on the island. The result was the Platt Amendment, and under its provisions American troops were withdrawn in exchange for Cuban acceptance in principle of Washington's right to intervene "for the preservation of Cuban independence, [and] the maintenance of a government adequate for the protection of life, property, and liberty." [105] The United States was given the right to buy or lease two naval stations—hence the origin of American control of Guantanamo Bay on Cuba's southeast coast.

Forced to choose between disagreeable alternatives, Cuba opted for the evacuation of troops and included the Platt provisions in its constitution. During the following decade the United States exercised its prerogatives on a number of occasions, and, ironically, was at times criticized by Havana for failing to intervene.

The determination of the Roosevelt and subsequent administrations to keep the sensitive Caribbean area free from European domination—fears of German naval bases in the region were not without justification—led to intervention in several Central American republics. It was reasoned that these republics, badly supported by marginal economic structures and riddled with debts, would eventually fall under the sway of European creditors. In fact, fear that such powers would use their claims as a device to gain extensive control over Venezuela and the Dominican Republic had provided a major impetus for the Roosevelt Corollary. Not surprisingly, in 1905 the Administration arranged for American supervision of customs collections in the Dominican Republic, reserving 55 percent of the receipts for the payment of foreign debts.

The potentially damaging effect of Caribbean instability upon American interests in the region was a preoccupation of Roosevelt's Vice President and successor, William Howard Taft. A conservative by temperament and conviction, Taft was heavily influenced by the nation's financial and industrial interests. A recent study of Taft's foreign policy demonstrates that the attitudes of both the President and his able Secretary of State, Philander C. Knox, were ill-suited for the task of redirecting America's policies toward the Latin states. The President lacked the imagination and the drive to accomplish the transformation and relied heavily on Knox, who found it difficult at best to mask his disdain for Latin American diplomats.[106]

The new Administration's approach to maintaining American

[105] The Platt Amendment printed in *Public Statutes at Large of the United States*, XXXI, Part II, pp. 895–98.

[106] Walter V. and Marie V. Scholes, *The Foreign Policies of the Taft Administration* (Columbia, Mo.: University of Missouri Press, 1970), pp. 6, 12, 13.

hegemony was markedly different from TR's, for Taft and Knox believed that the best way to contain foreign influence was to ensure the economic stability of Latin America. Economic intervention would preclude military intervention, it was theorized; dollars would substitute for bullets, as the Administration never tired of repeating. This policy, later dubbed "dollar diplomacy," sought the rapid expansion of American financial interests in the Caribbean and a corresponding weakening of European control. If successful, the benefits would have been desirable indeed: a diminished threat of European intervention; greater protection for the Canal Zone; and of course profits for American investors. Yet the Administration's strategy met with only very limited success. While Taft unsuccessfully attempted to win Senate ratification of a scheme which would have permitted private American banks to refund British-held Honduran bonds, in other republics, particularly Haiti, the Administration went far in supplanting European capital with American dollars.

Such efforts did not achieve Washington's goal of increased Latin American stability, causing Taft to add troops to his influx of dollars. Perhaps not unexpectedly given its proximity to the Panama Canal and its potential as an alternative isthmian route, Nicaragua became a major victim of dollar diplomacy and later of armed intervention. When in 1909 the violently anti-American dictator José Zelaya was challenged by rebels backed by American financial interests, the Taft Administration sympathized with the insurgents and agreed to recognize the new government only if it would permit an American reorganization of its finances, control of its customs, and refunding of its debt owed to Great Britain. When this plan met resistance a warship was sent and the Knox-Castrillo Convention (1911) providing for a financial protectorate was ratified. Renewed violence in 1912 led to the landing of 2,500 American marines—a contingency force remained until 1925, was withdrawn, and then reintroduced until 1933.[107]

In the end, dollar diplomacy failed on several fronts. The Senate, reflecting deeply felt reservations regarding Taft's fiscal interventions, refused to ratify several of the accords which would have resulted in the financial dependence of a number of Caribbean nations on the United States. The concept also failed because of its inevitable association with armed force. It predictably fostered Yankeephobia to the south. And most important of all, any claim to greater stability in Latin America was contradicted by the rising tide of American intervention in subsequent years.

[107] Incident considered in *Ibid.,* pp. 45–67.

Unfortunately, the Democrats under the leadership of Woodrow Wilson fared even worse. The first Democrat to occupy the White House since Cleveland, Wilson attempted to reconcile America's drive for economic expansion through trade and investment with his determination to win wide acceptance of his concept of a liberal-capitalist order. This dual goal—the exportation of liberalism and the protection of American economic and strategic interests—combined idealism with hardheaded opportunism but led, almost inevitably, to a violation of the sovereignty of a number of Latin American nations through armed intervention.

At first it seemed that the newly elected Democrats would eschew the "Big Stick" diplomacy of Roosevelt. But despite assurances and predictions of a fundamental change in Latin American relations, in point of fact the new Administration proved far more interventionist than its Republican predecessors. This was due, in part, to the Administration's tacit acceptance of a series of policies which had been initiated by the two previous administrations and which had deeply committed private American banking and investment interests in Latin America. It was also the product of Wilson's determination to be supreme in the Caribbean and thereby protect the Panama Canal. It soon became clear that the President never seriously considered renouncing the nation's "right" of intervention in Latin America which Roosevelt had enunciated so emphatically in his corollary. More generally, Wilson's failure was traceable to his determination to use the republics to the south as a source of economic expansion and as capitalist models to counter the threat of world revolution posed by the Mexican and Russian revolutions.

Wilson's biographer, Arthur S. Link, believes that the discrepancy between goals and practices in Latin America can be explained by the noble but misguided efforts of the Chief Executive and his first Secretary of State, William Jennings Bryan, to engage in a holy crusade to uplift and democratize Latin America. The pair had naively attempted to impose a moral order, fashioned after an American ideal, upon an area of the world which had historically viewed revolution as an essential part of the political process and which had considered democracy a "sham." [108]

But more cynical observers of Wilsonian idealism are apt to regard the Administration's holy cause as a "hypocritical disguise assumed by the wolf of imperialism when he disposed of Little Red Riding-hood's grandmother and took her place in bed to deceive the

---

[108] Arthur S. Link, *Wilson: The New Freedom* (Princeton, N.J.: Princeton University Press, 1956), p. 331.

next trusting and hoped-for victim." [109] It is certainly true that in Nicaragua, Santo Domingo, and Haiti, the United States intervened and thereby facilitated the establishment and control of military regimes which were of far more assistance to the United States than they were to their domestic constituencies. And while Link is apt to excuse much of the President's Latin American policies, it is doubtful that his reasoning will stand the ethical, if even the pragmatic, test. Link writes:

> [H]ad the people of these two republics [Santo Domingo and Haiti] demonstrated even a slight capacity to govern themselves and to discharge their international responsibilities, intervention in their affairs by the United States would not have occurred. . . . missionary diplomacy was not motivated by any ambition to promote the exclusive material interests of the United States.[110]

Just what is meant by "exclusive material interests" is uncertain, however, since trade and the protection of American banking interests in that part of the globe were obvious concerns of the Administration.

The most ambitious instance of American "missionary" diplomacy in the Western Hemisphere was directed toward Mexico, where the United States attempted to influence the course of a revolution to suit its concept of sound constitutional government respecting the social and economic needs of its people. It has not gone unnoticed that the Mexican Revolution of 1910 (which had evolved into a full-scale, bloody civil war by the time Wilson intervened) had as one of its goals the nationalization of natural resources, an accomplishment which would have deeply affected American economic interests. It is indicative of Wilson's general approach to the Mexican Revolution that in 1913 he refused to recognize a new Mexican government because it had come to power through a coup which witnessed the murder of the head of state, Francisco I. Madero, by his leading general, Victoriano Huerta. This may have been a moral position, but it violated America's long-standing policy of granting *de facto* recognition to revolutionary governments. "I will not recognize a government of butchers," [111] Wilson stormed, even though Huerta's government was constitutional in form and controlled most of Mexico. He also attempted to affect the outcome of the revolution by manipulating the availability of American-made arms to the various factions. The issue, for Wilson, was the political morality of the regime in question.

[109] Wilfrid H. Callcott, *The Caribbean Policy of the United States, 1890–1920* (Baltimore: The Johns Hopkins University Press, 1942), p. 430.
[110] Arthur S. Link, *Woodrow Wilson and the Progressive Era* (New York: Harper & Row, 1954), p. 103.
[111] *Ibid.,* p. 109.

Fearful of European intervention in the bloody Mexican civil war and determined to mold a foreign government to a preconceived image, the United States was led to the extreme of sending a so-called punative expedition, under the command of General John J. Pershing, to influence the course of the war. The long-range accomplishments of this heavy-handed diplomacy were pitifully few when compared with the bitter heritage which resulted. In the end Wilson was forced to concede that the United States could not impose its definition of legitimacy on another power.

A number of overriding policy objectives emerge from a consideration of American diplomacy in the pre-World War I era. Most dramatic was the decision of the nation's expansionist leadership to annex Pacific and Caribbean territory with small regard for the wishes of the subjugated peoples and little intention of drawing them into the American mainstream. The often sharp debate over motivations for this aggrandizement will be with us for a long while. Security considerations, economic factors, and messianic zeal have all been seen as paramount. However, one of the most important contributions of some recent scholarship has been the attention given to the extent to which late nineteenth-century policies were extensions of long-held economic objectives. Central here is an appreciation of the nation's determination to accelerate the momentum of its successful industrialization through the acquisition of territory or commercial rights.

A second major policy objective seems clear: the Far East, not the Caribbean, was viewed as the area most vital to the country's developing trade network. Not surprising therefore was the drive to acquire Pacific bases and the inclusion of Samoa, Hawaii, Guam, and the Philippines within the American orbit. Thirdly, of crucial importance to this strategic and economic policy was the construction and control of an isthmian canal, for such a waterway would facilitate trade with both the Far East and Latin America. Axiomatic was the drive for control of Caribbean territory so as to protect the vital Central American waterway; the keen interest in Cuba and the decision to take and retain Puerto Rico are indicative of this strategy. Such actions have been viewed as temporary "aberrations" of an "adolescent" nation and as carefully contrived, deliberate designs to foster America's security and economic position. The final verdict depends upon one's judgment regarding the nature of turn-of-the-century security considerations and the appropriate means of economic expansion.

Two

THE FIRST WORLD WAR

World War I is particularly significant in the course of American foreign policy. It was the first of a series of global wars fought by the United States in the twentieth century. As was to be the case in many of America's later involvements in foreign affairs, the nation's motivations were mixed. There was legitimacy in Wilson's contention that the country was fighting for idealistic aims—to uphold the concept of democracy against tyranny and to protect the ideal of self-determination of nations. Nevertheless, to a more profound degree the United States was engaged in this war, as in other wars in this century, because of self-interest. Washington intervened in World War I, finally, because of its conviction that a German victory would adversely affect American economic interests, the stability of the Western Hemisphere, national prestige, and the Administration's hope for postwar international order. To have given way to Germany's attempt to control the seas, Wilson would have had to abandon the nation's rights as a world commercial power. Considerations of economics and national prestige were both central factors in the final decision—had they not been, it is doubtful that the bias of the President and the public toward the Allied cause would have brought intervention. Concern for American security in the narrow sense was not, however, an important element in the final decision to join the Allies since there was never any serious threat of a direct German attack on the United States.

THE ONE GREAT NATION AT PEACE

The traditional characterization of the century bounded by the defeat of Napoleon and the outbreak of the First World War as a century of peace is somewhat deceptive since the structure of the European community by the end of the nineteenth century was such that the makings of a major explosion were clearly present. A delicate balance of power had evolved among the six major nations of Europe—England, France, Russia, Germany, Austria-Hungary, and Italy, but this equilibrium was constantly threatened by a bitter struggle for hegemony over the Balkan Peninsula. The European powers were linked into two blocs by a series of entangling alliances; the smoldering rivalries over the Balkans threatened to ignite all of Europe. This threat was particularly ominous because of an arms race which had dangerously accelerated European mobilization by 1914. The requisite spark to set off this powder keg was provided by a nineteen-year-old Bosnian student, Gavril Princip, who assassinated Archduke Franz Ferdinand, heir to the Austro-Hungarian throne, at Sarajevo on June 28, 1914.[1] By the first week of August, Austria, Serbia, Russia, Germany, France, and England were at war, to be joined by a number of lesser powers. Turkey and Bulgaria threw their weight to the side of Austria-Hungary and Germany, while Greece, Italy, and Japan supported England, France, and Russia.

The outbreak of general war in Europe profoundly shocked the American people and forced them, however reluctantly, to reconsider long-standing attitudes regarding the historical process and America's place within the world community. Most Americans had been lulled to complacency by the absence of a major war in Western Europe since 1871—a date which was beyond the memory of most Americans living in 1914. There had been, from the 1890s on, constant tension and unrest in Europe over armaments and the precarious balance of power, but to the American public these were confusing occurrences

---

[1] Bosnia was then an Austrian province and is now a part of Yugoslavia. For an account of the view that the assassin was actually sponsored by Serbia, see Vladimir Dedijer, "Sarajevo Fifty Years After," *Foreign Affairs*, XLII (July 1964), 569–84. For a generally sound interpretation of the origins of World War I, see Laurence Lafore, *The Long Fuse* (Philadelphia: Lippincott, 1965).

thousands of miles away which could not possibly have any connection with the well-being of the United States. And too, while those who had bothered to listen had heard predictions for decades of a major European cataclysm, these warnings were inevitably discounted because of their constant repetition.

In the years before the First World War, both Europe and the Far East failed to occupy the attention of most Americans. The nation's foreign policy since the close of the War of 1812 had been directed toward the protection of the Western Hemisphere from European expansion. This general objective was brought into sharper focus after the Spanish-American War when plans to build an isthmian canal caused the United States to seek hegemony in the Caribbean area. It was toward this goal that the McKinley, Roosevelt, and Taft administrations directed their efforts. European interference in the Western Hemisphere was jealously challenged, but the notion that a war between Europeans would constitute a direct threat to America would have seemed preposterous. Given this general attitude, the murder of the Austrian Archduke at Sarajevo caused little alarm at first, for the assassination appeared to be still another extension of the almost perpetual unrest in the Balkans. But the storm which followed, engulfing as it did England, France, Russia, and Germany by the early days of August, shattered the nation's complacent view of the world order. Yet even with their illusion of perpetual world peace blown apart, few Americans believed that the European holocaust would ever directly touch their lives.

The shock caused by the outbreak of world war was especially shattering because at the time nearly all Americans accepted the nineteenth-century view of history as a relentless, progressive phenomenon. Americans had, up to that time, subscribed to a species of practical idealism which argued that "the essential morality of the universe could be shown in the daily course of events." [2] The chaos which followed Sarajevo profoundly challenged the ideal of a gradual evolution of an earthly kingdom of peace and love. The comfortable, naive assumption that with the application of the scientific method to social problems, the world would move steadily, inevitably, toward harmony was blown apart by the European explosion. The war's cruel lesson was that powerful, irrational forces were still at large; the complacent view of human nature as fundamentally decent and civilized was abruptly crushed.[3]

The war also forced many Americans to renounce the theory that

[2] Henry May, *The End of American Innocence* (New York: Knopf, 1964), p. 361.
[3] For a fuller treatment of this interpretation, see *Ibid.*, pp. 360–61.

European civilization was somehow finer, more worthy of emulation, than the crude provincialism of the United States. With the ugly underside of the European model laid bare, such a notion could no longer be rationally sustained. The profoundly disturbing implication of the carnage in Europe was dramatically expressed by a writer for the *New Republic* who asked, early in 1915: "Is it not a possibility that what is taking place marks quite as complete a bankruptcy of ideas, systems, society, as did the French Revolution?" [4] Had others shared this vision, perhaps the movement from official neutrality, to preparedness, to intervention might not have been so painful.

This is not to imply that the United States was without its supporters of intervention. At a very early stage in the conflict, individuals such as the United States Ambassador to England, Walter Hines Page, warned of the grave threat to American security that would result from a German victory. Page poured out his concern in a passionate September 1914 letter to Wilson's closest confidant, Colonel Edward M. House: "If German bureaucratic force would conquer Europe, presently it would try to conquer the United States; and we should all go back to the era of war as man's chief industry. . . . It seems to me therefore, that [this] . . . idea must perish—be utterly strangled in the making of peace." [5] But a majority undoubtedly shared Walter Lippmann's confessed naivete: "I came out of college thinking . . . that war was an affair that 'militarists' talked about and not something serious minded progressive democrats paid any attention to." [6]

President Wilson gave voice to the official position of the nation on August 1, 1914, by issuing a strict neutrality proclamation. On the nineteenth the President delivered an impassioned plea for impartiality. Support for either of the belligerents, he warned,

> would be fatal to our peace of mind and might seriously stand in the way of the proper performance of our duty as the one great nation at peace, the one people holding itself ready to play a part of impartial mediation and speak the counsels of peace and accommodation, not as a partisan, but as a friend. [7]

It seems clear, however, that despite Wilson's desire that the

    [4] Quoted in *Ibid.*, p. 361.

    [5] Quoted in Ross Gregory, *Walter Hines Page: Ambassador to the Court of St. James* (Lexington, Ky.: University Press of Kentucky, 1970), p. 56. See also Chaps. III to VII.

    [6] Quoted in Charles Forcey, *The Crossroads of Liberalism* (New York: Oxford University Press, 1961), p. 223.

    [7] Quoted in Daniel M. Smith, *American Intervention: 1917* (Boston: Houghton Mifflin, 1966), p. 5.

nation be "neutral in fact as well as in name" he himself, as well as most Americans, were unable to abide by this standard. According to the 1910 census, Americans of English descent composed the largest single segment of the ethnic mix; moreover, the economic and political elite of the nation included proportionally more Englishmen than any other nationality. Perhaps more significant was England's attitude in the recent past—she had earned considerable respect as a peace-loving and cooperative member of the international community. And too, the United States was strongly linked to the British through ties of common language, tradition, literature, legal system, and the like. On another level, it was widely recognized in some circles that a pronouncement such as the Monroe Doctrine had been respected in good part because of the tacit support given by the British. As for the French, it was claimed that the legacy of Lafayette had not been forgotten.

An attempt at strict impartiality would thus prove visionary, and the British Ambassador to the United States, Sir Cecil Spring-Rice, was undoubtedly correct when he wrote: "All the State Department are on our side except [Secretary of State William Jennings] Bryan who is incapable of forming a settled judgment on anything outside party politics. The President will be with us by birth and upbring-ing." [8]

By contrast, the ambitious diplomacy and commercial ascend-ancy of the Germans was cause for much alarm. Germany had declared war against France and Russia, not vice versa, and, more provoking, had violated the neutrality of Belgium. It was obvious to some, but certainly not to a majority, that America's rights and interests as a major power would be severely compromised if the Kaiser triumphed. Perhaps the best expression of this view is in a letter by Elihu Root to an English friend. Root wrote in March of 1915: "Underlying all the particular reasons and occasions for the war, the principle of Anglo-Saxon liberty seems to have met the irreconcilable conception of the German State, and the two ideas are battling for control of the world." [9]

Given the dominant role of the President in the exercise of foreign policy, it was inevitable that Wilson's own ideological assumptions and world view would deeply influence the nation's response to the war.[10] In the conduct of domestic and international

[8] Stephen L. Gwynn, ed., *The Letters and Friendships of Sir Cecil Spring-Rice: A Record* (Boston: Houghton Mifflin, 1929), II, p. 220.

[9] Quoted in Philip C. Jessup, *Elihu Root* (New York: Dodd, Mead, 1938), II, 313.

[10] For a consideration of these factors, I am indebted to N. Gordon Levin, Jr., *Woodrow Wilson and World Politics* (New York: Oxford University Press, 1968).

affairs, Wilson had complete faith in what has been termed "liberal exceptionalism." N. Gordon Levin, Jr. has convincingly demonstrated that the United States was viewed by the President as representing:

> a new departure among the nations in both a moral and a political sense. . . . America had an historic mission to disseminate the progressive values of liberal-internationalism and to create a new world order. . . . imperialism and militarism were seen as essentially European phenomena associated with a past which America had escaped. . . . In Wilson's view, it was America's historic mission to bring Europe into a peaceful international order based on world law.[11]

In general, the President was faced with two alternative strategies to bring international politics closer to his view of America's mission. He could utilize the moral suasion of the United States to neutralize international conflicts through mediation and the establishment of a structure such as the League of Nations. This strategy was evident in his mediation efforts prior to America's entry into the war; it was also evident, of course, at Versailles, where he became the chief architect of the League. Wilson's other alternative was far less passive, for he had the option of employing America's military and economic power to compel the imperialist powers to enter a new international social order. This finally was his expectation in responding to the German submarine crisis in April 1917 with a declaration of war.

But the President's great hope was to avoid intervention, despite the imposing number of practical, immediate problems involved in his attempt to pursue strict neutrality. One of these difficulties might be demonstrated as follows: Great Britain controlled the seas, and so an American decision to continue to trade with all belligerents would automatically aid England since she could successfully blockade shipments to Germany. To refuse to trade with any belligerent would obviously aid the Germans. Wilson has been criticized for his failure to seriously consider an embargo of Europe as an effective method of keeping the nation neutral. The institution of such a ban, however, would have contradicted the President's conception of his duty to uphold the honor and secure the interests of the United States. As a major maritime power, Washington would have had to seriously compromise its principles and its standing in the world community if it were to bow to German control of the seas. It is also questionable that such a maneuver would have survived a political test, even taking into consideration the deeply felt national desire for peace. Moreover, there were basic economic ramifications of an embargo which could

[11] *Ibid.,* pp. 2–4.

not be ignored. At a time when loans to the Allies were being considered, the future Secretary of State Robert Lansing wrote the President that a decline in exports to the Allies would result in "restriction of output, industrial depression, idle capital, idle labor, numerous failures, financial demoralization, and general unrest and suffering among the laboring masses." [12] All this from the decline, not the total demise, of European exports.

Wilson's attempt to balance his definition of national honor and interest with his desire to stay out of war was greatly complicated by his relationship to his Secretary of State, William Jennings Bryan. Frustrated in his three attempts to win the Presidency, Bryan had been rewarded by the Democratic party for his efforts with the top cabinet post; but it was understood by Wilson at least that the appointment was politically motivated and that he would, in effect, serve as his own Secretary of State. Bryan consistently, if sometimes stridently, opposed any measure which threatened to transform the United States into a belligerent power. In June of 1915, distressed by what he viewed as conscious acts of unneutrality, Bryan resigned and was replaced by the pro-Allied Robert Lansing, counselor to the State Department. The move was not surprising since in May the President had told his private secretary, Joseph Tumulty, "England is fighting our fight. . . . I will not take any action to embarrass England when she is fighting for her life and the life of the world." In sympathy with this sentiment, Lansing insisted that "Germany must not be permitted to win this war. . . . American public opinion must be prepared for the time, which may come, when we will have to cast aside our neutrality and become one of the champions of democracy." [13] Supporting this view were two of Wilson's closest associates, Colonel House and the American Ambassador to England, Page. The nation's diplomacy before April 1917 should be viewed as a reflection of these attitudes.

All the same, Wilson's own bias in favor of the Allies and the sympathies of his advisors had to be weighed against the determination of the vast majority of the American people to remain neutral in deed if not in thought. A President's constituency is the entire nation, and the election of 1912 clearly demonstrated that Wilson's constitu-

[12] Ross Gregory, *The Origins of American Intervention in the First World War* (New York: Norton, 1971), p. 135. The embargo issue is considered in pp. 133–36. For the effect of the outbreak of war on the American economy, see Charles Gilbert, *American Financing of World War I* (Westport, Conn.: Greenwood, 1970), pp. 14–44.

[13] Robert Lansing, *War Memoirs of Robert Lansing* (Indianapolis: Bobbs-Merrill, 1932), p. 21. Bryan's opposition to intervention is effectively treated in John Milton Cooper, Jr., *The Vanity of Power: American Isolationism and the First World War, 1914–1917* (Westport, Conn.: Greenwood, 1969), esp. Chap. 3.

ency was overwhelmingly progressive-minded—in 1912 the two liberal-progressive candidates, Wilson (Democrat) and Roosevelt (Progressive) had won over 10.5 million of the 14 million votes cast. This was important because of the strong current of pacifism in the progressive movement, whose membership was primarily concerned with economic and social justice at home, and not campaigns abroad. Although Roosevelt and some of his followers were deeply interested in foreign affairs and their impact on the United States, this concern was not shared by most progressives.

In the South and the Midwest in particular, progressives viewed America's mission as one of self-purification since the nation was to provide a model for others. Pacifist agrarian progressives included Senators Robert M. La Follette (Wisconsin), William E. Borah (Idaho), George W. Norris (Nebraska), and Hiram Johnson (California). Their cause was considerably aided by the most charismatic of the anti-war group, William Jennings Bryan. While noninterventionist sentiment was not nearly as strong among urban progressives, both the rural and urban wings of the movement shared the belief that intervention would interrupt and eventually destroy the domestic reform crusade.

The determination of these reformers to stay out of the war was reinforced by their belief that modern warfare was the result of imperialist economic objectives. Many Americans, particularly farmers and laborers, saw a direct link between the war and the desire of bankers, munition makers, and industrialists for overseas markets. This conspiracy seemed all the more apparent since the very same elements which the progressives regarded (rightly or wrongly) as the bitter enemies of domestic reform were the strongest advocates of a vigorous preparedness program. Progressives were interested in arms limitation, international arbitration, and the renunciation of war. They were not surprised to find their enemies concerned with powerful armies, large navies, and foreign adventures. A leading progressive wrote to the publisher of the *Nation*: "War preparations and emphasis on militarism is national suicide to all the things I am interested in. I could stand the financial cost if it were equally distributed, but I can't stand the social cost. It is . . . taking poison into the system." [14]

BLOCKADES AND U-BOATS

The progressives and pacifists notwithstanding, the United States remained basically, though unofficially, pro-Allied during the 1914–

[14] Frederic C. Howe to O. G. Villard, quoted in Arthur S. Link, *Wilson: Confusions and Crises* (Princeton: Princeton University Press, 1964), p. 25.

17 period; Great Britain and not Germany most worked against American rights as a neutral in the early years of the war. An attempt had been made in 1908–09 to codify international maritime law, and the Declaration of London resulted, allowing for greater freedom of the seas for neutral nations. The British Parliament refused to ratify the declaration, arguing that as the major maritime power, it could not sign away its advantage in the event of war. With far less to lose, the American Senate ratified the declaration on the condition that other governments concur. But the declaration remained unapproved at the outbreak of war, and so each belligerent attempted to interfere with American trade with its opponent while avoiding incidents which might lead to America's formal declaration of war. When Secretary of State Bryan suggested that the belligerents abide by the unendorsed declaration, the Germans and their allies agreed, contingent upon London's concurrence. The British not only refused, but compounded Bryan's irritation by extending the contraband list and refusing to endorse a pledge not to interfere with the coasts or ports of neutrals. By March of 1915, via an order-in-council, the British had placed a virtual blockade on shipping not only to Germany but also to neutral ports in Denmark and the Netherlands. England's affronts to America's status as a neutral did not end with the etablishment of this near blockade against Germany. Indiscriminately, American ships were seized and searched at British ports; United States mail pouches were intercepted and letters opened; and American firms with German connections (often tenuous ones) were blacklisted by the British government.

Protests were of course issued, but never ultimatums. Lansing's sophisticated approach to the problem demonstrated his partiality toward Britain, for he wrote in his *War Memoirs*:

> The notes that were sent were long and exhaustive treatises which opened up new subjects of discussion rather than closing those in controversy. Short and emphatic notes were dangerous. Everything was submerged in verbosity. It was done with deliberate purpose. It insured continuance of the controversies and left the questions unsettled, which was necessary in order to leave this country free to act and even to act illegally when it entered the war.[15]

Officially, the Wilson Administration would ". . . insist only upon Britain's observance of traditional international law." [16]

All of this was of great importance because of the value of exports

---

[15] Lansing, *War Memoirs*, p. 128.
[16] Quoted in Ernest R. May, *The World War and American Isolationism, 1914–1917* (Cambridge, Mass.: Harvard University Press, 1959), p. 21.

shipped to the Allies. American commerce with the Allies in the two-year period 1914–16 rose from $825 million to $3.2 billion, while its trade with the Central Powers nearly disappeared (it plummeted from $170 million in 1914 to $1.6 million in 1916). The value of munitions purchased by the Allies between the outbreak of the war and American entry was over $2 billion. The influence of these purchases on the prosperity of the United States was self-evident.

While British violations of the rights of neutrals were countered with elaborately formal but toothless warnings, the Germans were held strictly accountable for any infringement of American neutrality despite their expressed willingness to cooperate with the Declaration of London, which would have insured America's rights as a nonbelligerent. At the outset this did not cause much difficulty because of the nature of German strategy. Her strong suit was her land army, and so she at first theorized that a series of humiliating blows to the armies of the Allies would ensure a successful conclusion of hostilities. But the opening of 1915 failed to bring victory and on February 4 the Kaiser issued an order which pitted his submarine fleet against enemy merchant ships found in British waters. The plan was a deceptively simple one—utilize the submarine to blockade the British Isles, cut off the food supply, and wait for England to fall.

The submarine in 1915 was a new and largely untried weapon of war; it was not only small in size, it was also ill-equipped to engage in sea battles with merchant ships it was attempting to intercept. The predicament of the German submarine was all the more serious because British captains had orders to ram such ships on sight. To be effective, U-boats were forced to attack without warning and without regard for the lives of those aboard, despite existing international law which dictated that enemy merchantmen might be searched (and sunk if they resisted) but provision must be made for passengers and crew. Since England was known to disguise her ships by flying neutral flags, Germany somewhat understandably warned neutrals that ships entering the war zone around the British Isles did so at their own peril. Finally, the Germans logically argued that if they were violating international law on the high seas, so was their enemy by the Allied blockade against food.

The German submarine policy was announced on the fourth of February and was to go into effect on the eighteenth. Even before the date of implementation, Secretary of State Bryan sent a message to the American Ambassador to Germany, James W. Gerard, instructing him to inform the German government of America's grave concern over the announced policy. In an attempt to compromise the differences between the two powers, Wilson suggested that Germany restrict its use of the U-boat in return for a relaxation of the British blockade; neither side was moved by the appeal.[17]

The first American victim of the new German policy, Leon C. Thrasher, was lost as a result of the sinking by a German U-boat of the British steamer *Falaba* on March 28, 1915. It was Bryan's contention that if an American chose to travel on a belligerent ship he was not only risking his own life, but the security of the nation as well. While at times persuaded by this argument, in the end Wilson adopted Lansing's interpretation that freedom of the seas guaranteed to neutrals, coupled with concepts of international law regarding search, seizure, and provision for passengers, had been violated by Berlin in the *Falaba* case. Tension continued to mount in April when a German airplane attacked the American vessel *Cushing* and on May 1 when the *Gulflight*, an American oil tanker, was torpedoed by a German submarine.

The obvious danger did not curtail American travel on British merchant and passenger ships. Wilson ignored the protests of his Secretary of State and continued to condone such trips. Complicating matters enormously was the tendency of British passenger liners to carry munitions—a practice which perhaps in part led the German government, on May 1, to place an advertisement in New York newspapers warning American nationals that they traveled on belligerent ships at their own risk. Six days after this warning was published the British liner *Lusitania* was torpedoed without warning by a German U-boat; it sank in 18 minutes. One thousand one hundred and ninety-eight persons were killed in the attack, and 128 of these were American citizens. The arguments raged, with Berlin defending its action on the grounds that the *Lusitania*, carrying munitions and other contraband of war, was under order to ram German submarines on sight. The British and many Americans countered that despite its cargo, the *Lusitania* was an unarmed ship, and provision should have been made for its passengers and crew.

While stopping short of an ultimatum to Germany, Ambassador Gerard was instructed on May 13 to inform the German government that it must "not expect the Government of the United States to omit any word or any act necessary to the performance of its sacred duty of maintaining the rights of the United States and its citizens and of safeguarding their free exercise and enjoyment." [18] And too, Wilson

---

[17] *Papers Relating to the Foreign Relations of the United States, 1915*, Supplement, pp. 98–100. Also see James W. Gerard, *My Four Years in Germany* (New York: Hodder and Stoughton, 1917). Perhaps the strongest statement of the role of the submarine in World War I is to be found in Charles Seymour, *American Diplomacy During the War* (Baltimore: The Johns Hopkins University Press, 1934).

[18] *Papers Relating to the Foreign Relations of the United States, 1915*, Supplement, p. 396.

continued to believe that he could both keep the nation at peace while persuading the Germans to relinquish their troublesome weapon. "There is such a thing as a man being too proud to fight," he told a Philadelphia audience on May 10. "There is such a thing as a nation being so right that it does not need to convince others by force that it is right." [19]

Officially, Berlin refused to discontinue use of U-boats; unofficially and by secret order, the Imperial Government instructed its submarine commanders to refrain from attacking passenger ships without warning. The shift in the German attitude can perhaps best be demonstrated in its reaction to what was apparently the unintentional sinking of the American liner *Arabic*—expressions of regret and offers of indemnity.

A significant turn in German-American relations occurred in March of the following year with the attack on the unarmed French passenger vessel, the *Sussex*. Although no American lives were lost in the incident, some United States nationals were wounded. The Wilson Administration chose to regard the attack as a violation of the assurances given to the nation after the *Lusitania* disaster. An ultimatum was issued to the German government: "Unless the Imperial Government should now immediately declare and effect an abandonment of its present methods of submarine warfare against passenger and freight-carrying vessels, the Government of the United States can have no choice but to sever diplomatic relations with the German Empire altogether." [20] This theme was sounded often in the months ahead.

Berlin reacted to the strongly worded *Sussex* Note on May 4, 1916, once again giving assurances regarding merchant and passenger vessels. However, concessions were offered with the understanding that the United States would urge the British to relax their blockade—if this did not come about, the Germans warned, they would have to reconsider their conciliatory position on the use of U-boats. Even before the *Sussex* crisis Wilson saw that with the belligerent armies stalemated, the only real hope the nation had of remaining free from conflict was to offer its services as mediator. To this end, the President sent his closest advisor, Colonel House, to Europe. On his arrival in London in January 1916, House discovered that the British had no intention of moderating the blockade; in Berlin Chancellor Theobald von Bethmann-Hollweg spoke of peace terms which House knew would be unacceptable to the Allies. For their part, the French were

---

[19] Quoted in the *New York Times*, 11 May 1915, p. 1.
[20] *Papers Relating to the Foreign Relations of the United States, 1916*, Supplement, p. 234.

determined to avenge the humiliation of the Franco-Prussian War and so were anxious to launch an all-out effort at victory.

House then reached a painful conclusion, but one which had Wilson's tacit approval: if a peace agreement could not be reached, the American government would enter the war. More pessimistic than the President, House believed that war with Germany was at this point all but inevitable.[21] He confided to his diary:

> In the event the Allies are successful during the next few months I promised that the President would not intervene. In the event they were losing ground, I promised the President would intervene. . . . I again told them that the lower the fortunes of the Allies ebbed, the closer the United States would stand by them. [22]

Returning to London, House concluded that American intervention was close at hand and so he reached an agreement with Sir Edward Grey, the British Foreign Secretary, which, according to Grey's account, all but committed the United States to join with the Allies if the Germans refused to enter peace negotiations or if a peace "on terms not unfavourable to the Allies" could not be reached.[23] This was not necessarily a combative position, for Wilson's biographer, Arthur S. Link, believes the agreement was viewed by Wilson as a peace measure and not as a preliminary to war.[24]

Subsequent to the House-Grey understanding the *Sussex* was attacked and Germany offered her assurances on the restricted use of submarines; for a nine-month period following the *Sussex* incident the American government experienced far more difficulty with England than with Germany. The Administration and millions of Americans were outraged by the brutal suppression of the Irish rebellion in the spring of 1916. The British action served in part to balance the image of the German as the barbaric invader of Belgium. The thoroughness of the British-imposed blockade was a further cause of irritation. Adding to the tension was the July 18, 1916, publication by the British government of a list of 80 firms and individuals (many with German connections) with which its subjects could not trade. Outraged, the Congress gave the President the authority, which he never exercised, to retaliate against nations blacklisting American nationals or firms.

[21] For an explanation of this interpretation, see May, *The World War and American Isolationism*, p. 350.

[22] Quoted in *Ibid.*, p. 353.

[23] Charles Seymour, *The Intimate Papers of Colonel House* (Boston: Houghton Mifflin, 1926), II, pp. 201–02, contains the confidential memorandum.

[24] Arthur S. Link, *Woodrow Wilson and the Progressive Era* (New York: Harper & Row, 1954), p. 205 (n).

Personally, Wilson was provoked to the point of setting aside (at least in mid-1916) his pro-Allied sympathies. "I am, I must admit, about at the end of my patience with Great Britain and the Allies. This blacklist business is the last straw. I have told [British Ambassador] Spring-Rice so, and he sees the reasons very clearly. . . . Can we any longer endure their intolerable course?" [25]

PREPAREDNESS

In the absence of American intervention, the war continued stalemated. Given the conviction of the vast majority of Americans that the war would not touch the United States directly, and given the determination of the progressives not to permit the war to interrupt the flow of social reform, the Wilson Administration confronted its most serious political test in its attempt to satisfy those critics who were demanding that the nation's military capability be strengthened while avoiding direct intervention. This effort by the Administration to provide for reasonable military preparedness was contained in two bitterly contested measures approved by the President in October 1915 and presented to the public at a New York City speech the following month. The naval bill called for the construction, in five years, of ten battleships, six battle cruisers, ten cruisers, 50 destroyers, 100 submarines, and some smaller ships, for a total cost of half a billion dollars. So ambitious was this program that it envisioned naval equality with England by 1925. The blueprint for the army's redesign was far more controversial since it proposed a substantial increase in the Regular Army while all but eliminating the National Guard's traditional role as the first line of defense; in its stead a national, rather than a state, reserve force was to be organized, consisting of 400,000 men and known as the Continental Army.

To the tiny, but at times exceedingly vocal, minority demanding outright intervention in the war, the President's preparedness proposal was an encouraging step, but a timid and less than satisfactory one. Influential national leaders such as Theodore Roosevelt, Senator Henry Cabot Lodge, Elihu Root, Robert Lansing, and Robert Bacon of the House of Morgan favored intervention; the more idealistic insisted that the United States must come to the aid of the European democracies so as to defeat imperialism, militarism, and autocracy. Others saw that America's fate was inextricably bound with that of the Allies and that the United States could not escape involvement in

[25] Quoted in Seymour, *American Diplomacy During the World War*, pp. 76–77.

the war. Within a month of Wilson's preparedness speech the interventionists, who were concentrated in New York, organized the American Rights Committee to further their appeal for participation. But until the late winter of 1916–17, when the submarine crisis and the publication of the Zimmermann Note had inflamed the public to the point of supporting intervention, this tiny group of northeasterners had little influence upon most Americans, who earnestly wished for continued noninvolvement.[26]

The applause of the interventionists for the Administration's preparedness measure was lost in the storm of indignation that was unleashed from progressives, moderates, and pacifists. Oswald Garrison Villard, publisher of the New York *Evening Post* and the *Nation*, and a strong supporter of Wilson, hotly objected to the 1915 preparedness scheme: "You are sowing the seeds of militarism," he wrote the President, "raising up a military and naval caste, and the future alone can tell what the further growth will be and what the eventual blossoms." [27] While the White House mail showed considerable support for the Administration among business and patriotic groups, the public and the Congress were fiercely, and bitterly, divided. Eastern pacifists had organized the League to Limit Armament nearly a year before the President's preparedness speech and 'this group, headed by Villard, George Foster Peabody, and a number of woman suffrage leaders such as Jane Addams, Lillian D. Wald, and Carrie Chapman Catt, mounted an impressive propaganda campaign to defeat the army and naval bills.

For many progressives, the preparedness flap occasioned their most profound disagreement with Wilson since his election three years earlier. Their dilemma was an extremely painful one since to break completely with the President would doubtlessly cripple, if not actually destroy, the reform movement. The solution was quite predictable: launch a massive effort against the President's plan, utilizing mass meetings, committees, the press, farm organizations, and labor unions; the political message to the President would soon be clear. In an impressive show of their political power, they enlisted the support of a core of 50 members of the Congress, dominated by Southern and Western Democrats and led by North Carolina's Claude Kitchin. Interviewed by the New York *Post* in mid-November, Kitchin charged that the war preparedness scheme was the concoction of war profiteers who were reduced to the use of scare techniques in

[26] See the interview of Arthur S. Link in John A. Garraty, *Interpreting American History: Conversations with Historians* (New York: Macmillan, 1970), II, p. 132.

[27] Quoted in Arthur S. Link, *Confusions and Crises*, p. 18. See also Cooper, *The Vanity of Power*, pp. 87–116, for positions of Democrats and Republicans toward the preparedness issue.

the absence of a real threat to national security. He named bankers, industrialists, jingoists, and militarists as the plotters.[28]

Undoubtedly the most dramatic of the dissenters was Bryan; since his July 8, 1915, resignation as Secretary of State, he was free to devote all his time to the peace movement. In personal appearances throughout the country and through his monthly journal, *The Commoner*, Bryan relentlessly battled the Administration and those he characterized as war profiteers.

In his effort to defeat the Administration's preparedness legislation, Bryan did not concern himself much with the political impact of his stance; but the President could not afford such a luxury, and knew it. Like it or not, it was clear by the autumn of 1915 that the preparedness campaign had become identified with and dominated by an influential coterie of Republicans and members of the financial and industrial establishment. Wilson shrewdly judged that in the event of a crisis the Republicans would be credited as the defenders of American security while the Democrats would be cast as weak vacillators. It would, nevertheless, be misleading to overemphasize Wilson's political motivations since the President's frustration in negotiating the submarine question after the sinking of the *Lusitania* was the most important factor moving him toward a preparedness position.[29]

Yet the Democrats remained bitterly split over the proposed legislation and the Republicans were planning to utilize the President's alleged lack of leadership in the upcoming 1916 Presidential campaign. Hence at the end of January 1916, the President toured the Midwest in an attempt to win converts and thereby pressure the Congress to ratify his legislation. The winter tour enabled Wilson to appear before an estimated one million persons and to regain the initiative; but it was a victory at considerable political expense since his deepened association with the drive further alienated many of the progressives who had supported him three years earlier, and who were so essential to his reelection in the fall. Worse still, the Congress was not influenced to any significant degree by the impact of the winter tour. It was only after the Administration modified its position, dropped the concept of a Continental Army, and agreed to rely on a strengthened, "federalized" National Guard, that the preparedness plan had any chance of achieving passage. Tensions between the Administration and the House Military Affairs Committee were further diminished with the replacement of Secretary of War Lindley

[28] The Kitchin statement is quoted in Link, *Confusions and Crises*, pp. 28–29.
[29] Link, *Woodrow Wilson and the Progressive Era*, p. 179.

M. Garrison (an unyielding supporter of the Continental Army scheme) with the progressive Mayor of Cleveland, Newton D. Baker.

Toward the end of March 1916, the House passed a watered-down version of the Administration's army bill by a vote of 402–2; it authorized a substantial increase in the size of the Regular Army and control of the National Guard by the War Department. The real victory in the House belonged to the anti-preparedness group, whose members withstood the combined pressure of the Administration, a vocal minority of the GOP, and the urgings of the prestigious metropolitan press. But a parallel victory in the Senate, where the Military Affairs Committee was dominated by big army advocates, proved more difficult. In a compromise measure the final legislation provided for a doubling of the Regular Army (to 208,000) and a federalized National Guard of 440,000, within five years. The Continental Army concept was never restored. Since the army bills were of far greater concern to pacifist, anti-preparedness groups, the Administration's proposal for naval expansion encountered less opposition and was passed in the summer of 1916.

An extremely sensitive detail remained: who was to pay for these armed forces increases—a particularly important question in a Presidential election year. Since the existing tax structure (authorized by the recently ratified Sixteenth Amendment) placed the burden of federal taxation on the lower and middle classes, liberals in both houses insisted that the more affluent members of society absorb the bulk of the cost. By September of 1916 this approach prevailed: the regular income tax was doubled (from 1 to 2 percent); the surtax on income over $20,000 was increased to 13 percent; a new tax was placed on corporate capital surplus and undivided profits; the estate tax was raised to 10 percent; and the tax on the munitions industry was hiked to 12.5 percent. The progressives were delighted with this victory, and with very good reason.

The preparedness controversy provided an inevitable backdrop for the Presidential election of 1916, although passage of the modified army plan greatly helped neutralize the issue in the campaign. Even so, the President occupied a less than commanding position in the race. The Republican party was a very potent force, and political pundits were well aware that no Democrat since Jackson had served two consecutive terms. Wilson was a minority president, having attracted only 42 percent of the popular vote in the three-legged 1912 election. If reelection was to be accomplished, the President had to win on three central issues: had he done enough in four years to satisfy the progressives; did his foreign policy stance, particularly in Europe and Mexico, appear to have a better chance of keeping the nation at peace than did the measures advocated by his Republican rival, former New York Governor and Supreme Court Justice, Charles Evans Hughes; could he successfully walk the tightrope between those who demanded strict pacifism and those who accused him of vacillation in the face of so grave a peril.

Yet despite his very credible record of progressive legislation, his success in steering clear of direct involvement in the war, and his moderate stance on the preparedness issue, the President nearly lost the election to Hughes. Wilson himself attempted to stress domestic issues in the campaign, but of course recognized that the European war was a central concern. His margin of victory was slim. With Hughes' early sweep of the East, it seemed certain that Wilson was to be returned to private life. But the President won heavily in the West and in enough marginal states to garner a 23-vote lead in the Electoral College and 500,000 more popular votes than his rival. The Democrats may have carried the day, if only barely, by their skillful, and unfair, manipulation of the dominant pacifist mood of the nation. The alternative to "Wilson and peace with honor" was marketed as "Hughes with Roosevelt and war."

An evaluation of the returns uncovered many surprises. The so-called German-American bloc, which seemed so solidly behind Hughes, was splintered by Wilson's identification with continued peace and by Roosevelt's jingoist, offensive attacks on Germany. The peace issue also kept Irish-Americans loyal to the Democratic party and swayed significant numbers of Scandinavian-Americans in the North Central states to Wilson. Labor was behind the President, as was the women's vote in the Middle and Far West. Given Roosevelt's decision not to run, the key to the 1916 victory was Wilson's ability to win the support of members of the Progressive party. Although he gained only about 20 percent of the total vote of the Progressive party, the President did so in strategic states. Socialist support (there were about 300,000 Socialists in 1916) was important to his victory in at least two key states, California and Ohio.[30] The Democrats' three-pronged pledge of peace-prosperity-and-progressivism had carried the day. The desire of the American people for continued peace was clear, and the British Ambassador in Washington was correct when he reported: "The United States does not want to go to war, and the elections have clearly shown that the great mass of the Americans desire nothing so much as to keep out of the war. It is undoubtedly the cause of the President's re-election."[31] The implications of the

---

[30] This analysis is found in Arthur S. Link, *Wilson: Campaigns for Progressivism and Peace, 1916–1917* (Princeton: Princeton University Press, 1965), pp. 157–64.

[31] Quoted in *Ibid.,* p. 162.

Democrats' manipulation of the peace issue would be apparent in the months ahead.

In some respects, the victory was a personal one for the Chief Executive but not for his party. The Democrats retained their majority in the Senate (54–42), but in the House each party had 215 seats, leaving the five swing votes in the hands of minority party representatives.[32]

In the long view, the election had a political impact which went far beyond the issue of Wilson's continuance in office, for the President was able (as Bryan was not) to combine the predominantly agricultural interests of the South and the West with Eastern progressivism. The resultant Democratic coalition had a decidedly liberal cast and it was openly suggested that Wilson bring this phenomenon to its logical conclusion by establishing a separate liberal party. This suggestion the President wisely turned aside, noting the "rigidity of party association as far as it affects a very large proportion of voters." [33]

WILSON CHOOSES BELLIGERENCY

Assured of power for another four years, Wilson resumed his attempt to gain a negotiated settlement. In mid-December he once again requested the belligerents to declare their war aims, only to discover the two sides as far apart as they had been nearly a year earlier when House made his pilgrimage to Europe. His gloom deepened when in January 1917 the German government announced that it was, in effect, disavowing the *Sussex* Pledge and resuming unrestricted submarine warfare. Chancellor Bethmann's determination to keep America neutral, even at the expense of gains that might be accrued by a more extensive use of the U-boat, was set aside by the military, which had become persuaded that unrestricted submarine warfare would bring victory to Germany before American intervention could cause serious harm. Unlimited submarine warfare became the official German policy on February 1, and in the war zone around France and England all belligerent and neutral ships were to be sunk without warning. As an added humiliation, the American government was informed that it could send one ship a week to Portsmouth provided that ship carried no contraband and was marked by red and white stripes. Two days later the German ambassador was requested to leave

[32] For this aspect of the election, see Seward W. Livermore, *Politics Is Adjourned: Woodrow Wilson and the War Congress, 1916–1918* (Middletown, Conn.: Wesleyan University Press, 1966), p. 10.

[33] Quoted in Link, *Campaigns for Progressivism and Peace*, p. 164.

the country, and the Wilson Administration broke diplomatic relations with Berlin.

With German-American relations tragically strained, the disclosure of the interception by the British intelligence network of the infamous Zimmermann Note electrified Washington and the nation. The public soon learned that Alfred Zimmermann, the German Foreign Minister, had sent a message to the German Minister in Mexico suggesting that if the United States and Germany went to war, Mexico (and Japan—at that time the ally of England) should join forces with the Central Powers. Mexico's reward for such an alliance was to be the restoration of territory that she had lost to the United States in 1848—namely Texas, New Mexico, and Arizona! The British informed the State Department of the existence of the note on February 24, and it was published on the first of March. The Southwest, which up to this time was largely disinterested in an armed confrontation with the Central Powers, now added its voice to the rising clamor for intervention.[34]

On February 26 Wilson asked Congress to grant him the authority to arm merchant ships; it was learned that same day that in the sinking of the British liner *Laconia* three American lives were lost. In mid-March three American merchant ships were torpedoed, thus verifying that neutral shipping was in word and deed included in the German order of February 1. When Wilson polled his cabinet, he found them unanimously in favor of war with Germany; a special session of Congress was called on April 2.

In the war message Wilson sought to combine two related themes. America was to engage in a great crusade to save democracy, a holy war against an enemy which had sinned against mankind. The United States could not let such a sin go unpunished. Yet the message also contained an account of specific grievances which had endangered the security of the nation. Hence the speech was at the same time both idealistic and practical, but it had a pervasive moral tone that was characteristically Wilsonian. The President's call to arms was read to the Congress on April 2, and it forcefully demonstrated the strength of the President's resolve.

> There is one choice we cannot make, we are incapable of making: we will not choose the path of submission and suffer the most sacred rights of our nation and our people to be ignored or violated. The wrongs against which we now array ourselves are no common wrongs; they cut

[34] An excellent account of this incident is to be found in Barbara W. Tuchman, *The Zimmermann Telegram* (New York: Viking, 1958). New information regarding the message is in the Appendix to Link, *Campaigns for Progressivism and Peace*, pp. 433–34.

to the very roots of human life. . . . [America's objective] is to vindicate the principles of peace and justice in the life of the world as against selfish and autocratic power and to set up amongst the really free and self-governed peoples of the world such a concert of purpose and of action as will henceforth ensure the observance of those principles.[35]

The outcome was never in doubt—the resolution passed the Senate with only six dissenting votes, and in the House the tally was 353 to 50. War was declared on April 6, and the United States designated itself an Associate Power.

One of the leading opponents of the resolution, Senator Robert M. La Follette of Wisconsin, contended that the nation need never have even considered entering the war had it remained truly neutral:

The present administration has assumed and acted upon the policy that it could enforce to the very letter of the law the principles of international law against one belligerent and relax them as to the other. That thing no nation can do without losing its character as a neutral nation and without losing the rights that go with strict and absolute neutrality.[36]

Nebraska's Senator George W. Norris objected on the grounds that economics had a preponderant role in the events leading to the decision to side with the Allied Powers. In a dramatic outburst he declared, "I would like to say to this war god, You shall not coin into gold the lifeblood of my brethren. . . . I feel that we are about to put the dollar sign upon the American flag." [37]

Although the noninterventionist majority had become a distinct minority by the spring of 1917, there remained pockets of dissent which supported La Follette's stance and which remained staunchly opposed to American participation in the European holocaust. There were, first of all, considerable numbers of German-Americans who continued sympathetic to the Fatherland, although their numbers had decreased by the opening of 1917. Irish-Americans who were hostile to England were staunch noninterventionists, as were those American radicals who viewed the war as the product of soulless capitalists, scheming munition makers, and others with economic interest in American participation. For a number of religious Fundamentalists the war was a contest between corrupt, Godless belligerents. Finally, a minority of American intellectuals, such as political scientist John W.

[35] All quotations from the war message are from the *Congressional Record*, 65th Cong., 1st sess., Vol. 55, Part 1, pp. 102–4.
[36] *Ibid.*, p. 233.
[37] *Ibid.*, p. 214.

Burgess, would not support the Allies because of their admiration for German culture.[38]

In the great outpouring of literature on the causes of America's eventual intervention in the First World War there emerge several basic interpretations. A view which gained popularity in the economically minded 1930s, and one which is increasingly invoked by revisionists of the past and current decade, is the concept that Allied purchases of American goods during the period prior to 1917 provided a bind so powerful and so fundamental to the economic health of the United States that the nation was compelled to support the Allied effort. It is true, as Charles C. Tansill argued many years ago, that the American economy was in a serious slump immediately following the inauguration of Wilson, a slump that became a boom once munition and other war materiel orders from Europe flooded the country. "In 1916 the value of American war supplies to the Allied Governments amounted to more than a billion dollars, and the intimate economic ties thus created," Tansill wrote, "served to supplement the sentimental bonds that had long attached America to the side of the Entente Powers." [39]

There is also the theory that it was American economic involvement in the form of loans to the Allies that led to intervention. Although the Allies at first paid cash for American war materiel, the strain on their economies was such that loans were soon requested. As early as August 1914 the French government sought loans from J. P. Morgan and Company, and when the firm asked Secretary of State Bryan's advice, he replied that while loans were not illegal, they certainly acted against the spirit of neutrality as outlined at the outset of the conflict. It was Bryan's belief that "money is the worst of contrabands—it commands all other things." [40] This position endured a brief two months. In October the State Department offered a distinction between loans made by the United States government (these would not be considered) and those made by private bankers acting as individuals. With the floodgates thus opened, by April of 1917 Great Britain had borrowed in excess of $1 billion; France $300 million; Canada $400 million; and Russia $50 million. The Central Powers were able to borrow only $20 million. Despite the apparent hypocrisy in the American position toward loans, no law prevented Germany from borrowing in the United States—it was the refusal of many of the large banking firms such as the House of Morgan to

---

[38] May, *The End of American Innocence*, pp. 367–70.

[39] Charles C. Tansill, *America Goes to War* (Boston: Little, Brown, 1938), p. 32.

[40] Quoted in Arthur S. Link, *Wilson: The Struggle for Neutrality* (Princeton, N.J.: Princeton University Press, 1960), p. 64.

cooperate with German attempts to secure American loans which accounted for the mere trickle of credits to the Central Powers.

The "economic interpretation" is generally supported by the findings of a Senate committee investigation of the 1930s headed by Senator Gerald P. Nye of North Dakota. This panel concluded that fantastic profits were earned by American munition makers and bankers in the period between 1914 and 1917, and that these businessmen and bankers had pushed the United States into war so that they might sell more war materiel and protect their outstanding loans. (A Central Power victory would have obviously jeopardized their chances of obtaining the repayment of loans to the Allies, for example.) [41]

An alternate explanation sometimes given for American intervention, but one which has lost considerable ground, is the role of British propaganda.[42] Although it is true that the British did launch a considerable campaign to keep the American people aware of German atrocities (particularly as they related to Belgium), the German government spent approximately $35 million in the United States to establish newspapers such as *The Fatherland* and in general to counter the effects of the British propaganda effort.

Finally, it is the much contested thesis of some that the United States pursued an unneutral policy and eventually entered the war not because of economic motivations or the pressures of propaganda, but rather because Wilson and the American people ultimately realized that it would be impossible to be secure if a hostile German ideology dominated Europe. Thus, at a time when the United States was debating entry into the Second World War, Walter Lippmann argued:

> [T]he great majority of Americans know by instinct and by reason that the control of the Atlantic Ocean is vital to the defense of the United States and of the whole Western Hemisphere. They know that for their physical security, for the continuation of the free way of life, it is necessary that the other shore of the Atlantic Ocean should be held by friendly and trustworthy powers. . . . [we intervened in 1917 in order to defend America by aiding the Allies to protect the Atlantic Ocean] against an untrustworthy and powerful conqueror.[43]

This thesis, and others like it, has been challenged by those who

[41] See John E. Wiltz, *In Search of Peace* (Baton Rouge, La.: Louisiana State University Press, 1963).

[42] H. C. Peterson, *Propaganda for War: The Campaign Against American Neutrality, 1914–1917* (Norman, Okla.: University of Oklahoma Press, 1939), p. 326.

[43] Walter Lippmann, "The Atlantic and America," *Life* (Apr. 7, 1941), p. 86.

insist that Lippmann misinterpreted the nation's true motivations in 1917, and instead projected contemporary attitudes (the desire to intervene in the second war against Germany) upon past history.[44] Lippmann's critics freely admit that a number of individuals in public and private life in the years between 1914 and 1917 did believe that the nation's self-preservation would be directly endangered by a German victory; but prior to March or April, 1917, this attitude was never adopted by the general public because a Germany victory had never seemed imminent. Robert Osgood concludes in his *Ideals and Self-Interest in America's Foreign Relations*: "Americans, as a whole, entered the war without a clear and reasoned perception of any enduring self-interest, such as their national survival. Instead, they drifted into war, largely oblivious of the practical consequences of momentary impulses, out of an aroused sense of national honor, combined with a missionary zeal to achieve world peace and democracy." [45]

Moving from this assessment of the attitude of the general public, Osgood tests the Lippmann thesis against the positions of four of Wilson's top advisors urging intervention: the American Ambassador in London, Page; Wilson's confidant, House; Secretary of State Lansing; and James W. Gerard, Ambassador to Germany. His conclusion is that while all four were alike in believing that American security was directly involved in a German victory, they did not urge intervention *primarily* on the basis of national self-interest. They too were swayed by the submarine issue to arguments of international morality and national honor rather than the more expedient issue of preservation. These men, like Wilson, recognized that the American public would be far more receptive to intervention based upon considerations of morality and national honor.[46]

There is substantial evidence for the view that Wilson was far more alert to the practical considerations of a German victory—his rhetoric notwithstanding—than his detractors will allow. In *Woodrow Wilson and the Balance of Power*, Edward H. Buehrig provides a strong argument for his conclusion that the United States and Germany "became embroiled because of their differing attitudes toward British control of the seas. Germany felt that she must challenge that control in the interest of her own future freedom of action. The United States, for its part, regarded British power benevolently, as a factor contribut-

[44] Robert E. Osgood, *Ideals and Self-Interest in America's Foreign Relations* (Chicago: University of Chicago Press, 1953), p. 111.
[45] *Ibid.*, pp. 111–12.
[46] *Ibid.*, pp. 154–71.

ing to American security." [47] For Buehrig, Wilson's concern for national security was the product of his belief that a German victory would disrupt the balance of power and shatter his hopes for world order.

In an interview published in 1970, Arthur S. Link, the scholar most closely associated with the biography and writing of Wilson, sidestepped the national security issue and concluded:

> [T]he most decisive factor which caused Wilson to move toward belligerency was his conviction that the war was grinding to a stalemate, that it would be impossible for Europe to endure another year of the agony. . . . He felt that the end of the war would be greatly hastened by American participation. . . . Finally, Wilson wanted a prominent place at the peace table.[48]

Despite the very considerable attention given to Wilson's idealistic and moralistic position toward the struggle, it is reasonable to conclude that he indeed had a keen appreciation of the practical implications of a German triumph. While some studies emphasize balance of power considerations, others hemispheric security, some economic interests, and others prestige factors, Wilson's war objectives obviously went far beyond making the world safe for that abstraction, democracy.[49]

THE DOMESTIC FALLOUT

Wilson moved cautiously in utilizing his increased leverage as a belligerent to bring about a settlement. But on January 8, 1918, he dramatically announced his Fourteen Points in the hope that the world might "be made fit and safe to live in; and particularly that it be made safe for every peace-loving nation which, like our own, wishes to live its own life, determine its own institutions, be assured of justice and fair dealings by the other peoples of the world against force and selfish aggression." [50] For the President, the Fourteen Points were the embodiment of his conception of the Allied war aims; that they were not necessarily the aims of his allies remains to be seen. In summary form, the Fourteen Points were as follows: open peace treaties, openly

[47] Edward H. Buehrig, *Woodrow Wilson and the Balance of Power* (Bloomington, Ind.: Indiana University Press, 1955), p. ix.

[48] The Link interview is found in Garraty, *Interpreting American History*, II, p. 134. See also Link, *Wilson: Campaigns for Progressivism and Peace*, pp. 390–419.

[49] An incisive analysis of a number of interpretations, particularly those of Link, Buehrig, May, and Osgood is Daniel M. Smith, "National Interest and American Intervention, 1917: A Historiographical Appraisal," *Journal of American History*, LII, No. 1 (June 1965), pp. 5–24.

[50] *Congressional Record*, 65th Cong., 2nd sess., pp. 680–81.

arrived at; freedom of the seas in peace and war; the removal of
economic barriers to trade among nations; armaments reduction;
settlement of colonial claims which account for the rights of the
populations concerned; the restoration of Russia, Belgium, and
France; the readjustment of Italian boundaries; autonomy for the
various groups within Austria-Hungary; restoration of the Balkan
nations and access to the sea for Serbia; sovereignty for Turkey and
free passage through the Dardanelles for all nations; the establishment
of an independent Polish state; and the formation of a general
association of nations.[51]

Idealistic in content and carefully timed for announcement when
Europe was on the verge of exhaustion after more than three grueling
years of war, the Fourteen Points undoubtedly represented the most
effective piece of American propaganda produced during the war.
Although well aware that this initiative would bolster homefront
morale, the Administration did not rely solely on this thrust, for
Wilson was at all times conscious of the need for a high level of
domestic support for the war. To this end, the Committee on Public
Information was established to market the war to the American
people. The President appointed George Creel, a progressive journalist from Denver who had actively campaigned for Wilson's reelection
in 1916, to direct the propaganda blitz. In addition to organizing
mammoth campaigns to sell war bonds, Creel directed much of his
energy toward newspapers, which were urged to exercise voluntary
censorship in suppressing stories that might be harmful to the battle
against Germany. In time there developed a conviction among
journalists that the Administration was being protected at least as
much as the war effort.

One thing at least is certain: the committee's sweep was massive.
More than 150,000 writers, lecturers, artists, actors, and directors were
engaged in the campaign; 75,000 volunteers were available to lecture
on the war and related issues, however tangential; 75,000,000
pamphlets and articles were distributed throughout the world, with
Germany a particular target. Five and a half million copies of one
such pamphlet, "The Kaiserite in America," were distributed by the
committee. The Creel group also sponsored a series of films depicting
Germans in a most unfavorable light: "Wolves of Kulture," "The
Prussian Cur," and the most popular of the genre, "The Beast of
Berlin." [52]

[51] *Ibid.*
[52] Figures are from Frank Freidel, *America in the Twentieth Century* (New York: Knopf,
1960), pp. 202–03, and Harvey Wish, *Contemporary America*, 4th ed. (New York: Harper & Row,
1966), pp. 234–36.

In the main, the committee successfully conveyed Wilson's idealism, his great hope for the postwar era, and, more specifically, his Fourteen Points. But Creel was also guilty of too often appealing to the easily aroused fear and hatred of things German and of the German people themselves. This aspect of his campaign tragically uncovered an ugly side to the much touted idealism of the war effort by lending support to the exaggerated accounts of German atrocities which were circulated by jingoist groups such as the National Security League. And too, in a quite direct sense, the propaganda effort fed the growing intolerance of dissenters and war critics. Exaggerated accounts of spies, saboteurs, and traitors led to demands for repressive measures; the Congress all too readily obliged by passing a number of loosely worded, harsh, and restrictive measures which were designed to ensure conformity while outlawing disloyalty.

The first of these measures, the Espionage Act of June 1917, provided for fines of up to $10,000 and 20-year prison terms for those engaged in espionage, sabotage, and obstruction of the war effort. Unfortunately this act, whose wording was too often vague and imprecise, was also directed toward any person found to "willfully cause or attempt to cause insubordination, disloyalty, mutiny, or refusal of duty . . . or . . . willfully obstruct the recruiting or enlistment service." [53] The Postmaster General was authorized to keep from the mails printed matter which he judged to be seditious. Less than four months later a sweeping "Trading-with-the-Enemy Act" sanctioned rigid censorship over the foreign-language press and international communications. The heavy-handed and at times vindictive enforcement of these measures was bitterly resented.

Yet the government continued to demand additional repressive measures. The Administration requested and the Congress passed a Sabotage Act in April 1918 and a Sedition Act the month following. The former was primarily directed against the Industrial Workers of the World (IWW or "Wobblies"), a much feared, antiwar, radical union whose militancy was considered a direct threat to the war effort.[54] The Sedition Act, surely one of the harshest measures enacted in all of American history, was a tragic reflection of the intolerance which the war and the government's propaganda campaign had spawned. Prior to the law's passage, scores of individuals had been arrested for speaking disloyally against the government, but the courts

[53] Act quoted in Zechariah Chafee, Jr., *Free Speech in the United States* (Cambridge, Mass.: Harvard University Press, 1941), p. 39.

[54] For a detailed account of the IWW's stormy relations with the Wilson Administration during the war, see William Preston, Jr., *Aliens and Dissenters: Federal Suppression of Radicals, 1903–1933* (Cambridge, Mass.: Harvard University Press, 1963), Chap. IV.

lacked a basis for conviction. The breadth of the 1918 Sedition Act provided the grounds by including "disloyal, profane, scurrilous, or abusive language, or language intended to cause contempt, scorn, contumely or disrepute as regards the form of government of the United States; or the Constitution; or the flag." It was also directed against "urging any curtailment of production of any things necessary to the prosecution of the war with intent to hinder its prosecution." [55] As interpreted, under the Sedition Act it became a crime to advocate increased taxation rather than new bond issues, to state that the draft was unconstitutional, to say that the sinking of merchantships was legal, and to argue that a popular referendum should have preceded the declaration of war. More than 1,500 persons were arrested for sedition after the law's enactment. Those who expressed pro-German or even pacifist sentiments and who did not face the federal courts were often snared by state sedition laws or, worse, by the lynch law of vigilante groups.

There was another form of repression of civil liberties during the war, more subtle but omnipresent. That repression was directed, predictably, against German-Americans and all things German. The teaching of German was prohibited in the Ohio public schools; German language books were banned in the Los Angeles public library system; and some communities would not permit German music to be played (thus silencing Beethoven). The conductor of the Chicago Symphony Orchestra, Bruno Walter, was suspended because he was not an American citizen. At times the repression degenerated to the ridiculous—sauerkraut was renamed "liberty cabbage" and German measles "liberty measles." Even the seemingly unoffending pretzel was banned from free lunch counters in Cincinnati. But there were other, personal tragedies, such as the tar-and-feather fate which met a pastor in Minnesota who was arrested by a vigilance committee while praying in German at the bedside of a dying German woman.[56]

In 1919 the Supreme Court agreed to hear appeals to a number of convictions under the Espionage and Sedition Acts. Unfortunately, the Court generally affirmed the lower rulings, thus signifying that it too was not impervious to the onslaught against civil liberties at a time of widespread intolerance and popular hysteria. But several of these cases have become landmarks because of the forceful dissenting opinions of Justice Oliver Wendell Holmes. In *Abrams* v. *United States* (involving the conviction of five persons—three for 20 years—for circulating a Communist leaflet) Holmes wrote: "I think that we

[55] Measure quoted in *Ibid.*, p. 145.

[56] For a brief account of the record, see Harry N. Scheiber, *The Wilson Administration and Civil Liberties, 1917–1921* (Ithaca, N.Y.: Cornell University Press, 1960).

should be eternally vigilant against attempts to check the expression of opinions that we loathe and believe to be fraught with death, unless they so imminently threaten immediate interference with the lawful and pressing purposes of the law that an immediate check is required to save the country." [57]

THE CRUSADE AT VERSAILLES

Fortunately, the Administration's abuse of civil liberties was short-lived, for in October 1918 the Germans sued for peace based on the Fourteen Points. By the twenty-third of the month Berlin had agreed to allow the Allies to set the armistice terms, to end submarine warfare, and to guarantee that the new government was an accurate reflection of the wishes of the German people. Since much of this was decided unilaterally by Wilson and the newly installed German government, Colonel House journeyed to Europe to win Allied approval of a peace settlement based on Wilson's understanding with Berlin. Although the British, French, and Italians at first balked, they eventually accepted the Fourteen Points as the basis for the proposed armistice (not, of course, for the final peace treaty) if two adjustments were made. England would not agree to the statement regarding freedom of the seas, and all demanded the inclusion of an item dealing with reparations for damages to Allied civilians.

In the meantime the Austrian empire, now in shambles, began negotiations with the Allies through Italy, and on November 3 the Austro-Hungarian faction of the Central Powers reached an agreement which was not based on the Fourteen Points. Thus abandoned, Kaiser William II abdicated on the ninth of November and a republican government was formed. Two days later, in Marshall Ferdinand Foch's private railway car (Foch was in command of all Allied troops in France), the armistice was signed.[58] Humiliated in defeat, the Germans nevertheless had the satisfaction of knowing that Allied soldiers had never set foot on their territory.

Ironically, despite Wilson's extraordinary role in the events

[57] Quoted in Chafee, *Free Speech in the United States*, p. 137. But also see Fred D. Ragan, "Justice Oliver Wendell Holmes, Jr., Zechariah Chafee, Jr., and the Clear and Present Danger Test for Free Speech: The First Year, 1919," *Journal of American History*, LVIII (June 1971), 24–45.

[58] In 1940 Hitler dictated his armistice terms to a crushed France in the very same railway car in which Foch accepted the German surrender. For details of the coordination of American and Allied military activities during the war, see David F. Trask, *The United States in the Supreme War Council: American War Aims and Inter-Allied Strategy, 1917–1918* (Middletown, Conn.: Wesleyan University Press, 1961).

leading to the signing of the armistice, his own nation turned against his party in the 1918 Congressional elections. In response to Republican objections to his Fourteen Points settlement—Senator Henry Cabot Lodge called for an unconditional surrender, while TR stammered that the nation should "dictate peace by the hammering guns and not chat about peace to the accompaniment of the clicking of typewriters" [59]—Wilson made the political blunder of requesting that the elections be viewed as a vote of confidence for his policies. After the balloting, the opposition party controlled the Senate by a 49 to 47 margin, and the House by 239 to 194. There exists, however, no convincing evidence that Democratic foreign policy was the main factor in the 1918 defeat. High taxes, the Eighteenth Amendment (prohibition), low farm prices, and the suppression of civil liberties during the war were all elements contributing to the Democratic defeat.

Campaign rhetoric proved to be an even greater harbinger of trouble when viewed in relation to stated Republican objections to Wilson's peace formula. "A general association of nations" had been the final item of the Fourteen Points, and much earlier there had been considerable interest in such a pact, leading to the establishment of the League to Enforce Peace in 1915. Former President Taft headed up the group, which included many notable Republicans and was supported by the Chairman of the Senate Foreign Relations Committee, Senator Lodge. Yet by mid-1918 the Republicans had shifted their position, apparently a reflection of the belief that there were political gains to be made of demands for a vindictive settlement against Germany. Membership in an overriding international organization, it was argued, would deprive the nation of the degree of self-direction that it had traditionally enjoyed. The historic warning against "entangling alliances," however misunderstood, was apparently still very much alive in some Republican circles.

Undaunted by the growing tide of opposition, Wilson decided to attend the peace negotiations at Paris personally—thus carrying with him a considerable amount of dangerous political baggage.[60] His major objectives were to secure a peace settlement based upon the principles of the self-determination of nations, one which would obviate the necessity of war in the future, and to create a League of Nations tightly interwoven into the fabric of the peace settlement. His

[59] Quoted in Thomas A. Bailey, *Woodrow Wilson and the Lost Peace* (New York: Macmillan, 1944), p. 40.
[60] The most authoritative account of the Versailles conference is Arno J. Mayer, *Politics and Diplomacy of Peacemaking: Containment and Counterrevolution at Versailles, 1918–19* (New York: Knopf, 1967).

most important advantage, and one which he used with great astuteness, was his enormous popularity with the peoples of Europe, who saw him as their savior. He could, and at times did, use the power of moral suasion to extraordinary effect. Blum has written that it was "Wilson's conviction that he was a special instrument of . . . moral force [which] was the strongest of several considerations prompting his determination to go to Europe to participate in making peace." [61] What he apparently failed to see was that the enormous crowds which cheered during his journeys to London, Paris, and Rome in January of 1919 because he stood for peace and a new world order were also determined to have their governments sign a vindictive peace.

But even aside from the vicissitudes of world opinion, Wilson was haunted by a number of practical problems which were to lead to his eventual defeat. A series of so-called secret treaties and agreements had been made by the Allies even before the American intervention. The French, for example, had been promised by the Russians the return of Alsace-Lorraine, occupation of the Saar Valley, and a "buffer state" to the west of the Rhine River. Italy had been offered portions of Austria which bordered her northern frontier; Japan was to be rewarded with a number of German islands in the Pacific; England, France, Italy, and Greece were to share slices of the Turkish Empire; and Russia had been promised Constantinople and additional territory, a pledge that was cancelled with the signing of a separate peace by the Bolsheviks.

Secondly, the very governments with which Wilson was allied (those of Lloyd George, Clemenceau, and Orlando) owed their existence to pledges that they would exact a vindictive peace at Paris. France had been invaded by Germany twice in a half century, and Clemenceau was not about to sign a "soft" peace; and too, Lloyd George had very recently been victorious in a campaign which stressed a hard line toward the Germans. So strong was the feeling against Germany that she was not even invited to the peace conference until the treaty was to be signed.

Another of Wilson's difficulties was his failure to recognize that he could not avoid domestic politics by making the Atlantic crossing. The defeat of his party in the recent Congressional elections, despite his call for a vote of confidence, was naturally viewed by the other Allied leaders as an enormous blow to his prestige and, consequently, to his leverage at the peace table. Wilson had, moreover, chosen to ignore the Republican party when appointing his peace mission.

---

[61] John M. Blum, *Woodrow Wilson and the Politics of Morality* (Boston: Little, Brown, 1956), p. 159.

Colonel House, Secretary of State Lansing, General Tasker H. Bliss (who had been a member of the Supreme War Council in Paris), and a career diplomat, Henry White, were appointed to the peace delegation. The only Republican in the group was White who, though having extensive experience in European diplomacy, was not a party regular. That Republicans of the stature of former President Taft, Senator Lodge, and Charles Evans Hughes were passed over was certain to cause serious repercussions.

The first item in Wilson's Fourteen Points had been a call for "Open covenants of peace, openly arrived at." Yet almost as soon as the negotiating nations gathered, the chiefs of state met in secret session, much to the annoyance of the throngs of American newsmen who had been sent to cover the conference. Wilson did, however, manage to win at least a partial victory early in the deliberations when it was agreed that the colonies of the Central Powers would become trustees of the soon-to-be-created League of Nations, thus saving them from automatic partition by the victors. But this compromise has since been widely criticized as but another ploy for naked imperialism.[62]

There has been a tendency among historians to excuse many of the errors and compromises made by Wilson at the conference on the grounds that he had one overall objective in mind—the acceptance of his League. Wilson's determination to incorporate the League in the peace settlement can be measured by the pressure which he brought to bear on Lloyd George, Clemenceau, and Orlando both to draft the covenant for the League immediately, and to weave it inextricably into the peace agreement. At the second plenary session on January 25 a League Commission with Wilson at the helm was created to sift through a series of drafts which had been in existence for some time and to decide upon a single presentation to the "Big Four." In ten scant days the commission had formulated the Covenant. The League was to be composed of an Assembly of all member nations, and a Council representing the United States, England, France, Japan, Italy, and four additional nations selected by the Assembly. It was recommended that in most decisions the unanimous agreement of the Council would be necessary.

It was Wilson's belief that the heart of the covenant was Article X, which pledged that "The Members of the League undertake to respect and preserve as against external aggression the territorial integrity and existing political independence of all Members of the

---

[62] See, for example, William Appleman Williams, *The Tragedy of American Diplomacy*, Chap. III. For the British position on self-determination, see Seth P. Tillman, *Anglo-American Relations at the Paris Peace Conference of 1919* (Princeton: Princeton University Press, 1961), pp. 176–228.

League." In case of aggression or of any threat or danger of aggression, the Council "shall advise upon the means by which this obligation shall be fulfilled." Article XI provided that it was the responsibility of each member to "bring to the attention of the Assembly or of the Council any circumstance whatever affecting international relations which threatens to disturb international peace or the good under-standing between nations upon which peace depends." Under this article, any threat of war was to be considered a matter of concern for each League member. The following article was more specific in terms of procedure:

> The Members of the League agree that if there should arise between them any dispute likely to lead to a rupture, they will submit the matter either to arbitration or to inquiry by the Council, and they agree in no case to resort to war until three months after the award by the arbitrators or the report by the Council.

But the teeth of the enforcement mechanism had been filed. Members disregarding the League's covenants were threatened with severance of trade and other economic measures, but the Council could only *recommend* the use of force to protect the covenants.[63]

With the final draft submitted to the Paris Conference, Wilson returned to the United States to sign bills passed by the outgoing Congress, and to initiate his defense of the League and his plan to incorporate it into the peace settlement with Germany. News of the terms of the proposed Covenant had preceded him to America, and so his opponents had considerable time to mobilize their forces—and mobilize them they did. Two days after his arrival from Paris the President met with Congressional leaders and discovered the depth of hostility against himself and the League. By the beginning of March, Senator Lodge, who had emerged as the leader of the faction opposing the League, had obtained the signatures of 37 Republican senators and two senators-elect to a so-called "Round Robin" which rejected the League as formulated and recommended that such an interna-tional organization not be considered until the peace settlement was signed. These 39 signatures were an ominous warning since they represented more than one-third of the membership of the Senate—a number sufficient to defeat any treaty presented to that body. Wilson was defiant in the face of this warning and announced to a New York audience on March 4 that with the return of the treaty from Paris the "gentlemen on this side will find the Covenant not only in it, but so many threads of the treaty tied to the Covenant that you cannot

---

[63] Quotations from Bartlett, *The Record of American Diplomacy*, pp. 464–65.

dissect the Covenant from the treaty without destroying the whole vital structure." Wilson warned that the peace could not survive without the League, and he did not intend to bring back a cadaver from Paris.[64] The world waited to learn the accuracy of this prediction as Wilson sailed for Paris a second time.

Despite the challenge hurled at his opponents, Wilson did return to Paris convinced by both Democratic leaders and sympathetic Republicans such as Taft and President Abbott Lawrence Lowell of Harvard that some amendments would have to be made to ensure acceptance in Washington. To this end Wilson reconvened the League Commission and won its assent to four amendments which allowed any member nation to withdraw from the League; permitted member nations to refuse colonial mandates; exempted such domestic issues as tariff and immigration policies from League jurisdiction; and guaranteed that the League would not interfere with those rights America claimed in the Monroe Doctrine. In return, he was forced to yield to the demands of France, Japan, and Italy regarding territorial acquisitions. Nevertheless, he too wrung some important concessions from would-be colonial powers. France relinquished her demand that the Rhineland be denied to Germany, and in return the United States and England pledged to protect France from future German aggression and established a demilitarized zone to be occupied by Allied troops for 15 years (an agreement the Senate never ratified). Italy, despite the temperamental outbursts of Orlando, was denied both Fiume and a number of African colonies. However, Japan was permitted to annex former German islands in the Pacific. (At the outset of the conference, in exchange for agreeing to place the League at the top of the agenda, Tokyo was given a sphere of influence over Chinese territory in the Shantung area. This eventually led to China's refusal to sign the treaty.)

Another compromise involved the settlement of Eastern Europe. The state of Czechoslovakia was established, containing more than three million Germans (a clear violation of the principle of self-determination). When Poland was resurrected, it was made up of German, Austrian, and Russian territory and it too contained millions of Germans and others who were not Polish.

After a degree of infighting at Paris that was somewhat commensurate with the intensity of the military operations during the war, the Germans were called to Versailles on May 7, 1919, to sign the treaty. Ironically, this was the fourth anniversary of the sinking of the *Lusitania.* Confronted with the 200-page treaty Berlin balked, protest-

---

[64] Blum, *Woodrow Wilson and the Politics of Morality,* p. 171.

ing it had agreed to stop fighting on the basis of a settlement reflecting the Fourteen Points. It was charged that the treaty, often vengeful in tone, was a violation of the terms of the original agreement. But the Allies, particularly Clemenceau, were adamant,[65] and so less than two months after their arrival the Germans signed the treaty (June 28, 1919). In many respects Germany's protest that the peace it was forced to accede to was a harsh and vengeful one was valid. Reparations were exacted; Eastern Europe had been divided in such a manner that Poland and Rumania received unjustifiably generous boundaries; there was no plan for disarmament; and if trade barriers were to be removed, the document failed to indicate how this aim would be implemented.

Several long-range problems resulted from the Versailles agreement. Europe and the world would have to contend with several disgruntled powers—Germany, Austria, and Italy. England, France, Poland, Rumania, and some others had little immediate cause for complaint—but they slowly realized how difficult it would be to coexist with dissatisfied and resentful neighbors, especially if the victorious powers were unwilling to maintain a large margin of military superiority. The willingness of the United States to involve itself in the affairs of Europe was also crucial to the maintenance of peace. A jealous and factious Europe had resulted from the war; more ominous, the United States, the one great power emerging from the war with its vitality intact and its stature enormously enhanced, at first seemed unwilling to cooperate in any meaningful way in the maintenance of peace in Europe and the world.

The day after the Germans signed the treaty Wilson left for the United States, confident that he would triumph over partisan opposition and well-intentioned criticism. On July 10 the Senate received the document, setting in motion a chain of events which would lead to a great and tragic personal defeat for the President. He had fulfilled his promise to attach so many threads of the treaty to the Covenant that the League Covenant could not be dissected from the treaty without destroying the whole vital structure." But the Senate dared what for Wilson was the unthinkable—to destory the vital structure, while leaving the President to mourn over the cadaver.[66]

The Upper Chamber was divided into three groups on the question. The first constituted those who were for ratification—40 in all, and all Democrats. The leader of this faction was Gilbert M. Hitchcock of Nebraska, minority leader of the Senate. On the other

---

[65] See Ray S. Baker, *Woodrow Wilson and World Settlement* (Garden City, N.Y.: Doubleday, 1922), II, p. 501.
[66] See above, pp. 89–90.

end were a dozen or more so-called irreconcilables who wished the treaty's death. Sharing the middle ground were a group of "reservationists" who were willing to sign the document if it contained a number of amendments; this group was led by Senator Lodge of Massachusetts. They reasonably argued that the League overly restricted the country's freedom of action by pledging it to go to war with nations designated by the League, but not necessarily by the United States, as aggressors. A further objection was that the combination of the treaty and the League reinforced the imperialistic position of England, France, and Japan. Some felt the treaty too weak, others too strong. To some extent, the opposition was motivitated by the Republicans' hope to deny Wilson an accomplishment which was—at least at the outset—quite popular.

It was in the interest of the Republican party to discredit the President in the eyes of the nation by attacking the treaty. Further, it was advantageous to such Republican millionaires as Andrew Mellon and Henry Frick to turn back the tide of progressive legislation, particularly tariff reform, with which Wilson was identified. An election for a new President was to be held the following year, and a triumphant Wilson might easily be carried to the White House on the back of the treaty's success.

In an even more subjective vein, the personality of the major figure in the battle against the treaty must be considered. Senator Lodge had earned a reputation as the "scholar in politics" before the emergence of Wilson. The President's meteoric rise from Princeton to the New Jersey State House to the Executive Mansion in a few short years challenged the Massachusetts Senator's position. The controversy over Lodge's motivations continues, unresolved by the Senator's publication in 1925 of his own explanation.[67] Lodge's biographer, John A. Garraty, suggests that the Senator's motivations were political rather than personal, and that he was far more interested in a Republican victory in 1920 than in a personal triumph over Wilson.[68]

Throughout the summer the Committee on Foreign Relations, chaired by Lodge and dominated by a republican majority, considered Wilson's handiwork. Lodge knew that he must stall if he was to turn public opinion from the treaty, for at the beginning of the summer public support for the measure was running high, particularly among members of influential professional groups. By September 10 the Committee was ready to publish its first report, and it proposed 45 amendments and four reservations to the treaty. This attempt was

[67] Henry Cabot Lodge, *The Senate and the League of Nations* (New York: Scribner's, 1925).
[68] See John A. Garraty, *Henry Cabot Lodge: A Biography* (New York: Knopf, 1953), p. 312.

beaten back on the Senate floor through a bipartisan coalition. Switching his strategy, Lodge then proposed that the Senate ratify the Treaty of Versailles, but that it do so with a series of understandings, commonly known as "reservations," that would be binding upon the United States. At the heart of this strategy was the second reservation which sought to guarantee that the United States could not be drawn into war without the express consent of the Congress.

Locked in a struggle of wills with his detractors, Wilson, now sixty-three, decided against the urgent appeals of his doctor to undertake an 8,000 mile speaking tour. His plan was simple and nearly successful—by barnstorming the country in favor of the League, he would so rally public support that the opposition Senators would be unable to pursue their crusade to defeat the settlement. The further west he penetrated, the greater his support; a possible reason for this was the large representation of German-Americans throughout the Midwest. It was states such as Washington, Oregon, and California that received the President's message eagerly and strongly expressed their desire to support his fight against the detractors of the League. Alarmed by this success, several Republican Senators closely followed the President's route, carefully undermining his support.

It is impossible to gauge the effect of Wilson's tour since on September 25 at Pueblo, Colorado, he collapsed. All the remaining speeches—including a group which were to be delivered in Lodge's native New England—were cancelled, and the President's private railroad car, with shades drawn, sped toward Washington. Several days after his arrival in the capital he suffered a paralytic stroke. The recovery was a slow and painful one, so slow that he was unable to meet with his cabinet for seven and a half months. Mrs. Wilson carefully secluded her husband from even his closest advisors for much of this period, and although his mind was unaffected by the stroke, the pressure of the ordeal seems clearly to have seriously impaired his judgment. The President never fully recovered from this illness.

While Wilson convalesced it was politics as usual, and the Senate voted to include the so-called Lodge reservations in the treaty. Believing these reservations, particularly the second, would have the effect of cancelling his accomplishment at Paris, the stricken President advised his supporters to refuse to endorse the Lodge formula. The changes, he believed, would "provide for . . . the nullification of the treaty." [69] The next day, November 19, the Senate voted down the amended treaty, 39 to 55. Those in favor of the revised document consisted of 35 of the "reservationist" Republicans and four Demo-

[69] *Congressional Record*, 66th Cong., 1st sess., p. 8768.

crats who chose to ignore the bidding of their party chieftain. Forty-two Democrats heeded Wilson's advice, and together with 13 "irreconcilable" Republicans they defeated Lodge's plan. A vote was then taken on the treaty without the reservations, and this attempt lost, 38 to 53.

It was not until March of 1920 that the treaty once again came to a vote—and only then because the public could not quite accept its defeat. There appears to have been considerable sentiment for the reservations which insured the independence of action of the United States,[70] but despite public pressure, Lodge bowed to those Republicans who threatened to bolt the party in that election year if he continued to plan a compromise measure with the Democratic leadership. The Senate voted on March 20 on the original League with 15 reservations (an additional one pertaining to Irish independence had been added). Wilson remained obstinate, warned his party that it was all a plot to destroy the League, and of course counseled rejection. This time a majority of the Senate, but not the requisite two-thirds, was in favor of the treaty plus reservations; the vote was 49 to 35. Only 23 Democrats sided with the President, but these 23, voting with the "irreconcilables," were able to keep the nation out of the world organization. Wilson's stubbornness, Lodge's political maneuvering, and the shortsightedness of many within and without the Congress had taken the United States a long step toward abdicating its responsibilities as a world power. The treaty and League as presented by Wilson were not flawless—but more astute, less selfish men would have found a way to both involve the nation in world affairs while remedying some of the obvious faults of the League. It might also be argued that had the American public been convinced that internationalism was necessary for the self-preservation of the nation, then the League Covenant might have had a far better chance of passage. But without massive public support, it was doomed.

There was one last chance for the treaty, which also failed. Wilson asked that the 1920 Presidential election be viewed as a solemn referendum on the question, but the two major parties were unwilling to cooperate. After rejecting the ailing Wilson, the Democrats nominated Governor James M. Cox of Ohio; his running mate was New York's Franklin Delano Roosevelt. Cox had not been identified with the League fight, and while the Democratic platform contained a plank supporting the treaty, it never explicitly voiced opposition to the reservations. Furthermore, Cox wisely chose to play

---

[70] For a discussion of this issue, see Thomas A. Bailey, *Woodrow Wilson and the Great Betrayal* (New York: Macmillan, 1945).

down the League in his campaign, thus rejecting Wilson's referendum concept. As for the Republicans, their choice for president was Senator Warren G. Harding of Ohio, who straddled the issue by advocating an "association of nations for the promotion of international peace" while insisting that this association "so definitely safeguard our sovereignty and recognize our ultimate and unmortgaged freedom of action that it will have back of it . . . the united support of the American people." [71]

Harding's landslide victory buried all hopes of American participation in the League. Few pictures in United States history are more moving and more tragic than the one depicting the brilliant, idealistic Wilson riding beside the vacuous Harding on the way to the latter's inauguration. Another Republican-dominated Congress was elected, and on July 2, 1921, by joint resolution, it declared the war with Germany ended. The final ratifications were exchanged at Berlin on November 11, 1921.[72]

INTERVENTION IN SIBERIA

The long-range consequences of the First World War have occasioned much critical interest. The German drive for hegemony over Europe was turned back, but not decisively since the attempt was to be repeated 20 years later. The enormous cost of the war—in men and resources—proved an all but fatal blow to England and France; they would never again rise to their former greatness. But the United States emerged as unquestionably the world's strongest economic power. Domestically, the war provided unforgettable lessons in the extraordinary possibilities of centralized control and economic integration, thus setting in motion changes in the nation's economic structure that may well have come to fruition even without the catalyst of the Great Depression of the 1930s.[73]

Perhaps the most controversial consequence of the war has been its effect on the course of the Russian Revolution and, more specifically, the attitude of Russia's allies toward the Revolution. The reaction of the United States to the internal upheaval in Russia must be viewed in light of Wilson's own attitude toward revolution. By the time the President took office, Lenin had already formulated a revolutionary philosophy which placed him in direct opposition to

[71] *New York Times*, 8 Oct. 1920, p. 2.
[72] *Public Statutes at Large of the United States*, Vol. 42, Part 2, pp. 1939–45.
[73] See the interview of Link in Garraty, *Interpreting American History*, II, pp. 141–42.

Wilson's determination to reshape the existing international order through gradual reform. The President's attitude toward Lenin was manifest in several ways. During the war Wilson attempted to support the pro-Allied Kerensky faction, which he hoped would liberalize Russia while continuing that nation's contribution to the struggle against Germany. But once the Bolsheviks came to power, Wilson, through intervention and diplomacy, sought the return of a more liberal, multi-party system.

Generally, Wilson and his followers believed that Lenin's concept of revolutionary-socialism would overrun Europe if the United States did not successfully sponsor the establishment of reform, progressive international movements. A victory for the Leninists would have destroyed the selfish imperialistic system, but in Wilson's view, it would also have destroyed liberal institutions and values. The President attempted to reform the international order from within—to weaken traditional imperialism, with its military rivalries, alliances, and wars for colonies and spheres of influence—while at the same time maintaining capitalism.[74]

Critics of Wilson's response to the establishment of the Bolshevik regime which came to power in November 1917 have stressed the President's decision to join with America's Japanese allies in a joint military expedition to Siberia in the summer of 1918. This action was taken against the wishes of the Russian government, which had signed an armistice with the Germans the previous December. The intervention, strongly encouraged by the French and the British, had three ostensible purposes: to protect Allied military equipment at Vladivostok; to aid in the evacuation of Czechoslovakian prisoners of war within Russia; and to improve Russia's ability to defend itself against Germany. The intervention itself was announced as part of the total war effort, and the Administration went to considerable lengths to assure the American public and foreign governments that it was not its intention to interfere with the internal affairs of the Soviet regime. Nevertheless, American soldiers remained on Russian soil for 15 months before the expedition had run its course.

There has been much interest in the last two decades in searching for underlying, more sinister motivations. Two general positions have emerged, the first advanced by those who accept the sincerity of the Administration's announced objectives, but who argue that Wilson's central concern was to moderate the aggressive Far Eastern designs of Japan by insuring that American military personnel were on hand when Japanese soldiers ventured on Russian soil.

[74] Levin, *Woodrow Wilson and World Politics*, pp. 13–49.

According to this interpretation the Japanese sought to absorb Siberia and were ready to capitalize on the precarious position of the recently installed Communist regime to gain control over that territory. Hence, in effect, Wilson was utilizing the American presence to maintain a sort of "open door" in Siberia until the Russian government was sufficiently strong to guarantee the area.[75]

But a number of scholars have challenged this view by attempting to prove that the President's central interest in Siberia had little to do with the war effort, the Czech prisoners, or the Japanese push into Siberia; rather, Wilson was determined to undermine and ultimately to topple the Bolshevik regime. The "open-door" consideration is also turned aside by the argument that the most effective and realistic method of maintaining a truly "open door" in the area was to unseat the Communists while blocking Japanese penetration. The Soviets, once their power was consolidated, would never permit open access to Siberia. The historian most closely associated with this view is William Appleman Williams, whose *American-Russian Relations, 1781–1947* was published in 1952. Characterizing the President as "deeply anti-Bolshevik," [76] Williams insists that Wilson was determined to effect a counterrevolution and thereby destroy the Soviet government.

This thesis is much complicated by Williams' economic bias and especially by his contention that although the pre-1917 American economic penetration of Russia had been endangered by the Communist regime, the Administration was determined to broaden this penetration in the postwar period. The Russian-American Chamber of Commerce reportedly had records of 2,500 American firms which were anxious to enter the Russian market. This thrust, according to Williams, was encouraged by the anti-Bolshevik provisional government which had assured the United States that its capital would receive "the warmest welcome in Russia." [77] It is perhaps important to note that one of the more traditional historians of the intervention also finds a strong economic bias in the American government's motiva-

[75] For the more traditional view, see John A. White, *The Siberian Intervention* (Princeton: Princeton University Press, 1950), and Betty Unterberger, *America's Siberian Expedition, 1918–1920* (Durham, N.C.: Duke University Press, 1956). In his sophisticated study of the intervention, former Ambassador to the Soviet Union George F. Kennan offers a more complex analysis of the President's motives, but he also defends Wilson against charges of manipulation of the crisis to undermine the Communist regime: *The Decision to Intervene* (New York: Atheneum, 1967), Chap. XVII. For a study of the intervention from the point of view of internal Japanese politics, see James William Morley, *The Japanese Thrust into Siberia, 1918* (New York: Columbia University Press, 1957).

[76] William Appleman Williams, *American-Russian Relations, 1781–1947* (New York: Holt, Rinehart & Winston, 1952), p. 149. Williams revised his thesis in two articles published in *Studies on the Left*, III (1963), 24–48, and IV (1964), 39–57.

[77] Williams, *American-Russian Relations*, p. 148.

tions, but a bias directed toward Japan rather than Russia. Betty M. Unterberger writes: "Throughout the course of the Siberian intervention the United States was engaged in a struggle to prevent Japan from gaining control of the Chinese Eastern Railway [linking Vladivostok with Siberia]." With the signing of the Inter-Allied Railway Agreement in January of 1919, "the primary concern of American military forces now became the restoration and protection of the railway instead of the rescue of the Czechs." [78]

Revisionists such as Williams believe the "touchstone" of Wilson's foreign policy to have been "the attempt to use economic and military force to create and guarantee the life of foreign governments modeled on his concept of the economic and political system of the United States." Intervention in Russia, therefore, became part of a comprehensive policy which included the President's attempt to affect the outcome of the Mexican Revolution through an arms embargo and the withholding of diplomatic recognition; his designs to transform the very nature of the German government as a condition of peace; and his determination to limit the Japanese thrust in the Far East. [79]

The difficulty with the Williams/revisionist interpretation is readily apparent. Wilson's personal hostility toward Communism and his desire for the downfall of the Bolshevik regime is a matter of record. But to infer from the President's anti-Communist stance a carefully conceived plot to depose the Russian government is to enter an arena of intense historical debate. [80] A very recent study of Wilson's actions in Siberia, however, does document and support portions of the revisionist interpretation by concluding that the President "intended preventing the establishment of Bolshevism in Russia, and intervention was but one of the methods he used to accomplish this end." [81] The President's true aims were obscured, according to this thesis, because he had learned in his attempts to influence the Mexican Revolution that unless his intentions were kept hidden, his policies were doomed. It would not do to place the Communists in the position—through an openly aggressive policy—of defending Russian political sovereignty against American interference. Secondly, powerful elements in the Congress were opposed to the Siberian expedition and so Wilson was forced to temper his anti-Soviet resolve.

But it is nevertheless insisted that the Chief Executive took

[78] Unterberger, *America's Siberian Expedition*, pp. 107, 117.

[79] Williams, *American-Russian Relations*, p. 158.

[80] See Chapter 5 for discussion of this issue.

[81] Robert James Maddox, "Woodrow Wilson, the Russian Embassy and Siberian Intervention," *Pacific Historical Review* (1967), p. 436.

several measures vis-à-vis Russia which demonstrated his wish to destroy the Soviet regime: the granting of loans by Executive order to British and French efforts against the Bolsheviks; the unofficial, but active, American cooperation in the blockade against Communist-held regions; and the Administration's use of the Russian embassy in Washington—which continued to be staffed by anti-Bolshevik person-nel—to undermine the Leninists.[82]

This interpretation of the Siberian intervention still lacks sufficient documentation to gain general acceptance. However, it is supported by a major study of Anglo-Soviet relations during the war years; although that study stresses the restoration of the Eastern Front against Germany as the basic British objective, the author freely admits that the expedition "was an attempt to apply a military solution to the political problem of the Bolshevik Revolution. As such, the surprising thing is not that its failure was so great, but that so many people allowed themselves to become convinced that it would succeed." [83]

From the point of view of American objectives, it is highly unlikely that the intervention had any important, positive results. Certainly the next two decades were to demonstrate that the attempt to control Japan's aggressive thrust in the Far East required far more than the presence of a few thousand American troops. The interven-tion did not do much to influence the Eastern Front of the war. Finally, if the revisionists are correct in their conclusions, then the strategy was a disaster. It was a disaster from a practical point of view in that foreign troops on Russian soil would almost inevitably drive the Russian people into the arms of the Bolshevik faction since the Leninists were demanding withdrawal. The attempt to weaken the Bolsheviks (if indeed that was Wilson's objective) constituted an indefensible violation of the political and territorial sovereignty of a nation which had so recently been America's ally. Importantly, it was a violation of Wilson's own much heralded goals for the postwar era, the Fourteen Points.

In a book entitled *The Aftermath*, Winston Churchill drew some interesting conclusions regarding the failure of the expedition, but he too missed the central point. Regretting that a larger force was not utilized, Churchill was

> certain that a resolute effort by a comparatively small number of trustworthy American or Japanese troops would have enabled Moscow

---

[82] *Ibid.*, p. 437.
[83] Richard H. Ullman, *Anglo-Soviet Relations, 1917–1921: Intervention and the War* (Princeton: Princeton University Press, 1961), I, p. 330.

to be occupied by National Russian [anti-Bolshevik] and Allied forces even before the German collapse took place. Divided counsels and cross-purposes among the Allies, American mistrust of Japan, and the personal opposition of President Wilson, reduced Allied intervention in Russia during the war to exactly the point where it did the utmost harm and gained the least advantage.[84]

While it is of interest that Churchill cannot be used to support revisionist views of Wilson's motivations, the statesman, like other critics of Allied diplomacy with the Bolsheviks, was obviously quite willing to utilize military force to reshape a government to his own liking. It is little wonder that contemporary historians, more sensitive to the pitfalls of excessive arrogance in dealing with other nations, have been highly critical of the whole Siberian debacle.

The First World War and its aftermath nearly slaughtered a generation of young men, altered the map of Europe, embittered Germany, provided the catalyst for the 1917 Bolshevik Revolution, fundamentally weakened England and France, and convinced many that the victors were more interested in perpetuating empires than establishing lasting peace. Domestically, the League battle, the "Red" hysteria, and the growing reluctance to enter into binding international commitments created an unhealthy underpinning for the seemingly glittering Twenties. The American attitude toward the League undoubtedly hastened the demise of that body while contributing to the growing global insecurity. Germany's unwillingness to accept a secondary role in Europe and the failure of the United States, England, and France to police the postwar settlement account in large measure for the disquieting European instability of the following two decades.

[84] Winston Churchill, *The Aftermath* (New York: Scribner's, 1929), p. 285.

Three

NATIONALISM
AND ISOLATIONISM
IN THE 1920s

The dozen years bounded by the elections of Warren G. Harding and Franklin D. Roosevelt constitute one of the most misunderstood and underrated periods in American diplomatic history. Overemphasis on the negative aspects of the League controversy has led to the popular notion that these years witnessed a wholesale American withdrawal from the responsibilities of world leadership. This idea, which has undergone extensive revision in recent years, stemmed in large measure from a failure to carefully define what is meant by isolationism. If the concept is understood in its narrow sense as seclusion from world affairs, then the nation was certainly not isolationist in that period; it was deeply involved in disarmament conferences, war debts and reparations negotiations, formulas for lasting peace, and a wide variety of social, economic, and cultural contacts with the rest of the world. Its outright interventionist policy toward Latin America continued, although by the end of the decade there evolved a very basic modification. American interest and involvement in a balance of power in the Far East continued long after the League question was dead. And throughout the period

101

American policy-makers actively sought the expansion of the nation's worldwide trade and investment network.

INVOLVEMENT WITHOUT COMMITMENT

Far from isolationist in any strict sense of the term, American foreign policy during the Twenties might best be defined as a refusal to enter into political commitments with powers or groups of powers, whether such agreements took the form of formal treaties or membership in world organizations. The period was one of "involvement without commitment." [1] During his last year as Chairman of the Senate Foreign Relations Committee, Senator Henry Cabot Lodge of Massachusetts wrote that except in times of war, there "never [has been] a period when the United States has been more active and its influence more felt internationally than between 1921 and 1924." [2]

But many historians have been far less generous; representative is Selig Adler, whose *The Isolationist Impulse* echoes the conclusion of many that a neo-isolationism characterized the Twenties and became much more profound after the Crash of 1929 shattered much of America's complacency.[3] A major challenge to this traditional view of the 1920s as an isolationist decade was presented by revisionist historian William Appleman Williams in a 1954 article for the liberal—some would say radical—journal, *Science and Society*. Williams wrote that an overemphasis on the League fight and a misunderstanding of the underpinnings of Republican foreign policy created an unwarranted legend; far from seeking the avoidance of international participation, American policy formulators sought the establishment of a world order based upon agreements reached by the major industrial nations. This was a conservative objective, Williams insists, because it was rooted in the belief in the sanctity of private property and in the prevention of revolution. Hence it did not rule out intervention to maintain the established order—particularly in Latin America. It is further argued that to realize this goal, successive Republican administrations directed their policies toward moderating the impact of the Soviet Revolution, preventing revolutions in colonial areas, winning Japanese and German acceptance of American

---

[1] L. Ethan Ellis, *Republican Foreign Policy, 1921–1933* (New Brunswick, N.J.: Rutgers University Press, 1968), p. 34.

[2] Henry Cabot Lodge, "Foreign Relations of the United States, 1921–1924," *Foreign Affairs,* II (June 1924), p. 526.

[3] Selig Adler, *The Isolationist Impulse: Its Twentieth Century Reaction* (New York: Abelard-Schuman, 1957), p. 219.

objectives, and gaining British acknowledgment of the preeminence of the American position in the new international order.[4]

The most controversial aspect of Williams's critique is his contention that the United States attempted to realize its goals primarily through economic policies, and that this conscious objective was the "basic theme" of American diplomacy during these years.[5] This thesis has been attacked on several grounds, but most generally because of Williams's tendency to use isolationism and seclusion synonymously. In point of fact, many traditional historians have acknowledged that the nation was isolationist in the sense of avoiding political precommitments, but they have also recognized that American policymakers were actively (though certainly not exclusively) seeking expansion through trade and investment. They do not agree with Williams's theory that American leaders utilized their economic position to create a new world order dominated by the United States—that is, that there was a more grand, or sinister, motivation behind Republican economic policies.[6]

It would seem that the most reasonable view of the Twenties, and a view reflective of the scholarship of several of the more convincing revisionists, is that of L. Ethan Ellis, who concludes that the period "manifested more of cooperation, less of arrant self-containment, than has usually been ascribed to it. . . . the time [was] a mixed one, combining traditional self-concern and imperviousness to outside factors with occasional, perhaps exceptional, but very real willingness to participate in international action." [7] This is an eminently fair characterization because it restores the balance that has been lost by an excessive emphasis on the League question. The defeat of Wilson's beloved Covenant so early in the interbella period has led historians to react at times as if that one event overshadowed the entire era. Although it is certainly true that political commitments were avoided and that the nation was preoccupied with narrow domestic concerns long before the Crash of 1929, it is nevertheless obvious that by the end of the Republican interregnum a notable degree of international cooperation had occurred.

The emergence of the United States from the war as the world's preeminent economic power made interaction inevitable. American economic supremacy was partly the result of the decline of the more

---

[4] William Appleman Williams, "The Legend of Isolationism in the 1920's," *Science and Society*, XVIII (Winter 1954), 16–17.

[5] *Ibid.*, p. 16.

[6] Robert James Maddox, "Another Look at Isolationism in the 1920's," *Mid-America*, LIII (Jan. 1971), p. 39.

[7] Ellis, *Republican Foreign Policy*, p. 34.

established powers after the war, and partly the result of the nation's shift from debtor to creditor status. The extent of this shift was most impressive; in 1919 private American investments abroad were $3 billion greater than foreign investments in the United States, and by 1929 this margin had grown to $8 billion. With the conclusion of the war, an additional $10 billion was owed to the United States government. In evaluating the significance of this economic leap, one must consider that by 1920 the United States was producing more goods and services, per capita and total, than any other nation; the national income of the United States was greater than the combined national incomes of Great Britain, France, Germany, Japan, Canada, and 17 smaller nations! [8]

America emerged from the war as the world's most prosperous state; it was the responsibility of three Republican administrations to formulate policies which would capitalize on this strength. Broadly, these policies were: economic expansion, both in trade and investments abroad; international stability in a peaceful world; and the prevention of revolution. It is important to view these goals as interrelated since international stability and the absence of wars and revolutions were clearly a prerequisite for continued expansion into foreign markets. This is not to suggest that peace and stability were not sought and valued for their own sake.

GLOBAL AND DOMESTIC DISLOCATIONS

An assessment of American foreign policy between the wars must also take into account, in 1919–32 terms, the state of the postwar world, the climate of opinion in the United States, and the dilemma of the nation's diplomatic leadership. The enormous destruction of the war, the disillusionment following the peace settlement, and the global suffering caused by the Great Depression, had destroyed the tenuous pre-1914 balance of power. The peoples of the embittered nations—particularly Germany, Japan, and Italy—soon became the enthusiastic supporters of demagogues who preached hate and advocated aggression. Germany, forced to surrender all her overseas colonies as well as the coveted Alsace-Lorraine region, was left with a 100,000-man army, a peace treaty which burdened the nation with sole responsibility for the holocaust, and a war reparations schedule which threatened bankruptcy. For the demagogic Adolf Hitler and his

[8] For statistics, see David A. Shannon, *Between the Wars: America, 1919–1941* (Boston: Houghton Mifflin, 1965), pp. 48–49.

National Socialist party, the postwar turmoil provided an ideal opportunity to win support for a nationalistic and militaristic solution. The fear of a communist takeover of Germany further strengthened Hitler's hand, as did his promise to save the nation from the Depression. Italy, greatly weakened by the economic drain of the war on her already wobbly economy, was deeply embittered by the division of the spoils at Versailles. The first of the Fascist dictators, Benito Mussolini, came to power legally in 1922. As early as the following year he demonstrated his determination to gain Corfu; four years later he had established virtual control over Albania.

The war had left Russia tragically divided, particularly after the February 1917 Revolution passed into a more radical phase with the Bolshevik coup in November. The civil war which followed the Leninist seizure of power, together with the devastating effect of the Depression, greatly debilitated that Asian power. Russia's internal weakness was of critical importance to the stability of the Far East, where a vigorous Russian presence might have provided a counter-weight to Tokyo's ambitions.

Japan had shrewdly joined the Allies in an attempt to strengthen its position in the Far East while the Europeans slaughtered one another. At Versailles, Japan received important German colonial mandates in the Pacific, but within a decade it was obvious that she would not be content with these gains. An island nation heavily dependent upon trade for raw materials and markets, Japan was deeply affected by the Depression's destruction of the world's trade network; Tokyo's solution was aggressive expansion throughout East Asia.

The catastrophe of the late Thirties might have been avoided had England and France not paid so dearly for their 1918 victory. The war had had a critical effect on the British economy by disrupting trade patterns and forcing the liquidation of foreign investments. In addition to the staggering financial burden of the war, France's physical loss was enormous because much of the contest was waged on her territory. These hardships caused many in both countries to resolve not to risk another conflict, but such timidity hastened the second holocaust by emboldening the aggressive nations. Given their post-1918 condition, it was virtually impossible for England and France to block the ambitions of these powers without the close assistance of the United States.

In responding to the global dislocations which followed the First World War, successive American Administrations formulated policies which were clearly reflective of the national temperament: the demand for demobilization and the return to "normalcy" after a disappointing and disillusioning victory; the fear of radicalism, influenced in part by labor's insistence that it not lose any of its wartime gains, and in part by revolutions abroad, particularly the Bolshevik triumph; and the determination to avoid formal political treaties with the European powers. The American public's apprehension was heightened by a serious recession in the early postwar period, the result of Wilson's failure to plan adequately for the restoration of the American economy to a peacetime footing. There was great hardship during the 1918–19 winter, followed by a severe depression in 1920–21. Farmers suffered intensely, and nearly one quarter of the work force were unemployed.[9]

It is little wonder during this period of economic hardship and fear of the spread of communism that many people exaggerated the threat to American institutions. The so-called Red peril had a brief, but frightening, flirtation with the American public as attempts were made to rid the country of "revolutionary" elements. In so doing, Americans sanctioned the violation of perhaps their most precious tradition—civil liberties. Labor militancy was too often seen as an extension of the Soviet's worldwide revolutionary thrust; retaliatory measures, at times vicious, were taken by the new American Legion, the revitalized Ku Klux Klan, and other ultranationalist groups. This class warfare and xenophobia soon directed itself not only against militantly radical activity, but also against individuals and groups considered undesirable—including liberals, Blacks, Catholics, Jews, and recent immigrants. A number of bitter strikes, particularly the 1919 Chicago steel strike (a major national effort to organize the industry's workers), and the coal strike of the same year, convinced many that revolutionary forces were determined to undermine and topple the government.[10]

When in the spring of 1919 a plot was uncovered, at first thought to be Communist-inspired, to murder anti-labor public officials, repression replaced reason. With little regard for historic American civil liberties, Wilson's Attorney General, A. Mitchell Palmer, conducted a series of raids without warrants to round up and prosecute suspected radicals or their sympathizers. The persecutions which followed resulted in the actual deportation of more than 600

[9] See George Soule, *Prosperity Decade: From War to Depression, 1917–1929* (New York: Holt, Rinehart & Winston, 1947), pp. 104–5.

[10] The most authoritative account of the phenomenon is Robert K. Murray, *Red Scare: A Study in National Hysteria, 1919–1920* (Minneapolis: University of Minnesota Press, 1955). Murray reviews the era in an interview conducted by historian John A. Garraty and published in Garraty, *Interpreting American History: Conversations with Historians* (New York: Macmillan, 1970), II, pp. 147–68.

"radicals." [11] Yet the fears were clearly exaggerated, for the best evidence available indicates that there were not more than 40,000 to 60,000 members of the Communist party in the United States in 1919–20. By 1925 party membership was reduced to no more than 20,000.[12]

Although Palmer's campaign was short-lived, it was a frightening example of governmentally-sanctioned excesses which were grounded in mass hysteria and fear. It is little wonder that two Italian immigrant radicals, Nicola Sacco and Bartolomeo Vanzetti, were condemned to death for murder in a trial that centered far more on their alleged radical activities than on evidence pertinent to the indictment. The case soon became symbolic the world over of the repression and fear that had resulted from postwar social and economic upheavals.

It was within this domestic context—the distrust of things foreign, the determination to avoid permanent entangling alliances, and the desire to concentrate on prosperity at home—that successive Republican administrations conducted the diplomatic relations of the nation.[13] One widely respected student of the era has concluded that "politics generally reflected, almost mirror-like, the state of opinion in this country on foreign affairs." [14]

The Harding, Coolidge, and Hoover constituencies were far more interested in prosperity at home than in formal overseas obligations. And when the glittering prosperity of the Twenties collapsed, men in private and public life had all the more reason to turn their attention inward. The newness of America's role as a rich and powerful nation was a major factor conditioning its responses in the 1920s, for both the public and its leadership were unaccustomed to and often unaware of the implications of the postwar realignment. Wilson had, after all, attempted to take the nation down a comparatively new path; non-involvement, although not always respected in fact, had a good deal of historical sanction behind it. The Republicans were much aware that they represented a people not especially concerned with matters beyond their continental boundaries and

[11] William E. Leuchtenburg, *The Perils of Prosperity, 1914–1932* (Chicago: University of Chicago Press, 1958), p. 80.

[12] For figures, see Murray interview in Garraty, *Interpreting American History*, II, p. 150.

[13] Important accounts of the Twenties are to be found in Frederick Lewis Allen, *Only Yesterday: An Informal History of the Nineteen Twenties* (New York: Harper & Row, 1931); Shannon, *Between the Wars*; John D. Hicks, *Republican Ascendancy, 1921–1933* (New York: Harper & Row, 1960); Paul A. Carter, *The Twenties in America* (New York: Crowell, 1968); Leuchtenburg, *The Perils of Prosperity*; and Arthur M. Schlesinger, Jr., *The Age of Roosevelt: The Crisis of the Old Order, 1919–1933* (Boston: Houghton Mifflin, 1957).

[14] Interview of Robert H. Ferrell in Garraty, *Interpreting American History*, II, p. 200.

understandably concluded that they would not be in power long if they moved much beyond the rather narrow restrictions placed upon them by a cautious public.

The policies of the party in power were also reflective of the delicate balance which always exists between the Executive Branch, Congress, and the public. While the Constitution grants primary responsibility to the President for the exercise of foreign policy, the Congress, and particularly the Senate, has at times exercised very considerable power. The President's action is further circumscribed by public opinion, the conflicting goals of other nations, internal critics, and the desire to be reelected.

Between the close of the First World War and the outbreak of World War II, the Congress played a far more critical role in foreign relations than we have become accustomed to in the nuclear age. The rejection of the Wilsonian concept of the postwar international order greatly reduced the prestige of the President as diplomatic leader, and throughout the Twenties the Congress was more powerful on an operational level than was the Executive Branch.[15] This phenomenon came about partly as a result of the Wilsonian debacle, and partly because Harding, Coolidge, and Hoover were all without formal training or practical experience in diplomacy. Although far more knowledgeable about European affairs than his two immediate predecessors, Hoover's involvement had centered on the making of his own fortune and the reconstruction of war-shattered Europe. (This generalization holds for the following decade as well, since Roosevelt's contact with foreign affairs before his inauguration was limited.) As a consequence, all three Republican presidents were forced to rely heavily on their Secretaries of State and the rest of the diplomatic entourage.

Harding was particularly fortunate in his choice of the brilliant Charles Evans Hughes as Secretary of State, and Hughes' biographer makes it clear that while never taking advantage of the President's trust, the Secretary "kept the reins of foreign policy securely in his own hands. . . . [He] was allowed perhaps the widest range of discretion ever permitted an American Cabinet officer in this field." [16] Although more actively interested in foreign affairs than Harding, Coolidge also left Secretary of State Frank B. Kellogg in almost complete control of foreign relations.[17] The interaction between Hoover and Henry L.

---

[15] Ellis, *Republican Foreign Policy*, pp. 38–39.

[16] Merlo J. Pusey, *Charles Evans Hughes* (New York: Columbia University Press, 1963), II, pp. 428–29.

[17] See L. Ethan Ellis, *Frank B. Kellogg and American Foreign Relations, 1925–1929* (New Brunswick, N.J.: Rutgers University Press, 1961).

Stimson, a wealthy Eastern lawyer and strong-minded internationalist, was far more complicated since the Secretary was very often at odds with his equally strong-willed chief.

To the contemporary eye, the relationship between the Presidents of the Twenties and the Congress seems particularly strange, since little attempt was made to influence the legislature in matters touching upon the foreign relations of the country. What relationship there was existed between the White House and the powerful Senate Foreign Relations Committee, whose leadership was shared by two particularly disparate political figures. Senator Henry Cabot Lodge of Massachusetts, who served from 1919 to 1924, was a Boston Brahmin, an expansionist, a leading opponent of Wilson's League, and a strict party regular. His successor, Idaho's William E. Borah, was prairie born and lacked the social, educational, and cultural advantages of the aristocratic Lodge. More importantly, their attitudes toward the role of the Senate in foreign affairs varied widely since Lodge was content if the Senate were merely consulted while Borah demanded all of the traditional prerogatives of the Congress in the execution of foreign policy. Whereas Lodge was comfortable with the workings of the regular diplomatic channels, Borah was impatient with anything that smacked of secret diplomacy and consistently strove for wide popular participation and debate. Unfortunately, as his biographer points out, the new chairman "never seemed to consider the possibility that popular sentiment might impose its will upon statesmen who wished to deal rationally with . . . issues." [18]

UNILATERIALISM AND THE INTERNATIONALISTS

To appreciate the position of the "isolationists" of the 1920s, those who opposed binding political commitments with other nations, one must understand their fundamental opposition to the collective security doctrine of the internationalists. Basically, adherents of collective security argued that the most effective means of settling international disputes and preventing aggression was not through the use of unilateral force (often seen as morally wrong as well as ineffective) but through a combination of states using their resources and influence to prevent an outbreak of hostilities or to deter aggressor nations. Opponents of collective security favored the retention of a national military force—but one for the defense of America and not

[18] Marian C. McKenna, *Borah* (Ann Arbor, Mich.: University of Michigan Press, 1961), p. 218.

for overseas campaigns. Their major tenent was "unilateralism," a theory which opposed commitments, through alliances, which would limit the freedom of action of the United States. Isolationists argued that the nation could better serve the cause of world peace through its example as a great, democratic, prosperous state than it could through entangling alliances and the use of force.

Many of the isolationists of the Twenties (and of the Thirties) were also noninterventionists who insisted that America should not have entered World War I and must not take any steps which might lead to entry in a second European conflagration. But this attitude toward Europe was not always, or even usually, manifest toward Latin America or the Far East. Many who sought to expand these regions were isolationist toward Europe. Used in this general sense, the designation isolationist included a broad range of national leaders—from Lodge, who was strongly interventionist before 1917, to Borah, who steadfastly opposed American entry into the First World War. Other isolationist leaders included Senators Robert La Follette (Wisconsin), Hiram Johnson (California), Burton K. Wheeler (Montana), Gerald P. Nye (North Dakota), and Arthur H. Vandenberg (Michigan); two early New Dealers, Raymond Moley and Hugh Johnson, were isolationists, as was the aviator and popular hero, Charles A. Lindbergh.

While generalizations of this sort are usually to be avoided, it is reasonable to conclude that isolationism in the Twenties was strongest in the Midwest and among certain ethnic groups, particularly German, Italian, and Irish Americans. It had a wide attraction for Roman Catholics, farmers, and agrarian progressives, and tended to be stronger in rural than in urban America. The Republican party was more the ideological home of the isolationists, but many urban Republicans were internationalists; the isolationist leadership also included Democratic Senator Wheeler. Since isolationism, as defined above, permeated the thinking of such a wide spectrum of Americans it is difficult to place geographical, ethnic, or social limits on the phenomenon.

Internationalists accepted the necessity of formal commitments to influence and maintain world peace. Those who have come to be regarded as "realists" argued that the United States could not avoid involvement in a major war since its own security interests would inevitably be directly involved. They advocated formal, cooperative efforts to stay the hand of would-be aggressors or, if this failed, the offer of military assistance to the victims of aggression. Internationalist leaders included Wilson; Henry L. Stimson, Hoover's Secretary of State; Cordell Hull, head of the State Department under Roosevelt;

Senators Tom Connally (Texas), James Byrnes (South Carolina), Alben Barkley (Kentucky), and Carter Glass (Virginia). The most consistent support for the internationalist position in the Twenties came from the Northeast and the South. Those of Anglo-Saxon origin, more than any other component of the ethnic mix, were closely associated with this philosophy, as were Eastern financiers, bankers, and large urban publications such as the *New York Times* and the *New York Herald Tribune*. In general, it was more an urban than a rural affiliation.

SINKING THE SHIPS

It is not surprising that among the most immediate reactions to the holocaust of World War I were attempts to limit what had come to be known as the arms race. By far the most productive of these attempts was the 1921–22 Washington Naval Conference which sought to control the competition between the great powers for naval superiority while resolving a number of problems related to the Far East. Japan had been one of the Allies during the First World War, but it had been widely acknowledged in the United States and elsewhere that Japan's central interest was in solidifying her position in the Pacific rather than in crushing the Central Powers. The evidence for this view was considerable. During the Versailles Conference the Japanese had demanded Germany's insular possessions in the Pacific north of the Equator and control of former German economic rights in Shantung. China had been so provoked by the treaty's inclusion of the second of these demands (Wilson apparently feared Japan would not join the League if she did not win control of Shantung) that she refused to sign the pact.

Even during the war the United States attempted to control the rate of Japanese economic expansion, particularly in China, with the November 1917 Lansing-Ishii Agreement endorsing the "open door" but acknowledging Japanese "special interests" in China.[19] The following summer the Wilson Administration sponsored a second scheme to curtail Japanese economic hegemony: a banking consortium of the United States, Britain, France, and Japan to extend loans to the Chinese government. And while China ultimately chose to seek loans on the world market rather than utilize the consortium, the very existence of the banking arrangement was evidence of America's fears

---

[19] *Papers Relating to the Foreign Relations of the United States, 1917,* p. 264. See Burton F. Beers, *Vain Endeavor: Robert Lansing's Attempts to End the American-Japanese Rivalry* (Durham, N.C.: Duke University Press, 1962).

about the expanding Japanese influence in the Far East. As noted in the previous chapter, the Wilson Administration's distrust of Japan was also a factor in the Siberian intervention decision.

The most effective deterrent to Japanese dominance in the Far East was the naval strength of foreign powers. The United States had initiated a major naval building effort with the Naval Appropriations Act of 1916, and even though the war effort had blunted the thrust of this program, by 1919 America had the second most powerful navy in the world; there was every indication that if the rate of ship construction continued, its navy would be more powerful than England's in less than a decade. In 1918 the Congress approved appropriations for a five-year building plan which envisioned a fighting fleet as powerful as the combined naval strength of the other world powers! A naval force of this size provided the United States with considerable diplomatic leverage, which was utilized by the 1919 transfer of the major portion of the battle fleet (nearly as large as the entire Japanese navy) to the Pacific.

Understandably, England was alarmed by American naval plans. At the close of the war she had the world's strongest fleet and believed that the continuance of a secure empire rested upon her naval superiority; yet a naval race with Japan and the United States would have been ruinous to the British postwar economy. For this reason Prime Minister Lloyd George obtained Wilson's pledge at the Paris Conference that in return for support of the League concept and of certain amendments to the treaty which Wilson was then spon-soring the United States would postpone a second five-year naval building plan. The American government did not consider itself bound by this pledge, however, once it rejected the League.

The world's third greatest sea power, Japan, had by this time initiated a major building program of its own, designed to compete with the American force in the Pacific. Eight battleships and eight battle cruisers were scheduled for the first phase of the program, and each year an additional battleship and battle cruiser were to be built. The threat to Washington and London was obvious.

All of this was complicated by the existence of an alliance between Britain and Japan, first concluded in 1902 and broadened in 1905, which pledged that if either should go to war to protect its Far Eastern interests, the other would remain neutral; but if either were attacked by a third power in such a war, the other would come to its aid. When this treaty was renewed in 1911, England sought to exclude the possibility of joint Anglo-Japanese action against the United States, a potential third power, but the attempt failed. Therefore, at least on paper, the British nation was committed to join Japan should her Far Eastern possessions be challenged by the United States. It was a most awkward position for England, especially since the continued existence of the treaty seemed to indicate at least tacit British support for Japanese expansion in the Pacific area. Neither American fears nor the fears of various Commonwealth countries such as Canada and Australia were quieted by British assurances that the alliance would not lead to a war with the United States.

An orderly disarmament, or at least an arms limitation, was thus clearly linked to stability in the Pacific. But the United States and Japan—and England to perhaps a lesser degree—could not agree to a reduction of naval strength unless they were guaranteed that their Pacific possessions and interests would not be threatened by such reductions. While the resources of the three nations would have been seriously strained by a naval race, each could not have survived the public outcry that would have resulted from its electing to economize at the expense of what was seen to be its national security interest.[20]

Much credit for the American initiative on arms limitation must go to Senator Borah, for although vehemently opposed to Wilson's League proposal for international stability, Borah embraced the limitations panacea. At a special session of the new Sixty-seventh Congress in April 1921 he introduced a resolution requesting the President to sponsor a naval conference of the United States, Great Britain, and Japan. While Harding preferred to pursue the 1916 naval building program, public support for Borah's alternative forced the President to reconsider his stance, and when the naval appropriations bill of 1921 was passed, it included Borah's resolution.

At first, a conference of the "big five" naval powers was proposed: the United States, Britain, Japan, France, and Italy. But soon the advisability of a broader conference was acknowledged, and four additional Asiatic powers, China, the Netherlands, Portugal, and Belgium, were invited. The success of the Bolshevik Revolution had soured the West toward Russia and so that essential participant was not included. Interestingly, in the months following the call of the conference the Harding Administration sought to convince the American people that this "Peace Conference"—the term was used very loosely for public relations purposes—had greater promise of meeting American objectives than Wilson's conference at Versailles. It

---

[20] These arguments are considered in Frederic L. Paxson, *Postwar Years: Normalcy, 1918–1923* (Berkeley, Calif.: University of California Press, 1948) and Harold and Margaret Sprout, *Toward a New Order in Sea Power* (Princeton, N.J.: Princeton University Press, 1946). Also useful here is Armin Rappaport, *The Navy League of the United States* (Detroit, Mich.: Wayne State University Press, 1962) because of its insistence that the "big navy" people were far less influential than is generally assumed.

was to be held on American soil and so presumably was less likely to be controlled by designing Europeans; unlike Wilson, the new President would not insist upon being a delegate; and both a Republican and a Democratic member of the Senate Foreign Relations Committee were appointed to the American delegation. To set the mood representatives were invited to witness the interment of the Unknown Soldier at Arlington Memorial Cemetery on the opening day of the conference, Armistice Day, 1921.

After the requisite ceremonies the conferees got down to business in a surprisingly short time. In his opening remarks the American representative and permanent presiding officer, Secretary of State Charles Evans Hughes, stunned his audience by proposing specific and sweeping naval reductions: the United States would dismantle 15 ships and halt the construction of 15 others; England would scrap 19 existing ships and pledge not to build four new ones; and Japan would eliminate ten ships from its navy and not complete the building of an additional seven. Hughes also indicated that he had plans for the limitation of other naval components such as submarines and aircraft carriers. The formula included the postponement of all major naval construction for ten years. The conference was greatly impressed by the sweep of Hughes' design and an observer is reported to have announced that in a half-hour the Secretary destroyed more ships "than all the admirals of the world have sunk in a cycle of centuries." [21]

The Hughes formula was not adopted as presented and extensive secret negotiations followed the "open diplomacy" of the initial day of the conference. As the representatives haggled about ratios, they negotiated an alternative to the Anglo-Japanese Alliance, since American endorsement of any ratio depended upon the disposition (or perhaps more accurately, the dissolution) of the alliance. The alternative to the Anglo-Japanese pact was the Four-Power Treaty, signed by the United States, Britain, Japan, and France on December 13, 1921. The signatory powers agreed to respect each other's rights in the Pacific and to refer differences to a four-power conference. Although this was not a mutual alliance treaty, it did contain a pledge to consult one another in the event of an attack on one of the powers.[22]

[21] Quoted in Mark Sullivan, *The Great Adventure at Washington: The Story of the Conference* (Garden City, N.Y.: Doubleday, 1922), p. 28(n).

[22] Van Alstyne points out that Hughes' success in "providing for mutual consultation regarding 'any Pacific question' . . . was short-lived: as the price for its approval, the Senate wrote in a reservation stipulating that 'under the terms of this treaty there is no commitment to armed force, no alliance, no obligation to join in any defense.' . . . This reservation, rather than the treaty itself, represented the spirit of the postwar period, and, except as paper documents, the Washington treaties passed into oblivion." Richard Van Alstyne, *The Rising American Empire*

The pact was to be in force for an initial ten years, and after the expiration of this period any one of the parties could withdraw following one year's notice. Specifically, the contracting parties had agreed "to respect their rights in relation to their insular possessions and insular dominions in the region of the Pacific Ocean." [23] By specifying insular possessions rather than all Pacific possessions, Hughes had safeguarded American interests in the Philippines without endorsing Japanese expansion on the Asian mainland.

Japan had lost much and gained very little, but was compensated in large measure by the Five-Power Treaty, signed two months later. Hughes had originally sought agreement on a 5:5:3 capital ship ratio for the United States, Britain, and Japan, respectively. But Japan would sign a naval limitations treaty only if she were given a higher ratio *or* if the limitations treaty contained guarantees of her special naval position in the Pacific. Demands for a higher ratio were dropped when the American government agreed to suspend further fortification of its Pacific island possessions (except Hawaii) and the British pledged not to fortify the western Pacific area (except for the islands near Canada, Australia, and New Zealand). Convinced that these additional guarantees would insure Japanese supremacy in that area of the Pacific of immediate concern and thus obviate the need for greater naval strength, Japan agreed conditionally to the modified formula. Hughes next sought to mollify France, which demanded a ratio equal to that of Japan rather than of Italy (the Hughes formula for the "big five" had been 5:5:3:1.67:1.67). The Secretary of State dramatically appealed personally to Premier Aristide Briand to rescue the stalemated conference, and France agreed to the 1.67 ratio, but only as it applied to battleships and battle cruisers.

Thus the Five-Power Treaty, signed February 6, 1922, established a ratio on capital ships, called for the destruction of some existing vessels and set limits on the size of battleships, cruisers, and aircraft carriers. The status quo as it applied to the fortification of the western Pacific area was guaranteed by a provision pledging that "no new fortifications or naval bases shall be established in the territories and possessions specified, that no measures shall be taken to increase the existing naval facilities for the repair and maintenance of naval forces, and that no increase shall be made in the coast defenses of the territories and possessions . . . specified." [24] The treaty was to remain in effect until December 31, 1936; a signatory nation wishing to terminate after that date was obliged to offer two years' notice.

(Chicago: Quadrangle, 1965), p. 204. This last comment would seem to be unfair since it was not the intent of the Four-Power Treaty to provide for mutual assistance.

[23] Bartlett, *The Record of American Diplomacy*, p. 490.

[24] *Ibid.*, pp. 487–88.

With Japan thus assured of her naval position in the Pacific, the other governments, and the United States Senate in particular, sought assurances that the Japanese would not use the Washington agreements to justify expansion in China. (It can, and has, been argued that the Washington treaties did not "give" Japan dominance over the Western Pacific since the United States had been weak in that area ever since it took the Philippines.)[25] Pressured by Hughes, the delegates molded the Nine-Power Treaty, binding them "To respect the sovereignty, the independence, and the territorial and administrative integrity of China"; and "To provide the fullest and most unembarrassed opportunity to China to develop and maintain for herself an effective and stable government." The treaty also contained a pledge to apply more effectively "the principles of the Open Door or equality of opportunity in China for the trade and industry of all nations." [26] The problem here and elsewhere in the Washington treaties was a noticeable absence of any mechanism to enforce the various provisions, if, indeed, any "mechanism" can render a treaty enforceable if the contracting powers do not wish to abide by the agreed terms. Much depended upon the slender reed of the good faith of the contracting parties, and Japan at least was soon to demonstrate slight regard for the agreements.[27] While the United States sharply curtailed its capital ship construction, Japan, France, Italy, and Great Britain continued to build warships since there was no limitation on submarines, destroyers, or cruisers under 10,000 tons. Nevertheless, a recent study of the conference agreements argues that American interests were furthered at Washington since the accord made it possible for Japan and Great Britain to end their alliance. The conference also moved the United States to a position of approximate naval parity with Great Britain and naval superiority over Japan.[28]

In the years between 1922 and 1930 Japan planned or built 125 warships; France, 119; Italy, 82; Britain, 74; and the United States, 11.[29] So even the relative advantage to the United States was short-lived. The failure of the Washington treaties to place limitations on cruisers, auxiliary craft, and aircraft was an obvious and much noted deficiency. But in the long run there was an even greater threat to American security implicit in the treaties, and that was the failure

[25] See Ferrell interview in Garraty, *Interpreting American History*, II, pp. 201–2.

[26] Bartlett, *The Record of American Diplomacy*, p. 489.

[27] See, for example, Sadao Asada, "Japan's 'Special Interests' and the Washington Conference, 1921–22," *American Historical Review*, LXVII (1961), 62–70.

[28] Thomas H. Buckley, *The United States and the Washington Conference, 1921–1922* (Knoxville, Tenn.: University of Tennessee Press, 1970), p. 187–188.

[29] *Senate Documents*: Miscellaneous, 78th Cong., 2nd sess., No. 202, p. 2.

of the American public to view the agreements as the beginning and not as the culmination of the efforts to rid the globe of war. This prerequisite political basis to the treaties was a matter of general indifference to the American public.[30]

Later in the 1920s Calvin Coolidge's Administration called upon the "Big Five" of the Washington Conference to meet at Geneva to discuss further naval limitations, particularly as such cutbacks might apply to craft not included in the Washington treaties. Both Italy and France, which had been given the smallest ratios, refused to participate in the 1927 Geneva Conference but sent delegates as observers. Of the remaining "Big Three" powers, Japan was clearly not interested in further restraints upon her mobilization efforts and England and the United States consumed much of the time arguing about the size and fighting power of vessels they ostensibly wished to limit. The 1927 Geneva Conference lasted six weeks and then dissolved without results; subsequently America sought to close the gap in the naval race in non-treaty vessels by a $5 billion authorization early in 1929 for the construction of a number of light cruisers and aircraft carriers.[31]

OUTLAWING WAR AND THE WORLD COURT

Coolidge's continued concern for world peace led to his interest in a universal disavowal of war. The idea had its roots in several sources, but the Chicago lawyer Salmon O. Levinson is generally credited with originating the proposal that the nations of the world band together in a pact pledging never to go to war and to treat any warring nation as an international outlaw. The American Committee for the Outlawry of War was established by Levinson at the close of 1921, and the committee soon published his "A Plan to Outlaw War." Predictably, Borah, who had been so instrumental in calling the Washington Conference, supported the committee's proposal and in February 1923 introduced a resolution in Congress making war an international crime. Neither the legislature nor the public, at the time, were much interested in Borah's proposal. Independently of Levinson, Dr. Nicholas Murray Butler, the president of Columbia University and of the Carnegie Endowment for International Peace (organized by

---

[30] Robert E. Osgood, *Ideals and Self-Interest in America's Foreign Relations* (Chicago: The University of Chicago Press, 1953), p. 342.

[31] Mertz Tate's *The United States and Armaments* (Cambridge, Mass.: Harvard University Press, 1948) and Harold and Margaret Sprout, *Toward a New Order of Sea Power* contain short accounts of the ill-fated Geneva Conference.

Andrew Carnegie in 1910 "to hasten the abolition of war, the foulest blot upon our civilization" [32]), had advanced the idea that wars could be eliminated by consent. The concept was vigorously supported by one of Butler's faculty members at Columbia, Professor James T. Shotwell. Ironically, these men had diametrically opposite views of the role of the League in their respective campaigns for peace. Neither Levinson nor his political patron, Borah, supported the League, while Butler and Shotwell were hopeful that an American endorsement of their proposal would move the country closer to the League. There were further differences in that Levinson believed that the very signing of such a pledge provided sufficient moral suasion for its success while Shotwell argued that the signatory nations must provide for the enforcement of the agreement.[33]

The opportunity to implement these ideas arose in 1927 when a general arbitration treaty between the United States and France was about to expire. Early in that year Professor Shotwell presented French Foreign Minister Briand with apparently convincing arguments for France's acceptance of the "outlawry" concept which he was just then sponsoring. Briand saw French acceptance of the concept as a means of building the United States into its system of alliances and so asked Shotwell to draft a message outlining France's willingness to sign such a peace pact. The message, much to the annoyance of Coolidge and the new Secretary of State, Frank B. Kellogg, was not sent through regular diplomatic channels, but was instead directed to the American people. Briand's ploy worked, for much of the American press and public embraced the idea. With the active assistance of Borah, steady pressure was applied for American participation,[34] and by the end of 1927 petitions containing the signatures of more than two million supporters of the Briand proposal flooded Washington.

Keenly aware of the scheme's political potency, Kellogg shrewdly raised the ante by suggesting to the French government that the pact include the other world powers. The American counterproposal was self-seeking, for a multilateral treaty would not link the United States to the series of defensive alliances which existed between France and other nations. The American public would be appeased by a device that was difficult for Briand, recipient of the Nobel Peace Prize, to refuse to sponsor. To win France's reluctant consent, however, it

[32] Quoted in Robert H. Ferrell, *Peace in Their Time: The Origins of the Kellogg-Briand Pact* (New Haven, Conn.: Yale University Press, 1952), p. 7.

[33] See, for example, James T. Shotwell, *War as an Instrument of National Policy* (New York: Harcourt Brace Jovanovich, 1929) and John E. Stoner, *S. O. Levinson and the Pact of Paris: A Study in the Techniques of Influence* (Chicago: University of Chicago Press, 1942).

[34] For Borah's role, see John C. Vinson, *William E. Borah and the Outlawry of War* (Athens, Ga.: University of Georgia Press, 1957).

was necessary to include in the so-called Kellogg-Briand Pact provision for waging "defensive wars"—war as "an instrument of national policy" only was outlawed. After delaying three months, the French agreed to sign. Interestingly, in the intervening time Kellogg became an enthusiastic convert and wrote to his wife in May of 1928: "If I can only get that treaty made, it will be the greatest accomplishment of my administration or of any administration lately." [35]

Eventually 64 nations, including all of the great powers except Russia, signed the pact which contained no provision for its guarantee except the good faith of the contracting parties. Kellogg carefully assured the Senate that the agreement would not draw Washington into the orbit of European affairs (an essential nod to the pervasive distrust of political commitments) and would not interfere with the nation's right of self-defense: "Every nation is free at all times and regardless of treaty provisions to defend its territory from attack . . . and it alone is competent to decide whether circumstances require recourse in self-defense." [36] The Senate easily ratified the Pact of Paris by a vote of 85 to 1 on January 15, 1929. In his eloquent defense of the pledge, Senator Claude Swanson of Virginia perhaps best stated the hopes for the agreement:

> Although this treaty is a mere gesture, yet it is a gesture of peace, not hostility; of good will and conciliation, not of irritation and defiance. While it may be powerless to prevent war, yet it legalizes no war. It permits but does not approve war. It is a noble gesture or declaration for world peace and as such I shall support it.[37]

Unfortunately good faith was exactly the element lacking, and although Kellogg was to win a Nobel Peace Prize for his effort, the world was left with a pathetically naive gesture.

A potentially more effective mechanism for the maintenance of international stability was the World Court. At the time the League Covenant had been formulated, Article Fourteen provided for the establishment of a court to arbitrate international disputes, a concept which had already won a considerable following. Republican Secretaries of State John Hay and Elihu Root had supported the idea and the League to Enforce Peace, headed by former Republican President William Howard Taft, had strongly advocated the establishment of just such a body during the war. Charles Evans Hughes, the

---

[35] Quoted in Robert H. Ferrell, *The American Secretaries of State and Their Diplomacy* (New York: Cooper Square, 1963), XI, p. 119.

[36] Quoted in Ferrell, *Peace in Their Time*, p. 197 (n).

[37] *Congressional Record,* 70th Cong., 2nd sess., Jan. 5, 1929, p. 1189.

GOP presidential nominee in 1916, had backed the Court concept in his campaign. Although the Republican party appeared to be strongly committed to the idea, after the Court was framed (ironically with the aid of the elder statesman of the Republican party, Elihu Root) the GOP leadership balked. Objections were raised because the Court was to apply principles from international law in rendering its decisions rather than serve merely as an arbitrator. But this expanded view of the Court's function sounded far more sweeping in theory than it was in fact since the Court could not compel disputants to appear before it. Rather it had jurisdiction only over cases where the affected parties agreed to use the Court and, practically speaking, this meant that the Court would be involved in relatively minor international disputes.

Although the Permanent Court of International Justice (its formal designation) had been established under the League Covenant, and although the United States was not and never would be a member of the League, provision had been made for American participation in the Court. All evidence points to the American public's expectation that the United States would be included. Harding clearly supported American participation, and the 1924 platforms of both major parties contained planks endorsing American involvement. But Wilson's old foes were tenacious and launched a vigorous campaign to prevent what they saw as a thinly veiled attempt to force the United States into the League through the back door. They insisted that the Court could be "packed" with jurists whose interests were antithetical to those of the United States, and they emotionally branded the Court the "League Court."

At the urging of Secretary Hughes, Harding requested Senate endorsement of the Court plan; at the same time Hughes drafted a number of reservations designed to assure the irreconcilables that the United States would be "protected" from the League. When the Foreign Relations Committee finally referred the measure to the full Senate in 1926, it passed by a vote of 76 to 17. This victory was a very qualified one since the bill's managers were forced to accept five reservations as a condition of passage. These reservations revealed a fixed determination not to become involved in the League by stipulating that the United States be permitted to participate fully in the selection of judges, that it pay only a fair share of the expenses of the Court, and that it be allowed to withdraw at any time.[38] The most serious reservation was the final one, which provided that the Court could not give an advisory opinion in a dispute involving the United States without Washington's consent.[39]

[38] *Congressional Record,* 69th Cong., 1st sess., pp. 2824–25.
[39] *Ibid.*

Since American membership depended upon the Court's agreement to these reservations, and since the Court found the fifth reservation unacceptable, the supporters of participation were again frustrated. The "Root formula" was then devised permitting the United States to object to a requested advisory opinion and to withdraw from the Court if the objection were not sustained. This compromise was submitted to the Senate in December 1930, and was stalled in the Foreign Relations Committee for four years. In March of 1934 pressure from the public and from President Roosevelt forced the committee to hold hearings on the measure and to submit the issue to the full Senate. After an intense effort in which old opponents of the League such as Senators Borah and Hiram Johnson joined forces with Senator Huey Long of Louisiana, publisher William Randolph Hearst, and radio priest Father Charles E. Coughlin, 52 Senators voted for the Court plan and 36 against. This January 1935 vote was seven short of the necessary two-thirds.

The political hostility toward the Court as late as the mid-1930s was an accurate reflection of the anti-Wilsonian and anti-League bias of the two decades between the war. The League of Nations, with 24 member states, had come into being in January of 1920; within 12 months its membership doubled. The scope of the League's affairs, the extent of its membership, and the support it received in its early years necessitated an official American stance toward the world body. The State Department at first took the implication of the Senate's final rejection to its logical conclusion by neglecting even to reply to communications from the organization, explaining that since the United States did not recognize the existence of the League it need not reply! Public pressure and his own inclinations soon led the new Secretary of State, Hughes, to order this diplomatic discourtesy discontinued.

Hughes had favored American participation, with the GOP reservations, and once the League was in operation recognized that many of its activities were of concern to the United States. His way out of the dilemma was the appointment of "unofficial representatives" to agencies of the League which were involved in matters of direct interest to the United States. Hughes insisted that these delegates, though "unofficial," represented the United States "just as completely as those designated by the President always have represented our Government in the conferences and negotiations which he properly authorizes in the conduct of our foreign relations." [40]

[40] Quoted in Charles Cheney Hyde, *The American Secretaries of State and Their Diplomacy,* Robert H. Ferrell, ed. (New York: Knopf, 1929), X, p. 368.

Throughout the Twenties there was a gradual recognition that at least unofficial cooperation with the League was necessary. Some, of course, wished to continue the fight for full participation and were joined by a series of prestigious organizations, such as the League of Nations Non-Partisan Association, The World Peace Foundation, the Carnegie Endowment for International Peace, and the Institute of International Relations. The efforts of these organizations, and of individuals such as President Nicholas Murray Butler of Columbia, Boston publisher Edwin Ginn, former Justice of the Supreme Court John H. Clarke, and journalist Walter Lippmann, were successful only insofar as the United States participated with, and not in, League commissions. Nevertheless, the government's refusal to broaden the base of American involvement accurately reflected the public's position.

Toward the end of the 1920s, with the Kellogg-Briand Pact completed and the League issue dead, the Hoover Administration attempted to extend further the naval disarmament initiatives of the decade's early years. Hence the President met with Britain's Labour Prime Minister Ramsay MacDonald in October 1929 to work out the details of a proposed London Naval Conference. The remaining members of the "Big Five" of the Washington Conference, Japan, France, and Italy, accepted MacDonald's invitation for a January 1930 meeting.[41] One of the central problems of the Washington Conference accords on naval limitations had been the failure of the powers to agree to place a ceiling on the construction of all types of warships; at London this was accomplished. Relatedly, Britain accepted parity with the United States not only in capital ships (this they had agreed to at Washington) but in all types of vessels. Another accomplishment was the delay for an additional five years in the replacement of capital ships. At the same time Britain, the United States, and Japan consented to scrap a total of nine capital ships, but the Japanese, still resentful of the second-class status accorded them at Washington, improved their ratio in destroyers and cruisers. Jingoist elements in Japan were far from satisfied and it is generally believed that the assassination of the Japanese Prime Minister was the direct result of his signing the London accord.

Much of what had been accomplished was threatened by the inclusion of the so-called escalator clause which stated that if a nation not bound to the treaty—such as France—instituted a naval building program which threatened the security of one of the signatory powers,

---

[41] The background for the meeting is presented in Henry L. Stimson and McGeorge Bundy, *On Active Service in Peace and War* (New York: Harper & Row, 1958).

the ratios could be disregarded. Despite obvious disappointment in the conference, the accord was signed on April 22, 1930, and ratified by a reluctant and suspicious Senate on July 21 by a vote of 58 to 9 (Hoover had refused to give the Senate his relevant confidential papers—hence the suspicion).[42] In retrospect it becomes clear that as the need for a basic agreement on arms limitation became more urgent the concerned powers grew increasingly unwilling to offer the requisite guarantees. The memories of the war were still very much alive and continued to cast a long shadow.

Hoover tried once again to marshall support for his peace plans by actively cooperating in the World Disarmament Conference at Geneva in February 1932. Unlike the Washington, Geneva (1927), and London conferences, this was to be a land disarmament conference. The conference, attended by 51 nations, was stalled for five months when on June 22, 1932, Hoover dramatically proposed that offensive weapons be abolished and that the existing armaments of the world (land, air, and naval) be reduced by one-third. Unable to clearly distinguish between "offensive" and "defensive" arms, and unable to convince France (which had Europe's most powerful army) to disarm at the expense of her security, the plan was lavishly praised and quickly killed. Proponents of disarmament were further discouraged by Japan's announcement in December of 1934 that she was offering the required two years' notice in anticipation of withdrawing from the Washington treaty agreements.

A second London Naval Conference gloomily convened toward the end of 1935 but when the United States refused to agree to parity with Japan, the latter's delegates quit the conclave. By 1938 Roosevelt, alarmed by the increased militancy of Japan, Germany, and Italy, requested and received a one billion dollar appropriation for the construction of a powerful two-ocean navy.

A GLOBAL ECONOMIC REALIGNMENT

The continuing interest in the extent and impact of American "isolationism" in the 1920s and 1930s has led historians to turn their attention to the economic policies of the era in an attempt to demonstrate that the United States, while at times a reluctant participant in the diplomatic arena, was far from retiring in its economic relations. In the years before the war, and indeed through-

---

[42] See Raymond G. O'Connor, *Perilous Equilibrium: The United States and the London Naval Conference of 1930* (Lawrence, Kan.: University of Kansas Press, 1962).

out its industrial revolution, the United States had been a debtor nation—borrowing for the construction of its railroads, canals, factories, and the like. The regularity, stability, and, perhaps most important, the rate of return which it offered to European investors caused overseas capital to flow to the United States. At the opening of the First World War Americans owed billions to European investors; but as the war progressed and the European nations were increasingly in need of funds to pay for the flood of war materiel streaming across the Atlantic, they sold their American securities, thereby steadily diminishing American indebtedness. By the end of 1915 the traditional debtor-creditor relationship was reversed when European governments asked J. P. Morgan and Company to assist them in the sale of war bonds valued at $500,000,000. From that moment to the entry of the United States into the war, America acted as a creditor to the often hard-pressed European belligerents. By the close of the war Europe's debt amounted to over $10 billion. The implication of this debt was far more important than its size, for as a creditor rather than a debtor nation the United States after 1918 sought investments abroad for its surplus capital. Within ten years it had invested in excess of $10 billion—then a staggering amount when added to Europe's war debt—in loans made by both the United States government and private investors.

Not only had the war resulted in a permanent realignment of the creditor-debtor positions of the various powers, it also greatly affected the rate of American industrialization. While the holocaust had debilitated much of Europe's industrial capacity, wartime demands had caused a rapid expansion of American industry. As a result, American dependence upon European imports decreased markedly at the very time that the European economies could have been at least partially salvaged by increasing their exports. And while European nationals had formerly earned substantial sums by investing in United States corporations, the liquidation of these securities during the war eliminated an important source of income in the decades between the wars. Locked in a battle to the death with Imperial Germany, the Allies were unable to export to a number of "underdeveloped" nations which had formerly contributed to their favorable balance of trade. American businessmen quickly moved into the vacuum and maintained their trade with these nations even after the war. Thus a dramatic global economic realignment had come about because European resources alone were incapable of sustaining the war effort. Successive administrations quite understandably took advantage of this realignment to strengthen the economic position of the United States, but they have been legitimately criticized for their unwillingness to adjust policies to ease the strain on other economies. In its attitude toward the war debts and in the selfishness of its tariff policy, the United States contributed to the economic, and eventually the military, disaster of the 1930s.

American capital which flowed to the Allies before, during, and after the war consisted of funds from the private sector (e.g., bonds sold by J. P. Morgan and Company on behalf of the Allies) and funds from the United States government. It was the government's contribution which caused most of the postwar controversy over the war debts. At the time these loans were made, individuals in the private and public sector had argued that they should be regarded as America's contribution to the war effort because the Allies had been fighting America's fight since 1914. Some contended that the funds represented Washington's just share of the prosecution of the war, while others prophetically warned of the great disruption which would result from an insistence that the war loans be repaid. Europeans bitterly recalled that although the Allies borrowed approximately two-thirds of the total debt of $10 billion during the war, gold did not flow from the United States—rather the loans were used as credit to purchase war materiel.[43]

On an international scale the entire debt question was made more complex by the fact that the United States was not the only creditor nation—during the war England, France, and Italy had extended loans to their allies, and Britain alone had been a creditor for $10 billion. Thus in large measure England could repay her debt only if her creditors honored their loans from Britain; in turn, the ability of these nations to repay England depended upon increasing their trade, particularly with the United States. It is of interest that England had faced a similar dilemma after the Napoleonic Wars when she had been creditor to several European states. Instead of crippling the economies of these nations by demanding repayment, England cancelled all debts, thus hastening the return of prosperity to Europe. In so acting, London knew full well that trade with a prosperous Europe would bring far more revenue than would repayment of the Napoleonic war debt.

But the United States chose not to benefit from this important precedent and instead, after waiting impatiently more than three years for Europe to begin repayment, Congress empowered a World War Foreign Debt Commission to renegotiate the debt with each of the reluctant borrowers, subject to Congressional approval. Eventually

[43] See Harold G. Moulton and Leo Pasvolsky, *War Debts and World Prosperity* (Washington, D.C.: The Brookings Institution, 1932).

agreements were negotiated with 13 debtor nations—the most important of these, England, had its interest reduced to 3.3 percent (the
interest on all loans had been 5 percent) and the maturity date
extended to 62 years. Similar but more generous arrangements were
made with other nations by 1926 so that in the end the average total
cancellation worked out .to just over 50 percent. The reduction was
very high for some nations: 60 percent for France and 80 percent for
Italy.[44]

Although the United States took pride in this apparent display of
largess, the work of the commission was decidedly unsatisfactory.
What was needed was a recognition by both the United States and its
former allies that an alternative to the debt structure (refunding,
cancellation, or reduction) could not be arranged until the question of
German war reparations was settled. That is to say, it had been agreed
at Versailles that reparations would be exacted from Germany, but
that the precise amount and the schedule for payment would not be
included in the final treaty since these decisions were to be made by an
Allied Reparations Commission. By April 1921 this commission had
set the reparations figure at approximately $33 billion, extended over
a still to be determined period. The conquered Germans were
obviously unable to honor this staggering figure and still remain
solvent. The attempt to do so resulted in the acceleration of economic
chaos within the nation, which was soon unable to meet the schedule
although a half-hearted effort was made. This burden, plus the
general disruption of the economy, worsened the already ruinous
inflation and caused great suffering, particularly among the middle
class. The financial crisis shook the fledgling Weimar Republic to its
very foundations and helped pave the way for Adolf Hitler.

It is now clear that a vicious circle was created by the Allies in
their attempt to repay war debts by collecting reparations from
Germany. The United States of course rounded the circle by
demanding that these debts be honored, and it is at least possible that
the European Allies, despite their publics' desire to "hang the Kaiser,"
might have eased their demands for reparations had the United States
cancelled the debt. In the absence of such action the European powers
thrashed about for a means of forcing Germany to continue its flow of
payments. By January of 1923 the Reparations Commission declared
the nation in default and then further undermined Germany's
economic base by giving France and Belgium authority to occupy the
industrial Ruhr Valley. An outraged Germany employed its only
available weapon to fight the occupation: passive resistance.

[44] *Ibid.*, pp. 91, 101.

It quickly became apparent to the Harding Administration that world trade would be seriously disrupted by Germany's inability to adhere to the reparations formula. Hence by the close of 1923 the President encouraged Allied plans to study the economy of the Weimer Republic; although the United States was not an official participant, the Chicago banker Charles G. Dawes, acting as a private citizen, chaired one of the committees investigating the German economy. The Reparations Commission adopted the so-called Dawes Plan in 1924, providing for a $200 million international loan to Germany (most of it funded by American bankers), Allied supervision of the Reichsbank, and a new German monetary unit, the reichsmark. A new reparations schedule was announced which greatly reduced Germany's annual payments and left the total sum undetermined.[45]

The early success of the Dawes Plan encouraged the Allies to seek a more permanent solution to the reparations issue and so a second committee was formed in September of 1928. The new panel was again headed by an American, New York financier Owen D. Young, who like Dawes acted as a private citizen. The Young Plan, as modified and accepted in January 1930, reduced the German reparation debt by $9 billion, with annual payments extended over 59 years. The plan is particularly important in its recognition that the reparation and war debt issues were inextricably linked; in a "concurrent memorandum" it was agreed that the reparations schedule would be further reduced if the United States agreed to lower the war debt. A new factor was thereby added to the Dawes Plan—the extent of Allied indebtedness to the United States.

In point of fact, however, the success of the Young Plan was more apparent than real, for one of the major reasons Germany was able to adhere to its schedule was that American bankers throughout the 1920s extended private loans to German state governments and to German industry (as well as to other European nations). Importantly, many of these loans helped the borrowers remain solvent, but they were not used for the expansion of basic industry.[46] Taken together, these factors made for an enormously complicated and delicate superstructure. As millions left Germany in reparations payments, additional millions flowed to Germany in the form of loans, mostly from the United States. It was a most perilous balance, soon to be shattered by the Depression, which all but precluded further private American loans abroad.

[45] See Bascom N. Timmons, *Portrait of an American: Charles G. Dawes* (New York: Holt, Rinehart & Winston, 1953) and Charles G. Dawes, *A Journal of Reparations* (London: Macmillan, 1939).

[46] Moulton and Pasvolsky, *War Debts,* pp. 283–300.

There is much to be said for Ambassador George Kennan's observation that on a theoretical level the web of loans, debts, and reparations had become a fatal trap for all the participants because of Allied insistence on viewing war "as a contest supposed to yield to the victor all the just fruits of virtue triumphant." But the holocaust which had so recently engulfed Europe was instead

> . . . a shocking, irreparable act of self-destruction . . . a debauch of violence so destructive and so injurious to all concerned that no hopeful approach to a repair of the damage could be founded on allegations about who had owed what to whom at one stage or another before or during the calamity. You couldn't draw blood from a turnip.[47]

The Great Bull Market came to a shattering halt in October 1929 and was replaced by the most serious depression in the history of the United States. Quickly spreading across the Atlantic the crisis threatened the very economic survival of Europe, and of Germany in particular. It was soon apparent that the carefully cultivated flow of loans, reparations, and war debt payments was doomed by the disaster; of special concern were the billions invested by private American citizens in European bonds, for a complete collapse of the European economy would render these investments worthless. Convinced of the possibility of such a disaster, a postponement of intergovernmental debts and reparation payments for one year was offered by Hoover on June 20, 1931. Although Congress was not in session at the time the proposal was made, the President received assurances from Congressional leaders of their support of his plan. Importantly, the proposed moratorium did not cover debts owed by governments to private individuals. The purpose of this action was clearly to help retard the ruinous erosion of the European economic system by offering an honorable alternative to default. American participation in the scheme was dependent upon the willingness of other European creditors (i.e., those receiving reparations from Germany) to cooperate in the pact. After demanding and receiving assurances that the moratorium was for one year only, the French removed their objections to the plan. When Congress convened it overwhelmingly upheld the President's decision but refused to consider proposals to cancel the debt outright in the face of the crisis.[48]

[47] George F. Kennan, *Russia and the West Under Lenin and Stalin* (Boston: Little, Brown, 1960), p. 201.
[48] The moratorium is reviewed favorably in Ellis, *Republican Foreign Policy,* pp. 25–27. Also see William Starr Myers, *The Foreign Policies of Herbert Hoover, 1929–1933* (New York: Scribner's 1940), pp. 180–87, and Robert H. Ferrell, *American Diplomacy in the Great Depression* (New Haven, Conn.: Yale University Press, 1957).

The relief provided by the moratorium was temporary, and in June and July of 1932 Germany met with its creditors in Lausanne, Switzerland, and negotiated a rescheduling of reparation payments. Under the plan approved, the new total was set at $714 million, representing a reduction of more than 90 percent of the adjusted total of the Young Plan. Unhappily, ratification of this sensible formula was made contingent upon American willingness to adjust (or hopefully to cancel) the European war debt. Heartened by both the moratorium and French Premier Pierre Laval's late 1931 meeting with Hoover (during which both rather ambiguously pledged to encourage "monetary stability"), the European nations assumed American willingness to acknowledge the interrelationship of reparations and the war debt. This expectation was unrealistic, especially after the United States government had declined to participate in the Lausanne conference; the Hoover Administration refused to cancel the war debts.[49]

The discouraged European nations decided to await the results of the November 1932 elections before pressing their claim. Unfortunately, it was Roosevelt's strategy to eschew major policy decisions until he was installed in office and so a new official response to the Lausanne formula was impossible. A solution was not found even after FDR took office, and so on December 15, 1935, six of the debtor nations defaulted; eventually all but Finland followed suit. Without formal agreement the inevitable occurred: reparations and war debt payments ceased. By failing to acknowledge the interdependence of the reparation, debt, and tariff questions, Washington helped bring Germany and much of Europe to the brink of ruin by the mid-1930s. Nor was the new Democratic Administration acting responsibly when it informed the World Economic Conference in July of 1933 that it would not endanger its goal of domestic recovery by supporting the conference's objective of stabilizing currencies as a means of alleviating the worldwide Depression.[50]

The intensity of economic nationalism in the period between the wars was clearly apparent in the nation's tariff policy. With perhaps understandable lapses in sophistication, the postwar administrations sought to expand the nation's trade and investment network while at the same time restricting the ability of foreign powers to sell their goods to the United States. The expectation was naive and doomed to failure.

[49] William Starr Myers, ed., *The State Papers and Other Public Writings of Herbert Hoover* (Garden City, N.Y.: Doubleday 1934), II, p. 235.

[50] For an interesting account of Roosevelt's so-called bombshell message to the conference, see James MacGregor Burns, *Roosevelt: The Lion and the Fox* (New York: Harcourt Brace Jovanovich, 1956), and especially Herbert Feis, *1933: Characters in Crisis* (Boston: Little, Brown, 1966), pp. 169–258.

The Republican party had long been identified with a protectionist tariff philosophy, which it had advanced with great success in the half-century following the Civil War by steadily mounting walls against competitive foreign imports. The Wilson-Gorman Act of 1894 (passed during the Democrat Cleveland's second term) and the Underwood Act of the first year of Wilson's Administration, were the only meaningful attempts in 50 years to scale the barriers erected by successive Republican administrations. One of Wilson's last acts in office was to veto a hike in the tariff on raw materials and certain agricultural imports. True to form, shortly after Harding's triumph the Republicans called a special session of the Congress to stiffen the tariff; determined to bypass Wilson's rejection of the protectionist proposal, the Republican majority quickly gave its approval to the Emergency Tariff Act of May 1921, which reenacted legislation vetoed only months earlier, while increasing the rates on additional agricultural products. The farmer thus had his day and the manufacturers demanded payment in kind. The scope of these demands was contained in the Fordney-McCumber Act of September 1922, which sheltered heretofore unprotected commodities and raised the ceilings on items already covered by earlier legislation.

Passage of such legislation served in the long run to depress rather than to spark the American economy. As a creditor nation since the war, the only way the United States could continue to expand its foreign sales was to open its doors to European goods and thereby provide its potential customers with capital to buy American products. The Republican exclusionary tariff policy limited the ability of the rest of the world to trade with the United States; in retaliation, barriers soon were erected against American goods. Such economic nationalism in a highly technological international economy quickly proved disastrous.

Yet illogic gave birth to even greater folly, and with the opening of the new decade the highly protectionist Hawley-Smoot Act was approved, despite the predictions of a thousand economists that it would be ruinous to the international trading community. The petitioners wrote:

> There are few more ironical spectacles than that of the American Government as it seeks, on the one hand, to promote exports through the activity of the Bureau of Foreign and Domestic Commerce while, on the other hand, by increasing tariffs it makes exportation even more difficult. . . . A tariff war does not furnish good soil for the growth of world peace.[51]

[51] Statement reprinted in the *New York Times,* 5 May 1930, p. 4. For Hoover's

Hoover ignored the warning, but within two years, 25 governments retaliated against the measure; by 1932 the value of American exports was only one-third of what it had been in 1929 ($1,611,016,000 compared with $5,240,995,000 three years earlier).[52]

Hoover only very reluctantly acknowledged that the Depression was an international catastrophe requiring global remedies. It is possible that had he remained in office after 1933 he might have recognized the central importance of expanded trade to the restoration of a healthy national and international economy. But the task was left, instead, to Franklin D. Roosevelt and the Democratic majority in Congress.

JAPAN AND MANCHURIA

While the United States and the European powers attempted to resolve some of the problems which resulted from the postwar economic realignment, storm clouds gathered over Asia as Japan sought to secure and expand her interests in the Pacific. At the 1921–22 Washington Conference, Japan had only reluctantly agreed to the 5:5:3 naval ratio which placed her in a decidedly inferior position to the United States and Great Britain, but which maintained her regional superiority. To understand Tokyo's decision to expand one must consider that the nation had undergone a spectacular industrial revolution, resulting in an increased dependence upon world markets for continued national growth. The reasonably self-contained group of islands which Commodore Perry knew had vanished. The onset of the Depression and the drastic reduction in world trade, coupled with steadily rising world tariff barriers, deprived Japan of markets and of foreign capital with which to buy food and raw materials.

Japan's aggressive designs coincided with renewed instability in the Far East, for the Chinese Empire was undergoing its second revolution of the century as Sun Yat-sen's Nationalist Party forces slowly wrested control from the government at Peking. After the death of Sun, Chiang Kai-shek assumed leadership of the Kuomintang forces and concentrated on the removal of foreign influence—particularly influence gained by treaty—from China. As the level of violence increased the rift between Chiang's moderates and the Communist

---

involvement, see *The Memoirs of Herbert Hoover: The Cabinet and the Presidency, 1920–1933* (New York: Macmillan, 1952), Chap. 41.

[52] Shannon, *Between the Wars*, p. 167.

radicals within the Kuomintang deepened; by 1928 Chiang had purged the party of its Communist elements. That same year the United States, anxious to ease tensions over the issue of foreign influence in China, agreed to full Chinese autonomy over her tariff. The resultant treaty broke the stranglehold of the sphere-of-influence nations.

Although American relations with the new Chinese government were improving by the end of the decade, Chiang's purge of the Communist faction within his party had adversely affected his relations with Russia. When the Chinese leader attempted to extend the authority of his government to Manchuria despite Russia's predominant sphere of influence in North Manchuria, Moscow invaded Manchuria, crushed the Chinese forces, and dictated the terms of the surrender. This action was taken not long after the formulation of the Kellogg-Briand Pact; Russia's successful clash with China—clearly the kind of aggressive action "outlawed" by the Pact—demonstrated the futility of such an arrangement. Japan, whose special interests in South Manchuria were jealously guarded, anxiously watched global reactions to the Russo-Chinese struggle of 1929. It noted well that when Secretary of State Stimson attempted to apply the terms of the Kellogg Pact to Russia, he was coldly informed that his intervention was "considered as a pressure, which nothing justifies . . . and consequently, it can in no way be considered as a friendly act." [53] Stimson's position was made all the more awkward by Washington's refusal to recognize the Soviet Union.

At this time about 40 percent of Japan's trade was with Manchuria and the province was looked upon as a symbol of the nation's status as an imperial power. Understandably, China's attempt to regain control of this highly valued sphere led to a series of incidents: the execution of a Japanese army officer; a clash between Chinese police and Japanese consular police; an anti-Chinese riot in Japanese-controlled Korea; and an anti-Japanese boycott in China. Finally, in mid-September, 1931, the Mukden incident occurred. A section of track on the Japanese-controlled South Manchurian railroad was damaged by an explosion set by Japanese soldiers who were apparently acting as individuals and not on instruction of their government.[54] Having manufactured a rationale for the takeover of South Manchuria, the Japanese army first overpowered the Chinese in Mukden and surrounding cities and then swiftly extended their aggressive thrust to the rest of South Manchuria. The speed and

[53] *Papers Relating to the Foreign Relations of the United States, 1929,* II, p. 406.
[54] Robert H. Ferrell, "The Mukden Incident: September 18–19, 1931," *Journal of Modern History,* XXVII (Mar. 1955), 66–72.

effectiveness of this push lends credence to the theory that the attack had been planned before, if not in anticipation of, the Mukden incident. Shortly after the invasion the Chinese sharply protested Tokyo's action as a violation of the League of Nations, the Nine-Power Pact of 1922, and the fledgling Kellogg-Briand Pact; importantly, all three agreements did not provide for mandatory military intervention in the face of such aggression. Even had such a provision been operative, it is most difficult to assume that all contracting parties would have been in agreement as to what constituted "aggression."

When the League met to discuss the Manchurian invasion the United States took the unexpected step of sending a representative to the conference. Early in the deliberations, France, England, and Italy sent notes to the disputants invoking the Kellogg-Briand Pact. It was a hopeful sign, but at best just a beginning; unfortunately the Council members lacked the resolution to intervene meaningfully and so the sessions continued without result. Toward the end of October the Council lamely resolved that Japan and China should settle their differences and requested Japanese removal from occupied Manchuria. The Council met again in mid-November and a five-member Lytton Commission was established to investigate the Far Eastern situation and report to the League. Although well-meaning, the Council had tailored a most convenient device for delay as Japan increased her control over the affected area. Surprisingly, Hoover's internationalist Secretary of State, Stimson, believed that this action of the League would be effective and that Japan would listen to reason, halt its advance, and possibly pull back.[55]

These expectations were of course not realized, and by the opening of 1932 the Japanese had made further gains at China's expense. Stimson believed that the United States should now act unilaterally, but given the attitude of President Hoover and the American people, a peaceful move was required. His solution was to adopt Hoover's suggestion that the United States refuse to recognize any treaty between Japan and China which had been brought about by the exercise of force. Thus the Stimson Doctrine was drafted, endorsed by Hoover, and sent to the interested parties on January 7, 1932:

> . . . [T]he American Government deems it to be its duty to notify both the Imperial Japanese Government and the Government of the Chinese Republic that it cannot admit the legality of any situation *de facto* nor does it intend to recognize any treaty or agreement entered into

[55] See Ferrell, *The American Secretaries of State*, XI, pp. 233–35.

between those Governments, or agents thereof, which may impair the treaty rights of the United States or its citizens in China, including those which relate to the sovereignty, the independence, or the territorial and administrative integrity of the Republic of China, nor to the international policy relative to China, commonly known as the open door policy. . . .[56]

In issuing the doctrine, Stimson was fully aware that America's prestige in Asia was intimately associated with its support of the territorial and political integrity of China. Like so many others, the secretary had been wooed and won by visions of the impact that a powerful, unified, and democratic China would have on the stability of the Far East. A major study of the role of self-interest in twentieth-century American foreign policy concludes that the Hoover-Stimson reliance upon moral coercion and the reiteration of principle, in the absence of a commitment to coercion or collective action,

> was the most ineffective means possible for achieving the desired end. It did not strengthen any treaties or vindicate international morality; it did not protect America's interests in the Far East; it did not avoid war.

Instead, by arousing Japanese hostility and by fixing conditions which were clearly unacceptable to the Japanese, the imperialist ambitions of radical elements were encouraged.[57] The results of Stimson's efforts were both predictable and understandable, for neither the President nor the American people wished to take forceful action. Japan on the other hand seemed determined to follow the path of the United States only a few decades earlier and obtain an empire. By October of 1932 the Lytton Commission had made public its report condemning Japan for both the invasion and the establishment of the puppet state of Manchukuo. It recommended autonomy for Manchuria, albeit under China's political control, and the guarantee of Japanese interests in the area. When the League adopted the commission's report the following February, an indignant Japan simply gave the requisite two years' notice of her intent to resign from the international body.

While it is tempting to conclude that Japan's flouting the League, the Kellogg-Briand Pact, and the Nine-Power Treaty provided a telling example for aggressors about to make their debut,[58] it is

---

[56] *Ibid.*, pp. 238–39.

[57] Osgood, *Ideals and Self-Interest*, p. 356. An authoritative study of the Manchurian episode is Sara R. Smith, *The Manchurian Crises, 1931–1932: A Tragedy in International Relations* (New York: Columbia University Press, 1948).

[58] See Sumner Welles, *The Time for Decision* (New York: The World Publishing Company, 1944).

not possible to establish a direct link between America's failure to take action against Japan and Hitler's increased boldness. The growing tension in Europe had its own motivations which did not have any clear connection with events in the Far East. It was the British attitude toward Nazi Germany, particularly London's decision to make naval concessions to Germany in violation of the Treaty of Versailles, which encouraged Hitler to think that any action which he took short of war would be condoned.[59]

Hitler announced Germany's withdrawal from the League in 1933 and two years later, boldly ignoring the provisions of the Versailles agreements, gave notice of his intention to rearm Germany. Italy's Mussolini followed the lead in October of 1935 when his forces poured into all-but-defenseless Ethiopia. This time the League declared Italy an aggressor and announced economic sanctions (importantly, oil was excluded from the list). But faced with an emergent Germany and the continuing Depression, the two major European powers, England and France, were unwilling to engage Italy in the defense of the African state. The Fascists grew stronger and bolder. Germany further dismantled the crumbling and soon-to-be-abandoned Treaty of Versailles by occupying the Rhineland in March 1936. Stimson's dogged attempt to move the United States to a more internationalist position appeared to be forgotten.[60]

THE LATIN AMERICAN PROTECTORATE

Closer to home, in Latin America, the United States moved in the Twenties toward a more reasoned and reasonable policy. The Roosevelt Corollary to the Monroe Doctrine (1904), the determined efforts by the McKinley, Taft, and Roosevelt administrations to facilitate economic expansion to the South, and the blatantly interventionist nature of Wilson's so-called missionary diplomacy had by the 1920s created very serious strains in relations with Latin America. By the opening of the new decade the interventionist tradition which had led to direct American control over Haiti, Santo Domingo, Panama, Cuba, and Nicaragua was firmly entrenched. But even before the Republicans gave way to Roosevelt, there was clear evidence of a gradual, sometimes sporadic, move toward the renunciation of imperialist ambitions and the adoption of policies long

---

[59] See Ferrell interview in Garraty, *Interpreting American History,* II, pp. 209–10.

[60] For studies of Stimson, see Richard N. Current, *Secretary Stimson: A Study in Statecraft* (New Brunswick, N.J.: Rutgers University Press, 1954) and Elting E. Morison, *Turmoil and Tradition: A Study of the Life and Times of Henry L. Stimson* (Boston: Houghton Mifflin, 1960).

associated with the Good Neighbor effort of the Thirties. This change
was due in large measure to the defeat of Germany and the signing of
the Washington naval treaties limiting Japan to the Western Pacific,
since both reinforced American hegemony in the Caribbean and the
entire Western Hemisphere. The United States was thereafter free to
liquidate its protectorate in Latin America and to adopt a more
peaceful policy respectful of the sovereignty of the republics to the
South.[61]

There was in addition an economic motivation for the policy
shift since by 1925 the value of American trade with the Latin
republics was greater than the combined total of American trade with
Great Britain, France, and Germany. By the end of the decade, direct
United States investments in Central and South America totaled 3.5
billion dollars, or more than twice the value of American investments
in any other area of the globe.[62]

From the point of view of the Latin American leadership and
public, no meaningful adjustment in relations was possible until the
United States formally renounced its "right" to intervention. The
prospects for such a radical shift in attitude at first seemed dim. At the
sixth International Conference of American States (Havana, January–
February 1928) the Monroe Doctrine, and, more generally, interventionist policies, were hotly debated. The American representative,
former Secretary of State Hughes, skillfully sidestepped the central
issue by insisting on the nation's right to "interpose" in the affairs of its
Hemispheric neighbors "for the purpose of protecting the lives and
property of its nationals."[63]

The Roosevelt Corollary to the Doctrine, together with it's "big
stick" implications, had been seriously undermined by the end of the
1920s; but until Hoover became President, much more attention was
paid to the possible grounds for intervention than to outright
renunciation of the concept. Latin America was somewhat encouraged
by the shift in policy toward Haiti, where intervention and occupation
since 1915 had rendered that nation a political captive of the United
States. President Hoover's determination to withdraw led to a
September 1932 agreement outlining plans for the complete separa-
tion of Haiti from American control. And although the Haitian

[61] John A. Logan, Jr., *No Transfer: An American Security Principle* (New Haven, Conn.: Yale
University Press, 1961), pp. 275–76.

[62] Donald M. Dozer, *Are We Good Neighbors?* (Gainesville, Fla.: University of Florida Press,
1959), p. 9.

[63] Quoted in Bryce Wood, *The Making of the Good Neighbor Policy* (New York: Columbia
University Press, 1961), p. 43.

National Assembly at first rejected the proposal, thus permitting the Roosevelt Administration to win credit for the final settlement, the major impetus for disengagement occurred during a Republican regime.

Closely associated with Latin hostility toward intervention was its resentment over a shift in American policy regarding diplomatic recognition. By substituting his own test of "constitutional legitimacy" for the long-established practice of granting *de facto* recognition, Wilson had deeply offended Latin American sensibilities. This change in basic policy was continued through the Republican era, for Hoover withheld recognition from Guatemala (1930) and El Salvador (1931) because they had come to power through revolutionary means. Wilson's doctrine, nevertheless, was doomed. In the first two years of Hoover's Administration there were revolutions or serious internal unrest in 19 Latin American republics—to attempt to determine strict legitimacy for each of these regimes was clearly unrealistic. In 1930 Secretary of State Stimson was authorized to announce that Wilson's policy was no longer in effect, except for Central America, and that *de facto* recognition would once again be extended to new governments. This decision was based on Hoover's belief that it would be virtually impossible to continue Wilson's formula given the almost continual unrest to the South, and on his sincere conviction that the time had come for the United States to renounce many of its earlier practices. It is not surprising that in the past two decades the view that Hoover, and not FDR, is the true father of the Good Neighbor Policy has won a respectable following.[64]

Practice, unfortunately, at times lagged considerably behind theory, and in the 1920s tiny, unstable Nicaragua became a prime target of the Roosevelt Corollary. The United States had a long-standing interest in this republic because of its proximity to the Panama Canal and because of its potential as an alternate canal route (the Bryan-Chamorro Treaty of 1916 gave the United States authority to construct and fortify an isthmian canal on Nicaraguan territory). During the Taft Administration, Nicaragua experienced difficulty in meeting its obligations and so marines were dispatched and a customs collection mechanism established in 1911 and 1912. By 1923 the affairs of that republic appeared to be sufficiently stable for Hughes to pledge withdrawal of the military force if an election reflective of the wishes of the Nicaraguan people were held; the marines were

[64] Alexander DeConde, *Herbert Hoover's Latin-American Policy* (Stanford, Calif.: Stanford University Press, 1951); also Ferrell, *American Diplomacy in the Great Depression*.

withdrawn by President Coolidge in 1925. But shortly thereafter a coup replaced the elected government and Washington refused to grant diplomatic recognition to the new regime. The Nicaraguan Congress then took matters in hand, unseated the revolutionary leadership, and designated Adolfo Diaz, a long-time friend of the United States, head of state.

Diaz, however, found little favor with revolutionary groups in his country—not surprising given his close identification with American interests—and new unrest followed his installation. Coolidge's solution was to send in more marines than he had withdrawn. Continued insurgent opposition to the Diaz regime and the American presence led to marine-supervised elections in 1928, 1930, and 1932. And while Coolidge's personal envoy, Henry L. Stimson, repeatedly and skillfully attempted a negotiated settlement, the last American forces did not leave until 1933, signaling the end of a 22-year presence, with a brief interlude in 1925.

In 1931 the Hoover Administration served notice on American citizens living in Central America that if they felt their lives or their property threatened in the interior of those republics, they were to come home, move to more settled regions, or accept the consequences. This was a far cry from Coolidge's 1927 position that American lives and property would be protected "where ever they may be."[65]

A second, more satisfactory test of the gradual alteration of American attitudes in the Twenties can be found in the nation's relations with Mexico, which Wilson had deeply offended by authorizing a "punative expedition" under General Pershing in 1917. Mexico was particularly important in the postwar era because for a while it was the world's second largest producer of oil. European and American interests had been seriously threatened by the 1911 Revolution, which sought economic, political, and social democratization. A central goal of the revolution, which flared intermittently for decades, was the lessening of control over Mexico's economy by foreigners who had been granted outrageous concessions by the ousted dictator, Porfirio Diaz.

The specific difficulty in the 1920s stemmed from the decision of Mexican President Plutarco Calles to observe the spirit of the 1917 Mexican Constitution by decreeing that subsoil rights belonged to the state. The concessions granted by Diaz to American oil companies were clearly threatened, and Coolidge's Secretary of State, Kellogg, at first attempted to return to a Wilson-styled solution by threatening to

---

[65] Quoted in Ellis, *Republican Foreign Policy*, p. 260. The Nicaraguan episode is considered in detail in Wood, *The Making of the Good Neighbor Policy*, pp. 13–47.

support the overthrow of Calles if American "rights" were not respected. The Secretary then deepened the offense by insisting that Bolsheviks were behind the Mexican Revolution.

Fortunately, American public opinion was not receptive to such truculence and the Senate instead called for arbitration of outstanding differences. Coolidge was most fortunate in his appointment of Dwight Morrow to replace the recently resigned ambassador to Mexico, for Morrow soon hammered out a compromise formula which acknowledged Mexican control of subsoil rights, but permitted Americans with pre-1917 concessions (which had already been worked) to continue to operate. This peaceful accommodation, together with the gradual if belated withdrawal of troops from Nicaragua, was a clear indication of a new posture toward Latin America years before the announcement of Franklin Roosevelt's Good Neighbor Policy.

It has long been claimed that the Hoover Administration's most dramatic commitment to nonintervention took the form of a 1930 *Memorandum on the Monroe Doctrine* (more commonly, the "Clark Memorandum"). But diplomatic historian Robert H. Ferrell convincingly demonstrated a few years ago that the memorandum had never been adopted as official policy by the Hoover, or any other, Administration.[66] The history is as follows: In 1928 Secretary of State Kellogg requested that an undersecretary, J. Reuben Clark, Jr., prepare a scholarly commentary on the Monroe Doctrine which would demonstrate that the doctrine was aimed at European intervention and could not be used to justify American interference in Latin American republics. One of Clark's assistants actually wrote the report, which did not explicitly repudiate the Roosevelt Corollary to the doctrine. Yet in a 17-page letter of transmittal, Clark concluded: "it is not believed that this corollary is justified by the terms of the Monroe Doctrine, however much it may be justified by the application of the doctrine of self-preservation."[67]

Through a process still not clearly understood, both the report and the covering letter were published by the Government Printing Office in 1930. The following year, despite the memorandum's continued lack of official sanction by the Hoover Administration, Secretary of State Stimson told a Council of Foreign Relations meeting that the Monroe Doctrine had to do with American relations with Europe and not with Latin America. This was the essence of the Clark Memorandum, although Stimson did not mention the docu-

---

[66] Robert H. Ferrell, "Repudiation of a Repudiation," *Journal of American History,* LI (Mar. 1965), pp. 669–73.

[67] Quoted in *Ibid.*, p. 669.

ment by name. Throughout the remainder of the Hoover presidency, and into the Roosevelt period, officials insisted that the memorandum constituted nothing more than Clark's private opinions.

Having repudiated the repudiation, historian Ferrell concludes that both the Hoover and Roosevelt administrations "missed a good opportunity to detach an embarrassing and unnecessary corollary from the Doctrine. The national interests of the United States in Latin America could easily have found protection either in the Doctrine itself, in the developing Pan-American system, or in the age-old right of national self-defense." [68] But since the Latin Americans were by that time seeking outright American repudiation of intervention, whatever its ideological basis, it is doubtful that in the long run much would have been gained.

The Crash, Depression, and Fascist aggression abroad provided catalysts for an accelerated accommodation with the Latin American republics. After 1929, the reduced American economic involvement with its Hemispheric neighbors—both in trade and investments— forced a thorough reconsideration of past policies and presumed prerogatives. But as long as troops remained and the theory of intervention continued to be upheld, a true transformation in relations was impossible.

Barbara Tuchman has described World War I's impact in *The Proud Tower*:

> The Great War of 1914–18 lies like a band of scorched earth dividing that time from ours. In wiping out so many lives which would have been operative on the years that followed, in destroying beliefs, changing ideas, and leaving incurable wounds of disillusion, it created a physical as well as a psychological gulf between two epochs.[69]

In the face of so traumatic an upheaval, it is little wonder that the American public and its leadership moved cautiously in responding to the post-war realignment and refused to enter into political commitments with foreign powers.

Still, the Republican era was far from sterile despite its failures. Any final assessment must consider that the position of the United States in the postwar years was dramatically different than anything experienced in its history. Perhaps a cautious adjustment was inevitable. The economic nationalism of the era was shortsighted and doomed; it constituted a selfish attempt to capitalize on the nation's

---

[68] *Ibid.*, p. 673.
[69] Barbara W. Tuchman, *The Proud Tower* (New York: Macmillan, 1966), p. xiii.

creditor status, its mature industrialization, and the economic opportunities arising out of the global realignment. Unfortunately, such policies proved limited and poorly suited to the immense need for creative leadership in a climate of political and economic instability.

Four

NEUTRALITY
TO BELLIGERENCY

The determination of Japan, Germany, and Italy to ignore the sovereign rights of the community of nations, the unwillingness or inability of the major democracies to control the rising tide of aggression, and the social and political consequences of the economic collapse of the 1930s led to the Second World War. The outbreak of war was made all the more inevitable by the Western democracies' naive reliance upon a series of well-intentioned but meaningless pacts which had been formulated at a time when so many wished to believe that legislated world order was possible. The United States discouraged more rigorous attempts at peace-keeping and only slowly acknowledged that an isolated, secure Western Hemispheric bastion was no longer possible if, indeed, it had ever been possible. And although President Franklin D. Roosevelt and Secretary of State Cordell Hull understood that the security of the United States was inextricably bound to the general world order, throughout much of the 1930s the Congress continued to act as if the most reasonable solution to the crisis was to legislate away the nation's rights as a neutral. In all of this, the President has been viewed either as the pawn of public and Congressional isolationism, or as a sagacious

142

politician who slowly guided the nation toward his own internationalist philosophy.

The isolationists of the Thirties, following the tradition of the earlier postwar period, sought to retain America's freedom of action by avoiding actual or implied long-term political commitments to other nations. The dictates of national self-interest, rather than overseas alliances, were seen as the legitimate basis for the nation's foreign policy.[1] This approach, inevitably, rested upon each individual's conception of the most effective manner of ensuring and furthering the national self-interest. It is well to keep in mind, nevertheless, a valuable clarification offered by Senator Borah in 1934 while addressing the Council on Foreign Relations. In matters of trade, finance, and compassion for human suffering, Borah declared, the United States has "not been isolationist and never will be. . . . But in all matters political, in all commitments of any nature or kind, which encroach in the slightest upon the free and unembarrassed action of our people, or which circumscribe their discretion and judgment, we have been free, we have been independent, we have been isolationists." [2] This, then, was the thread of commonality between the two decades. Opposition to collective security was more intense in the Thirties, but the basic ideology had not changed from that of the previous decade.

Senator Borah's attitude toward overseas commitments was widely shared by the people of the United States, who viewed Wilson's ideal of making the world safe for democracy with bitter cynicism; this attitude was also voiced by novelists and historians who wrote of the First World War as a futile, unnecessary gesture. In the "Meester Veelson" section of his novel of disenchantment, *Nineteen Nineteen*, John Dos Passos expressed the current disenchantment:

> First it was *neutrality in thought and deed*, then *too proud to fight* when the Lusitania sinking and the danger to the Morgan loans and the stories of the British and French propagandists set all the financial centers in the East bawling for war, but the suction of the drumbeat and the guns was too strong; the best people took their fashions from Paris and their broad "a's" from London, and T.R. and the House of Morgan.
>
> Five months after his re-election on the slogan *He kept us out of war*, Wilson pushed the Armed Ship Bill through Congress and declared

---

[1] Manfred Jonas, *Isolationism in America, 1935–1941* (Ithaca, N.Y.: Cornell University Press, 1966), p. 5.

[2] William E. Borah, *Bedrock: Views on Basic National Problems* (Washington, D.C.: National Home Library, 1936), p. 58.

that a state of war existed between the United States and the Central powers:

> *Force without stint or limit, force to the utmost.*[3]

UNILATERALISM AND PACIFISM

The internationalists' major confrontation with their ideological opponents occurred in the Thirties rather than in the postwar decade because of the convergence of a number of complex and diverse factors. As late as FDR's first inauguration, and indeed well into his second term, Americans continued to labor under a pair of nine-teenth-century misconceptions: that the absence of war was a characteristic of the natural order; and that through a determined detachment the nation could steer clear of international conflict. The leading study of this phenomenon concludes that the isolationists of the decade were centrally concerned with the preservation of the American government's "absolute control over its foreign policy by avoiding any long-term political commitments, either actual or implied, to other nations." Instead, they advocated a species of unilateralism by calling for a policy of independence in foreign relations which "would leave the United States free at all times to act according to the dictates of national self-interest."[4] This attitude was, perhaps, most clearly expressed by Norman Thomas's *The Choice Before Us*, which urged the national leadership to "support no consultative pact that goes beyond the promise to confer."[5]

Those of Thomas's persuasion viewed events abroad in the early years of the decade with growing alarm, for Germany, Italy, and Japan obviously had designs which were not tempered by a reasonable concern for international stability. Heightened international tensions, particularly the Japanese thrust against Manchuria in 1931, the outbreak of the Italo-Ethiopian War in 1935, and Hitler's flagrant violations of the Versailles Treaty were clear warnings that another global holocaust was near. It was therefore not particularly illogical for the isolationists to conclude that unless the United States government was exceedingly circumspect in its response to the succession of crises, the nation inevitably would be drawn into a future war.

---

[3] John Dos Passos, *Nineteen Nineteen* (New York: Washington Square Press, 1961), p. 263. The novel was first published in 1932. Critical "revisionist" historians of the 1930s include: Charles C. Tansill, *America Goes to War* (Boston: Little, Brown, 1938); Walter Millis, *Road to War* (Boston: Houghton Mifflin, 1935); and Charles A. Beard, *The Devil Theory of War* (New York: Vanguard, 1936).

[4] Jonas, *Isolationism in America*, p. 5.

[5] Norman Thomas, *The Choice Before Us: Mankind at the Crossroads* (New York: Macmillan, 1934), p. 179.

At the same time, a grueling depression caused the American public to turn its attention inward to matters closest at hand, an economic crisis which would not respond to Roosevelt's prescriptions. When alarms from abroad became insistent, the public demanded that insulation be provided through highly restrictive neutrality legislation. The Depression had additional, more subjective effects on the exercise of foreign policy, for its profound impact on American self-confidence substantially affected the nation's willingness to accept overseas obligations. People suffering deeply because of their government's inability to arrest an economic decline were not likely to be sanguine about that government's ability to affect the destinies of other nations. Moreover, the considerable discredit suffered by bankers and industrialists after 1929 denied this potentially powerful voice for internationalism the broad support of the citizenry.

Not only were business and financial leaders castigated for their role in the economic crisis of the Thirties, they were also the subject of one of the most publicized of Congressional investigations, Senator Gerald P. Nye's 1934–35 inquiry into the role of bankers and munitions makers in the events leading to America's World War I intervention. The direct impact of the Nye Committee's findings on American public opinion remains a matter of sharp controversy; there is considerable logic in John E. Wiltz's conclusion that the committee's findings did not directly influence the prewar neutrality legislation since the relationship between intervention and the munitions industry was never convincingly established.[6] But there can be little doubt that popularizations of Nye's findings, such as Walter Millis' *Road to War*, published in 1935, did much to influence public opinion. When Charles C. Tansill's *America Goes to War* (1938) appeared, those seeking more scholarly documentation of the conspiracy thesis were served.[7]

Isolationists of the Thirties stressed negative solutions to the nation's dilemma by opposing the establishment of a massive military capability, the alignment of the United States with Britain and France, and the liberalization of certain foreign trade practices. But their program had more positive aspects, for at a time when the major world powers were increasingly drawn together in economic and security pacts, it was argued that the United States could maintain a free hand, just as it had done in the previous century. By so doing America could participate in global affairs, yet remain a model of democratic tradition for the rest of the world. For this reason

---

[6] See John E. Wiltz, *In Search of Peace: The Senate Munitions Inquiry, 1934–36* (Baton Rouge: Louisiana State University Press, 1963), and Selig Adler, *The Uncertain Giant, 1921–1941: American Foreign Policy Between the Wars* (New York: Macmillan, 1965), Chap. VII.

[7] Osgood, *Ideals and Self-Interest,* pp. 364–402.

isolationists viewed themselves as heirs to a tradition which advocated international contacts without relinquishing freedom of action.

Whether such an approach was feasible in the twentieth century was quite another thing. Isolationists of the decade were fond of quoting Washington's cautionary Farewell Address which urged America to "steer clear of permanent alliances by artificial ties in the ordinary vicissitudes of her politics and the ordinary combinations and collisions of her friendships and enmities." Jefferson, too, had insisted that the first principle of American foreign policy should be "peace, commerce and honest friendship with all nations, entangling alliances with none." [8]

Throughout the nineteenth century this philosophy prevailed. Rather than adhere to a strict isolationism, the United States sympathized with Latin American revolutions, issued the Monroe Doctrine, sought to wrest Canada from the British, challenged England for Oregon, made inroads into Japan and China, and fought Mexico in the 1840s and Spain at the century's close. It did all of this without mutual defense pacts; formal treaties were utilized to resolve questions related to boundaries, immigration, fishing rights, and the like.[9] It was earnestly believed by those seeking to keep America uninvolved in the 1930s that although certain conditions had changed by the twentieth century, the Washington-Jefferson approach was still workable. But the United States was a major power with an overseas empire by 1900; a transportation and communication revolution had shattered the protection afforded by the two oceans, and military technology had greatly altered the stakes of war. The majority rigidly believed that these changes could be provided for through legislation and a modification in public attitude. Unilateralism and pacifism thus became the key elements of isolationism in the decade before the Second World War.

Unilateralism and pacificism were not linked historically, and they were not joined in the docrines of Washington and Jefferson; the United States in the nineteenth century subscribed to unilateralism but fought England, Mexico, and Spain. But for the isolationists of the 1930s, unilateralism was not possible without pacificism because modern wars were viewed as leading inevitably to overseas entanglements. By insisting upon both traditions, the movement attracted

---

[8] James D. Richardson, *A Compilation of the Messages and Papers of the Presidents, 1789–1897* (Washington, D.C.: Government Printing Office, 1899), I, p. 323.

[9] As Jonas points out, the Clayton-Bulwer Treaty of 1850 was an exception, but this treaty was far from popular. Jonas, *Isolationism in America*, p. 13. For a very useful, if brief, introduction to the background of American isolationism, see Donald F. Drummond, *The Passing of American Neutrality, 1937–1941* (Ann Arbor: University of Michigan Press, 1955), pp. 1–20.

genuine pacifists, those who believed that a nation could remain both uninvolved and secure, and those who, while understanding and accepting the unilateralist tradition, were happy to "accept noninvolvement in war as an unexpected bonus." [10]

Even a brief examination of the isolationists' attitude toward the crises in Europe and Asia illuminates their profound determination to have America go it alone. While hopeful that their country would not become involved in crises on either continent, it is clear that Europe represented the greater danger since in Asia the United States would be involved with only one power, Japan, which it could oppose without entangling treaties. Belligerency in Europe would almost certainly necessitate alliances with England and France, during and after the conflict. Thus isolationists were at the same time confident that the nation could under certain circumstances act unilaterally yet fearful that under other circumstances conflict would undermine both America's freedom of action and its institutions.

Although many who accepted such a doctrine in the Thirties were Midwesterners, the phenomenon was apparent throughout the nation; its leadership represented both coasts, as well as the more insulated interior.[11] Although the Republicans have been more closely associated with the movement—it is often charged that they were isolationist for rather transparent partisan purposes—the Democrats were not without influence. Hence the isolationist leadership in the House and Senate bridged regional and party lines: Senators Homer T. Bone (D-Washington) and Bennett C. Clark (D-Missouri); Representatives Louis Ludlow (D-Indiana) and Maury Maverick (D-Texas). Republican adherents included Midwesterners such as Senator William E. Borah of Idaho, but also Senator Hiram W. Johnson of California and Representative Hamilton Fish (New York) and George H. Tinkham (Massachusetts). The movement cut across political ideology as easily as it cut across political affiliation: the Socialist Norman Thomas was as outspoken an isolationist as was the conservative, Republican, former President, Herbert Hoover.

The perhaps understandable tendency to identify isolationism of the Thirties with political conservatism has been misguided since many of the same liberal intellectuals who had been greatly disillusioned after the First World War were quick to agree that idealistic motivations must not again become the mainspring of national policy.

[10] For this analysis, see Jonas, *Isolationism in America*, p. 16.

[11] There is, however, reason to believe that Midwestern Congressional delegations were more isolationist than was the public of that region. See Ray Allen Billington, "The Origins of Middle Western Isolationism," *Political Science Quarterly*, LX, Mar. 1945. For the Southern attitude, see Charles O. Lerch, Jr., *The Uncertain South* (Chicago: Quadangle, 1964), pp. 288–90.

In an attempt to be "objective" there was a strong tendency to excuse Hitler's policies as legitimate responses to the selfish Versailles settlement; moral judgments on such policies were distrustfully viewed as shortsighted simplifications. Hence Stuart Chase, Charles Beard, George Soule, Norman Thomas, and Oswald Garrison Villard stubbornly insisted upon noninvolvement even in the face of obvious Fascist threats to democratic ideals.[12]

There has been some attempt to prove that pro-German and anti-British ethnic prejudices, along with their political exploitation, played a crucial role in the resurgence of American isolationism. A major study of the impact of ethnics on American foreign policy concludes that the ethnic version of isolationism in these years was "detrimental to the true meaning of traditional isolationism" since hyphenate Americans were all too often committed to Anglophobia and anti-Communism; not surprisingly, they derived considerable support from anti-Semitic, pro-Fascist, and pro-Nazi elements. Other ethnics, however, were staunchly anti-German, interventionist, and internationalist. Although vocal, this group had decidedly less impact than their isolationist brethern.[13]

Efforts directed toward establishing parallels between isolationist sentiment and socioeconomic identifications have proven unsuccessful; the movement encompassed exceedingly disparate elements of the social structure: Socialists and the American Legion, labor unions and Henry Ford, Midwestern Progressives, Herbert Hoover, and the *New Republic*. It was, rather, unilateralism and fear of war which afforded the movement its limited cohesiveness. But there were, certainly, wide variations. Many conservative adherents, for example, justified isolationism on the grounds that the United States represented an impregnable fortress. America's security, according to men such as Hoover, Senator Robert A. Taft, and Charles A. Lindbergh, was tied to the defense of the Western Hemisphere and not to the European balance of power or international adventures. Thus Hoover insisted that the Western Hemisphere was guarded by a "moat of 3,000 miles of ocean on the east and 6,000 miles on the west," while Taft reasoned that "the difficulty of attacking America across those oceans will forever prevent any such attack being even considered, if we maintain an adequate defense on the sea and in the air." [14]

Such concepts captivated a majority of Americans until slowly,

[12] Osgood, *Ideals and Self-Interest*, pp. 369–77.

[13] Louis L. Gerson, *The Hyphenate in Recent American Politics and Diplomacy* (Lawrence: University of Kansas Press, 1964), pp. 111–12.

[14] Hoover quotation in the *New York Times*, 2 Feb. 1939, p. 6; Taft in Osgood, *Ideals and Self-Interest*, p. 380.

but quite perceptibly, the public came to realize that its security was threatened by fascist aggression abroad. This transformation was exceedingly painful despite American pro-Allied sympathies before and after the outbreak of war in 1939. In the years just prior to American entry into World War II, however, idealistic motivations and concern for national security were far less mixed than they had been in the 1914–17 period. Neutral rights, national honor, and democratic ideals, though of course debated, were less fundamental causes of the policy shift than was self-interest.[15] It was the dramatic German blitz in the spring and summer of 1940, toppling Denmark, Norway, the Netherlands, Belgium, Luxembourg, and France, which dramatically shifted American public opinion. By July of 1940, the Gallup poll showed that a large proportion of those surveyed believed that they would be personally affected by a German victory.[16]

RUSSIAN RECOGNITION

Just as an overemphasis on the failure of the United States to join the League contributed to the characterization of the 1920s as a rigidly isolationist decade, so too has the critical attention lavished on isolationism and the neutrality legislation of the 1930s resulted in a tendency to de-emphasize several solid diplomatic accomplishments of the first half of Roosevelt's tenure. A number of dramatic policy shifts away from fixed Republican positions were undertaken: the establishment of formal diplomatic relations with the Soviet Union; the formation of the Export-Import Bank in 1934 to encourage foreign purchases through American loans; and the reduction in tariff rates. The disappointing economic impact of the decision to extend diplomatic recognition to Moscow is considered below. Far more successful was the Export-Import Bank scheme, for it provided foreign buyers with loans in the form of credits from American firms. A similar objective was contained in the loan policy of the Reconstruction Finance Corporation, which by 1941 had financed the export of over $47,000,000 of American agricultural surpluses.

As described in the previous chapter, one of the results of the nearsightedness of the 1920s' economic nationalism was the erection of disastrous tariff barriers to international commerce. Clearly the leader in the struggle for expanded trade was FDR's internationalist

---

[15] *Ibid.*, p. 408.

[16] Hadley Cantril *et al.*, "America Faces the War: Shifts in Opinion," *Public Opinion Quarterly*, Dec. 1940, p. 654. This shift is explained in detail in William L. Langer and S. E. Gleason, *The Challenge to Isolation, 1937–1940* (New York: Harper & Row, 1952).

Secretary of State, Cordell Hull. A Wilsonian who strongly believed that expanded foreign trade would bring relief from the Depression, Hull knew that the most effective way to invigorate international trade was through an across-the-board reduction in tariffs. But the American public had become accustomed to equating protectionism with increased employment at home, and such a policy would have been political suicide. Hull pragmatically set aside his long-standing advocacy of tariff reduction for a more practical measure—reciprocal trade agreements. Under his leadership the Administration success-fully lobbied for a 1934 law which authorized the President to negotiate tariff reductions of up to 50 percent on specific items in exchange for reciprocal reductions by the negotiating power or powers. By the opening of the Forties, the State Department had concluded over 20 such trade agreements—although most such arrangements were with Latin American nations, France and Great Britain joined the list by the end of the decade.[17]

This legislation had a greater impact than might at first be assumed because of a "most favored nation" clause which stipulated, for example, that a reciprocal tariff reduction between the United States and Argentina on beef would be extended to all nations importing beef to the United States, with the exception of powers specifically excluded by the Executive Branch. In 1942 the govern-ment estimated that reciprocal trade agreements and the "most favored nation" approach had led to an over-all tariff reduction of 30 percent in 10 years.[18]

This desire for increased markets to relieve the stagnation of the Depression was as important as any other single factor motivating the Roosevelt Administration to reverse the stand of its predecessors and to seek diplomatic ties with the Soviet Union. An ally in World War I, but a much feared ideological enemy since the Bolshevik Revolution, Russia presented a serious dilemma for the American public and its leadership. Wilson and his three successors had refused to grant formal diplomatic status to the Soviet regime on the grounds that it was ruled by those advocating aggressive force and the destruction of the democratic-capitalistic system. Russia's repudiation of its war debt and its refusal to acknowledge the claims of American nationals were further barriers to recognition. Yet throughout the Twenties many were enticed by the possibility of expanded trade through a formaliza-

[17] William R. Allen, "Cordell Hull and the Defense of the Trade Agreements Program, 1934–1940," in Alexander DeConde, ed., *Isolation and Security* (Durham: Duke University Press, 1957), pp. 107–32.

[18] David A. Shannon, *Between the Wars: America, 1919–1941* (Boston: Houghton Mifflin, 1965), p. 170.

tion of diplomatic relations; during the following decade the need for potential allies in Europe and Asia provided considerable impetus for the development of a new diplomatic posture.

But any such major revision in Washington's relations with the Bolshevik regime required a long gestation. The American public's enthusiastic response to news of the Czar's overthrow in the February 1917 revolution was quickly chilled when the Bolsheviks came to power in November. The separate Russo-German peace pact at Brest-Litovsk in March 1918 was regarded as an unpardonable breach by a traitorous Russian leadership. Even with the war's successful completion, most Americans remained adamantly against recognition. Soviet propaganda in the United States was bitterly resented and it was argued that Russian embassy and consulates—which would be authorized after recognition—would breed still further propaganda excesses. The open hostility of the Soviet regime toward religion, together with the disestablishment of the Greek Orthodox Church and the 1923 execution of Roman Catholic Monsignor Buchkavich, set millions of Americans against the Leninists. Moreover, the obviously dictatorial nature of the Soviet government, which ruled through a small, authoritarian Communist oligarchy, was deeply offensive to American democratic traditions. Finally, millions of Americans feared that by granting recognition the nation would appear to condone the Bolshevik regime's bloody terrorism, forced labor camps, persecutions, and violations of the most basic civil liberties.

The openly hostile attitude of the Bolsheviks toward the Western governments was a major factor influencing four American administrations to withhold recognition. Russian hostility went far beyond propaganda campaigns, for in a most fundamental way the very legitimacy of democratic governments was challenged, their social systems openly attacked, and their survival threatened. The Soviets sought revolution in Western capitalistic nations and actively supported internal efforts toward that end. It is little wonder that during the "Red" hysteria of the early 1920s, the Republicans dared not risk the political censure which would have followed any serious attempt at a rapprochement. Of course, all three Republican presidents also were personally antagonistic to such a notion.[19]

On a less subjective level, relations were strained by Moscow's refusal to acknowledge responsibility for the foreign debts of either the Czarist regime or the 1917 provisional government (which held power after the February Revolution). In 1914 the Czar's government owed

[19] See Edward M. Bennett, *Recognition of Russia: An American Foreign Policy Dilemma* (Waltham, Mass.: Blaisdell Publishing Company, 1970), pp. 47–86.

an estimated four billion gold rubles, or about two billion dollars. This was the largest foreign indebtedness of any nation on the globe. By 1917 this debt had risen 300 percent. When the Leninists came to power they nationalized foreign property valued by its owners at two billion rubles. The United States was not much affected by the pre-1914 debt since France, Britain, Germany, and Belgium were the Czar's major creditors; only 6 percent of the expropriated property belonged to American citizens. However, during the war the United States lent considerable sums to the Russians, particularly to the 1917 provisional government. These debts and credits were important factors in international relations in and of themselves, but they took on even greater importance when considered in tandem with the complexity of international monetary claims and reparations following the war.[20]

Debts, claims, and propaganda excesses notwithstanding, most American liberal and radical intellectuals were sympathetic to Lenin's goals, thought the Brest-Litovsk agreement necessary for Russian survival, and denounced the Siberian intervention.[21] Support for this perspective came from an unexpected source—major business interests who envisioned huge profits from an expanded Russian trade. These seemingly disparate factions were at the forefront of the movement for recognition in the Twenties, but the public at large supported the nonrecognition policy of the Republican administrations.[22]

The Soviets themselves were most eager for diplomatic sanction, which was viewed as a means of obtaining foreign capital and credits, provided this goal could be attained without affecting the revolutionary regime's freedom of action. Trade was a second and closely related goal of the Leninists. The quite subjective desire for the prestige which flowed from recognition should not be discounted. Former Ambassador to Russia, George F. Kennan, has judged the Soviet recognition objective "amazing," given Moscow's open hostility in the Twenties to the institutions and ideals of the Western capitalist nations, and its threats to destroy those powers through the exportation of revolution. The Ambassador concludes that the Soviet leadership's attitude toward Western governments "psychologically and politically, was equivalent to that which would prevail toward an enemy in time of war. This regime was indeed waging, on every front except the overt

[20] Figures are from George F. Kennan, *Russia and the West Under Lenin and Stalin* (Boston: Little, Brown, 1960), p. 200.

[21] For a study of the complexity of the liberals' reaction to the revolution, see Christopher Lasch, *The American Liberals and the Russian Revolution* (New York: Columbia University Press, 1962).

[22] Peter G. Filene, *Americans and the Soviet Experiment, 1917–1933* (Cambridge, Mass.: Harvard University Press, 1967), pp. 269–71.

military one, every form of warfare it knew how to wage, and with the most deadly intent." [23]

The one important American contact with the Soviet Union in the postwar decade had been commercial; in 1920 the Wilson Administration lifted the ban on trade with Russia, and in the ensuing years the Bolshevik leadership carefully assured American financial interests of its dependability as a trading partner. By the mid-Twenties, the United States exported more to the Soviet Union than it had to Czarist Russia. In 1924–25 American goods constituted the greatest single component of Russian imports, and during the following four years Russian imports from the United States were second only to those from Germany.[24]

In these early years, Russia was greatly hampered by the decision of the United States to prohibit the importation of gold from Russia. (It was claimed that the gold had been confiscated from its owners by the Bolsheviks.) This was a serious matter since the Soviets could only pay for American imports with gold or exports of their own. With a balance of trade in favor of the United States, and with a paucity of export commodities in the early transitional years, the American ban on gold from Russia was a cruel blow to hopes for expanded commerce.

This dilemma was compounded by the Soviet's inability to obtain widespread credits for long-term financing of American purchases. While some American giants, such as Standard Oil, General Motors, General Electric, and International Harvester, did extend long-term credits, most smaller corporations thought it too risky to do so. Yet despite these very considerable handicaps, cotton, rubber, nonferrous metals, semi-finished goods, automobiles, and agricultural machinery were sold to Russia, even though the United States did not provide an important market for Soviet exports.

The first Five-Year Plan (begun 1928–29), which sought agricultural collectivism and the expansion of heavy industry, marked an important change in United States-Soviet commercial relations. The plan rested on Russia's ability to import large quantities of heavy industrial and agricultural machinery, and the United States was an obvious source of supply. The effect of the Five-Year Plan on American exports was quickly felt—orders in 1929 were nearly 300 percent above the previous year's, and by 1930 the United States had surpassed Germany in the value of exports to the Soviet Union; in turn, the largest purchaser of American agricultural and industrial

[23] Kennan, *Russia and the West*, pp. 184, 187–88.
[24] See Robert Paul Browder, *The Origins of Soviet-American Diplomacy* (Princeton: Princeton University Press, 1953), p. 25.

equipment in 1930 and 1931 was the Soviet Union. To facilitate the exchange, American technicians were sent to assist in the utilization of equipment.

The depressed state of international commerce following the Crash of 1929 greatly enhanced the attractiveness of the Russian market, and those firms enjoying the bulk of this trade were at the forefront of the campaign for a normalization of relations. They were supported by a number of public officials, particularly Senator Burton K. Wheeler of Montana, who warned that the Soviets would seek out German and British imports if recognition did not occur.[25] When in 1932 Russian-American trade plummeted 89 percent, critics charged that nonrecognition, continuing criticism of the Bolshevik regime (particularly the charge that it was utilizing forced labor), and restraints on credit arrangements in the United States, had caused Moscow to turn elsewhere for its supply sources. While it was certainly true that German and British goods often replaced those from the United States, the Russians had also sharply curtailed all imports: the 1933 total was only half that of the previous year, and only 30 percent of the 1930 total.[26] It is most likely that this decline had more to do with the impact of the Depression than with the absence of diplomatic recognition or the difficulty in obtaining credits.[27]

A flurry of Congressional interest in recognition followed news of the decline in Russian imports, and many stood behind Senators Wheeler and Borah's long campaign to win that objective. California's Senator Hiram Johnson charged: "There are billions of dollars' worth of future orders in Russia for American workers to fill, and in these times it is simply economic idiocy for America, by its policies, to preclude Americans from trade and commerce which so readily could be obtained." [28] But as long as Hoover remained in the White House the chances for recognition were dim, for the President was steady in his resolve not to recognize a regime built on the brutal repression of its citizens.

By the end of the decade the implications of the first Five-Year Plan, the Crash, and the worldwide Depression, greatly altered American attitudes toward Russia. As the Depression deepened the concept of national economic planning was of greater and greater interest to the Roosevelt Administration and to the public. The

---

[25] See Filene, *Americans and the Soviet Experiment*, pp. 259–62.

[26] Figures from Browder, *The Origins of Soviet-American Diplomacy*, p. 45.

[27] For a view of the relationship of trade and recognition from the point of view of a critic of American policy in these years, see William Appleman Williams, *American-Russian Relations, 1781–1947* (New York: Holt, Rinehart & Winston, 1952), pp. 177–229.

[28] *New York Times*, 24 Apr. 1932, p. 7.

Depression also increased the determination of business leaders to spur an economic revival through expanded trade, regardless of the ideological views of trading partners: businessmen, liberals, newspaper editors, and the Protestant clergy demanded recognition in the interest of commerce, world peace, and common sense.[29]

In the midst of the worsening economic crisis the Bolshevik default on debts and claims was far less of an issue since other nations, such as Great Britain, France, and Italy, had either defaulted themselves or made only token debt payments by 1933. The decision of England and France to grant recognition despite repudiation was a further reason for the United States to reconsider its position. This was particularly sensible since Russia had by this time negotiated some individual adjustments with private American corporations affected by the expropriations.

Even Russian propaganda seemed less virulent in the 1930s, for after more than a decade of dedicated effort, it became apparent that so-called "suitcase revolutionaries" would not create any serious threat to the American system. The Russian regime, moreover, was stable despite its origins and seemed to be winning a larger measure of international support. There was considerable sophistication in the acknowledgment, however belated, that recognition did not imply sanction of the Bolsheviks; America's traditional policy, after all, was one of de facto recognition. Early in 1933 the eminent authority on international law, John Bassett Moore, had attacked the notion of granting recognition only to "genuinely friendly" powers:

> [T]he establishment of diplomatic relations with a government never was formerly supposed to imply approval either of its form or of its acts. Our establishment of such relations with the Barbary "Pirates" probably was hastened by our disapproval of what they did, and by our desire to obtain redress.[30]

Recognition seemed all the more imperative as the threat of Japan, Germany, and Italy impelled the United States to cast about for potential allies. Finally, FDR's personal leadership in the decision for recognition, and his astute judgment that such a policy would win the acceptance of the American public, was the decisive factor.

In October 1933, Roosevelt communicated personally with

[29] Filene, *Americans and the Soviet Experiment*, p. 272. See also, Thomas A. Bailey, *America Faces Russia: Russian-American Relations from Early Times to Our Day* (Ithaca, N.Y.: Cornell University Press, 1950), pp. 262–68.

[30] John Bassett Moore, *The Collected Papers of John Bassett Moore* (New Haven, Conn.: Yale University Press, 1944), VI, p. 479.

President Mikhail Kalinin of the Soviet Union, suggesting an opening of negotiations on the recognition question. The response was enthusiastic. Foreign Minister Maxim Litvinov was dispatched to Washington, and on November 17 a final agreement was announced. In exchange for formal recognition the Soviets agreed to the following: grant freedom of worship to Americans living in Russia; curtail propaganda directed at the United States; drop claims for damages arising from the 1918–20 Siberian intervention; and continue negotiations on the debt issue.[31]

The establishment of formal diplomatic relations was generally supported by a majority of the American people.[32] The *New York Times*, for example, published a survey of editorial opinion in the United States which concluded that in the absence of unanimity on the question, there existed a general acknowledgment that the step was "inevitable." [33] Peter G. Filene, author of a major work on American reactions to the Soviet Union prior to the recognition decision, concludes: "a decade earlier, Roosevelt could not have acted so easily, or would not have even dared to act, because of an inevitable deluge of popular protest. He took the bold step only because, by the early thirties, open-mindedness had finally surpassed hostility toward the USSR." [34] But Filene cautions that this positive reception represented a wide variety of attitudes which depended in large measure on what individual Americans thought of the war, prosperity, the Depression, and the value of democracy.

While vicious attacks on the decision by ultranationalist groups may be discounted, much legitimate criticism was directed toward Roosevelt's overly optimistic, seemingly naive, predictions of the salutary consequences of his initiative. A very recent study of the policy switch charges: "the United States approached the Soviet Union in November 1933 as though it were about to take a wife. . . . The Russians on the other hand were destined to take the view that the USSR had been engaging in a seduction and had been successful in winning a paramour." [35]

It is certainly true that Roosevelt's reversal of Hoover's position did not lead to the anticipated economic windfall. While 1934 trade totals were double those of 1933, they represented only one-seventh the value of goods exported to Russia in 1931. And while trade

---

[31] These eventually broke down completely. Donald G. Bishop, *The Roosevelt-Litvinov Agreements: The American View* (Syracuse, N.Y.: Syracuse University Press, 1965), Chaps. V and IX.

[32] Filene, *Americans and the Soviet Experiment*, p. 272.

[33] *New York Times*, 18 Nov. 1933, p. 2.

[34] Filene, *Americans and the Soviet Experiment*, p. 273.

[35] Bennett, *Recognition of Russia*, pp. 125–26.

expanded in succeeding years, these increases had relatively little effect on the total value of American exports.[36] Yet the fact remains that recognition of a major world power made sense, for it was apparent from almost the first that a head-in-the-sand attitude would accomplish nothing except to stall an accommodation. By extending recognition, the United States freely accepted the Bolshevik regime's existence and, more importantly, acknowledged a willingness to coexist in a world of conflicting ideologies. The disintegration of this accommodation will be the subject of later chapters.

INCREASED HEMISPHERIC SOLIDARITY

Although early New Deal diplomacy deserves much credit for its creative reversal of Republican positions toward protectionism and the recognition of the Soviet Union, the Roosevelt Administration could claim only limited gains in extending the Republican accommodation toward Latin America. Despite a marked improvement in United States-Latin American relations in the 1920s, the major diplomatic objective of the republics to the South remained unfulfilled: the repudiation of the theory of intervention in hemispheric affairs. Roosevelt's triumph in 1932 encouraged optimism, for the Democratic platform of that year had pledged "no interference in the internal affairs of other nations" and "cooperation with nations of the Western Hemisphere to maintain the spirit of the Monroe Doctrine." In his Inaugural Address, the President both coined a phrase and made a promise for a "policy of the good neighbor—the neighbor who resolutely respects himself and, because he does so, respects the rights of others—the neighbor who respects his agreements in and with a world of neighbors." [37]

This pledge was honored at the Seventh International Conference of American States at Montevideo (1933), where Secretary Hull asserted that "No state has the right to intervene in the internal or external affairs of another. . . . no government need fear any intervention on the part of the United States under the Roosevelt administration." [38] The renunciation was not unequivocal, however, since a reservation was issued stipulating in effect that while the United States had renounced interference in the internal political

[36] Browder, *The Origins of Soviet-American Diplomacy*, p. 194.

[37] Both quotations from Donald M. Dozer, *Are We Good Neighbors?* (Gainesville, Fla.: University of Florida Press, 1959), pp. 17–18.

[38] Quoted in Bryce Wood, *The Making of the Good Neighbor Policy* (New York: Columbia University Press, 1961), pp. 118–19.

affairs of Latin American republics, it might still intervene to protect the lives and property of its nationals. Nevertheless, the Administration had gone a long way toward renouncing the theory of forceful intervention, and in the next few years demonstrated its good faith by withdrawing all troops from Haiti and Santo Domingo; the negotiation of a new canal treaty more favorable to Panama; the abrogation of previously negotiated transit rights across Mexico's Isthmus of Tehuantepec; and the ratification of a number of reciprocal trade agreements.

In February of 1936 Hull outlined the Administration's basic policy in a radio address:

"(1) to promote better understanding among our sister republics of this hemisphere; (2) to lend every assistance to the maintenance of peace and the perfection of peace machinery on this continent; and (3) to eliminate excessive artificial barriers to inter-American trade." [39]

A long step toward the achievement of these goals was taken at the Conference of American States at Buenos Aires in 1936, a conference which FDR personally attended.

At Buenos Aires the United States signed a protocol declaring intervention inadmissible, "directly or indirectly, and for whatever reason, in the internal or external affairs of any other of the Parties." [40] It was Washington's understanding that this referred to the use of armed force to influence the internal affairs of a sister republic; Hull stoutly denied the interpretation of some participants that the pledge also prohibited traditional, peaceful intervention for the protection of American nationals. Intervention, for the United States, continued to be defined as the use of armed force.[41]

Hull's initiatives for increased trade with hemispheric neighbors were well received. By 1932 the effects of the Depression had drastically reduced the value of Latin American trade; by the time of FDR's election it was approximately 70 percent off the 1929 level.[42] At the Montevideo, Buenos Aires, and Lima conferences, Hull repeated his pledge to scale protectionist Republican tariff walls through bilateral reciprocity treaties based upon mutual concessions. This was particularly important since the economic nationalism of many European nations (adopted in part in retaliation for American exclusiveness) had sharply reduced the value of Latin American exports across the Atlantic. By 1938 Hull succeeded in negotiating

[39] Quoted in Dozer, *Are We Good Neighbors?*, p. 24.
[40] Quoted in Wood, *The Making of the Good Neighbor Policy*, p. 162.
[41] For a discussion of this point, see *Ibid.*, pp. 162–65.
[42] Shannon, *Between the Wars*, p. 170.

reciprocal trade agreements with ten Latin republics, resulting in a 166 percent increase in the value of American exports and a corresponding increase of 114 percent in Latin American imports to the United States.[43]

The approaching holocaust in Europe and Asia provided an inevitable backdrop for the 1938 Lima conference of American states, which witnessed a significant and totally understandable shift of interest away from hemispheric squabbles. Since 1936 the Roosevelt Administration had intensified its efforts to ensure that the collective action of all American nations would safeguard the security of the hemisphere, and in his opening remarks at the Lima conference Hull stressed the necessity of a strengthened inter-American security system to protect the hemisphere from invasion. The defense of the Americas was pledged in the "Declaration of Lima" which called for "continental solidarity . . . against all foreign intervention or activity that may threaten them." Consultative procedures were provided should the security of any American state be threatened; importantly, the powers were *not* limited to *peaceful* measures.[44]

The decade's most significant test of the workability of the Good Neighbor initiative was Mexico's 1938 expropriation of agricultural and petroleum property belonging to American nationals and valued at $200,000,000.[45] This expropriation was part of a broad land redistribution policy and was not directed specifically at American holdings. The Administration's response was distinctly low-keyed, for it did not threaten intervention or other forms of retaliation: Hull quickly acknowledged the right of Mexico to nationalize the land, but insisted upon compensation for American owners. In the end, a joint commission was established to determine compensation levels as well as provisions for the stability of Mexican currency in the transition period.

Generally, the Good Neighbor policy during Roosevelt's first five or six years in office involved questions of intervention, recognition, commercial reciprocity, protection of nationals, and the like. After 1938 a dramatic shift occurred, with increased emphasis on hemispheric solidarity and security, accompanied by an acknowledgment on both sides that only through close association could the Americas be secure.

There is, nevertheless, a regrettable tendency to view the policies

---

[43] Figures from Dozer, *Are We Good Neighbors?*, p. 26.

[44] The text of the Declaration of Lima is reprinted in J. Lloyd Mecham, *The United States and Inter-American Security, 1889–1960* (Austin: University of Texas Press, 1961), p. 142.

[45] This figure according to American estimates. Wood, *The Making of the Good Neighbor Policy*, p. 203.

of the Roosevelt Administration as the full-flowering of the Good Neighbor concept. Decades after the close of the Roosevelt era the attitude of the United States toward the Latin American republics continues to be a source of widespread bitterness. The violent demonstration against Vice President Nixon during his 1958 "good-will tour" of Latin America for the Eisenhower Administration, and the open hostility a decade later toward President Nixon's special envoy to South America, Governor Nelson Rockefeller, attest to a continuing resentment toward the United States long after Roosevelt's death.

ATTEMPTING QUARANTINE

Latin American good will, Russian recognition, and expanded international trade were major concerns of the Roosevelt Administration; they were not, of course, its central concern. Overshadowing all else was the Administration's preoccupation with formulating an appropriate response to the impending catastrophic blow to world order. In October 1935 Italy's Blackshirts rolled over Ethiopia and the following year Germany, in violation of all post-World War I settlements, occupied the Rhineland. Beginning that same year and ending in 1939, a bloody civil war exhausted Spain as General Francisco Franco's Fascist forces, backed by Germany and Italy, crushed the Republican government (aided by Russia).

Congress confronted the gathering crisis by acceding to the predominately isolationist mood of the country. A 1935 neutrality measure enjoined the nation from armaments trade in wartime. Roosevelt had sought a somewhat more sophisticated formula by suggesting that the President be permitted to exercise his discretion in prohibiting arms exportation to belligerent nations so that they might be sold to the victims of aggression. The Congress turned aside this recommendation and passed its own version, which came to be known as the First Neutrality Act.

The 1935 legislation explicitly stated:

> That upon the outbreak or during the progress of war between, or among, two or more foreign states, the President shall proclaim such fact, and it shall thereafter be unlawful to export arms, ammunition, or implements of war from any place in the United States, or possessions of the United States, to any port of such belligerent states, or to any neutral port for transshipment to, or for the use of, a belligerent country.[46]

[46] *Peace and War: United States Foreign Policy, 1931–1941* (Washington, D.C.: Government Printing Office, 1943), pp. 266–67.

The act further stipulated that the President was to enumerate the nature of the materiel to be prohibited; that the embargo was to be extended to nations which appeared to be on the verge of war; and that the manufacturers of such war materiel were required to register with the Secretary of State. With the *Lusitania* and similar tragedies in mind, the Congress ordered that once the President declared that two or more nations were at war, American shippers were forbidden to carry arms, ammunition, or implements of war to either a belligerent nation or to a nation which might transship such items to a belligerent. Finally, American nationals were firmly warned that they traveled on vessels belonging to belligerent nations at their own risk. Despite his strong belief that the measure's "inflexible provisions might drag us into war instead of keeping us out," [47] FDR bowed to the wishes of the Congress and the bill became law on August 31.

Italy's fascist government provided the First Neutrality Act with an early trial—less than two months after it became law Mussolini invaded Ethiopia. Even though Il Duce did not actually declare war, Roosevelt understandably proclaimed that a state of war existed and applied the neutrality legislation. The weakness, to say nothing of the inhumanity, of the measure was almost immediately apparent. The Blackshirts were well prepared for the African campaign and clearly capable of bringing it to a successful conclusion without American arms. Haile Selassie's nation was doomed without outside assistance. (It can, however, be argued that to some extent the measure may have operated in Ethiopia's favor. That is, as a landlocked nation with a primitive transportation system, it is highly unlikely that Ethiopia would have been able to receive many American arms; the Italians, although able to prosecute this phase of the campaign without American supplies, were nevertheless eager to obtain them and would have availed themselves of the opportunity had it not been for the 1935 legislation.)

Ironically, while much American war materiel could not be sent to Italy or Ethiopia, oil, the single most important overseas commodity needed by Mussolini, was not covered by the embargo. And although Roosevelt and the State Department called for a "moral embargo" on the shipment of oil and other items to Italy, it was largely ignored.[48]

The League of Nations responded to the Italo-Ethiopian conflict

[47] Samuel I. Rosenman, *The Public Papers and Addresses of Franklin D. Roosevelt* (New York: Random House, 1938–50), IV, p. 346.

[48] See Henderson B. Braddick, "A New Look at American Policy during the Italo-Ethiopian Crisis, 1935–36," *Journal of Modern History*, XXXIV (Mar. 1962), 64–73. Also George W. Baer, *The Coming of the Italo-Ethiopian War* (Cambridge, Mass.: Harvard University Press, 1967).

by branding Rome the aggressor. The League's Council imposed a series of economic sanctions: member states were forbidden to ship arms, ammunition, and implements of war to Italy; all loans, private or public, were disallowed; League nations were not to accept imports from Italy; and an embargo was placed upon the exportation of a number of commodities. The great weakness was that the sanctions did not apply to oil, iron, steel, and coal. The League was also enormously hampered by England and France's playing a most delicate game: while they wished to cooperate they were at the same time seeking to appease Italy in an attempt to forestall Rome's alliance with Germany. And while Britain sent her Mediterranean fleet to the Suez Canal area—threatening by implication to close the canal, an act which would have seriously hampered the Italian offensive—it did not take any stronger action. At one point in the tortured deliberations of the Council an oil embargo was seriously discussed. But in March 1936, before definitive action could be taken, Hitler moved his troops into the Rhineland and withdrew from the League. Both England and France became more anxious than ever to discourage a pact between the two European dictators and so despite the rhetoric, which continued, all effective countermeasures ceased. By early summer Italy had annexed Ethiopia, and the League ended its sanctions in July of 1936.[49] It was hardly one of the more inspiring episodes in the short history of the international body.

The American public was quick to condemn the Italian aggression, but the dominant isolationist current continued to run strong.[50] The First Neutrality Act was slated to expire on February 29, 1936, and in anticipation of its reenactment, the State Department attempted to win Congressional acceptance of a basic modification which would give the Chief Executive freedom to determine whether or not to apply the embargo against belligerents. The department had originally sought an amendment granting the President the power to discriminate between belligerents in applying the embargo, but given the political climate this sensible proposal was doomed. Hull had also sought to extend the embargo to cover items—such as oil—which had not been included in 1935. Yet despite repeated appeals by the Secretary of State to the Senate Foreign Relations Committee, the Upper House refused to give the President the discretionary powers which he sought. It was feared that he would use those powers to

[49] For the League's response to the Italo-Ethiopian War, see F. P. Walters, *A History of the League of Nations* (New York: Oxford University Press, 1952), II, Chap. 53. Also Herbert Feis, *Seen from E.A.: Three International Episodes* (New York: Knopf, 1947), pp. 193–275.

[50] Brice Harris, Jr., *The United States and the Italo-Ethiopian Crisis* (Stanford, Calif.: Stanford University Press, 1964), p. 146.

attempt to coordinate the policies of the nation with those of the League (Wilson's ghost still stalked the Senate chamber) or to maneuver the United States into another European war.

Thus the State Department's revisions were set aside and the Congress, by joint resolution, voted to extend an amended version of the Neutrality Act of 1935 until May 1, 1937. The Second Neutrality Act differed in its prohibition against loans to belligerents, a modification which was supported by the State Department. In addition, whereas the earlier measure had *empowered* the President to extend the embargo to other states as they became involved in an existing war, the 1936 act *directed* him to do so. The implication of this second amendment was considerable since the United States was placing individual League nations on notice that should they assist a victim nation they could not then receive war materiel from the United States! Not only did the Congress preclude Washington from acting responsibly in the face of aggression, it also hampered other nations from implementing their own mutual assistance pacts. Finally, it was agreed that the new act would not apply ". . . to an American republic or republics engaged in war against a non-American state or states, provided the American republic is not cooperating with a non-American state or states in such war." [51] Given the long-range objectives of the Executive branch, the legislation was not an improvement over the earlier measure. It is quite possible that the President's desire not to have his domestic legislative program threatened by bitter debates over the nation's foreign policy caused him to acquiesce to the neutrality bill.

Italy's invasion of Ethiopia had provided a telling proving ground for the merits of the First Neutrality Act, and to an even more profound degree the Spanish Civil War was to test the effectiveness of the revised legislation. In July 1936 a bloody civil war erupted in Spain between insurgents led by General Francisco Franco and the Spanish Republican government. Even if one accepts FDR's strategy of complying with the predominant isolationist sentiment so as not to endanger his domestic program, it is difficult to defend the President's initial reaction to the Spanish Civil War, which was to act as if Franco's forces constituted a foreign state. Operating under this assumption, he imposed moral embargoes against both sides while urging the Congress to amend the Second Neutrality Act to include embargoes against nations embroiled in civil wars. This was done in both the Arms Embargo Act of January 8, 1937, and the Third Neutrality Act of May 1, 1937.

[51] *Peace and War*, p. 314.

In his strong defense of the Arms Embargo Act—which passed
the Congress by an overwhelming majority—Hull has sharply attacked those who with "keen hindsight" have criticized the Administration's handling of the civil war.

> Had we reversed our moral embargo, had Congress later repealed the
> Arms Embargo Act, American arms, ammunition, and implements of
> war might have gone not only to the Spanish Government but also to
> the Franco forces, if not directly at least indirectly. In any event,
> shipments of arms to either side or both would have served to lengthen
> the war and hence conflicted with our [policy] . . . which was to
> prevent prolongation of the conflict. The longer the Spanish War went
> on the greater was the likelihood that other nations would become
> involved.[52]

But critics have repeatedly charged that despite their pledges of
nonintervention, the Italian and German governments were actually
providing Franco with massive amounts of aid, including troops.[53]
Hence while Hull attempted to forestall a spread of hostilities,
American policy indirectly aided the fascists and thereby made
increased aggression inevitable.

A month after the completion of the Rome-Berlin Axis of
October 1936, Italy and Germany formally recognized Franco's fascist
government, thereby further facilitating the General's victory. Unexpectedly, it was the isolationist Senator Nye who urged the Administration to repeal the embargo so as to permit arms shipments to the
Loyalists. Secretary of the Interior Harold Ickes, who supported Nye's
attempt to permit a discretionary lifting of the embargo, has written
that Roosevelt told him he would not accede to the demand because to
do so "would mean the loss of every Catholic vote next fall and that
the Democratic Members of Congress were jittery about it and didn't
want it done." Ickes confided to his diary that the "mangiest, scabbiest
cat ever" was out of the bag.[54] In the long run Roosevelt's policies
vis-à-vis Spain proved to be most unwise since they encouraged the
general European and American mood of appeasement. The American Ambassador to Spain, Claude Bowers, wrote in July 1937:

> My own impression is that with every surrender beginning long ago
> with China, followed by Abyssinia [Ethiopia] and then Spain, the

---

[52] Cordell Hull, *Memoirs of Cordell Hull* (London: Macmillan, 1948), I, p. 483.

[53] Relatedly, for the view that Russian aid was not as slight as was previously believed, see
Kennan, *Russia and the West*, p. 309, and Hugh Thomas, *The Spanish Civil War* (New York:
Harper 1961), pp. 634–38.

[54] Harold Ickes, *The Secret Diary of Harold Ickes* (New York: Simon & Schuster, 1954), II,
p. 390.

fascist powers, with vanity inflamed, will turn without delay to some other country—such as Czechoslovakia—and that with every surrender the prospects of a European war grow darker.[55]

With the passage of the Third Neutrality Act (1937) the Administration once again requested, although not very strongly, inclusion of discretionary powers for the President in the implementation of the embargo. Once again the request was denied. In addition to the civil war provisions, the Congress strengthened the neutrality measure by failing to place a time limit on the embargo sections. And while the earlier measure had warned American nationals that they traveled on belligerent ships at their own risk, the Congress now forbade such travel. Importantly, the law included a "cash and carry" provision which permitted the President to prohibit the exportation (in American ships) of items not considered arms, ammunition, or implements of war to belligerent nations until title of such articles had actually been transferred to the foreign buyer.

Although the machinations of Italy, Germany, and Spain caused the Administration to be intensely concerned with European affairs in the mid-1930s, the Far East could hardly be characterized as stable. In July 1937 a detachment of Japanese troops battled with Chinese soldiers at the Marco Polo Bridge, ten miles from Peking. This "incident" provided the Japanese with sufficient reason to invade China in force. The situation was somewhat analogous to the Italo-Ethiopian War in that both conflicts were undeclared, but this time Roosevelt chose not to apply the neutrality legislation; the strength of pro-Chinese sentiment had much to do with his decision. While Japan at this time was importing significantly more American goods than was China, China's advantage was proportionally greater. The decision not to employ the neutrality legislation thus favored the Chinese, even though it was technically correct.

Frustrated in his attempts to avert war between the democracies and the dictatorships, Roosevelt experimented with another scheme after the "China incident" by delivering his so-called Quarantine Speech in Chicago on October 5, 1937. The speech, prepared in large part by the State Department—except for the "quarantine" idea, which apparently took Hull by surprise—was very much a product of the President's "groping and intermittent" efforts to ward off the impending catastrophe. Roosevelt told his Chicago audience:

[55] Quoted in F. Jay Taylor, *The United States and the Spanish Civil War* (New York: Bookman Associates, 1956), p. 15. Probably the best study of the civil war as it related to the United States is Allen Guttman, *The Wound in the Heart: America and the Spanish Civil War* (New York: Free Press, 1962).

"There is a solidarity and interdependence about the modern world, both technically and morally, which makes it impossible for any nation completely to isolate itself from economic and political upheavals in the rest of the world, especially when such upheavals appear to be spreading and not declining. . . . International anarchy destroys every foundation for peace. . . . When an epidemic of physical disease starts to spread, the community approves and joins in a quarantine of the patients in order to protect the health of the community against the spread of the disease."[56]

There now exists considerable evidence for the view that much of the public responded favorably to the "quarantine" thesis but that Roosevelt, caught unprepared and without specific plans to implement his Chicago proposal, acceded to the shrill denunciations of the isolationists. By his quick retreat he frustrated and alienated his supporters while giving the impression that the isolationists' outrage represented the general consensus.[57] The concept of isolating aggressor nations by a deliberate policy, rather than isolating the United States from aggressors, was startling to those who believed that the neutrality legislation was a fixed point in American foreign policy. But the greatest consternation in the isolationist ranks was caused by FDR's statement that "The peace loving nations must make a concerted effort in opposition to those violations of treaties and those ignorings of humane instincts which today are creating a state of international anarchy and instability from which there is no escape through mere isolation or neutrality." [58] While he certainly was not calling for a resumption of Wilson's crusade to join the League, the President was suggesting that war could be averted "by providing for a collective neutrality or nonbelligerency, the mere threat of which would act as a restraint upon aggression." [59]

The well-organized reaction to the quarantine proposal forced Roosevelt to back down quickly. Secretary of State Hull concluded that it set back by at least six months the Administration's campaign to strengthen public support for a policy of international cooperation. Not only had Roosevelt failed to mobilize his constituency, he might actually have encouraged overseas aggressors by offering them a view of the United States as a deeply divided nation.

Isolationist concern over the drift of American policy was

[56] Dorothy Borg, "Notes on Roosevelt's 'Quarantine' Speech," *Political Science Quarterly*, LXXII (Sept. 1957), 405. Text in *Peace and War*, pp. 383–87.

[57] See Travis Beal Jacobs, "Roosevelt's 'Quarantine Speech,'" *Historian*, XXIV (Aug. 1962), pp. 493, 501. This general view is also contained in Dorothy Borg, *The United States and the Far Eastern Crisis of 1933–1938* (Cambridge, Mass.: Harvard University Press, 1964), pp. 386–98.

[58] For the text of the speech, see *Peace and War*, pp. 383–87.

[59] Borg, "Notes on Roosevelt's 'Quarantine' Speech," p. 413.

heightened the day after the quarantine speech when the State Department announced its concurrence with the League Assembly's findings that in invading China, Japan had violated both the Nine-Power Treaty and the Kellogg-Briand Pact. Internationalists received a further opportunity to encourage American cooperation with the League when the Belgian government invited the signers of the Nine-Power Treaty to meet in Brussels to settle the dispute between Japan and China. Predictably, Japan refused the invitation, explaining that by announcing its findings on October 6, 1937 without giving Japan a hearing, the League had already prejudged the case and so had made the Brussels meeting pointless. With 19 nations in attendance, the conference met most of November but took no action stronger than holding the Japanese in contempt of the Nine-Power Treaty and the Pact of Paris. The Japanese government steadfastly insisted that its actions in China were taken in self-defense and that since neither the Nine-Power Treaty nor the Kellog-Briand Pact were applicable to the "China incident" the matter could only be settled by China and Japan.

In an attempt to avoid incidents involving American nationals, and perhaps to assure those at home that he was indeed backing down from the "quarantine" position, Roosevelt ordered a general evacuation of United States nationals from China. The move followed several ugly incidents involving Americans who were assaulted by Japanese soldiers; there had also been some bomb damage to American schools and hospitals in China, despite the policy of placing or painting large American flags on the roofs of such buildings. A turning point was reached on December 12, 1937, with the bombing of the United States gunboat *Panay* and the destruction of three Standard Oil Company tankers.[60] Three Americans were killed and several others wounded. The Japanese apologized profusely and offered reparations for the damage and injuries; nevertheless the Administration, with good reason, remained convinced that the action was a deliberate attempt to underscore Japan's determination to have a free hand in the Far East.

The bombing and sinking of the *Panay*, with the resultant loss of American life, understandably reminded the American public of the series of events leading to Wilson's war message to the Congress in 1917. Fear that the United States once again would be manipulated into war caused much concern and accounted for renewed interest in a scheme to allow the American public, and not the President and Congress, to determine whether or not the nation should go to war.

[60] For background, see Borg, *The United States and the Far Eastern Crisis*, pp. 486–518.

The idea was not a new one, for in 1916 Congressman Denver Church of California proposed just such a referendum. He was supported by William Jennings Bryan, Robert M. La Follette, and William Randolph Hearst. Church made little headway with his proposal, but two decades later a Democratic Congressman from Indiana, Louis Ludlow, revived the idea. Ludlow was considerably encouraged by public opinion polls which indicated his idea had a wide following; a Gallup poll found in the fall of 1937 that seven out of every ten Americans believed that the Congress should not declare war without the approval of the American people.[61]

Roosevelt and his supporters in both parties launched a vigorous campaign against the isolationist measure. During the Congressional debate Speaker of the House William Bankhead dramatically stepped down as presiding officer to read a letter from the Chief Executive denouncing Ludlow's proposal on the grounds that such a referendum ". . . would cripple any President in his conduct of our foreign relations . . . and would encourage other nations to believe that they could violate American rights with impunity."[62] Despite FDR's efforts, which included Postmaster-General James Farley's warning to wavering Democrats that unless they supported the President their patronage would be cut, Ludlow was barely defeated by a vote of 209 to 188 (the vote was taken on January 10, 1938). The Congressman's misguided attempt at mass participation in the formulation of foreign policy represented the strongest statement of American isolationism in the years preceding the outbreak of World War II. That a measure as extraordinarily naive as Ludlow's could come as close as it did to succeeding was a telling commentary on the limitations placed on Administration attempts to respond to the threats of European and Far Eastern aggressors.

GLOBAL WAR

As the bitterness between isolationists and internationalists within and without the government intensified, fascists and aggressors abroad grew bolder. The year that began with the narrow defeat of the Ludlow Amendment undoubtedly represented the last opportunity of the Western democracies to stop the aggressive dictatorships. Hitler's brutish persecutions of German Jews had been in operation for some time, but in early 1938 he increased the extent and frequency of these

---

[61] Robert A. Divine, *The Reluctant Belligerent* (New York: John Wiley, 1965), p. 48.
[62] *Congressional Record*, 75th Cong., 3rd sess., p. 277.

outrages, thereby instigating widespread American criticism and public notice. On the evening of March 11, 1938, to the surprise of very few European officials, Hitler's armies invaded Austria and quickly absorbed it into the Reich. The European democracies did nothing about the invasion; neither did the United States. Hull, FDR, and others, still smarting from the reaction to the Quarantine Speech and the narrow defeat of the Ludlow Amendment, reasonably concluded that little could be done about Austria in the face of the apparent determination of England and France to regard the takeover as irreversible. Yet the Administration was well aware that the situation was ominous: Austria was in the hands of Hitler, China was in the grip of Japanese forces, and Franco was close to success in Spain. In an attempt to move the American public at least a step closer to a recognition of its international obligations, the Administration intensified its preparedness campaign.

The threat of a general European war became all the more apparent later in the summer when the Sudeten Germans, who occupied those border areas of Czechoslovakia which were adjacent to Germany, increased their demands for local autonomy. Hitler of course supported these efforts and plans were announced for military maneuvers in September. It was expected that despite England and France's attempts at peace France would support Czechoslovakia and England in turn would support France. Europe in the summer of 1938 was very close to the brink of war. By September, Hitler had promised to aid the Sudeten Germans in their effort to gain self-determination, and three days later a very alarmed British Prime Minister Neville Chamberlain traveled to Germany to meet Hitler. There he learned from the Führer that the price for peace in Europe was secession to the Reich of the area populated by Sudeten Germans. Pressured by England and France, Czechoslovakia reluctantly agreed to this formula. Hitler then raised the ante by demanding the right to designate those areas to be ceded; his hand was considerably strengthened by assurances from Mussolini that Italy would support the Reich in the event of a general European war. England and France were notified that if the Czechs did not accede to Berlin's territorial demands, Germany would mobilize against that nation. At virtually the last minute a hurried Munich Conference convened on September 29, attended by Hitler, Mussolini, Chamberlain, and French Premier Edouard Daladier. By capitulating to Hitler's demands, war in Europe was postponed, but Chamberlain's assurances that the Munich agreement guaranteed "peace in our time" proved a pathetic and tragic miscalculation.[63]

[63] Langer and Gleason, *The Challenge to Isolation*, pp. 32–35; John McV. Haight, Jr.,

As the war fever spread in Europe, Japan courted a crisis in the Far East. Taking advantage of the Marco Polo Bridge "incident" Japan forcibly brought limited areas of China under her control and puppet governments were established reminiscent of Manchukuo in Manchuria.[64] Japan's military activities in China included the bombing of Chinese cities from the air; such action, not yet considered routine, led Hull in July of 1938 to encourage a "moral embargo" against the sale of airplanes to Japan. The moral embargo against Italy had been a disaster, but Hull was quite successful in his appeal to withhold airplanes and related equipment to nations engaged in the bombing of civilian populations. Yet the Japanese offensive continued as if unaffected by the American retaliation. The Chinese capital of Nanking was overrun, and many major cities, ports, and railroad centers fell to Tokyo's invading forces. To American protests that the Japanese onslaught was in violation of both Chinese sovereignty and the Open Door, Tokyo replied that once the "China incident" was settled—presumably with the complete takeover of China—the Open Door would be respected.

The American Government's uneasiness over the Japanese position was greatly heightened in November of 1938. Ambassador Grew characterized the Japanese position: "Japan must, for her own strategic and economic safety, control certain sources of raw material in China and certain industrial opportunities." [65] Ominously, Prime Minister Konoye would no longer give the United States assurances regarding the Open Door in China. At the end of 1938 the State Department formally responded to this "new order" by informing the Japanese Foreign Office that it did not recognize ". . . that there is need or warrant for any one Power to take upon itself to prescribe what shall be the terms and conditions of a 'new order' in areas not under its sovereignty and to constitute itself the repository of authority and the agent of destiny in regard thereto." Specifically referring to the Open Door, the message asserted that ". . . the people and the Government of the United States cannot assent to the abrogation of any of this country's rights or obligations by the arbitrary action of agents or authorities of any other country." [66]

It is most tempting to assume that Hitler's success in Munich less

---

"France, the United States, and the Munich Crisis," *Journal of Modern History*, XXXII (Dec. 1960), pp. 340–58); and Neville Chamberlain, *In Search of Peace* (New York: Putnam's, 1939). Also Keith Eubank, *Munich* (Norman, Okla.: University of Oklahoma Press, 1963).

[64] Excellent background for the Sino-Japanese War is provided in Borg, *The United States and the Far Eastern Crisis*, pp. 138–275.

[65] Joseph C. Grew, *Ten Years in Japan* (New York: Simon & Schuster, 1944), pp. 271.

[66] Quoted in Julius W. Pratt, *The American Secretaries of State and Their Diplomacy* (New York: Cooper Square, 1964), XIII, p. 455.

than two months before the announcement of the "new order" had greatly encouraged Japan to new heights of aggression. By the opening of 1939 both Germany and Japan appeared to be very much in control of their respective spheres and an increasingly alarmed Roosevelt ordered the United States Pacific Fleet back to its regular base in the Spring of 1939, cutting short its Atlantic cruise. (Two months earlier the Congress complied with the President's request and appropriated funds to strengthen fortifications in Guam, Samoa, and Alaska.)

Despite the "new order" and the threat of a complete absorption of China, 1939 was to be Europe's year. The Führer was not satisfied with Chamberlain's formula for "peace in our time" and an apprehensive Roosevelt began to alter his response to the growing crisis. The change in emphasis was set forth in a January 1939 statement in which the President seriously questioned the legitimacy and the validity of existing neutrality measures.

> We have learned that when we deliberately try to legislate neutrality, our neutrality laws may operate unevenly and unfairly—may actually give aid to the aggressor and deny it to the victim. The instinct of self-preservation should warn us that we ought not to let that happen any more.[67]

Senator Key Pittman, Chairman of the Foreign Relations Committee, agreed to sponsor a measure supported by Hull which would permit the sale of arms and armaments to belligerents so long as they were paid for in cash and transported in the purchasers' ships. It was widely anticipated that such a measure would be of great assistance to England and France.

Such steps were in line with the President's assertion in his 1939 Annual Message to Congress that "There are many methods short of war, but stronger and more effective than mere words, of bringing home to aggressor governments the aggregate sentiments of our own people." [68] But even before the Congress could act upon the suggested shift in its neutrality stance Hitler intervened in an internal dispute between the Czechs and Slovaks and on March 15, 1939, absorbed Bohemia-Moravia and Slovakia into the Reich. Hungary and Poland were by this time appropriating those portions of Czechoslovakia which were populated by Magyars and Poles. The general dissolution of the European order was irresistible to Mussolini and on April 7 his troops rolled over the tiny kingdom of Albania.

[67] Rosenman, *Papers of Franklin D. Roosevelt*, VIII, pp. 3–4.
[68] The message is reprinted in *Ibid.*, pp. 1–12.

The President once again attempted to influence events, now by a dramatic personal appeal to Hitler and Mussolini. On April 14, 1939, he sent a note directly to the two European dictators stating that in return for assurances not to attack 31 nations in Europe and the Near East for at least ten years the United States would participate in international talks related to disarmament and the reduction of trade barriers. Such assurances were, of course, not forthcoming. At the end of the month Hitler told the Reichstag of the President's message and brazenly informed the membership that he had been in contact with the countries referred to in FDR's message and that each had assured him that it did not feel threatened by Germany.[69] Less than a month after the Reichstag speech Hitler and Mussolini's obvious intentions were furthered by the formulation of a military agreement commonly known as the "Pact of Steel" (May 22, 1939).

Relatedly, it had long been Hitler's hope to conclude mutual assistance pacts with imperial Japan and Soviet Russia. His strategy vis-à-vis Japan was obvious: a formal alliance with that nation would not only help neutralize the military might of England and France, it would also intimidate the United States. Although such a pact was popular with the Japanese army, civilian business interests, supported by the navy, were hardly inclined to twist the tails of England, France, and America. Furthermore, Ambassador Grew's warning that such an alliance would have an adverse affect upon American public opinion was undoubtedly a sobering consideration.[70] After lengthy Cabinet debates Japan informed Hitler in early June that although it was quite willing to join in common cause against the Soviet Union it could not agree to a formal pact. Historian and former State Department official Herbert Feis has theorized that Japan's Prime Minister Hiranuma greatly feared the implications of his country's fighting alongside Germany with China unconquered and Russia uncommitted. Grew's biographer has concluded that the Foreign Ministry's unwillingness to involve Japan automatically in a European war, together with the navy's fear of the effect of American economic retaliation on rearmament, kept Hitler from committing Japan completely to the Axis cause.[71] And too, it is most probable that Roosevelt's decision to send the American fleet back to the Pacific had considerable influence on the Japanese government's decision not to link its fate with Germany's. Finally, Ambassador Grew's diary reveals

---

[69] See Hull, *Memoirs*, I, pp. 622–23.

[70] Langer and Gleason, *The Challenge to Isolation*, p. 102.

[71] Herbert Feis, *The Road to Pearl Harbor* (New York: Atheneum, 1967), p. 20; Waldo H. Heinricks, Jr., *American Ambassador: Joseph C. Grew and the Development of the United States Diplomatic Tradition* (Boston: Little, Brown, 1966), p. 282.

that he let it be known in influential Japanese circles that it would be almost impossible for the United States to remain neutral in a general European war.

With his designs for a Japanese alliance thwarted, Hitler turned to the Soviet Union. Stalin had been understandably suspicious of Berlin's intentions and in the summer of 1939 sought to negotiate a defensive alliance with Great Britain and France. This attempt ultimately failed, most probably because the Soviets demanded what amounted to a free hand in the Baltic States and Finland. The Germans were greatly heartened by this development and promptly opened negotiations of their own with the new Russian Foreign Minister, Vyacheslav Molotov. The result was a tremendous shock to the Western democracies: the signing of a nonaggression pact between Hitler and Stalin, dated August 23, 1939. Hitler was thus assured of Russian neutrality when the inevitable attack upon Poland occurred while Stalin, by secret agreement, was to receive a portion of Poland and a sphere of influence in the Baltic area. In addition, Russia gained enormously from the assurance that she could not be attacked by both Germany and Japan. Roosevelt responded to the resultant increased pressure on Poland by offering to act as conciliator in the dispute.[72] And while Poland expressed her willingness to participate in such a plan the Führer did not respond to the offer.

With Russia neutralized Hitler issued his ultimatum to Poland, hopeful that England and France would not honor their agreements but nevertheless willing to battle the European democracies. German troops massed at the border invaded Poland on September 1, and two days later both Great Britain and France declared war on the Reich. German bombers over Warsaw extinguished the last flickering lights in Europe.

A PRECARIOUS NEUTRALITY

In assessing Germany's strategy in Europe in the years prior to the outbreak of war, one is immediately struck by Hitler's tendency to minimize and grossly miscalculate the potential effect United States intervention might have on his designs. In *The Swastika and the Eagle*, James V. Compton concludes that Hitler's image of the United States, gained through random, unofficial sources, was highly colored by a

---

[72] James E. McSherry, *Stalin, Hitler and Europe* (Cleveland: World Publishing Company, 1968), I, pp. 196–252, gives valuable background material.

"clutter of prejudices." [73] More often than not, such information was utilized to disparage rather than to assess realistically Washington's potential to thwart the Führer's plans. Almost everything that Hitler learned of the United States—capitalism, the large Jewish minority, the free press, liberal democracy, and the racial and ethnic mix—increased his contempt and disdain. These were not, in his view, the elements of national greatness. Moreover, long accustomed to utilizing a variety of scapegoats for Germany's defeat in the first war, Hitler consistently refused to acknowledge America's contribution to the Allies' victory. The German leader, according to Compton,

> convinced himself that the internal condition and external position of the United States rendered an American role in Europe out of the question. A picture of isolation, military weakness, social division, economic distress and racial decay . . . allowed Hitler to tend to more congenial continental problems. Toward American aid to Germany's enemies and even a possible entry into the war, he professed the most complete indifference.[74]

Wilson's initial reaction to the outbreak of war in Europe had been to ask the American people to be neutral in thought as well as in action; it would have been unreasonable of Roosevelt to expect as much. In a September 3 radio "fireside chat" he acknowledged that while the nation's official stance was neutrality, he could not "ask that every American remain neutral in thought as well." [75] Two days later the President announced that he was activating the arms embargo authorized by existing neutrality legislation. The ban was automatic even though it was immediately apparent that the curb conflicted with the public's strong desire to stay "neutral" but aid the Allies.

From the very outset official Washington recognized that an Allied victory was essential to American security. "[E]very word that comes through the air, every ship that sails the seas, every battle that is fought does affect the American future," FDR told a "fireside" audience.[76] It was imperative to dismantle the neutrality legislation. To this end a special session of the Congress was called to convince the legislators that revision was the best way to protect the nation's neutrality and security. Throughout the six weeks of debate the Administration goal of denying victory to the Germans was obvious.

[73] James V. Compton, *The Swastika and the Eagle: Hitler, the United States, and the Origins of World War II* (Boston: Houghton Mifflin, 1967), p. 261.

[74] *Ibid.*, p. 261. Also see pp. 7–23.

[75] Wilson's position outlined in Chapter II, p. 60, above. For FDR quote, see Rosenman, *The Public Papers of Franklin D. Roosevelt*, VIII, p. 463.

[76] Rosenman, *The Public Papers of Franklin D. Roosevelt*, VIII, p. 462.

As a compromise to outright repeal an Administration-sponsored measure advocated the continuance of the prohibition against Americans traveling on belligerent vessels and the ban against American ships entering combat zones. In an impassioned address attacking the Administration's revision Senator Borah pleaded with his colleagues to learn from the lessons of World War I. He predicted that any peace treaty which might settle the present conflict ". . . will devote itself, as did the Versailles Treaty, to the unquenchable imperialistic appetites of those who sit around the table." [77] The final version of the Fourth Neutrality Act (1939) represented a compromise between the Administration and the isolationist faction. While the ban on loans to belligerents remained, it was modified to the extent that short-term (90 day) credits could be extended; American ships were forbidden from coastline combat zones of belligerent countries. For Roosevelt and Hull's purposes the most useful aspects of the new law were the repeal of the existing arms embargo and the reenactment of the expired "cash and carry" provision, permitting belligerents—in reality, the Allies—to purchase war materiel paid for in cash and transported in their own vessels.[78] Since it was the clear intention of the government to favor the Allies in the implementation of these changes the act must be viewed as an Administration victory. The new legislation permitted a resumption of the traditional commercial ties between England, France, and the United States, while the superiority of the British navy insured the Allies maximum utilization of this opportunity.

It was soon clear that the Allies would need all the assistance they could obtain. The apparent strength of France's Maginot Line and the quality of the British navy had caused many journalists to predict an early and easy victory, but the journalists' "phony war" soon grew deadly. Although Stalin received his prearranged slice of Poland after the Germans crushed that nation, the Russian Bear remained distrustful of its ally. Hence late in 1939 Stalin began placing enormous pressure on neighboring Finland in an attempt to obtain a territorial buffer against Germany. Stalin further demanded the "lease" of the strategic port of Hango as a naval and air base fortified with Russian troops, but Finland stoutly withstood the pressure. As the only nation which had repaid in full its World War I debts Finland enjoyed considerable popular support in the United States. It was therefore difficult for Roosevelt to deny that government's request that the United States intercede with the Kremlin.

[77] Borah's address in *Congressional Record*, 76th Cong., 2nd sess. (Oct. 2, 1939), p. 74.
[78] The legislation is printed in *Peace and War*, pp. 494–506.

Moscow remained adamant, arguing that the security of the Gulf of Finland and of Leningrad depended upon Soviet fortification of Hango and Russian control of a considerable amount of nearby territory.

With Finland determined to retain her neutrality and independence the crisis continued throughout November; at the end of the month, without a formal declaration of war, Russian troops crossed the border while Soviet aircraft bombed Helsinki. Roosevelt considered breaking diplomatic relations with Moscow but instead placed a moral embargo on the sale of aircraft and other materiel of war to the USSR. The League, acting with unaccustomed speed, expelled Russia. By mid-March Finland's brave resistance was crushed, and while submitting to Russia's terms she managed to retain her independence.[79]

Thus by the spring of 1940 Soviet fortifications against Germany were strengthened, while Hitler's blitzkrieg succeeded in defeating Denmark, Norway, the Netherlands, Luxembourg, and Belgium. With the miraculous escape of the British Expeditionary Force from Dunkirk, France was left isolated on the continent of Europe. Her fate darkened when the supposedly impregnable Maginot Line crumbled under a German invasion from the north. Mussolini, already committed to Germany, ignored a series of appeals from FDR, declared war on June 10, and struck the beleagured France from the south. Roosevelt bitterly informed a University of Virginia audience that ". . . the hand that held the dagger has struck it into the back of its neighbor." Despite the President's great disappointment over not being able to dissuade Italy from further aggression, unlike many other statesmen neither he nor Hull believed that the combination of dramatic German victories and the Italian entry necessarily spelled defeat. Rather there was a keen determination in the Executive branch to provide England and the defeated democracies with as much American aid as possible. In the Virginia speech the President promised:

> "[I]n our American unity, we will pursue two obvious and simultaneous courses; we will extend to the opponents of force the material resources of this nation; and, at the same time, we will harness and speed up the use of those resources in order that we ourselves in the Americas may have equipment and training equal to the task of any emergency and every defense." [80]

[79] The war is discussed in Andrew J. Schwartz, *America and the Russo-Finnish War* (Washington, D.C.: Public Affairs Press, 1960), and Robert Sobel, *The Origins of Interventionism: The United States and the Russo-Finnish War* (New York: Bookman Associates, 1960).

[80] Rosenman, *The Public Papers of Franklin D. Roosevelt*, IX, p. 264.

Given the state of existing legislation there was little that Roosevelt could do to prevent the fall of France. Several days before the Italian attack the President authorized the sale of surplus World War I military supplies, but this was only a finger in a dike about to burst. France's defense quickly crumbled and on June 22, 1940, Hitler, with a sure feel for historical irony, ordered that the surrender take place in the same railway car and in the same spot in France where Germany surrendered in 1918.

The shock of France's fall coupled, finally, with the realization that Hitler would soon be in control of Europe and very possibly of the British fleet turned the tide of American public opinion. Soon after the French surrender Roosevelt fought for and received an $18 billion dollar appropriation for military preparedness; by September of 1940, after acrimonious Congressional debate, the first peacetime draft in American history was passed. Both actions represented a very significant shift in American posture, but a shift which occurred tragically late. Some of the credit for the transition must go to a pressure group, the Committee to defend America by Aiding the Allies.[81] Founded in May of 1940 and headed by William Allen White, a Republican newspaper editor from Kansas, the committee was primarily interested in preventing American direct intervention by strengthening the Allies. A more hawkish line was taken by influential members of the Eastern establishment who met regularly at the Century Club in New York City and were known as the Century Club Group. This faction—which included Joseph Alsop, Herbert Agar, Elmer Davis, Henry Luce, Dean Acheson, Allen Dulles, James B. Conant, James P. Warburg, and Henry Sloane Coffin—argued that White's work might easily precipitate American belligerency. They strongly urged Washington to take the offensive by declaring war on Germany immediately.[82] The opposite tack was taken by the isolationist America First Committee, whose most popular spokesman was the aviator-hero, Colonel Charles A. Lindbergh. Founded in September 1940, by the end of 1941 the organization boasted 450 chapters and 850,000 members; nearly two-thirds of the membership lived within 300 miles of Chicago.[83]

As the situation grew more desperate the United States, still

[81] The standard history of the committee is Walter Johnson, *The Battle Against Isolation* (Chicago: University of Chicago Press, 1944).

[82] William M. Tuttle, Jr., "Aid-to-the-Allies-Short-of-War versus American Intervention, 1940," *The Journal of American History*, LVI (Mar. 1970), pp. 840–58. For a study of the most outspoken propagandists for intervention in 1940 and 1941, see Mark Lincoln Chadwin, *The Hawks of World War II* (Chapel Hill, N.C.: University of North Carolina Press, 1968).

[83] Wayne S. Cole, *America First: The Battle Against Intervention, 1940–1941* (Madison: University of Wisconsin Press, 1953), p. 30.

acting as a nonbelligerent, intensified its efforts to ensure Hitler's defeat. Thus thousands of British pilots were trained in Florida; American aircraft and other military equipment was sent to Canada for transshipment to Great Britain; and damaged British warships were repaired in American shipyards. The Century Club Group, which had argued that the United States should have entered the war in 1940, was convinced that such patently unneutral activity could only lead to war. Throughout the summer of that year the crisis in Europe worsened, for with France securely under Hitler's control Berlin turned its full and brutal power toward the British Isles. The combination of aerial bombings and a submarine blockade threatened the extinction of Churchill's forces.

Those in the United States lobbying for intervention in the form of massive assistance to England had numerous schemes, the most popular of which was to provide London with 50 aging destroyers currently in "mothballs" in American harbors. The ships would be of great use for convoys and anti-submarine patrols, but the problem of getting them transferred to England without violating existing neutrality legislation loomed. Since Churchill could not wait out a bitterly debated adjustment to the Neutrality Act, Attorney General Robert Jackson and some Century Club Group lawyers devised what was hoped to be a defense of the legality of such a transfer. The scheme involved Great Britain's "giving" the United States a 99-year lease on bases in both Newfoundland and Bermuda while at the same time granting rent-free leases for 99 years on sites in the Bahamas, St. Lucia, Jamaica, Trinidad, and British Guiana. The "price" paid by the United States was the 50 aging destroyers. Congress was officially informed of the transaction on September 3, 1940, the day after the formal papers completing the transfer were signed. FDR defended the exchange by arguing that it "is not inconsistent in any sense with our status of peace. Still less is it a threat against any nation. It is an epochal and far-reaching act of preparation for continental defense in the face of grave danger." [84]

Churchill later wrote of the transfer as "a decidedly unneutral act by the United States," [85] and the isolationists were neither convinced nor placated by Roosevelt's remarks. The move represented an Executive order of great import, implemented without Congressional consultation at a time when consultation may well have endangered the very existence of the British nation. Roosevelt had taken an enormous risk, one a President can never assume without considerable

[84] *Peace and War*, p. 565.
[85] Winston S. Churchill, *Their Finest Hour* (Boston: Houghton Mifflin, 1949), p. 404.

assurance of clear public support: a Gallup poll published two weeks before the signing had concluded that 62 percent of the American public were favorably inclined toward the destroyer-bases scheme.[86] Yet there was a serious risk that Hitler might have considered such an obviously unneutral act sufficient justification for a declaration of war.

The destroyer-bases swap called for considerable political courage since FDR had already decided to shatter the two-term tradition and run for reelection in November. The destroyer deal had brought war closer to the United States at a time when a September public opinion poll had found 83 percent of the Americans surveyed opposed to entry into the war.[87] Although the President's Republican opponent, Wendell Willkie of Indiana, represented the internationalist wing of his party and had acquiesced to the destroyer agreement, Willkie was continually prodded by GOP isolationists to capitalize on the antiwar sentiment. Ominously, late in the campaign Willkie began questioning the President's desire and ability to keep America out of the war. Such a strategy was politically understandable, and it is to Willkie's credit that he resisted in the main the great temptation to ride to the White House on the back of a "scare" campaign. Nevertheless, with questionable judgment Roosevelt lashed back at his Republican critics in a speech in Boston at the very end of October, stating: "I have said this before, but I shall say it again and again and again: Your boys are not going to be sent into any foreign wars." [88] He omitted to add the cautionary "unless we are attacked," which had been included in the Democratic Platform. The victory over Willkie, though not as great as the 1936 landslide, was still substantial and may legitimately be viewed as an endorsement of the President's foreign policy and particularly of his consistent pro–Allied bias.[89]

Fortified by an election which he viewed as a mandate for his handling of the crisis, Roosevelt sought to formalize the nation's commitment to England. Only weeks after the election the British Ambassador, Lord Lothian, and the Under Secretary of the British Treasury, Sir Frederick Phillips, were in the United States explaining to the public and to official Washington that the "cash and carry" policy had so dwindled England's dollar reserves that soon she would be unable to purchase war materiel in the United States. This message was dramatically underscored in a long letter from Churchill in which the Prime Minister insisted that both American and British security

[86] See *Public Opinion Quarterly*, IV, p. 713.

[87] Hadley Cantril, ed., *Public Opinion, 1935–1946* (Princeton, N.J.: 1951), pp. 971–72.

[88] Quoted in Robert E. Sherwood, *Roosevelt and Hopkins: An Intimate History* (New York: Harper & Row, 1948), p. 191.

[89] Divine, *The Reluctant Belligerent*, p. 101.

were dependent upon an Axis defeat. Although deeply committed to the British cause the President knew that the aid required to sustain Churchill necessitated Congressional approval and could not be gained by Executive order. His solution, characteristically pragmatic, was to suggest that the United States "lend" war materiel to nations resisting aggression in the same way, and for the same reason, that a man lends his garden hose to a neighbor whose house is burning. In a "fireside chat" at the end of the year the President described the United States as an "arsenal of democracy," and in January, 1941, he formalized his proposal to the Congress.

> Let us say to the democracies: "We Americans are vitally concerned in your defense of freedom. We are putting forth our energies, our resources, and our organizing powers to give you the strength to regain and maintain a free world. We shall send you, in ever-increasing numbers, ships, planes, tanks, guns. This is our purpose and our pledge." [90]

The message touched off two months of intense debate during which Senator Robert A. Taft of Ohio denounced Lend-Lease as a device to give the President power to engage in undeclared wars throughout the world.[91] But neither isolationist Congressmen nor the America First lobby were successful. The measure passed by approximately two-to-one margins in each House and was signed into law on March 11, 1941. Its delegation of authority to the President was exceedingly broad, for he now only had to designate a country "vital to the defense of the United States" to provide it with any defense article, service, or information.[92] The line between neutrality and open belligerency had become very fine indeed.

In the same measure proposing the Lend-Lease formula Roosevelt set forth a powerful statement of his desire to see world order based upon four essential human freedoms: freedom of speech and expression; freedom of every person to worship God in his own way; freedom from want; and freedom from fear. It was a call for a moral order, ". . . the very antithesis of the so-called new order of tyranny which the dictators seek to create with the crash of a bomb." [93]

[90] Rosenman, *The Public Papers of Franklin D. Roosevelt*, IX, pp. 669. For background, see James MacGregor Burns, *Roosevelt: The Soldier of Freedom, 1940–45* (New York: Harcourt Brace Jovanovich, 1970), pp. 43–49.

[91] Quoted in Charles A. Beard, *President Roosevelt and the Coming of War, 1941* (New Haven, Conn.: Yale University Press, 1948), pp. 67–68. (Interestingly, Joseph P. Kennedy, who had just resigned as Ambassador to Great Britain, lobbied against the bill.)

[92] Reprinted in *Peace and War*, pp. 627–30. It was entitled "An Act to Promote the Defense of the United States." For a characterization of the shift in FDR's strategy, see Drummond, *The Passing of American Neutrality*, pp. 375–76.

[93] Rosenman, *The Public Papers of Franklin D. Roosevelt*, IX, p. 672.

The need for Lend-Lease legislation became almost immediately apparent when in April of 1941 Germany overran both Yugoslavia and Greece while making impressive gains against the British in North Africa. British survival was further imperiled by Berlin's extension of the combat zone to include Iceland and Greenland. Submarines, surface craft, and the German air force were dramatically employed in this Battle of the Atlantic which all but crippled British shipping. In responding to the crisis Roosevelt increased American aid to the British, including the direct transfer of a number of Coast Guard cutters for the anti-U-boat campaign. Dozens of Axis ships were seized in American ports. By greatly extending the Atlantic neutrality zone the President was able to use American patrol ships to site the positions of Nazi raiders and submarines and to transfer the information gathered to the British.

The necessity of getting Lend-Lease materiel to England understandably quickened the tempo of American participation in the Battle of the Atlantic. At one point the President seriously considered ordering American craft to convoy ships carrying Lend-Lease goods; but widespread support of the position that such action would lead directly to war caused him to abandon the plan. Yet a month later, in May, three battleships, an aircraft carrier, and several other vessels were ordered from Pearl Harbor to the Atlantic to join the anti-submarine patrol. Soon after, the *Robin Moor*, an American freighter headed for Cape Town with noncontroversial cargo, was sunk by German submarines despite its clear markings. In a strongly worded message to the Congress Roosevelt said: "We must take the sinking of the *Robin Moor* as a warning to the United States not to resist the Nazi movement of world conquest. It is a warning that the United States may use the high seas of the world only with Nazi consent." [94] In retaliation all German and Italian assets in the United States, and the assets of all occupied countries, were frozen. Soon all German and Italian consulates were closed.

Tension between the United States and Germany grew in the spring of 1941 when the Danish minister in Washington, Henrik Kauffmann, signed an agreement permitting the United States to occupy Greenland while the emergency lasted. At that time Greenland was a colony of Denmark, a nation already overrun by Hitler. Kauffmann alone authorized the transfer, which was to be temporary and not to affect Danish sovereignty. By late spring of 1941 a majority of Americans acknowledged that a Germany which could tyrannize defenseless nations of Europe would, if it could, violate the rights of the

[94] Quoted in Hull, *Memoirs*, II, pp. 944–45.

United States. The destroyer-bases transfer, Lend-Lease, the Battle of
the Atlantic, and the occupation of Greenland by American troops
were all clear indications of the nation's unofficial co-belligerent
status.

In January of 1940 FDR sent Under Secretary of State Sumner
Welles to Europe to attempt to determine if a negotiated peace were
possible. American self-interest motivated the visit, for the Chief
Executive saw two alternatives to a protracted struggle. Either victory
for Hitler, which would directly threaten American security, or victory
for the democracies, but only after what Roosevelt described as a
"long and desperately fought contest which would bring Europe to
total economic and social collapse, with disastrous effects on the
American people." [95]

The failure of the Welles mission was quickly followed by Hitler's
blitz in the spring of 1940; Roosevelt was prepared (some would add
"at long last") to be more forthright in his attempts to aid Britain. Not
only did he rapidly accelerate the nation's preparedness, but he
disavowed the hemispheric fortress philosophy of his isolationist critics
by insisting that England and France were vital to the American line
of defense. And although in the summer of 1940 the President had to
trim his sails somewhat because of the political implications of his
unprecedented third term bid for the White House, his new tack was
everywhere apparent after the November victory. Roosevelt's theme,
repeatedly voiced, was that the fundamental danger to American
security was a fascist victory. The solution involved the dramatic
conversion of the United States into a "great arsenal of democracy." [96]

ROOSEVELT'S STRATEGY

Before discussing events in Asia which led to the attack on Pearl
Harbor, it would be useful to consider the often repeated criticism that
had Roosevelt been a more skillful and forceful diplomatic leader the
nation would not have been mired in a disastrous isolationism at the
very time when the democracies were fighting for their survival. It is
charged that had the President pursued a policy of boldness, the
global disaster of the late Thirties and early Forties may well have
been averted; at the very least, a more constructive response by the
President would have more adequately prepared the United States for
its role in the battle against totalitarianism.

[95] Welles's paraphrase of FDR in Sumner Welles, *The Time for Decision*, (New York: World
Publishing, 1944), p. 73.
[96] For this view of FDR's diplomacy in this critical period, see Osgood, *Ideals and
Self-Interest*, pp. 410–17.

The most forceful, recent restatement of this thesis is Robert A. Divine's *Roosevelt and World War II*, which argues that FDR's great political skills as a tactician and pragmatist were well suited to domestic politics but were most inadequate to the exercise of foreign affairs. The President pursued an isolationist policy in the 1930s, Divine charges, by "refusing to commit the United States to the defense of the existing international order." [97] By acquiescing to a series of neutrality measures, the Italian invasion of Ethiopia, Japan's aggression against China, and the takeover of Austria and the Sudetenland in Czechoslovakia, Roosevelt denied to the United States a constructive role in maintaining international order. Divine rejects the thesis that FDR was at heart an internationalist who for political purposes—continuance in office and passage of his domestic reform program—reluctantly acceded to the dominant isolationist mood of the American public.[98] Instead, he offers support for Charles Beard's thesis of 1948 that FDR was an isolationist "out of genuine conviction." [99] The Chief Executive is seen as the product of his age, fearful of war and international commitments, and determined to have the United States play its legitimate role as the peaceful model of a civilized, democratic society. Such a thesis refutes the more popular view of the President as an unwilling victim of the nation's prevailing isolationism and pacifism; instead, the President is held responsible for the nation's pacifism because of his own paralyzing fear of war and because of his naive conviction that moral suasion could be effective in the face of the European crisis.

The Divine thesis also indicts Roosevelt for tragic vacillation even after his transformation late in 1938 from an isolationist to a reluctant internationalist. For example, while in June 1940 he pledged all-out aid short of war to Britain, he waited months before transferring the desperately needed destroyers to Churchill. The problem, Divine concludes, is that FDR was attempting to please the interventionists with "his rhetoric . . . [while] reassuring his isolationist critics. . . . Movement in a straight and unbroken line seems to have been alien to his nature—he could not go forward until he had tested the ground, studied all reactions, and weighed all the risks." [100] In the second and final volume of his biography of FDR, James

---

[97] Robert A. Divine, *Roosevelt and World War II* (Baltimore: Penguin, 1969), p. 5–6.

[98] For this view, see Leuchtenburg, *Franklin D. Roosevelt and the New Deal*, pp. 275–98. Also Adler, *The Uncertain Giant* Chap. VII.

[99] Divine, *Roosevelt and World War II*, p. 7. Also Beard, *President Roosevelt and the Coming of War*.

[100] Divine, *Roosevelt and World War II*, p. 37. In an earlier work Divine somewhat dramatically charged that FDR, by his indecision, caused the United States to become the "silent accomplice of Hitler," Divine, *The Reluctant Belligerent*, p. 63.

MacGregor Burns also concludes that the President had done much to cultivate the dominant isolationist mood of the Thirties by his "obeisances to the God of No Foreign War" and by his insistence that the United States would not use its military might to influence the international order unless it were actually invaded. In the initial volume of the biography, Burns charges that during his first term the President was "more pussyfooting politician than political leader." [101]

While there now exists sufficient reliable evidence to fault Roosevelt's diplomatic leadership in responding to the Far Eastern and European crises, it would appear on balance that the Divine thesis suffers from its failure to take an accurate measure of the public and Congressional pressure on the President in his role as diplomatic leader. FDR was a humanitarian idealist of the Wilsonian mold, with strong internationalist convictions.[102] But unlike Wilson, he was endowed with a sufficient measure of American pragmatism to protect him from his predecessor's tragedy. And while FDR may have had less than a total grasp on the complexities of world power politics, the President was realist enough to understand the most important fact in the isolationist-internationalist struggle of the 1930s: that the security of the United States, and indeed the Western Hemisphere, would be gravely threatened by fascist domination of either Europe or Asia.

The President was privately an internationalist and, later, an interventionist; but he often acted as an isolationist because of very serious domestic pressures. It is well to remember that throughout the Thirties the nation was suffering the worst depression in its history, and Roosevelt viewed as his first priority domestic reform legislation; the President was obviously unwilling to jeopardize such legislation by diverting attention from those internal questions which were his greatest concern. And while at first glance it might appear that the very impressive, lopsided Democratic majorities in the House and Senate throughout the decade gave him a relatively free hand, a simple count of his party's seats does not reveal the deep and often bitter division within the Democratic party over the proper response to the growing international crisis. Furthermore, the potentially powerful Senate Foreign Relations Committee was headed by Key Pittman of Nevada, a weak chairman whose committee soon came to

---

[101] Burns, *Roosevelt: The Soldier of Freedom*, p. 42; James MacGregor Burns, *Roosevelt: The Lion and the Fox* (New York: Harcourt Brace Jovanovich, 1956), p. 262.

[102] I am following here the argument of Robert E. Osgood in his *Ideals and Self-Interest*, Chap. XVII. For the view that although Roosevelt was late in recognizing the depth of the threat presented by the Nazis, he understood how closely American security would be affected by a German victory, see Sherwood, *Roosevelt and Hopkins: An Intimate History*, pp. 125–26.

be dominated by two of the Congress' most determined isolationists, William E. Borah of Idaho and California's Hiram Johnson.

Nor were FDR's major advisors of one mind—Secretary of State Hull, Secretary of the Treasury Henry Morgenthau, and Louis Howe were internationalists, but Assistant Secretary of State Raymond Moley, Harry Hopkins, Hugh Johnson, and Secretary of the Interior Harold Ickes were strongly inclined toward isolationism. Even Hull was an erratic supporter of a more forceful policy since as a former Senator he tended to overreact to Congressional isolationism.

While Roosevelt may be legitimately criticized for publicly adopting an isolationist posture so as not to endanger his goal of winning the 1936 election, it is nonetheless true that when polled in December 1936 the American public ranked employment and economy in government as the two issues which most vitally concerned them.[103] In the summer and early fall of 1940, only one-third to one-half of the American people were willing to help England win at the risk of getting into war. Statistics such as these undoubtedly have led diplomatic historian Robert H. Ferrell to conclude that even as late as 1941 FDR would have found it exceedingly difficult to convince the Congress to declare war in the absence of an attack on American territory.[104] Divine would most probably respond that Roosevelt's vacillation had reinforced the public's reluctance to aid the Allies.

Even so, one must still evaluate the nature of a proper response. There are few who would disagree that a President's mission as political and diplomatic leader is not simply to follow prevailing currents of opinion, but rather to mold and guide opinion to more closely reflect his assessment of American interests. Roosevelt's strategy after the 1936 election was to cautiously cultivate internationalist sensibilities while slowly escalating American involvement in the anti-fascist struggle. While it is true that he professed support of traditional attitudes toward political commitments to foreign powers, FDR nevertheless sought means short of belligerency to assist England and France. That this strategy was conservative and undramatic is not in question; whether it is correct to characterize the President as confined to a policy of "pinpricks and righteous protest"[105] is quite another matter.

[103] George Gallup and Claude Robinson, "American Institute of Public Opinion—Surveys, 1935–38," *Public Opinion Quarterly*, II (July 1938), p. 384.

[104] 1940 statistics from Hadley Cantril *et al.*, "America Faces the War: Shifts in Opinion," *Public Opinion Quarterly*, IV (Dec. 1940), p. 652. Ferrell interview in John A. Garraty, *Interpreting American History*, II, p. 215.

[105] Burns, *Roosevelt: The Lion and the Fox*, p. 385.

TOKYO'S DECISION

Japan, not the European powers, brought the United States to war and thereby ended Roosevelt's dilemma. In February 1939 Tokyo moved a step closer to its recently announced "New Order for East Asia" by occupying the Chinese island of Hainan, which was then within the French sphere of influence. The island was of considerable importance because of its strategic position between Singapore and Hong Kong, two major British trading centers in the Far East. In March the Spratly Islands in the South China Sea were seized, a matter of grave concern partly because they were claimed by France, but more importantly because of their proximity to both French Indochina and the Philippines. The security of British, French, Dutch, and American possessions in the Far East were thus immediately threatened by the Japanese push in that area. The long-range interests of the Western democracies were further threatened by a deliberate and constant erosion of their trading "rights" in China by restrictive Japanese policies in areas controlled by Tokyo. In partial retaliation for these moves the United States informed Japan in July of 1939 that it was abrogating its 1911 commercial treaty in six months and that beginning in 1940 it was free to impose any manner of restrictions upon Japanese trade.

The fall of France, which represented a psychological watershed in the relations between the United States and England, also had a powerful effect upon Japanese-American relations. Briefly put, by the summer of 1940 England alone battled Germany, leaving the possessions of the defeated democracies—especially French Indochina and the Dutch East Indies—at the mercy of Tokyo's ambitions. When on August 1, 1940, the Japanese Prime Minister, Prince Konoye, announced that the "New Order for East Asia" was to be supplanted by a "New Order for Greater East Asia" more than semantics were involved. The new policy was omniously more ambitious than the old. Its imperialistic implications were outlined in a series of decisions reached at a September 4, 1940, conference attended by Konoye and the ministers of War, Navy, and Foreign Affairs:

> The sphere to be envisaged in the course of negotiations with Germany and Italy as Japan's Sphere of Living for the construction of a Greater East Asia New Order will comprise: The former German Islands under Mandate, French Indo-China and Pacific Islands, Thailand, British Malaya, British Borneo, Dutch East Indies, Burma, Australia, New Zealand, India, etc., with Japan, Manchuria and China as the backbone.[106]

[106] Quoted in Ruhl F. Bartlett, ed., *The Record of American Diplomacy* (New York: Knopf, 1964), p. 629.

The Philippines was noticeably absent from the list—apparently the Japanese cabinet was determined to retain some semblance of normal relations with the United States. However, nothing in the cabinet statement precluded a further widening of Japan's sphere in the future. Thus it is clear that in the period between July 1940 and July 1941 it was the goal of the Konoye government to successfully conclude its struggle with China, to advance southward with all deliberate speed, and to avoid war with the United States. Japan believed it could accomplish all three goals because a German victory in Europe would cause the United States to be "quiescent, if not acquiescent," leaving Tokyo free in the Far East.[107] The flaw in this strategy was Japan's certainty that America would acquiesce to a German victory and to vigorous Japanese expansion southward. Even before the issuance of the Japanese cabinet's policy statement the Roosevelt Administration responded to overt threats to French Indochina by ordering the removal of the Pacific fleet from San Diego to Pearl Harbor. And too, on the very day the Konoye cabinet announced its position (the timing was coincidental) Roosevelt ordered a licensing system for the exportation of scrap metal and oil from the United States. This restriction did not lead to a total embargo of such items to Japan for some time—the embargo was still only partial, in good measure because of Roosevelt's desire to keep Japan out of the European conflict. Nevertheless both the licensing order and the partial embargo represented the beginning of economic sanctions against Japan. The general direction of American policy at this time was demonstrated by the Administration's attitude toward the Japanese offensive against French Indochina in August of 1940. Although refusing to accede to the desperate appeals of the French in Indochina for direct American assistance, late in September Roosevelt announced a $25 million loan to Chiang Kai-shek's government and a total embargo on iron and steel scrap to Japan.

Such overt action by the United States was overshadowed by the unsurprising announcement of September 27, 1940, that Germany, Japan, and Italy had signed a formal military alliance. The three-power pact was important in its recognition of Germany's "new order" in Europe and of Japan's design for Greater East Asia. The pact, moreover, was directed against the United States: Article Three stated that the contracting parties would assist one another politically, economically, and militarily if any one of them were attacked by a power not presently involved in either the war in Europe or the conflict between Japan and China. Since Article Three was not to be

---

[107] See Herbert Feis, *The Road to Pearl Harbor* (New York: Atheneum, 1967), p. 86.

applied to the Soviet Union the intent of the Axis was clear. Although it was undoubtedly Japan's hope that the Tripartite Pact would keep the United States from interfering in the Far East, this strategy backfired when news of the agreement precipitated a hardening of the American position.[108] For its part, Germany intended to use the threat of a two-ocean war to keep the United States from intervening on the side of Churchill's beleaguered forces. As if to assure Britain on this count, Hull issued a public statement denying that the pact would have any effect on the general direction of American policy.

Although FDR refused to place a total embargo on oil to Japan, export restrictions to that nation were tightened following the announcement of the Tripartite Pact. The further exportation of chemical and machine tools was halted, Chiang Kai-shek was given additional assurances of American support (although not the formal alliance which he so actively sought), and Britain strengthened the Generalissimo's position by reopening the most important overland supply route to China, the Burma Road. Additionally, the Philippines was reinforced, Guam was fortified, plans were laid for American, British, and Dutch defense of the East Indies and Malaya, and warships were sent to Australia and New Zealand.

By the end of 1940 a vicious circle had developed. Japan was determined to expand her influence in the Far East by moving south, and the United States reacted with a series of increasingly strong countermeasures. But every item (e.g., chemicals, scrap metal) withheld from Japan increased Tokyo's need to gain a stranglehold over the centers of raw materials in the Far East. Accelerated Japanese imperialism led to further American restrictions on exports. Faced with Washington's determination to halt Japan's southward push even at the risk of war, Konoye sent his Foreign Minister, Yosuke Matsuoka, to negotiate with the Russians. In the event of a war with the United States it was imperative that Japan be assured that Russia would not descend upon Manchuria (Manchukuo) and China. Matsuoka met with enviable success in Moscow, for on April 13, 1941, a five-year treaty was concluded in which each side pledged neutrality in the event of the other's becoming involved in war.

The neutrality pact—barely two months old—suffered a severe strain when on June 22, 1941, Hitler broke his treaty with Stalin and invaded Russia. The invasion strongly tempted Japan to disavow its agreement with the USSR, side with Hitler, and attempt to defeat the only other Pacific power which could interfere with its "new order," and especially with its designs on China. But the Konoye government

---

[108] See *Ibid.*, pp. 110–121. Feis reprints the text, pp. 119–20.

instead utilized the growing European turmoil to pressure the German-controlled Vichy government to accede to its demand for bases in southern Indochina. The helpless French agreed to Japanese demands for air and naval stations in south Indochina, and for the positioning of air, ground, and naval forces in the area; by the end of July Japanese forces were in Saigon. It is important to note that by this time the United States had broken the Japanese diplomatic code, and Hull and several other high-ranking officials had considerable knowledge of Japanese strategy.

In response to the occupation of Indochina, all Japanese assets were frozen in the United States. A further squeeze was put upon Japan by the decision of Great Britain, the Commonwealth nations, and the Dutch East Indies to discontinue trade with Japan. Should Japan decide to go to war to achieve her goals, she could no longer depend on the resources of the United States to prepare her for the fight.

According to Tokyo, Japan was in Indochina to guarantee that the area not fall to an unfriendly power. But when Roosevelt suggested that the United States and Japan cooperate in an international guarantee of the neutrality of Indochina the offer had no effect upon Japanese policy. With the issue deadlocked, Tokyo's Ambassador, Admiral Kichisaburo Nomura, proposed that summit level talks be held between Foreign Minister Matsuoka and Roosevelt; the suggestion, however, came at the very time that Roosevelt was leaving for the so-called Atlantic Conference with Churchill in Newfoundland.

During the four days of secret meetings the two Western leaders agreed that American and British vessels would be made available to convoy both American and British ships in the North Atlantic. Churchill had also sought an American pledge to go to war if Japan attacked either Malaya or the Dutch East Indies, but Roosevelt cautiously asserted that he could not make such a commitment without Congressional approval. The most noted development of the conference was the issuance of the Atlantic Charter on August 14, 1941. A joint accord issued in the form of a press release, the charter was a declaration of the basic principles of the two nations. Their aims included: the right of peoples to choose their own form of government; no aggrandizement; no territorial changes opposed by the peoples concerned; access to trade and raw materials; improved labor standards, economic advancement, and social security; international security; freedom of the seas; and disarmament.[109] Significantly, the

[109] Hull, *Memoirs*, II, p. 975.

charter expressed the hope that a permanent system of international security would be developed. The Atlantic Charter was perhaps most important for its psychological value, since the United States, as a nonbelligerent, signified that its goals and those of England were parallel.

On his return from the Atlantic Conference the President met with Ambassador Nomura to inform him that continued Japanese efforts toward military domination by force or threat of force of neighboring countries would compel Washington to take all necessary steps to safeguard the legitimate rights and interests of the United States and American nationals. There was a conciliatory tone to the President's suggestion that wide ranging talks might be arranged— talks which could include discussion of an economic program for the Pacific area—if Japan agreed to suspend its expansionist activities.

In an attempt to reach an accord Nomura proposed that Roosevelt meet with the Japanese Premier, Prince Konoye. The President at first embraced the idea but was soon persuaded by Secretary of State Hull that agreement in principle on major issues should be reached prior to any such meeting. In retrospect, it is certain that an agreement in principle was not possible. On September 6, 1941, a secret Japanese Imperial Conference agreed to withdraw from the Indochinese peninsula only after a just peace was assured in the Far East. By definition, a just peace included major American concessions: the restoration of normal trade with Japan; guarantees that Japan would be able to obtain raw materials from the Southwest Pacific area; and the suspension of military preparations in the Far East. Philippine neutrality would be guaranteed, and British-American trade in China would continue if Japan were given the special sphere of influence in Indochina granted to her by the intimidated Vichy government. Moreover, neither the United States nor England was to interfere with a Japanese settlement of the "China incident"; in fact the two democracies were to further a Japanese settlement by pledging to end all aid to the still resisting Chinese government. Relatedly, there was to be no question of Japan's "right" to station troops in China. The Imperial Conference, in the vaguest terms possible, announced that should the United States and Germany go to war Japan would determine if the terms of the Tripartite Pact would apply to the United States. Finally, it was decided that the negotiations and the preparations for war would continue concurrently.

The gulf between the two nations' positions can best be measured by comparing the conclusions of the Imperial Conference with the four basic principles which Hull had outlined in a note to Ambassador Nomura on April 16. The four principles were:

(1) Respect for the territorial integrity and the sovereignty of each and all nations; (2) Support of the principle of noninterference in the internal affairs of other countries; (3) Support of the principle of equality, including equality of commercial opportunity; and (4) Nondisturbance of the status quo in the Pacific except as the status quo may be altered by peaceful means.[110]

Accepting Hull's judgment that the differences between the two nations were far too profound to warrant a top-level meeting, Roosevelt asked the American Ambassador to Japan to meet with Prince Konoye. At this meeting the Prime Minister agreed to Hull's four principles of April 16. But since he was unwilling or unable to make any commitments regarding specific issues the President refused to confer with him; on October 16 all hope for a summit meeting was lost when the Konoye ministry resigned and was replaced by one headed by the hawkish General Hideki Tojo.

There has been considerable debate over Roosevelt and Hull's decision not to meet with the Japanese leadership until a willingness to discuss specific issues was evidenced. Ambassador Grew has insisted that such a conference would have been extremely valuable; according to Grew, Konoye was unable to offer specific commitments in advance because if they were "leaked" it would lead to the downfall of his ministry.[111] Others have pointed out that Konoye's *Memoirs* reveal that the Prime Minister was able to win the military's acceptance of the proposed meeting only by promising that the establishment of the "Greater East Asia Co-Prosperity Sphere" was nonnegotiable. Tokyo was fully prepared to go to war on this issue. It has been suggested that Roosevelt deliberately attempted to push Japan into war by refusing to meet with Konoye,[112] but decoded messages revealed that Tokyo had no intention of withdrawing from occupied areas or even of halting its southern advance.[113]

Two factors must be considered in assessing Japan's moves in the period immediately preceding the Pearl Harbor attack. The embargo, freezing of assets, and (later) the total trade ban were causing very serious disruptions of the Japanese economy. With oil reserves dwindling rapidly, the nation desperately sought a supply source. And too, Tokyo's policies must be considered as reflections of the enormous

---

[110] *Ibid.*, p. 995.

[111] Joseph C. Grew, *Turbulent Era: A Diplomatic Record of Forty Years, 1904–1945* (Boston: Houghton Mifflin, 1952), II, p. 1301–4.

[112] See, for example, Beard, *President Roosevelt and the Coming of War.*

[113] Robert J. Butow, *Tojo and the Coming of War* (Princeton, N.J.: Princeton University Press, 1961) argues that this decision had been made by early September. Also see F. C. Jones, *Japan's New Order in East Asia: Its Rise and Fall, 1937–45* (London: Oxford University Press, 1954), pp. 293–329.

influence of the military in the nation's policy-making structure. The American tradition of civilian authority over the military did not exist in Japan. Hence it was General Tojo who rejected Konoye's plan to present a more conciliatory reply to Roosevelt's request for a statement of Japanese intentions, and it was Tojo and the military who were most willing to go to war with the United States in pursuance of national policy. At the end of October Tojo announced that Japan's position was "immutable and irrevocable. . . . If a hundred million people merge into one iron solidarity to go forward, nothing can stop us." [114]

Japan was working within a life or death timetable—because of her desperate need for oil and other raw materials she had to continue her push south, but that push had to be made quickly, before the United States decided to declare war. Conversely, the longer Washington contained Japanese expansion southward, the more effective the economic sanctions. The United States had time on its side and the Tojo government was not about to haggle while its tiny oil reserves became further depleted. Thus by early November plans were made final for war with the United States, England, and the Netherlands; by this time the date of the Pearl Harbor attack was also set. Despite these decisions Nomura was authorized to resume his conversations with Secretary Hull. The November seventh proposal, which offered nothing new except a provision regarding trade in the Pacific area, was rejected by Hull. It was then suggested that in exchange for a relaxation of the American embargo Japan would offer "assurances" regarding expansion southward. And while this second plan was not presented as an ultimatum, Hull knew through the intercepted and decoded Japanese messages that a time limit had been placed upon American acceptance. This November 20 Japanese proposal for peace in the Pacific was as follows:

1. Both the Governments of Japan and the United States undertake not to make any armed advancement into any of the regions in the Southeastern Asia and the Southern Pacific area excepting the part of French Indo-China where the Japanese troops are stationed at present.

2. The Japanese Government undertakes to withdraw its troops now stationed in French Indo-China upon either the restoration of peace between Japan and China or the establishment of an equitable peace in the Pacific area. In the meantime the Government of Japan declares that it is prepared to remove its troops now stationed in the southern part of French Indo-China

---

[114] Quoted in Langer and Gleason, *The Undeclared War, 1940–41* (New York: Harper & Row, 1953), p. 837.

to the northern part of the said territory upon the conclusion of the present arrangement which shall later be embodied in the final agreement.

3. The Governments of Japan and the United States shall cooperate with a view to securing the acquisition of those goods and commodities which the two countries need in Netherlands East Indies.

4. The Governments of Japan and the United States mutually undertake to restore their commercial relations to those prevailing prior to the freezing of the assets.

   The Government of the United States shall supply Japan a required quantity of oil.

5. The Government of the United States undertakes to refrain from such measures and actions as will be prejudicial to the endeavors for the restoration of general peace between Japan and China.[115]

With full knowledge that nonacceptance meant war, the Administration refused the terms and instead prepared a counter proposal. A modus vivendi—temporary agreement—was offered, providing for mutual pledges that the policies of each nation would be directed toward lasting peace. Specifically this meant that neither would make further advances in the Pacific area by either military force or a threat of force. The draft further called for the withdrawal of Japanese troops from southern Indochina. In turn the United States would agree to resume limited trade with Japan, including the exportation of oil for civilian use, and to cooperate with a settlement between Japan and China "based upon the principles of peace, law, order, and justice." [116] Such a plan, Hull believed, had little chance of success; the proposal was formulated because the army and navy were seeking more time to prepare for what seemed an inevitable confrontation with Japan.

It is perhaps somewhat easier to understand the attitude of members of the armed forces if one considers that at the very time the United States and Japan were engaged in crisis negotiation over the Far East, an undeclared naval war was in operation in the Atlantic. The Atlantic Conference had resulted in a secret agreement to use American ships for convoy purposes in the Atlantic, and the opportunity to inform the American people of this decision came in September when a German submarine which had been followed by the U.S.S. *Greer* fired two torpedoes at the destroyer. The torpedoes missed their mark and the *Greer* retaliated by dropping depth charges. The destroyer had seriously provoked the submarine by following it for several hours and reporting its position to British air patrols;

---

[115] *Peace and War*, pp. 801–2.
[116] Hull, *Memoirs*, II, p. 1073.

nevertheless several days later the President used the attack on the *Greer* to announce to a world-wide radio audience that American ships would hereafter fire upon all Axis vessels in areas defended by the United States. The following month the destroyer U.S.S. *Kearny* was torpedoed with a loss of 11 American lives. Roosevelt reacted to the incident by announcing that "We will not let Hitler prescribe the waters . . . on which our ships may travel." [117] Within days the destroyer *Reuben James* was torpedoed with a loss of 115 American lives. Outrage over these incidents led the Congress to approve—but significantly by only slim margins—an Administration-sponsored revision of existing neutrality legislation. By November, United States merchant ships were armed and allowed to sail to belligerent ports; a two-ocean war seemed imminent.

Hull's modus vivendi with Japan was never issued because of Chinese opposition, fears that it would signify appeasement, and the Churchill government's obvious lack of enthusiasm. In its stead a ten-point program, which was to serve as a basis for settlement, was substituted on November 26. There was little optimism about the acceptability of the program since item three called for a complete Japanese military withdrawal from Indochina and China, and item one all but required Japan to renounce the Tripartite Agreement.[118] Any hope that this program would even delay the onset of hostilities was soon dashed. Intercepted Japanese messages included instructions to envoys to destroy codes and code machines. At the same time a large segment of the Japanese naval force moved southward. It was generally thought that this force would attack one or more of the British or Dutch colonies, or Thailand; few seriously considered that American territory would be attacked. Meaningful negotiation after delivery of the November twenty-sixth note was all but precluded. On December 1, Tokyo made its final decision to go to war with the United States. Although the ten-point proposal was rejected, the government ordered that negotiations with the United States continue, supposedly in an attempt to keep Washington off its guard. Japan of course was still unaware that its code had been broken.

It is important to recognize the importance of China in the final deadlock, for to the very end the United States insisted that Japan withdraw from that nation. Having fought in China for four and one-half years, and having staked its reputation in Asia upon its future role there, Japan looked upon China as a nonnegotiable issue. It is difficult to support the thesis that American economic interest in

[117] Rosenman, *The Public Papers of Franklin D. Roosevelt*, X, p. 411.
[118] Reprinted in *Peace and War*, pp. 810–12.

China motivated the Roosevelt Administration to draw the line there. American trade and investment in that area, although long-standing, was slight if viewed in the context of the total investment and trade pattern.[119] Rather it was American interests in the entire Far East, security and economic interests, which would have been profoundly affected by Japanese hegemony over China. Moreover, the American public would not have supported Japan's design for China following the Sino-Japanese war.[120] The fall of China was unacceptable because of what it signified for all of Asia and indeed the world.

Despite the long-range importance of China, America's immediate concern was Japanese suspension of its activities to the south. On the very eve of the attack on Pearl Harbor Roosevelt sent a personal message to Emperor Hirohito requesting that troops be withdrawn from Indochina. The note did not reach the Emperor before the attack on Hawaii plunged the United States and Japan into war.

The Japanese strike at Pearl Harbor the morning of December 7, 1941, was a stunning surprise to the United States. The Pacific fleet anchored in the harbor provided an easy target and every battleship was either sent to the bottom or seriously disabled; most of the planes at the base were destroyed and nearly 2,500 men were killed. The attack lasted less than two hours and resulted in the virtual destruction of American power in the area. Capitalizing on its advantage, the Tojo government ordered attacks on the Philippines, Siam, Malaya, and other points in the Pacific. Roosevelt's confidant, Harry Hopkins, has left an interesting description of the meeting following news of the attack, including the following entry:

> The conference met in not too tense an atmosphere because I think that all of us believed that in the last analysis the enemy was Hitler and that he could never be defeated without force of arms; that sooner or later we were bound to be in the war and that Japan had given us an opportunity.[121]

In a brief, emotional message to Congress the following day Roosevelt referred to December 7 and Pearl Harbor as ". . . a date which will live in infamy,[122] and asked that Congress recognize that a state of war existed between the United States and Japan.

[119] For American policy in Asia from the point of view of economic considerations, see Lloyd C. Gardner, *Economic Aspects of New Deal Diplomacy* (Madison: University of Wisconsin Press, 1964), pp. 133–51.

[120] Jones, *Japan's New Order in East Asia*, pp. 457–59. Also see Paul W. Schroeder, *The Axis Alliance and Japanese-American Relations, 1941* (Ithica, N.Y.: Cornell University Press, 1958), pp. 198–99.

[121] Quoted in Sherwood, *Roosevelt and Hopkins*, p. 431.

[122] *Peace and War*, p. 839.

"America First" sentiment had become an additional casualty of the surprise attack, and so the Senate accepted the war resolution without a dissenting vote on December 8. That same day, by a vote of 388 to 1, the House concurred (the sole negative vote was cast by Congresswoman Jeannette Rankin of Montana, who had also voted against going to war with Germany in 1917). On December 11 both Germany and Italy formally declared war and Congress responded with separate war resolutions against each. These declarations of a state of war passed without a negative vote.

There has been some support for the theory that Germany convinced Japan to attack. Secretary of War Stimson's diary indicates that this belief led him to support a December 8 declaration of war against both Germany and Japan. Stimson's suggestion was not accepted by the President's inner circle, and most historians have tended to discount the idea.[123] It seems clear that Hitler, dangerously extended on two fronts because of his decision to invade Russia, would have welcomed a continuance of American nonbelligerency—at least until he had brought Moscow to terms.

THE ROMAN GOD JANUS

Athough the Pearl Harbor attack ultimately represented a monumental Japanese blunder, it was a source of deep humiliation to the people of the United States. As a result there has been intense interest in explaining away this most tragic embarrassment. It is easy to reach the conclusion that given the advances in technology and intelligence-gathering it would have been impossible for the United States to have been unaware of the impending attack. It has been argued that as early as January, 1941, Ambassador Grew had been reporting rumors of Japanese plans for an assault on Pearl Harbor. Grew's reports aside, it seemed logical to many that Japan would strike at the concentration of American might in the Pacific if she was to have a reasonable chance of conquest in the area. Having presumed that a surprise attack was impossible, some students of the disaster have concluded that the Roosevelt Administration deliberately offered a target to the Japanese to entice them into war. Once America was attacked, all critics of Roosevelt's policy of aiding the Allies would be quelled, and Tojo and Hitler would be brought to heel by a united America. Hence it is argued that the President, with the cooperation

[123] Sherwood, *Roosevelt and Hopkins*, p. 431–37; Hans L. Trefousse, *Germany and American Neutrality, 1939–1941* (New York: Bookman Associates, 1951), pp. 148–53 contains accounts of German reaction.

of men such as General George C. Marshall and Admiral Harold R. Stark, baited the Japanese with the Pacific fleet. To follow such a theory to its logical conclusion, one must then charge that Roosevelt planned to cripple his country in the Pacific by the deliberate destruction of the fleet, and planned the slaughter of nearly 2,500 men in a baited attack.

In his *President Roosevelt and the Coming of War, 1941,* Charles A. Beard asked;

> Did the course of American-Japanese affairs as conducted during the months preceding Pearl Harbor, however it "looked," actually point in the direction of peace with Japan? Were those affairs in such a state at any time during this period that the President actually expected them to eventuate in the maintenance of peace in the Pacific? . . . Was the Japanese offensive really a surprise to the Administration?[124]

William Henry Chamberlin replied in *America's Second Crusade:*

> America was stealthily maneuvered into war behind the backs and without the knowledge of the elected representatives of the American people. . . . Like the Roman god Janus, Roosevelt in the prewar period had two faces. For the American people, for the public record, there was the face of bland assurance that his first concern was to keep the country out of war. But in more intimate surroundings the Chief Executive often assumed that America was already involved in war. . . . Seldom if ever in American history was there such a gulf between appearances and realities, between Presidential words and Presidential deeds.[125]

George Morgenstern's *Pearl Harbor* charged;

> [N]o amount of excuses will palliate the conduct of President Roosevelt and his advisers. The offense of which they stand convicted is not failure to discharge their responsibilities, but calculated refusal to do so. They failed—with calculation—to keep the United States out of war and to avoid a clash with Japan. . . . The "warnings" they sent to Hawaii failed—and were so phrased and so handled as to insure failure.[126]

These charges are perhaps the most serious ever brought against an American President. Roosevelt's defenders have outnumbered his accusers, although one would be hard pressed indeed to refute the

---

[124] Beard, *President Roosevelt and the Coming of War,* p. 484–485.

[125] William Henry Chamberlin, *America's Second Crusade* (Chicago: Henry Regnery, 1950), pp. 130–31, 147.

[126] George Morgenstern, *Pearl Harbor: The Story of the Secret War* (Old Greenwich, Conn.: Devin-Adair, 1947), p. 329.

charge that he was not very reluctant to mask or even to misrepresent his pro-Allied bias. However, a close examination of Japanese source material reveals a determination to continue expansionist policies regardless of the nature of American opposition. And so while there may at times have been room for limited compromise, the entire course of American relations with Japan was colored by Japan's decision to pursue its Greater East Asia Co-Prosperity Sphere at any cost. This irrestible force met an immovable object in the American policy to resist such expansion, which was viewed as a threat to both the nation's security postion in the Far East and the security position of allies such as Great Britain. Also to be considered was the moral commitment to China—a historic and long-standing commitment which very likely should never have been made but which existed, by 1941, as a major factor in Roosevelt's calculations. The argument that Roosevelt used Pearl Harbor as a "back door" to war with Germany[127] is considerably weakened when one considers that Hitler's alliance with Japan was defensive in nature; even if Japan were to claim that the Pearl Harbor attack was "defensive" (the longer Japan was kept from sources of oil, the less her chances of survival) there was no guarantee that Hitler would honor his pledge. One is immediately reminded of his June 1941 attack on ally Russia.

Recognition of the inevitability of a clash between Japanese designs and American intentions does not, however, explain away the surprise nature of the Pearl Harbor strike. Once one rejects the theory that the Japanese government's precise plans were known to Roosevelt and Hull, one must explain why they were not, especially since the Japanese code had been broken long before the attack. This question led to a full-scale joint Congressional investigation between November 15, 1945, and May 31, 1946, and the accumulation of 30 volumes of evidence. In all of that documentation certain factors stand out in bold relief. Although Washington had sent "war warnings" to both Admiral Husband E. Kimmel and Lieutenant General Walter C. Short, the naval and army commanders at the Hawaii base, these warnings failed to convey adequately the very real possibility of a surprise offensive. The knowledge gained from code interceptions was communicated to only a very few in Washington, and the messages were not shared with those in Hawaii even though they indicated that war was close at hand. In large part this was the result of a widespread refusal to believe that Pearl Harbor would be Japan's target. And while many critics have noted that the intercepts clearly signaled

---

[127] See Charles C. Tansill, *Back Door to War: The Roosevelt Foreign Policy* (Chicago: Henry Regnery, 1952).

considerable Japanese interest in the location of ships at Pearl Harbor it has been demonstrated that the Japanese were as curious about the location of ships at Panama, San Diego, San Francisco, Portland, Vancouver, and other ports.[128] Still, the obviously strategic importance of Pearl Harbor, to say nothing of its location, should have caused Washington to react with a greater degree of alarm. With the Japanese in Formosa, with Japanese convoys headed for Malaya, and with similar threats of force throughout the Far East, it was understandable—although perhaps not justifiable—for the spotlight to have been off Pearl Harbor.

A less dramatic explanation of the tragedy, but an extremely important one, involves the operation of the intelligence network. As Roberta Wohlstetter points out in her searching examination of the surprise attack, although the code had been broken, the governmental agency responsible for such work was so understaffed and overworked that there was often a delay of several days in the decoding efforts. More important, once decoded, the messages had to be interpreted; Wohlstetter found the quantity and quality of personnel engaged in this operation to be wanting. But the problem involved more than the quality of American staff, since the messages were written for individuals who knew infinitely more of the Japanese government and the Japanese mentality than those involved in the decoding and interpretation efforts. Given the virtual flood of messages dealing with Japanese intentions in many corners of the globe it was perhaps unreasonable to expect those providing the interpretation to pinpoint the relevant wheat in so much chaff. Finally, in retrospect it is far easier to look through the documentation and identify clear signs pointing to Pearl Harbor—it was obviously much more of a riddle before December 7.

The "back door" thesis has lost much of its following. More specialized studies have undercut most of the documentation provided by Beard, Tansill, and others. Common sense had something to do with the demise of the thesis, for in the absence of supportable evidence it is difficult to sustain the notion of a demonic Roosevelt diabolically plotting to involve the United States in total war at a hideous price in men and treasure. A far more rewarding, and relevant, field for further study would involve an investigation of the political, economic, social, and cultural forces which appeared to

---

[128] See Roberta Wohlstetter, *Pearl Harbor: Warning and Decision* (Stanford, Calif.: Stanford University Press, 1962), pp. 386–95.

justify America's disastrous isolationism in the decade of the Thirties. The attempt to maintain the nation's freedom of action by avoiding long-term political commitments proved highly impractical in the face of determined efforts by Germany, Japan, and Italy to pursue their global designs. Had Roosevelt and Hull's internationalism influenced the public and the Congress in the early Thirties, the democracies might have been able to thwart the aggressor nations. Instead, the globe was engulfed in a holocaust which produced, by 1945, increased levels of bitterness, mistrust, and instability.

Five

FROM HOT TO COLD TO LIMITED WAR

Richard Rovere has observed that as late as the 1920s "it was only now and then (generally in times of economic stress) that even the domestic policies of the federal government impinged noticeably on the lives of most Americans. As for foreign policy, when we had any, it was a matter of almost complete indifference to all but a handful. There was very little that either a true statesman or a demagogue could say that would bring responses from every part of the country. Aspirations and anxieties could be exploited by politicians, but not very often by politicians dealing with national and international issues." [1] The Cold War, the "McCarthy Scare," and the Korean conflict abruptly reversed this phenomenon and quickened the American public's interest in, if not understanding of, the conduct of foreign affairs. The outcome of the Second World War inflamed the sensibilities of the American people, for it forced the United States to share world power with a regime whose objectives seemed so profoundly threatening to American security.

[1] Richard A. Rovere, *Senator Joe McCarthy* (New York: Harcourt Brace Jovanovich, 1959), p. 259.

THE CONTRADICTORY ALLIANCE

"So we had won after all. . . . [A]fter seventeen months of lonely
fighting and nineteen months of my responsibility in dire stress, we
had won the war. . . . Britain would live. . . . How long the war
would last or in what fashion it would end, no man could tell, nor did
I at this moment care. . . . All the rest was merely the proper
application of overwhelming force." [2] In this moving passage from his
history of the Second World War, Winston Churchill recorded his
reactions to learning of the assault on Pearl Harbor and the entry of
the United States into the global struggle. The Prime Minister's
jubilation was understandable, but his use of the word "merely" was
not; a strange partnership had been forged by the Japanese attack.
Russia, Great Britain, and the United States were fused in a Grand
Alliance against a common enemy, yet given the divergent objectives
of the three powers the merger was perhaps as unnatural as it was
"grand." The disparate goals of the erstwhile partners, together with
the mutual distrust and suspicion between Russia and the West, serve
as a logical backdrop for the emergence of the Cold War.

Necessity rather than trust bound the three powers together:
Britain was determined to uphold her hegemony over the Mediterranean and, together with France, to preserve African and Asian
colonialism. Churchill in particular believed that his American ally
actively sought to dismantle the British Empire and to assign his
nation to a position of decided inferiority. In turn, the United States
was obviously suspicious of British colonial designs and of Churchill's
advocacy of a traditional balance of power arrangement for the
postwar world.[3]

The Soviet Union wished the maps of Europe and Asia redrawn
to reflect its special interests, while the United States was seeking to
undermine the sphere-of-influence demands of its partners and to
guarantee its traditional prerogatives in the Western Hemisphere. It is
little wonder that Churchill hurried to Washington two weeks after
Pearl Harbor to gain assurance that the United States would support
his military objectives and not let Europe languish while it concentrated on its Pacific opponent. This early Anglo-American war
conclave, known by its code name "Arcadia," designed the broad
military strategy for the war and unified the military command.

[2] Winston S. Churchill, *The Second World War* (Boston: Houghton Mifflin, 1950), III,
pp. 606–7.
[3] See Gaddis Smith, *American Diplomacy During the Second World War, 1941–1945* (New York:
John Wiley, 1965), p. 10.

Importantly, it forged the Declaration of the United Nations binding Russia, the United States, Great Britain, and 23 other governments in a pact against the Axis powers. This alliance was to be based on the principles of the Atlantic Charter, and all agreed not to conclude a separate peace with the enemy. It was anticipated that such a step would lay to rest Soviet fears regarding a separate peace, but throughout the war Stalin apparently remained deeply distrustful that the Western powers would abandon him to the Nazis.

But this was hardly the only antagonism among the Allies, for the United States in particular failed to acknowledge that Stalin's postwar aims were essentially those which motivated him to sign the infamous nonaggression pact with Germany in 1939—that is, Russian control of the Balkan area, the Persian Gulf, and the Dardanelles. Although the Atlantic Charter had pledged no acquisition of new territory, Moscow stood firm on its right to retain the three Balkan states and portions of Poland, Finland, and Rumania since all had been obtained before Hitler's invasion. Stalin's suspicions regarding Anglo-American support for his territorial claims were heightened in the summer of 1942 when his partners refused to ease the pressure on the Eastern Front through the invasion of Europe which he had so anxiously sought and which FDR had informally pledged. Instead, the British call for a North African operation, to relieve and save British territory there, was approved by Roosevelt.[4] So less than a year after the Grand Alliance was created its internal contradictions became starkly apparent. The antagonism which lay so close to the surface was not lost on Lord Moran, a close associate of Churchill, who observed in 1944: "Winston never talks of Hitler these days; he is always harping on the dangers of Communism. He dreams of the Red Army spreading like a cancer from one country to another. It has become an obsession, and he seems to think of little else." [5]

The necessity of rescuing North Africa brought the complex Allied relations with the French into sharp focus. After the Fall of France in June of 1940 three separate French political entities had emerged. A group supportive of the leader of the Vichy government, Marshall Henri Pétain, was willing to collaborate with the German conquerors. Those loyal to General Charles de Gaulle (who had fled to England and formed both a Free French government in exile and a Fighting Free French resistance group) constituted a second faction. There was also a Vichyite resistance organization which would not join de Gaulle's Fighting French. Unfortunately, London and Wash-

[4] Samuel E. Morison, *Strategy and Compromise* (Boston: Little, Brown, 1958).
[5] Lord Moran, *Churchill: Taken from the Diaries of Lord Moran* (Boston: Houghton Mifflin, 1966), p. 185.

ington failed to acknowledge the same entity: Roosevelt accepted the Pétain government at Vichy while the British favored de Gaulle's exile group. The matter understandably went far deeper than diplomatic recognition since Churchill in effect supported de Gaulle's determination to retain the French empire while Roosevelt was cool to the restoration of both the British and the French colonial structures. However, in 1944, with the successful counterinvasion of France, London, Moscow, and Washington acknowledged de Gaulle as head of the provisional government.

Confronted by a series of internal contradictions in the wartime alliance, Roosevelt chose to play the role of the "broker" between Great Britain and the USSR and remained steadfast in his faith that if he could not reform Stalin at least he might convince the Soviet leader of his "universalist" plan for a durable and equitable peace after the war. While the Chief Executive's attitude toward Stalin has been much criticized, his position was, after all, the product of his belief that the Soviet armies were indispensable to an allied victory. It was mainly for this reason that approximately $11 billion in Lend-Lease aid was extended to Russia during the war. Roosevelt clearly believed that the Soviet attitude could be effectively worn down by assuring Moscow that its legitimate interests and its security would be upheld by the West through the United Nations. If FDR's belief that he could establish the basis of a postwar peace through Russian cooperation proved unrealistic, then at least the President must be given credit for his goal. After a meeting of the Big Three in Tehran, Iran, in the winter of 1942, FDR told the American people of his confidence in continued cooperation among Russia, Great Britain, and the United States. But that same year Major General John R. Deane returned from a fact-finding mission to the Soviet Union with an assessment which would be echoed for decades.

> The truth is that they want to have as little to do with foreigners, Americans included, as possible. We never make a request or proposal to the Soviets that is not viewed with suspicion. They simply cannot understand giving without taking, and as a result even our giving is viewed with suspicion. Gratitude cannot be banked in the Soviet Union.[6]

SAVIOR OR EMPIRE-BUILDER?

The nature and origins of the Cold War, and particularly the role of the United States in producing the bitter schism, has been one of the

[6] John R. Deane, *The Strange Alliance: The Story of Our Efforts at Wartime Cooperation with Russia* (New York: Viking, 1947), p. 84–85.

most intensely debated issues of recent diplomatic history. A generation has been raised in the frosty climate and now, with the passage of
time and hopeful signs of a realistic thaw, a certain perspective is
possible. The Cold War was the product of economic, political, and
ideological differences between the two superstates which emerged
during and after the Second World War. While allied against a
common enemy the two powers were able to repress many of the basic
differences between them. But with victory in sight and then achieved
the mutual antagonisms, and the inability of the Moscow and
Washington leadership to reconcile them, created so volatile an
atmosphere as to threaten a third, and this time nuclear, holocaust.

The disagreements between the two powers are perhaps more
comprehensible than the fear and hostility which they generated. It is
not unusual for allies to fail to concur on the division of the spoils or on
the structure of the peace. The World War II alliance had its share of
reasons for discord—the reconstruction of Europe, geopolitical boundaries, atomic weaponry control, colonialism—but in themselves these
problems do not explain the intensity of the rivalry. Rather, one must
consider that the economic, political, and ideological objectives of the
Soviet Union and the United States had not been altered by the war.
As has been outlined in earlier chapters, the United States has
consistently sought the expansion of its liberal-capitalistic order, the
expansion of its international trade network, and the containment of
revolution. It has understandably sought to be paramount in a world
dominated by like-thinking states. The Soviets, in turn, had early in
the twentieth century accomplished a spectacular political and, later,
economic revolution; the ideology of this upheaval threatened America's conception of world order and challenged its opposition to
revolution.

Given the implications of a "victory" by either side, the level of
distrust, and the Soviet and American capacity for messianic zeal and
bombast, the frost of the pre-1945 period quickly thickened and
hardened. As one commentator describes it:

> [R]hetoric on both sides rose above actual points of conflict into the
> realm of global crusading, with each side assuring the unconverted and
> unanointed that earthly salvation lay exclusively in the voluntary or
> enforced acceptance of their particular form of political and economic
> organization. . . . [T]hose who dallied with neutralism or trafficked
> with "them" faced the moral, political, and perhaps nuclear wrath of
> the other side.[7]

[7] James V. Compton, ed., *America and the Origins of the Cold War* (Boston: Houghton Mifflin,
1972), pp. x–xi.

But how, more specifically, did this disastrous state of affairs come about? There does not exist any widely accepted synthesis; perhaps the best that can be said is that in the last decade or so there has been a growing challenge to the conventional theory that Russia must bear the major responsibility for the Cold War. A substantial number of historians have shifted the burden of guilt to the United States for its failure to acknowledge that Moscow's perception of a just peace was strongly influenced by a genuine and realistic concern for its national security and economic recovery.

The orthodox, or Nationalist, view is ably presented by John W. Spanier in his *American Foreign Policy Since World War II,* which emphasizes Russian designs on Eastern and Western Europe. The Soviets are presented as having an "almost paranoid fear of hostile Western intentions" coupled with an "enmity toward all non-Communist nations." The United States erred—in this presentation—because of the "unsuspecting and utopian nature of American wartime thinking"; that is, its expectation that with Germany crushed the "natural harmony would be restored." But throughout Spanier's analysis Moscow is the aggressor:

> The power vacuum created by Germany's defeat provided the opening for Soviet power to fill, and Communist ideology made a clash inevitable. Because democratic principles could not be extended beyond Western power, Russian dominance in the Balkans and Poland became firmly established, and Soviet power now lapped the shores of the Aegean, the Straits of Constantinople, and . . . the Adriatic.[8]

The diplomat-historian George F. Kennan has written extensively on Soviet-American relations and along with Hans J. Morgenthau and Robert E. Osgood has emerged as a leading spokesman of the Realists. It is Kennan's contention that the war, after all, was never fully "winnable" for the West without Russia; the postwar arrangement, the Ambassador insists, was not a "tragedy" and not the result of unbridled Soviet aggression since Moscow had earned certain fruits of victory because of her strategic importance to the Allied victory.[9] This is not to suggest that Kennan dismissed Soviet designs on all of Europe. Rather, he has argued that Washington had overestimated the military capacity of Russia to capture Europe after the war. Kennan has also suggested that in the absence of Western support of an Eastern Europe dominated by Moscow, the Soviets

---

[8] John W. Spanier, *American Foreign Policy Since World War II,* 4th rev. ed. (New York: Praeger, 1971), pp. 22, 23, 28.

[9] See George F. Kennan, *American Diplomacy, 1900–1950* (New York: New American Library, 1950), pp. 66–68.

would "probably not be able to maintain their hegemony successfully over the entire area they had taken under their control in Eastern Europe."

A key to Kennan's evaluation, and to the position of the Realists, is the conviction that a close collaboration between the United States and Russia was not essential to the preservation of peace since this goal could be accomplished by accepting the existence of a balance of power and various spheres of influence for each of the major states. Finally, Kennan denies that the real danger for world stability was further Soviet military advance into Europe; the threat to order came instead from the "Communist parties in the Western countries themselves, plus the unreal hopes and fears the Western peoples had been taught to entertain." [10]

In quite different ways, both Spanier and Kennan view the United States since 1945 in a basically defensive posture, reacting against Soviet initiatives. But others, those termed "radical" or "revisionist" or "New Left" historians have viewed the United States as the major offensive power in the postwar era. Most representative of this group is Gabriel Kolko, whose studies of American foreign policy in the nuclear age have been sharply critical of Washington's efforts to dominate the globe both politically and economically. It is Kolko's contention that American diplomacy during and after the war can be understood only in terms of the carefully articulated political and economic aspirations of the United States. America applied its enormous strength to its expansionist goals.

For Kolko, the Roosevelt and, later, Truman administrations were "anxious to attain a highly organized world economic and political community as a precondition to the realization of [their] vital peace aims. . . . America's foreign policy at the end of World War II necessitated the ability and desire to employ loans, credits, and investments everywhere, to create a world economic order according to its own desires. In this the United States did only what was functional to its own needs and objectives." The tragedy, writes Kolko, is that in its single-minded obsession to obtain this preeminence the United States failed to acknowledge that Moscow would not have Bolshevized Eastern Europe in 1945 had it been offered an alternative to the American determination to dominate the postwar world. For the United States, any economic bloc or sphere of influence outside its control was a threat to its goal of "an integrated world capitalism." [11]

[10] George F. Kennan, *Memoirs, 1925–1950* (Boston: Little, Brown, 1967), pp. 250–51.

[11] Gabriel Kolko, *The Politics of War: The World and United States Foreign Policy, 1943–1945* (New York: Random House, 1968), pp. 619, 620, 624, 625.

In disputing the conventional wisdom regarding the origins of the Cold War, Kolko is also challenging a more moderate theory of "accidental" imperialism: "That there was something accidental or unintended about the American response to the world is a comforting reassurance to those who wish to confuse the American rhetoric and descriptions of intentions with the realities and purposes of operational power." [12] He is attacking here a position most closely associated with Ronald Steel's *Pax Americana*. Steel has argued that at the conclusion of World War Two the United States had the choice of assuming political and economic responsibility for much of the German and Japanese empires or having them fall to our "ideological adversaries." In accepting the former alternative a "counter-empire of anti-communism" was created, reflecting the idealism of the United Nations, the altruism of the Marshall Plan, the pragmatism of the Truman Doctrine, and the military strategy of NATO. "We engaged in a kind of welfare imperialism, empire building for noble ends rather than for such base motives as profit and influence. . . . This is not an imperial ambition, but it has led us to use imperial methods." [13]

The Washington policymakers have therefore been seen variously as righteous crusaders against an aggressive communist advance, calculating, powerful advocates of global political and economic dominance for the United States, or somewhat surprised recipients of an unintentional empire. The events recounted below have led observers to draw a startling variety of conclusions.

COLLECTIVE SECURITY AND YALTA

The enormous and terrible destruction of the war, together with mounting support for the theory that the holocaust might not have occurred had the United States joined Wilson's League, ensured the requisite public pressure in favor of Roosevelt's call for an international organization responsible for the collective security. By mid-1943 there were encouraging signs of an ultimate Allied victory; in September of that year the House of Representatives enthusiastically endorsed the Fulbright Resolution "favoring the creation of appropriate international machinery with power adequate to establish and to maintain a just and lasting peace." Two months later the Senate passed the Connolly Resolution, which was very similar to the Fulbright measure. These twin resolutions placing the Congress in support of a plan for the establishment of a United Nations meant

[12] *Ibid.*, p. 625.
[13] Ronald Steel, *Pax Americana* (New York: Viking, 1967), pp. 16–17.

that Roosevelt would not have to endure the torments of Wilson's futile struggle.

The Soviet Union's attitude toward the scheme, however, was still very much in doubt since Stalin had not shown much interest in the appeal for a postwar major power collaboration. Stalin's interests, after all, remained in large measure inimical to those of the Western allies. Any enthusiasm he showed for the future organization was based on his expectation that the body would further the Big Three's control of world affairs. But this arrangement, and any other hope for postwar harmony, depended on British and American acceptance of Stalin's sphere of influence in Central and Eastern Europe.[14] By the time negotiations on the United Nations were well underway, the Soviets were ensuring the establishment of their Eastern European sphere.

The design for cooperation through an international organization took its first great stride forward at a summer 1944 meeting of the Big Three at Dumbarton Oaks, a mansion outside Washington, D.C. The general structure of the United Nations was established, and the construct which emerged corresponded with the American President's expectation that in time all nations would be admitted to the world body, but that the responsibility for keeping the peace would rest with the United States, England, Russia, and China (France was soon to be added to this group). Unfortunately, Roosevelt was not sufficiently concerned with the possibility that these nations might prove unable to work in concert. Structural adjustments to the initial assumption of Big Four cooperation did not come about until later revisions of the operation of the General Assembly. (The November 3, 1950, "Uniting for Peace Resolution" authorizes the General Assembly to consider certain questions when the Security Council, because of a lack of unanimity on the part of its permanent members, is unable to exercise its responsibility to maintain peace and security.) From the very outset there was constant friction over the authority of the Security Council, the utilization of the veto power, the admission of new members, and a host of procedural matters. It was not until Stalin, Churchill, and Roosevelt met in Yalta in 1945 that most of these questions were resolved; the suspicions, nevertheless, endured.

Sharp exchanges over the United Nations' structure and function were symptomatic of the growing rift among the Allies as they moved toward victory in the closing days of the war. The strain became particularly acute during 1944, when Russian armies occupied Poland and the Balkans. Although FDR was much inclined to believe that an

[14] Kennan, *Memoirs, 1925–1950*, p. 220.

amicable solution could be arrived at in the face of Russian designs over this area, Churchill remained deeply concerned. With the President unable to leave the United States because of his upcoming and unprecedented fourth race for the White House, the British leader traveled to Moscow in October to meet with Stalin and divide the Balkans into Russian and British spheres of influence. Hence it was decided that Russia was to have 90 percent control over Rumania; England, 90 percent control of Greece; both would exercise equal authority in Yugoslavia and Hungary and share a 75 percent–25 percent division of control over Bulgaria, in favor of Russia.[15] Although absent, Roosevelt made it clear through his representative, American Ambassador to Russia W. Averell Harriman, that he would not consider himself bound by the agreements until a full-dress Big Three meeting could be held after the November elections. Nevertheless, the Realpolitik of the Russian occupation of Eastern Europe, coupled with the Polish question, afforded massive complications which helped significantly to dispel Washington's expectations of a peacetime concert of interests.

The purpose of the Yalta Conference, which took place between the fourth and eleventh of February 1945 was to resolve all unsettled problems involving the peace; this was the face-to-face meeting of the Big Three which Roosevelt had required as a prerequisite to his endorsement of the substance of the Moscow Conference. Much has been made of the fact that the talks were held at the Russian resort city on the Black Sea—Russia was assumed to have benefited greatly by her role as host, an argument usually not advanced in discussing the relationship between the structure of the United Nations and its formulation on American territory.

Yalta has clearly aroused more bitter criticism and dispute than any of the wartime conferences. A good deal of this controversy rests on the contention that FDR offered unnecessary concessions on the strength of his faith in the United Nations, much as Wilson is said to have frittered away many of his potential advantages at Paris because of his determination to have the League of Nations included in the Treaty of Versailles.[16] Often called into question are: Roosevelt's

---

[15] Winston S. Churchill, *The Second World War* (Boston: Houghton Mifflin, 1953), VI, p. 227.

[16] For criticism of the Yalta agreement, see William H. Chamberlin, *America's Second Crusade* (Chicago: Henry Regnery, 1950); Chester Wilmot, *The Struggle for Europe* (New York: Harper, 1952); John T. Flynn, *While You Slept: Our Tragedy in Asia and Who Made It* (Old Greenwich, Conn.: Devin-Adair, 1951); and Freda Utley, *The China Story* (Chicago: Henry Regnery, 1951). For a more balanced, though semi-official account, see Herbert Feis, *The China Tangle* (Princeton, N.J.: Princeton University Press, 1953). Also, John L. Snell, ed., *The Meaning of Yalta* (Baton Rouge: Louisiana State University Press, 1956).

decision-making procedures at the conference (e.g., was he sufficiently willing to take advice and, if so, did he choose the right advisors); his freedom of action in the negotiations as a democratically elected head of state who was directly responsible to his constituency; and, of course, the substantive merits of the decisions themselves. It is perhaps fair to conclude that the Chief Executive was willing to go to considerable lengths to assure the success of the United Nations, even if this meant making concessions to Stalin, who feared a lack of safeguards for his nation's security. So-called New Left historians now view Stalin's concerns over national security as less than obsessive.

The substantive agreements at Yalta were as follows:

(a) *The United Nations.* A veto for the five permanent members of the Security Council. This can hardly be viewed as a concession to Russia since other nations insisted on this point. Secretary of State Edward R. Stettinius, Jr., has written that the Joint Chiefs of Staff, key Cabinet officials and Congressional leaders were determined that "the United States should not join any world organization in which its forces could be used without its consent." [17]

(b) *Poland.* The Russian armies by February of 1945 were already in Warsaw and the Anglo-American forces had not as yet crossed the Rhine. Thus Russia had a distinct advantage here. The entire issue was unfortunately complicated by the existence of two Polish governments: the pro-Western government in exile in London and the provisional government at Lublin established by the Polish Communist Committee of National Liberation. Both Roosevelt and Churchill refused to recognize the latter structure. By way of compromise, it was agreed that the Lublin government would be reorganized to include both factions so as to establish a broadly democratic governing base. Once this was accomplished, free elections were to be held by secret ballot.

While this seemed to guarantee the Poles freedom of choice, there was no way of assuring that such elections would indeed be "free." As it turned out, the Polish elections were far from unfettered and the country soon became a satellite of Russia. While Roosevelt is often blamed for the enslavement of Poland, it should be remembered that the final decision was greatly influenced by the control of almost all of Poland by Russian forces in February of 1945. Similarly, the Italian settlement was colored by the Anglo-American occupation of Italy, and the Japanese settlement was overshadowed by American

[17] Edward R. Stettinius, *Roosevelt and the Russians: The Yalta Conference* (New York: Doubleday, 1949), p. 296.

domination of that defeated nation. Despite the democratic principles which were written into the conference's "Declaration on Liberated Europe," Poland's fate awaited other Eastern European countries occupied by Soviet troops at the opening of 1945.

(c) *Germany*. It was decided that Germany would be divided into four sectors: American, British, French, and Russian. Officially, this was to be a temporary measure, but was actually the result of an interesting compromise. At the outset Stalin was much opposed to giving France a share on the rather logical grounds that as a nation long occupied by Hitler's troops, France could hardly be viewed as a victor. The Marshal later agreed to a share for France with the understanding that it would come from the American and British zones. On the other hand, while the Soviet leader at first insisted upon a huge $20 billion reparation from Germany (despite the absence of American demands for reparations and comparatively minor British requests) he eventually settled for a much lower figure, but one which did include provision for the use of German labor for the reconstruction of Russia. It should once again be remembered that the physical presence of Russian troops in Germany influenced this aspect of the settlement.[18]

(d) *Japan*. The last important issue to be decided at Yalta was Russia's participation in the Japanese phase of the war. In February, American military experts were predicting that it might very well take 18 months to defeat Japan after Germany surrendered. While the success of the atomic bomb was to influence greatly these estimates, at Yalta the Americans lacked assurances that the bomb would work. Hence General MacArthur strongly urged FDR to "secure the commitment of the Russians to . . . vigorous prosecution of a campaign against the Japanese."[19] In return for Moscow's agreement to assist in this phase of the war Churchill and Roosevelt promised to return to Russia territory she had lost in the Russo-Japanese War of 1904, plus dominant economic and political interest in Manchuria. Practically, this meant the transfer of Japan's Kurile Islands; Russian control of Outer Mongolia; the return to the Soviets of the southern half of the Sakhalin Island; the "internationalization"

---

[18] The reparations issue is reviewed in William L. Neumann, *After Victory: Churchill, Roosevelt, Stalin and the Making of the Peace* (New York: Harper & Row, 1967), Chap. VIII. Neumann reprints the "Secret Protocol on Reparations," p. 144. For a discussion of the debate over the Eisenhower policy toward Russian penetration of Germany, see Stephen E. Ambrose, *Eisenhower and Berlin, 1945: The Decision to Halt at the Elbe* (New York: Norton, 1967). Favorable assessments of Roosevelt's negotiations as they related to Germany are in John Snell, "What to Do with Germany?" in Snell, ed., *The Meaning of Yalta*, and Kolko, *The Politics of War*.

[19] Walter Millis, ed., *The Forrestal Diaries* (New York: Viking, 1951), p. 31.

of Darien (a port); the restoration of Port Arthur as a naval base; and dominant interest in Manchuria—although Stalin pledged to recognize Chinese sovereignty over the area.

On balance, it would seem illogical to blame the Yalta agreements for what occurred after the war. Roosevelt believed that it was necessary to obtain Russia's cooperation to achieve world peace, and to obtain this cooperation some concessions had to be made. The unfortunate fact is that by February of 1945 the disposition of the postwar world had been largely determined, and it was the military and political decisions before Yalta which were most responsible. For example, the previous November at Tehran, the Iranian capital, the Big Three had already agreed to give Russia an ice-free port in Manchuria, that portion of prewar Poland east of the Curzon Line, and a portion of Germany and Berlin. The Soviets remained essential to an Allied victory over Germany and they were studiously courted for their potential assistance against Tokyo. It is also well to remember that in the winter of 1944–45, while the Anglo-American forces were struggling to hold Belgium and the northern front in the West, the Russians had undertaken a spectacularly successful campaign in the East. Their military accomplishment by February 1945 was most impressive.

Moreover, not only were the Yalta accords an acknowledgment of the tremendous military contribution Stalin had made to the war effort, they were equally an undisputed recognition of the power and prestige Russia had gained in Europe and Asia through the defeat of the Axis powers. It is for this reason that the revisionists object so strenuously to the view that the Soviets received far more than they deserved at Yalta. Kolko concludes: "[T]he Russians came in a position of tactical military superiority and with a vast credit of blood and aid to the West, both of which they failed to exploit fully. . . . The 'betrayal of Yalta' . . . was really a deflation of the illusions cultivated, not in the results obtained." [20]

Although Churchill is often presented as the great realist while Roosevelt is at best seen as naively idealistic, publicly the Prime Minister was quite satisfied with the Yalta accord. He told the House of Commons on his return that the meeting

> leaves the Allies more closely united than before, both in the military and in the political sphere. . . . The impression I brought back from the Crimea, and from all my other contacts, is that Marshal Stalin and the Soviet leaders wish to live in honourable friendship and equality

[20] Kolko, *The Politics of War*, p. 368.

with the Western democracies. I feel also that their word is their bond. I know of no Government which stands to its obligations, even in its own despite, more solidly than the Russian Soviet Government. . . . Sombre indeed would be the fortunes of mankind if some awful schism arose between the Western democracies and the Russian Soviet Union.[21]

The debate over the success of Yalta has been complicated by the issue of Roosevelt's health at the time of the meeting. The 1944 campaign had placed considerable strain on a President already weakened by the tremendous burdens of 12 years in office. FDR appeared exhausted when he returned from the Crimea. Thus much has been made of the Chief Executive's physical—and mental—condition; it is true, for instance, that the weight of his leg braces forced him, for the first time in his long tenure, to sit while addressing the Congress on his return. Yet the argument that he was too ill to negotiate remains unconvincing. His decisions would appear to have been dominated by the opinion of his military advisors that they had to have Russian support in the Far East, and not by any debilitating illness. The most recent study of the conference concludes: "The decisions at Yalta involved compromise by each nation, probably more by the Soviets than by the Western nations." [22]

TRUMAN'S RESPONSIBILITY

Exhausted by his trip, the President left Washington at the end of March for Warm Springs, Georgia, and there, on the twelfth of April, died of a massive intracerebral hemorrhage. At the time of Roosevelt's death, Harry Truman had served as Vice President for less than three months. Eight American Vice Presidents have succeeded to the Presidency, but none have entered that office at a more critical time than did Truman. A one-time haberdasher, Truman's rise to the United States Senate had been made possible in large measure by the maneuverings of one of the nation's most notorious big city machines, that of Kansas City's Tom Pendergast. The new President had no training in the Executive Branch of the Government; he was not considered part of FDR's "inner circle" and so had been witness to only a minimal number of briefings concerning American policies and commitments; and he had very few intimate friends in Executive

[21] Churchill, *The Second World War*, VI, pp. 399–401.
[22] FDR's health is considered in Ross T. McIntire, *White House Physician* (New York: Putnam's, 1946), pp. 216–17; quotation from Diane Shaver Clemens, *Yalta* (New York: Oxford University Press, 1970), p. 290.

departments, coming as he did from the Senate only a few months earlier.[23] Yet to the Missourian fell the tasks of ending the war; establishing a new international order; and guiding the country in its transition to peacetime. It is no wonder that many people seriously doubted his capacity to assume the responsibilities of Chief Executive and Commander in Chief. Fortunately, Truman was consistently underrated by both supporters and political foes and in the current reassessment of his tenure he has emerged with high grades.

Ever a controversial figure, Truman has been warmly praised for his stand against Stalin's designs for communism's spread and roundly damned as the "father" of the Cold War. There is of course no completely accurate way of determining if Roosevelt would or could have persisted in his conciliatory policy toward the Soviet Union in the final phase of the war and after the peace. But it is clear that ominous signs of a serious strain in the Grand Alliance were present long before FDR's death and that the rift was widening as the German and Japanese threat was beaten back. There were endless occasions to rekindle old suspicions, particularly the failure of London and Washington to include the Soviets in the Italian settlement and the unwillingness of Stalin to concur with his allies' interpretation of the Yalta understanding.

As noted earlier the established theory regarding the origins of the Cold War has instructed that the United States moved with the greatest reluctance away from FDR's basically accommodating posture toward the Soviet Union. It was only when the Truman Administration became firmly convinced that Stalin had replaced Hitler as the paramount threat to peace, it is argued, that the United States took increasingly stern measures to prevent a broadly-based Soviet advance and the resultant destruction of the precarious European equilibrium. Those who have most vigorously assaulted this interpretation have sought to demonstrate the extent to which American policy in the formative years of the Cold War was profoundly the product of selfish national interest and a determination to reshape the postwar world to America's image even at the expense of legitimate Soviet concerns for its hard-won security.

Truman has, inevitably, occupied center stage in this battle over cause and effect; those who have emerged as the revisionists have stressed the new President's determinedly hard line. Hence William

[23] For an assessment of Truman's disposition of FDR's policies, see Lloyd C. Gardner, *Architects of Illusion: Men and Ideas in America's Foreign Policy, 1941–1949* (Chicago: Quadrangle, 1970), pp. 55–83.

Appleman Williams in an early revisionist study characterized the
situation as follows:

> [Truman] made it clear very soon after he took the oath as President
> that he intended to reform the world on American terms. He casually
> told one early visitor "that the Russians would soon be put in their
> places; and that the United States would then take the lead in running
> the world in the way that the world ought to be run." [24]

It is well to keep in mind that those who have strongly attacked
Truman for his role in the Cold War have hardly exonerated
Roosevelt; Gabriel Kolko's *The Politics of War*, for example, charged
that the "major distinction between Roosevelt and Truman was their
phraseology in achieving the same ends, for Truman had none of
Roosevelt's grace and bearing, and was blunt where Roosevelt could
be diplomatic or at least pleasant." [25] The Missourian's peppery
delivery, as well as his increasingly hard line toward the Soviets, has
been the occasion of much comment. Often quoted is Truman's harsh
analysis of the deterioration of Washington's relations with its
communist ally. "Our agreements with the Soviet Union so far . . .
[have] been a one-way street. . . . If the Russians did not wish to join
us, they could go to hell." [26]

Soviet Foreign Minister Molotov was one of the earliest victims
of the new President's barbed tongue. Only days after FDR's death
Truman decided to risk an open breach with Moscow by making an
issue of Stalin's interpretation of the Yalta decisions affecting Poland.
In an unusually frank exchange Truman outlined his understanding
of the Yalta agreement by which the provisional government in
Warsaw (dominated by the communists) would be reorganized in
order to establish a new broadly-based representative structure. When
Molotov attempted to assure the President of his government's desire
to resolve the Polish question, Truman snapped that the issue had
been resolved at the Crimea.

> I wanted it clearly understood that [friendship with Russia] could be
> only on a basis of the mutual observation of agreements and not on the
> basis of a one-way street.
>
> "I have never been talked to like that in my life," Molotov said.
>
> I told him, "Carry out your agreements and you won't get talked to like
> that." [27]

[24] Williams, *The Tragedy of American Diplomacy*, p. 240.
[25] Kolko, *The Politics of War*, p. 381.
[26] Quoted in Barton J. Bernstein, "American Foreign Policy and the Origins of the Cold
War," in Bernstein, ed., *Politics and Policies of the Truman Administration* (Chicago: Quadrangle,
1970), p. 26.
[27] Harry S. Truman, *Memoirs* (New York: The New American Library, 1955), I, p. 99.
Also, W. Averell Harriman, *America and Russia in a Changing World: A Half Century of Personal*

Soviet-American relations were further strained the next month when following the German surrender Truman abruptly curtailed Lend-Lease assistance to Russia. According to the Chief Executive's own account, he had signed "without reading" an order drafted for Roosevelt which cut back Lend-Lease assistance to a number of powers following Germany's defeat. Zealous administrators took the order on its face value and went so far as to turn back ships already bound for Russian and European ports. Although several European nations, particularly Britain, were dramatically affected by the move, the Soviets interpreted the unannounced action as a further example of its estrangement with Washington. The order was subsequently modified, but its damaging effect on relations with Moscow was irreversible.[28] Understandably, the affair has gained a good deal of notoriety among revisionist historians who have utilized it as an example of the Administration's attempt to coerce the Soviet Union by economic threats into abrogating its claims in Eastern Europe.[29]

In an effort to achieve a more stable relationship with Stalin, Truman sent FDR's closest confidant, Harry Hopkins, to Moscow in May of 1945. Long associated with attempts by the Roosevelt Administration to achieve a meaningful accommodation with the Soviets, Hopkins's standing with Stalin was regarded as an invaluable asset; it was hoped that the by now frail, seriously ill envoy would symbolize a continuity in policy while emphasizing Washington's willingness to work with Moscow. More specifically, the Hopkins mission was to break a deadlock over voting procedures in the Security Council, seek an accommodation over Poland, and encourage a meeting of the Big Three. (Truman relates that he instructed his representative not to stand on formalities: "I made it plain to Hopkins that in talking to Stalin he was free to use diplomatic language or a baseball bat if he thought that was the proper approach." [30]

The envoy's open discussions with the Soviet leader led to a break in the logjam over the United Nations and a reciprocal pledge to resume Lend-Lease. But Poland was destined to remain a major irritant—while Stalin pledged to uphold his understanding of the Yalta pact he disavowed any interpretation which might lead to Poland's once again serving as a corridor to the Soviet Union. Importantly, the communist chief not only denied any intent to

---

Observation (Garden City, N.Y.: Doubleday, 1971), p. 40.

[28] Truman, *Memoirs,* I, pp. 254–55.

[29] Walter La Feber, *America, Russia and the Cold War, 1945–1966* (New York: John Wiley, 1967), p. 22.

[30] Truman, *Memoirs,* I, p. 288.

Sovietize Poland, but also asserted the inability of the Soviet Union to do so.[31] Yet despite these assurances the only real headway Hopkins had made on the Polish question was to smooth the path for a resumption of discussions.

Paralleling the Hopkins mission, Truman dispatched former Ambassador to Russia Joseph E. Davies to confer with Churchill over the alarming deterioration in relations between the Soviet Union and its two major allies. Davies shared with the Prime Minister Truman's concern that the situation had worsened because of Stalin's belief that the United States and Britain were in league against him and would be aided by the new United Nations structure. Both the Hopkins and Davies missions were of great importance for their efforts to finalize the United Nations agreement, their attempts to set a constructive tone for the forthcoming Potsdam Conference, and most particularly their evidence that Truman had sought to mend the serious breach in the alliance.

AGONIZING DECISIONS

Among the earliest decisions which Truman had to make involved the impending meeting of 50 nations in San Francisco to finalize the United Nations Charter. The meeting had been planned by Roosevelt so as to avoid many of the criticisms that had been heaped upon Wilson for his handling of the negotiations at Paris. For example, at San Francisco both the Senate and House were represented by two members each, and the eight-member American delegation contained a nearly even distribution of Republicans and Democrats, including the highly influential Republican Senator Arthur H. Vandenberg of Michigan. Equally important, Roosevelt had avoided another Wilsonian pitfall by separating his world organization scheme from the general terms of the peace. It might be argued that the memory of Roosevelt encouraged a spirit of determination on the part of the delegates: flags flew at half mast, and Stalin, who had planned to have his government play only a minor role in the proceedings, decided instead to send his Foreign Minister, Vyacheslav M. Molotov.

In the face of a multitude of problems—not the least of which was Soviet opposition to regional groups such as the Pan American Union—an agreement was designed:

(a) All members were to have equal representation in the General Assembly.

(b) The Security Council was to have 11 members, five of whom were to have

[31] Kolko, *Politics of War*, p. 400.

permanent seats (the United States, England, Russia, France, and China) and the remaining six were to serve two-year terms.

(c) The main purpose of the General Assembly was to consider questions which threatened the peace and which might lead to war. The central concern of the Security Council was to maintain international peace.

(d) The Security Council was empowered to utilize armed forces provided by member nations to safeguard or restore the peace.

(e) The permanent members had veto power in the Security Council, except on procedural matters.

Truman personally attended the closing sessions in San Francisco, rightly confident that he would suffer none of the bitter political attacks which had finally defeated Wilson. Unlike the League, the charter swiftly cleared the Senate in July by a vote of 89 to 2.

That same month the major powers confronted one another at the Potsdam Conference, held in good part because of the new President's desire for assurance that the Soviet government intended, as it had pledged at Yalta in February, to enter the war against Japan.[32] Thus from mid-July to early August, Truman met with Stalin and Churchill (who was later replaced by Clement Attlee, the result of an electoral defeat for Churchill). Truman was particularly anxious to meet with the Soviet leader because of recent violations of the Yalta agreements: the direct intervention by the Russians in the reorganization of the Rumanian government; the attempt to undermine the agreement concerning free Polish elections; and the Soviet accusation that Roosevelt had been attempting to make a separate peace with the Germans.

The day before the meeting at the Potsdam palace near Berlin, America's first atomic bomb was exploded at Los Alamos, New Mexico; Truman relates in his *Memoirs* that Stalin did not seem particularly surprised when informed of the success of the project[33] although American monopoly over so formidable a weapon could have only increased the Soviet Union's anxiety about its own security. It was the desire of Stalin to participate in the spoils of the Japanese surrender—especially since there were strong indications that the Japanese were close to the end of their resistance—which caused the Soviet leader to demonstrate a degree of cooperation at Potsdam which was not again to be experienced by his Western allies.

Nine days after the conference began an ultimatum was issued

---

[32] Truman, *Memoirs,* I, pp. 420–21. For details, see Neumann, *After Victory,* pp. 161–81.

[33] Truman, *Memoirs,* I, p. 458. For a history of the Cold War stressing the enormous impact of the atomic bomb on Soviet relations with the West, see Herbert Feis, *From Trust to Terror: The Onset of the Cold War, 1945–1950* (New York: Norton, 1970), esp. Parts IV and VI.

spelling out the dire consequences for the Japanese Empire if the nation did not surrender unconditionally. Japan would be permitted to retain her historic access to raw materials, and would be encouraged to develop a democratic form of government, but she was to be occupied, disarmed, and denied the fruits of her conquests since the turn of the century. Unmoved, Tokyo refused to accede to Allied demands, and so on August sixth—after the formal termination of the Potsdam Conference—the United States demonstrated its success in producing a nuclear fission bomb by laying waste to Hiroshima and killing an estimated 80,000 persons.

It was, ironically, the unexpected success of the nuclear device which led to the bitter attack on Truman for his decision to employ it. Prior to initial tests it had been estimated that the bomb's explosive power would be between 500 and 5,000 tons of TNT; in point of fact, the nuclear bomb dropped on Hiroshima equaled 20,000 tons of TNT and caused an unanticipated level of destruction to life and property. The weight of this action on the American conscience has been understandably great, but in fairness to the Administration a number of contemporary considerations must be kept in mind. Since it was not known whether or not the bomb could be successfully detonated before the end of the war, it was difficult at best to incorporate it into the diplomatic calculations for ending the war; in fact, Truman did not even know of the existence of the bomb until after he became President. Not only the size, but also the effects of the resultant radioactivity were tragically underrated by scientists involved in the project. And too, the already terrible destruction of the war perhaps numbed the leadership's sensitivity to the use of still another instrument of death. A major argument for using the bomb was the near consensus that in the absence of dramatic proof to the Japanese of the enormous destructive capability in the hands of the Allies they would surrender only after a massive invasion of the islands. The potential loss of American life was estimated between 500,000 and 1,000,000 men. A swift, terrible strike on a major industrial city was viewed as the most effective means of forcing a Japanese surrender.[34] That these estimates of Tokyo's ability to sustain its war effort were overly pessimistic is obvious only in retrospect.

The Japanese phase of the war was hardly the only item on the Potsdam agenda, for the conferees were also concerned with the disposition of Germany. The Yalta formula of four zones was endorsed; Germany was to be disarmed; her leaders treated as war criminals and thus punished (this led to the infamous Nuremberg trials); and her physical resources were to be used as reparations to her

[34] See Smith, *American Diplomacy During the Second World War*, pp. 157–72.

former enemies. In sum, her capacity to make war was to be destroyed. Relatedly, it was decided that in lieu of fixed reparation payments, the four occupying powers could collect their claims from what was available in their own zones, provided sufficient resources remained in Germany to allow the nation to function without outside assistance.

The final settlement of the fate of Poland was tabled until the end of the war. In the meantime, Russia was extending her influence in that country so that she could eventually claim a boundary farther west than England, France, and the United States desired. In all, the spirit of harmony that Roosevelt and Churchill spoke of after returning from Yalta had not made a successful passage to Potsdam, and Truman and Attlee left in a decidedly different frame of mind. But Potsdam differed from Yalta in more than its spirit. With the exception of the secret agreement involving Soviet entry into the war against Japan, most of the 21 "conclusions" either referred questions to future meetings of the Council of Foreign Ministers or were phrased so as to leave each participant free to formulate his own interpretations. Ominously, Acting Secretary of State Joseph C. Grew noted at this time that the triumph of American arms meant only "the transfer of totalitarian dictatorship and power from Germany and Japan to Soviet Russia which will constitute in [the] future as grave a danger to us as did the Axis." [35] It can of course be argued that it was precisely this bias which precipitated the Cold War.

Three days after the bombing of Hiroshima a second nuclear device was dropped on Nagasaki which, like Hiroshima, was a war production center of secondary importance. Although Japan sued for peace the next day (an unconditional surrender had been demanded and received) it was agreed on August fourteenth that Emperor Hirohito would remain titular head of his country, subject to the orders of the soon-to-be-designated authority, General Douglas MacArthur. In the meantime, on August eighth, Russia entered the Japanese phase of the war.

THE GERMAN QUESTION

Following the Japanese surrender, disputes over the eventual disposition of Austria and Germany heightened tensions between Russia and the West by exposing the raw edge of mutual suspicions. At the Moscow Conference of 1943 the Big Three Foreign Ministers had agreed that Austria, the first independent country to be crushed under

[35] Joseph C. Grew, *Turbulent Era* (Boston: Houghton Mifflin, 1952), II, p. 1445. For a generally critical view of Soviet diplomacy at Potsdam, see Feis, *From Trust to Terror*, Part III.

the Nazi boot, would be reestablished as a "free" and "independent" entity. The Potsdam accord further provided that Austria would not be required to pay reparations. Yet the practical problem here as elsewhere was that at the time of peace Vienna and other important industrial and agricultural districts were controlled by Soviet troops.

When the Austrians were permitted in November of 1945 to select a Parliament of their own choosing, it was decidedly anti-Communist in composition. The Russians therefore continued to delay ratification of the Austrian treaty and, in apparent disregard of the Potsdam agreements, were moving Austrian resources out of their zone by claiming that military and industrial materiels were in fact German. It was not until May of 1955, after years of acrimonious debate, that a peace treaty was finalized ending the occupation and establishing Austria once again as an independent state.

If the Russians were reluctant to cooperate with their former allies in the Austrian settlement, they proved far more inflexible in their position on the final disposition of Germany. Immeasurably complicating the division agreed to at Yalta and Potsdam was the concomitant decision to section Berlin, which was more than 100 miles within the area to be occupied by the Soviet Union, into four corresponding parts. Administratively, an Allied Control Council was formed of the military commanders of each sector. The problem here was that decisions affecting Germany as a whole had to be unanimously agreed to by the council, an arrangement which all but guaranteed endless deadlock.

The French also proved troublesome to the Americans and British because of their demands to annex the Saar Valley and to control the Rhineland; this was perhaps understandable in light of three German occupations of France since 1870. For their part the Russians helped undermine the spirit of the Potsdam agreement by refusing to treat the administratively partitioned Germany as an economic unit. Instead, Russia established what amounted to a communist state in her sector; insisted that the $10 billion reparation figure mentioned at the wartime conferences was fixed and could be exacted from her zone by the removal of both capital goods (factories and the like) as well as the fruits of production; and refused to merge her zone with the economic union created by the Americans and British in their sections in 1946. Many shared Admiral Leahy's view that the positioning of Berlin deep within the Russian sector led to "a state of virtual armed truce . . . with the Russians enforcing a land blockade." [36]

In an attempt to ward off the specter of a permanently divided

[36] W. D. Leahy, *I Was There* (New York: Whittlesey House, 1950), p. 382.

Germany, the United States offered a formula in September of 1946 whereby a federal system of government would be established for that country. The Americans sweetened the proposal, for the benefit of the alarmed French who were envisioning a revival of the German army under unification, by offering to include a 25- or 40-year disarmament agreement. Thus Secretary of State James F. Byrnes stated at Stuttgart, Germany, that the Potsdam accord provided for a combined program of demilitarization and reparations by which Germany's war potential was to be reduced by the elimination and removal of her war industries and the reduction and removal of her heavy industry plants. Under this plan, Germany was to be able to support a standard of living commensurate with that of the rest of Europe without assistance from other countries. But Byrnes also warned that the Allied Control Council's failure to ensure Germany's functioning as an economic unit had frustrated this key provision of the Potsdam agreement.[37]

The failure of these bids for German economic and political unification in both 1946 and 1947 led to the establishment of West Germany as a separate entity. It also was responsible for a dramatic shift in American relations with the Russians from 1947 on, a change that was to be characterized by a new policy concept, "containment." Before considering this notable adjustment in policy, the one area in which Russia and the West did manage to cooperate should be mentioned briefly. This was the so-called Nazi war crimes trial at Nuremberg, Germany, an outgrowth of the establishment of the United Nations War Crimes Commission in 1943. Meeting as a court of what might be termed ex post facto justice (the German atrocities had never been formally defined as "crimes," and hence the justification for the trials coincided with the trials themselves) the Big Four, after nearly a year of hearings, convicted 19 leading Nazis, 12 of whom were sentenced to death.

CONTAINMENT

Despite evidence of some cooperation by the Soviet government during the Nuremberg trials, the Truman Administration soon became convinced of Russia's intention to replace Germany as the world's aggressor nation. It would seem clear that by 1947 at least public opinion was behind the President's belief that Roosevelt's dreams for a postwar entente were not to be realized, and that a tougher line toward the former ally was definitely in order. The bases for this view were not hard to find, for in 1946 Moscow showed clear

[37] Department of State, *Bulletin*, Vol. XV, pp. 496–501.

evidence of expansionist tendencies in Manchuria, Iran, Greece, and Turkey. At the very opening of the second volume of his *Memoirs,* Truman establishes his administration's mood by 1946: "[I]n spite of these efforts [formation of the United Nations and the Potsdam agreements] relations with Russia had become strained. Victory had turned a difficult ally in war into an even more troublesome peacetime partner. Russia seemed bent upon taking advantage of war-shattered neighbors for imperialistic ends."[38] In an extremely revealing section of this same volume Truman outlined his feelings toward the Soviets in remarks to Chief Justice Fred Vinson:

> In our dealings with the Russians we had learned that we had to lead from strength and that any show of weakness was fatal. But there was never the suggestion of belligerency in our attitude. We made every effort to talk reason and cooperation with them, and we meant it. But for reasons best known to them they either could not, or would not, believe us.[39]

This attitude was quickly transformed into policy. The catalyst proved to be the British announcement in February of 1947 that London would no longer be able to support (economically) the existing anti-Communist government of Greece; the implication of this was the very real possibility that communist guerrilla activity, kept underground by British support to the Greek government, would now be relatively free to transform Greece into a Soviet satellite. On March twelfth Truman addressed a joint session of the Congress to request aid for Greece.

> One of the primary objectives of the foreign policy of the United States is the creation of conditions in which we and other nations will be able to work out a way of life free from coercion. . . . We shall not realize our objectives, however, unless we are willing to help free people to maintain their free institutions and their national integrity against aggressive movements that seek to impose on them totalitarian regimes. This is no more than a frank recognition that totalitarian regimes imposed on free peoples, by direct or indirect aggression, undermine the foundations of international peace and hence the security of the United States.[40]

Shrewdly, he pointed out that the cost to the United States to participate in World War II's crusade to keep the world safe from

[38] Truman, *Memoirs,* II, pp. 13–14.

[39] *Ibid.,* p. 249. Also see Gardner, *Architects of Illusion,* pp. 55–83, for Truman's growing firmness.

[40] Text reprinted in the *New York Times,* 13 Mar. 1947, p. 2. For background, see Cabell Phillips, *The Truman Presidency: The History of a Triumphant Succession* (Baltimore: Penguin, 1966), pp. 167–76.

totalitarian rule was $341 billion, and thus the $400 million requested for the aid of Greece and Turkey under the "Truman Doctrine" (a label attached to the concept by the press) represented approximately one-tenth of one percent of that amount; it would be used to safeguard the investment of World War II. The message, enthusiastically received by the Congress, remains a highlight of Truman's Administration and one of his most popular measures.

Its critics, nevertheless, charged that the proposal was far too sweeping and imprecise and might well appear to commit the United States to an endless line of wars against communism's advance.[41] There was also the very real possibility that the promulgation of such a theory was hard evidence of Washington's admission of the United Nations' inadequacy to ensure global stability. Yet it was difficult to dispute the telling effect that Soviet use of its Security Council veto was having on the effectiveness of the world body. Truman has, therefore, been more praised than damned for his marshaling of efforts against a Sovietized Europe.

A month later, during the course of a speech at Columbia, South Carolina, Presidential Advisor Bernard Baruch made reference to the existence of a "Cold War," and Walter Lippmann helped popularize the concept through his widely syndicated column. So these two words, taken together with Churchill's reference during a May 1946 speech at Westminster College in Fulton, Missouri, to an "Iron Curtain" across Europe, came to characterize the postwar period. In the face of this growing polarization, a far more comprehensive plan for the salvation of Europe was soon to be designated the "Marshall Plan." Britain's financial woes were hardly solved by the expedient of withdrawing its aid to Greece, and in May of 1947 Churchill took note of the desperate economic condition of his own country, and of France, Italy, Norway, and others when he declared: "What is Europe now? It is a rubble-heap, a charnal house, a breeding-ground of pestilence and hate." [42] The Marshall Plan represented an explicit acknowledgment of Churchill's assessment of Europe's plight; it provided that Europeans themselves formulate a comprehensive economic recovery plan which would be financed in part by the United States. The emphasis was to be placed on economic recovery rather than military aid, and on cooperative action among the European nations, not simply the solution of individual problems by individual states.

The offer was made to the European powers in June of 1947

[41] For example, Kennan, *Memoirs, 1925–1950*, pp. 320–21, 341. Also see Richard M. Freeland, *The Truman Doctrine and the Origins of McCarthyism* (New York: Knopf, 1972).

[42] Quoted in Eric Goldman, *The Crucial Decade–And After* (New York: Random House, 1960), p. 66.

when Secretary of State George Marshall proposed to the Harvard graduating class—and to Europe—

> . . . the revival of a working economy in the world so as to permit the emergence of political and social conditions in which free institutions can exist. . . . [T]here must be some agreement among the countries of Europe as to the requirement of the situation and the part those countries themselves will take in order to give proper effect to whatever action might be undertaken by the government. It would be neither fitting nor efficacious for this government to undertake to draw up unilaterally a program designed to place Europe on its feet economically. This is the business of the Europeans.[43]

Moscow had been invited to participate in the project, and Soviet Foreign Minister Molotov met with the Ministers of Foreign Affairs of England and France in Paris. But any expectation of cooperation was doomed since the Russians could not have been expected to grant the United States a voice in their economic planning and development. (Ironically, Stalin's rejection aided passage by more closely associating the bill with the anti-communist effort.) Spain, with dictator Franco at its head, was not invited to participate.

A second Paris conference, with 16 nations in attendance, met in July, established a Committee on European Economic Cooperation, and informed the United States in September that a four-year recovery program had been designed which required $22.4 billion in American assistance. Three months later Truman formally submitted the $17 billion Marshall Plan (formally known as the European Recovery Program) to the Congress; the success of the bill was considerably aided by the establishment of a Communist government in Czechoslovakia in February of 1948 and the threat that the Italians would democratically choose a Communist majority government in their April elections. Hence in March the bill passed both houses of Congress and during the next four years the American government contributed $13.2 billion to European economic recovery. Measured in terms of the increased stability of the Western European economy, the Marshall Plan has been judged "spectacularly successful" [44] by international economist Isaiah Frank.

Nevertheless, those openly suspicious that the Truman Adminis-

---

[43] Quoted in Truman, *Memoirs*, II, p. 138. For background, see Joseph Marion Jones, *The Fifteen Weeks: February 21-June 5, 1947* (New York: Harcourt Brace Jovanovich, 1955). Also Harry Bayard Price, *The Marshall Plan and Its Meaning* (Ithaca, N.Y.: Cornell University Press, 1955).

[44] See Professor Frank's essay, "The Economic Constraints," in Robert E. Osgood, ed., *America and the World: From the Truman Doctrine to Vietnam* (Baltimore: The Johns Hopkins University Press, 1970), p. 243.

tration was being far from altruistic in its offer of massive aid have charged that the true motivation behind the plan was to bolster the American, not the European, economy. The state of European resources after the war, and particularly the shortage of dollars or credit to purchase American goods, threatened to stagnate American commerce with its traditional (and hoped for) trading partners. It is therefore theorized that rather than risk a depression similar to the one which had followed the First World War, the United States decided to export dollars: "By June 1947," two critics have written, "what Washington desired was the opportunity not only to subsidize United States exports but to permanently influence and shape Western Europe's internal economic policies." [45] Yet to view the measure from this perspective is to ignore Washington's very legitimate concern that economic decline and chaos abroad would have had tremendous political consequences. The instability which would have resulted from widespread economic dislocations would have given rise to revolutionary politics; how long could the United States have remained at peace under such conditions?[46]

It would seem appropriate then to view both the Truman Doctrine and the Marshall Plan as part of a larger foreign policy objective of the Truman Administration—one that has come to be termed "containment." One of the most important, if not the most important, long-range consequences of the Second World War was its destruction of the existing balance-of-power arrangement. The world power structure before the war had consisted of at least seven countries—Germany, Japan, Italy, France, England, the United States, and the Soviet Union. The first five of these emerged from the war with their power either seriously in decline or completely destroyed. The United States and Russia ascended to the rank of "superpowers" attempting, via the Cold War, to tilt the balance in their own favor.

In this charged climate, the Truman Administration sought a new diplomatic strategy, and one was formulated by Ambassador Kennan and his Policy Planning Staff (created under the aegis of the State Department). As the name implies, containment was not designed to capture from the Soviet government areas which it had absorbed during and after the war. Rather, Kennan explained that the policy was directed toward holding the line against further expansion of communism since "political intimacy" with the Soviet

---

[45] Joyce and Gabriel Kolko, *The Limits of Power: The World and United States Foreign Policy, 1945–1954* (New York: Harper & Row, 1972), p. 360.

[46] See Thomas G. Paterson, "The Quest for Peace and Prosperity: International Trade, Communism, and the Marshall Plan," in Bernstein, ed., *Politics and Policies of the Truman Administration*, pp. 92–97.

regime could not be expected in the foreseeable future. The American leaders, therefore, were to regard the Soviets as "rivals," confronting them with "unalterable counter-force at every point where they show signs of encroaching upon the interests of a peaceful and stable world." [47] In his *Memoirs,* Kennan has explained that the purpose of containment

> as then conceived was not to perpetuate the status quo to which the military operations and political arrangements of World War II had led; it was to tide us over a difficult time and bring us to a point where we could discuss effectively with the Russians the drawbacks and dangers this status quo involved, and to arrange with them for its peaceful replacement by a better and sounder one.

And, two decades after its formulation, Kennan found it necessary to "emphatically deny the paternity of any efforts to invoke that doctrine today [1967] in situations to which it has, and can have, no proper relevance." [48] A respected critic of the Vietnam War, Kennan has strongly resisted the application of a 1940s concept to vastly changed situations in the 1960s and 1970s.

The apparent reaction of the Soviet government to the intensified determination of the United States to forestall further Russian gains after the Second World War was to increase its pressure upon what was perhaps the most sensitive arena of the Cold War: Berlin. As has been noted above, tension was rising in the region because of Russian disinclination to cooperate with the other Allied powers in a plan that would lead to the unification of Germany. A step toward that objective came in an announcement of currency reform in West Germany in June of 1948, and the extension of that reform, over Russian protests, to the 2,500,000 Berliners in the three Western sectors. Soviet retaliation consisted of a land blockade of the city—air corridor guarantees had already been established. Moscow hoped to either force the other powers to back down on their unification efforts or, more ambitiously, to "starve" those powers out of Berlin.

Truman, with the option of forcing Berlin open with the use of troops, decided that such action would bring the United States too close to war with the Russians.[49] And so "Operation Vittles," American shorthand for the Berlin Airlift, began. By the spring of 1949, 8,000 tons of food, fuel, medicine, and other essential supplies were flown to Berlin on a daily basis. The Russians at times threatened the air corridors, but never actually attacked any of the

[47] Kennan, *American Diplomacy,* p. 104.
[48] Kennan, *Memoirs, 1925–1950,* pp. 365–67.
[49] Truman, *Memoirs,* II, p. 149.

planes used in this most dramatic show of Western determination to keep the city and to turn back any further Soviet attempts to advance in Europe. Defeated, and clearly unwilling to risk total war over Berlin, the Russians lifted the blockade on May 12, 1949. Any assessment of Moscow's strategy in the Berlin crisis must, of course, be conjectural since Soviet archival material is not open to Western researchers. While most commentators have seen the blockade as symbolic of Russia's determination to keep Germany and the rest of Europe weak and divided, there is some evidence that Moscow was far more pragmatic than had been earlier assumed, and that before 1950 the Soviets lacked a cohesive German plan.[50]

Eleven days after the blockade was lifted the German Federal Republic, with Bonn as its capital, was established. To offset this move, the Russians installed the German Democratic Republic in their zone, thus forestalling hopes for the reunification of the nation until two decades later when West German Chancellor Willy Brandt gained a Nobel Prize for his Ostpolitik.

The Berlin blockade and resulting airlift had implications far beyond an immediate concern for that city. The Administration by 1948 had become convinced that in addition to the peace-keeping functions of the United Nations, some kind of regional defense arrangement would have to be designed for the protection of the Western European area. Such a policy had been advocated by the State Department, and, fortunately for Truman, had been warmly received by the foreign policy spokesman of the Republican party, Senator Arthur H. Vandenberg of Michigan. Thus Vandenberg agreed to sponsor a Senate resolution placing the Upper Chamber on record as favoring regional arrangements based on continuous and effective self-help and mutual aid.[51]

Vandenberg's help, and indeed the support of the Republican party, was especially welcome at this time because of the impending 1948 presidential election. In this contest between Governor Thomas E. Dewey of New York and President Truman (a race complicated somewhat by the entry of the Southern Democratic Dixiecrat ticket and of former Secretary of Commerce Henry A. Wallace's Progressive Party) both major candidates supported bipartisanship in foreign policy. Despite a deeply split Democratic party, and public opinion

[50] See John Gimbel, *The American Occupation of Germany: Politics and the Military, 1945–1949* (Stanford, Calif.: Stanford University Press, 1968), p. 202. For more complete treatment, see Jean Edward Smith, *The Defense of Berlin* (Baltimore: The Johns Hopkins University Press, 1963); W. Phillips Davison, *The Berlin Blockade: A Study in Cold War Politics* (Princeton, N.J.: Princeton University Press, 1958); and Robert Rodrigo, *Berlin Airlift* (London: Cassell, 1960).

[51] Arthur H. Vandenberg, Jr., ed., *The Private Papers of Senator Vandenberg* (Boston: Houghton Mifflin, 1952), pp. 493–98.

polls pointing to a Dewey landslide, Truman won the election[52] thereby strengthening his bid for the establishment of the North Atlantic Treaty Organization and the acceptance of other aspects of his foreign policy.

The NATO mutual defense pact had actually been anticipated by an agreement signed at Brussels by England, France, Belgium, the Netherlands, and Luxembourg in March of 1948. But the United States was not a party to that agreement—hence the Vandenberg Resolution. With the polls strongly indicating that the public now wished the United States to abandon its historic policy of avoiding "entangling alliances," Washington was ready in April of 1949 to meet with 11 other nations to sign the treaty. It was clearly underscored that such an accord was not in violation of the United Nations Charter because its intent was defensive rather than offensive. The "teeth" of the NATO agreement was the provision that an attack upon one of the signatory nations would be considered an attack on all. The individual nations were anxious to retain the power to declare war, and so the document stipulated that in the event of aggressive action against one of the members, each of the others would take "such action as it deems necessary," including "armed force," [53] to meet the aggressor.

The mutual defense plan was ratified by the Senate in July with 82 members voting in the affirmative, and within a month a sufficient number of nations had taken similar action to enable the pact to go into effect. America's departure from traditional attitudes toward engagement by the summer of 1949 was dramatic: the Truman Doctrine, the Marshall Plan, and NATO all indicated a clear willingness on the part of the nation to recognize its preeminent position in the Western world and to accept the responsibilities of that position. As Secretary of State Dean Acheson testified before the Senate Foreign Relations and Armed Services Committees in June of 1950·

> The interests of the United States are global in character. A threat to the peace of the world anywhere is a threat to our security. Vigorous, intelligent and sustained action on our part is essential to the preservation of our liberty.[54]

[52] The Truman upset is discussed in Phillips, *The Truman Presidency*, pp. 225–51. Also, Irwin Ross, *The Loneliest Campaign: The Truman Campaign of 1948* (New York: New American Library, 1968), esp. pp. 230–54; and Jules Abels, *Out of the Jaws of Victory* (New York: Holt, Rinehart & Winston, 1959).

[53] The most authoritative work on NATO is Robert E. Osgood, *NATO: The Entangling Alliance* (Chicago: University of Chicago Press, 1962).

[54] Text reprinted in the *New York Times*, 3 June 1950.

THE REVISIONIST CRITIQUE

In considering the aftermath of the Second World War, some of the tensions between those who concur with the traditional view of the roots of the Cold War and those who vigorously dissent from such an analysis have been observed. Those who defend Truman and Acheson regard Russia as a hostile, aggressive force seeking to expand to unreasonable limits, and the United States as the upholder of the ideals of national sovereignty, self-determination, and the objectives of the United Nations. This attitude toward the Cold War was widely shared by American historians until about 1960, when the "New Left" or "revisionist" historians set about to offer alternative, and sometimes shrill, interpretations of the origins of the postwar condition.[55] It is not a coincidence that the revisionist attack on accepted interpretations came at a time when the communist monolith seemed to be disintegrating. It was difficult for some to react to the Soviet threat in quite the same way as many had in the 1950's. (In the earlier decade some Americans advocated the right to shoot people who, having failed to build their own "bomb shelters," attempted to occupy those of others!) Many had been seriously shaken by Eisenhower Administration officials' accounts of how close to the brink of war the United States had come in the 1950s.[56] Finally, the deep and continuing unrest in the country over the conduct of the Vietnam War has led to a reconsideration of America's foreign policy in general, and to a greater willingness to criticize aspects of that policy.

The operative assumption of the revisionist historians is that the policies, actions, and attitudes of the United States, and not of the Soviet Union, led to the polarization which followed the war. Gar Alperovitz, for example, asserts in his highly critical *Atomic Diplomacy*:

> It is now evident that, far from following his predecessor's policy of cooperation, shortly after taking office Truman launched a powerful foreign policy initiative aimed at reducing or eliminating Soviet influence from Europe. . . . I believe new evidence proves not only that the atomic bomb influenced diplomacy, but that it determined much of

[55] For this account, I am much indebted to the synthesis provided by Arthur Schlesinger, "Origins of the Cold War," *Foreign Affairs*, Vol. 46 (Oct.), 22–52. Some of the more important of the "revisionist" works would include: Gar Alperovitz, *Atomic Diplomacy: Hiroshima and Potsdam* (New York: Simon & Schuster, 1965); D. F. Fleming, *The Cold War and Its Origins* (Garden City, N.Y.: Doubleday, 1961); David Horowitz, *The Free World Colossus* (New York: Hill and Wang, 1965); William A. Williams, *The Tragedy of American Diplomacy*; L. C. Gardner, *Architects of Illusion*; and Joyce and Gabriel Kolko, *The Limits of Power*.

[56] See James Shepley, "How Dulles Averted War," *Life*, Jan. 16, 1956 p. 70.

Truman's shift to a tough policy aimed at forcing Soviet acquiescence to American plans for Eastern and Central Europe.[57]

The more extreme revisionists argue that America's sense of its own power led it to the belief that it could sponsor democratic and capitalistic countries at the very doorstep of Russia. Since the Soviet Union viewed the establishment of such states as a direct threat to its own security, it had no alternative but to retaliate by sponsoring governments which would afford greater security. This throws an entirely different light upon Russian actions in the period under discussion, for it leads one to the conclusion that Soviet strategy was defensive rather than aggressive in nature. The revisionist school also borrows heavily from George Kennan's theory[58] that the positioning of the armies at the time of the armistice determined to a large extent the eventual political outcome of the war.

In considering the arguments of the revisionists, it is important to distinguish between the leading theories concerning the preservation of world order after the war. The theory championed by the United States is commonly termed "universalist." Its advocates believe that the only effective way to attain and retain world peace is through an international organization, such as the United Nations, which has the authority to guarantee national security. The opposing view, often labeled "sphere-of-influence," contends that the world can be made secure if each of the great powers is given assurances by the others that it will be preeminent in areas of specific concern to it; this was the theory supported by Moscow. The reasons for Soviet support of a "sphere-of-influence" formula have much to do with Russia's past history. She had been repeatedly attacked from her Western border, a border which is not defined by a natural barrier such as an ocean, mountain range, or desert. In 1944 Kennan wrote of the permanent feature of Russian psychology: "Behind Russia's stubborn expansion lies only the age-old sense of insecurity of a sedentary people reared on an exposed plain in the neighborhood of fierce nomadic peoples." [59]

In the reevaluation of the origins of the Cold War, the revisionists have revealed certain inconsistencies in the actions of the West. For example, although Russia was not involved in the Italian campaign, she was an ally in 1943, when Italy fell. Nevertheless she was studiously ignored in the Italian (not to mention the Japanese)

---

[57] G. Alperovitz, *Atomic Diplomacy*, p. 13.
[58] See Alperovitz, p. 211–12.
[59] Quoted in Schlesinger, "Origins of the Cold War," p. 30.

settlement, just as she was in turn to ignore American and British demands that they be consulted in the Eastern European arrangements. Hence it is pointed out that if the West refused the Russians a hand in the Italian peace settlement, it was unreasonable to expect her to give the West a part in Rumania, particularly when that country (and all of East Europe) lay in a sphere which the Russians considered their private domain. Furthermore, while much criticism has been leveled at the Soviet government for stalling its troops on the Polish border for more than two months while the anti-Soviet Polish underground was massacred by the Nazis, Stalin was quick to defend these actions by explaining that Poland had been the traditional corridor of attack to Russia. Any attempt to deny Moscow hegemony over that area was thus interpreted as a hostile act against Soviet security. Finally, adhering to the "sphere-of-influence" concept, and with the Moscow Conference agreements still fresh in their minds, the Russians adopted a "hands off" policy in Greece when the British supported the pro-Western Papandreou government in its fight against the communist underground in that country.

It is therefore argued that had the United States not been tied to a "universalist" formula for the postwar world, Russia, in exchange for the sphere she most wanted—Eastern Europe—probably would have guaranteed England's predominance in Greece and might well have allowed the United States considerable influence in China. All of this makes for very interesting speculation and points once again to the belief of the revisionists that the Russians sought security rather than world domination. Nevertheless, the United States rejected this formula, partly because of its belief that balance-of-power formulas have been historically unsuccessful, and partly because accedence to such a plan could be viewed as a denial of one of the most publicized American goals—self-determination. However, Washington's tendency to regard the USSR as a threat to its security cannot be used to justify policies which flowed from that perception—it can only be used to explain those policies.

Too much can be made of the revisionist hypothesis regarding the origins of the Cold War. It is important to consider that communism views the Western democracies as an alien force. Stalin informed a delegation of American workers in 1927 that

> In the course of further development of international revolution, there will emerge two centers of world significance: a socialist center, drawing to itself the countries which tend toward socialism, and a capitalist center, drawing to itself the countries that incline toward capitalism. Battle between these two centers for command of world economy will

decide [the] fate of capitalism and of communism in [the] entire world.[60]

And too, when considering the conduct of Soviet foreign policy, the personality of Stalin must not be ignored. Khrushchev has written of the "nervousness and hysteria" of the leader during the war, and he noted that after the war

> the situation became even more complicated. Stalin became even more capricious, irritable and brutal; in particular, his suspicion grew. His persecution mania reached unbelievable dimensions. . . . He decided everything, without any consideration for anyone or anything. Stalin's wilfulness showed itself . . . also in the international relations of the Soviet Union. . . . He had completely lost a sense of reality; he demonstrated his suspicion and haughtiness not only in relation to individuals in the USSR, but in relation to whole parties and nations.[61]

It would seem that in the intervening years there has been a decided moderation of the starkness of communist ideology; Stalin himself has been dead two decades and new leaders have demonstrated new attitudes.

The Cold War was produced by a complex grouping of pressures exerted by and upon the United States and the Soviet Union. It was partly the outcome of Moscow's unwillingness to compromise on questions influencing the Russian definition of security interests, particularly as these interests related to Eastern Europe. The ideological conflict was also a consequence of Soviet determination to achieve prewar goals as they affected the Balkans, the Persian Gulf, and the Dardanelles. However, for the past decade and a half a number of historians have insisted upon viewing post-1945 events from a radically different perspective—the Cold War, they claim, grew out of America's determination to expand its global economic position, to win converts for its particular ideology, and to prevent disruptions of the existing order which appeared to be injurious to American interests. Despite much rhetoric to the contrary, the United States has insisted upon the retention of its own economic and political "special interests" in various parts of the globe while denying the legitimacy of such spheres when controlled by others.

[60] Quoted in Kennan, *Memoirs, 1925–1950*, p. 547.
[61] Quoted in Schlesinger, "Origins of the Cold War," p. 49.

Six

COLD WAR IN ASIA

The most powerful nation on earth at the close of the Second World War, the United States was soon forced to acknowledge its inability to dictate the course of world events. Resolute nationalistic movements, the aggressive policies of China and the Soviet Union, and the willingness of desperate peoples to engage in bloody guerrilla warfare have convulsed the globe since the end of World War II. The United States' short-lived monopoly over atomic weapons did not enable the nation to dominate the globe and once its atomic monopoly was lost, the balance of power became infinitely more precarious.

In Asia, the stakes of the Cold War increased as the scope of conflict widened. With global warfare unthinkable, the United States was forced to stand on the sidelines while Chiang Kai-shek's China became a communist state. This defeat was only partially balanced by the spectacularly successful reconstruction of Japan and that nation's emergence as one of the bulwarks of the Free World. Within five years of World War II's close the United States was plunged into a bloody, frustrating battle to prevent South Korea from falling to the communists. An unclear objective, a limited war, and an inconclusive armistice deeply undercut popular support for the policy of "containment." Yet the Korean War, despite its unsatisfactory resolution, was to emerge as a model for post-1945 conflict. It is little wonder that a confused, embittered nation rallied behind President Dwight D. Eisenhower's self-styled "normalcy."

THE CHINESE REVOLUTION

The development of Asia and the entire postwar world was fundamentally altered by the Chinese Revolution. The basic elements of the civil strife and of the eventual Communist Chinese victory lie in the century of internal upheaval which preceded the founding of the People's Republic of China in 1949. The communist phase of the revolution, dating from about 1920, was ultimately successful because its leaders were able to seize the opportunities created by General Chiang Kai-shek's utter failure to cope with the profound internal crisis. By 1920 the nation was beset with political disunity, a ruinous inflation, and corrupt administration. The unwillingness of Chiang's Nationalist government to address itself responsibly to the need for economic and social reform (particularly as it related to the distribution and ownership of land in a nation of millions of landless peasants) provided the communists with the grass-roots support so essential for victory in guerrilla warfare.

By the middle of the nineteenth century European and American commercial interests had gained a toehold on the potentially vast China trade market, but they were at first limited to the southern port of Canton. With China's loss in the so-called Opium War of 1839–42, Great Britain not only demanded that the Chinese pay the entire cost of the war, but also forced the opening of additional ports, exacted rights of "extraterritoriality," and established the "most-favored-nation" principle vis-à-vis China.[1] The victim of economic imperialism, China was seriously undermined by rising nationalist movements demanding widespread social and cultural reforms. The substance of Chinese life was fundamentally challenged—its political and economic systems, its class and value structures.[2] The extent to which the nation was weakened by these upheavals was made dramatically clear by Japan's stunning victory over China in 1895. Militarily humiliated and politically shaken, the once-powerful Manchu Dynasty helplessly witnessed further economic encroachments by maritime powers demanding ever-widening spheres of influence. Despite their ostensible concern for the Chinese nation, Washington's Open Door Notes were self-serving attempts to ensure American participation in the continuing economic exploitation of that hapless nation. By the opening of the twentieth century many portions of China had been reduced to colonial status.

Continuing Western economic imperialism, the consequences of

[1] See Arthur Waley, *The Opium War Through Chinese Eyes* (London: Allen & Unwin, 1958).
[2] For the diplomacy of the period, see Te-Kong Tong, *United States Diplomacy in China, 1844–60* (Seattle: University of Washington Press, 1964).

the Sino-Japanese War of 1895, and the growing frustration of those attempting to modernize China, led to the emergence of a powerful revolutionary force under the leadership of Sun Yat-sen. Born a peasant, Sun became a doctor. He studied in Japan and Europe, moving throughout the Far East in the early years of the new century in an attempt to establish revolutionary groups. By 1905 he had combined several small revolutionary parties into a secret society pledged to overthrow the Manchu Dynasty, which had reigned since 1644. After a series of failures, sporadic subversive activity succeeded in plunging China into civil war in October 1911. Widespread opposition to the Manchu Dynasty, directed by the many underground revolutionary societies which had developed throughout China, led to the swift and comparatively bloodless demise of the ruling elite.

By February of 1912 the last of the Manchu emperors formally abdicated, and the Republic of China was established; a parliamentary cabinet government was to be formed under a new constitution. Predictably, since the revolution had been held together by little more than anti-Manchu sentiment, the new republic was soon rocked by a profound internal crisis over the government's new structure. It was quickly apparent that a Western-styled democracy could not be superimposed on a political system which for centuries had rested upon imperial rule through entrenched bureaucracies. Yet the demands of the powerful landlord class which still dominated the provinces had to be reconciled with the new attempt at greater centralization and with the needs of rising commercial interests. So powerful were these conflicting forces that when the provisional President of the Republic, Yuan Shih-k'ai, died in 1916 the nation was again plunged into chaos. Sun Yat-sen's new political party, the Kuomintang, was at this time unable to provide the unifying force needed by the nation.

The renewed political power of the landlords, together with the continuing concentration of land ownership, led to increased peasant dissatisfaction, and at times open revolt, in the years following the virtual demise of the republic. This peasant unrest was supported by Chinese intellectuals who, with their increased exposure to Western education and Western society, demanded a powerful, unified, modern nation. At the same time, there developed a fundamental rift among the reformers: though all were in favor of Chinese nationalism, distinctions were made between modernization and Westernization. In the 1920s there was an increasing tendency to view the Western nations as imperialists caught in a declining political-economic structure. The way to a revitalized and independent China was not through identification with Western ideology, but rather through acceptance of a Marxist/Leninist position.[3] The rising labor class, which had resulted from the growing industrialization of China's major cities, provided still another base for the Marxists.

The domination of the government at Peking by rival and largely ineffective warlords led not only to a maladministration of Chinese political affairs, but also to a near collapse of the nation's economic base. Suffering was most acute in the countryside where landowners, large and small, brutally exploited the peasantry. The communists' effectiveness in organizing millions of the desperate landless provided the base for a revolutionary force which Mao Tse-tung predicted would "rise like a tornado or tempest . . . and rush forward along the road to liberation." [4] The farmers' not unreasonable expectation of forceful central government intervention to arrest the steadily worsening economic crisis led to a widespread acceptance of the theory of state socialism. This proved to be an immense boon to the communists; unlike European socialism, which had been introduced gradually and in a variety of guises, Leninism provided the only available route to a Chinese collectivist state. Moreover, communism attacked two of the central targets of the Chinese revolutionary, imperialism and feudalism. This frontal assault on both foreign influence and the landlords had great appeal. According to China expert John K. Fairbank, communism

> would allow China to expunge her modern humiliations by leaping over the capitalist phase of universal development to stand as she should in the forefront of the nations. For the faithful believer the Party would provide. A new China would result.[5]

On this ideological base the communists brilliantly organized the farmers by going to the heart of their concerns—increased food production, land reclamation, transportation and production cooperatives, and labor exchange. Since cooperatives were rigidly opposed by a ruling class fearful of organized attacks on its authority, the communists sponsored peasant cooperatives on the village level, ostensibly for agrarian reform. These ventures provided a powerful political base and an ideal forum for propaganda.

The Chinese Communist Party was formed in Shanghai in 1921, and by the middle of the decade Sun Yat-sen had accepted its participation in his nationalist movement; Russian assistance to China

---

[3] This aspect of Chinese politics in the 1920s is discussed in Akira Iriye, *Across the Pacific: An Inner History of American-East Asian Relations* (New York: Harcourt Brace Jovanovich, 1967), pp. 145–50.

[4] 1927 statement quoted in O. Edmund Clubb, *Twentieth Century China* (New York: Columbia University Press, 1964), p. 135.

[5] John K. Fairbank, *The United States and China*, rev. ed. (New York: Viking, 1958), p. 228.

soon followed. Members of the Communist party were admitted to the Kuomintang on an individual basis since it was assumed that the goals of the two groups were fundamentally alike. But with Sun's death in 1925 there developed a deep ideological rift in the Kuomintang, leading to Chiang Kai-shek's emergence at the head of the right wing, anti-communist faction. Chiang "purged" his party of its Marxist element in the late 1920s.

This anti-communist stance took on great significance when, in 1928, Chiang's Nationalist armies were victorious over the Northern warlords. A successful, if shaky, unification of China was now at least possible. Unfortunately, the Nationalist government at Nanking was undemocratically controlled by the Kuomintang and was unable to effect the basic social, economic, and political reforms which had created the impetus for the successful revolution in 1911. The growing dictatorial tendencies of the Nanking leadership (which was increasingly dominated by Chiang Kai-shek), continuing insurrections by still powerful warlords, and Japanese aggression in Manchuria, Shanghai, and elsewhere, all undermined the new Nationalist party. Chiang seemed singularly unprepared and unwilling to confront these challenges. The economic and social plight of the peasants continued unabated, further weakening the General's position.

During the Second World War, while China's very survival was threatened by Japanese aggression, Chiang's tenuous hold deteriorated further. Along with the disruption of normal trade and investment patterns, the nation was forced to bear huge military expenditures which led to a ruinous inflation. Threatened from without and locked in a desperate guerrilla civil war, the Nanking government lost much of its popular support.

China's internal chaos and its ineffective response to Japanese aggression led the Roosevelt Administration to pressure Chiang into exerting greater leadership in resolving his differences with the communists. Hence in January of 1942 a China-Burma-India Theater of War was created under the direction of the Chinese head; Lieutenant General Joseph W. Stilwell was named United States commander and was appointed Chiang's Chief of Staff. It soon became obvious, however, that while American energies were directed toward Tokyo's defeat Chiang was at least as interested in utilizing the war effort to weaken the Chinese communists. Hence much of the military equipment requested was used to fight the enemies of the Nationalist government. And while the Army leadership remained loyal to Chiang, the individual foot soldiers were badly treated, poorly fed, and often neglected; morale suffered in predictable proportions.

In the last two years of the war the situation further deteriorated. The Nationalists' continued disinclination to launch effective, large-scale efforts against the Japanese, their insistence upon massive American assistance (including a billion-dollar loan), and their preoccupation with the struggle against the Chinese communists led Roosevelt to sternly warn Chiang of impending disaster. In a September 1944 message, the President bluntly stated his position:

> I have urged time and again in recent months that you take drastic action to resist the disaster which has been moving closer to China and to you. . . . Only drastic and immediate action on your part alone can be in time to preserve the fruits of your long years of struggle and the efforts we have been able to make to support you. Otherwise political and military considerations alike are going to be swallowed in military disaster.[6]

In August of 1944 Roosevelt sent Major General Patrick J. Hurley to the Generalissimo to urge the unification of Communist and Nationalist forces in the struggle against Japan. Although the Communist party indicated a willingness to cooperate if the Kuomintang dictatorship were ended and a democratically elected coalition government formed, Chiang would agree only to the unification of all Chinese troops under his command. This of course the Communists would not do. Given the widely divergent goals of the two factions (particularly since the Kuomintang's right wing had gained ascendancy) it was most doubtful that the two forces would have cooperated for a protracted period. This is not to imply, however, that a temporary, uneasy coalition against the Japanese could not have been successful.

At the Yalta Conference of February 1945 the relationship between the United States and China was further complicated by Roosevelt's attempt to gain Russian support for a postwar Chinese government under the direction of the Nationalists. In return, Stalin was to receive control of that portion of Northeast China which had been in the hands of the Russians at the opening of the Russo-Japanese War (essentially, the Russians would dominate Manchuria even though China maintained official sovereignty). The terms of this agreement had been kept from Chiang, and by the time the Sino-Soviet Treaty was signed Russia was in control of Manchuria, although China retained title to the territory.

Japan surrendered to the Allies on the very day of the signing of the Sino-Soviet Treaty, August 14, 1945. No longer threatened by Japan, the Nationalists and Communists continued their civil slaughter on a larger scale. Mao Tse-tung's objectives were clear:

---

[6] Quoted in Clubb, *Twentieth Century China*, p. 240. For the most recent study of Stilwell's ordeal in China, see Barbara W. Tuchman, *Stilwell and the American Experience in China, 1911–1945* (New York: Macmillan, 1971).

[A]ll Chinese Communists . . . must struggle against foreign and feudal oppression and for the deliverance of the Chinese people from their tragic fate of colonialism, semi-colonialism, and semi-feudalism, and for the establishment of a new democratic China under proletarian leadership and with the liberation of the peasantry as its main task.[7]

Even before the armistice, Communist Chinese troops captured Japanese positions and demanded control of the surrender of Japanese forces. At the urging of the new American Ambassador to China, General Patrick J. Hurley, Mao Tse-tung arrived in Chungking on August 16 to discuss a possible coalition (the Nationalist capital had been moved from Nanking in the late 1930s). After protracted negotiations proved fruitless, the Nationalist cause was aided by an American decision to transport approximately 500,000 of Chiang's troops to strategic positions within China. American armed forces were also utilized to hold key ports and airfields. Such activity—together with American backing of Chiang's position on the surrender of Japanese troops—short-circuited, at least temporarily, major Communist victories in the south.

Such was not the case in the northern portion of China. There the Chinese Communists gained wide control of the countryside, and were it not for an American directive ordering the Japanese to hold their positions, the Communists would have made dramatic advances in the large northern cities. Forces loyal to Mao were, nevertheless, able to capture huge amounts of Japanese military stores and so to strengthen their position. As early as October of 1945 the Communists had infiltrated Soviet-controlled Manchuria, and Russian complicity in the Chinese Communist drive further undermined Chiang's authority in the north.

Frustrated in his attempt to impose some order on the chaotic Chinese situation, Ambassador Hurley resigned his post in late November 1945, charging that his policies in China were doomed to failure because of the career foreign service officers who "sided with the Chinese Communist armed party. . . . These same professionals openly advised the Communist armed party to decline unification of the Chinese Communist Army with the National Army unless the Chinese Communists were given control." [8] The Ambassador's charge, according to Tang Tsou's major study of United States-Chinese relations in the 1940s, represents the first official statement of what

---

[7] Mao Tse-tung, *Selected Works* (London: Lawrence & Wishart, 1954), IV, p. 275.

[8] Hurley's letter of resignation is quoted in full in a highly laudatory and largely uncritical biography, Don Lohbeck, *Patrick J. Hurley* (Chicago: Henry Regnery, 1956), pp. 428–32.

was to become the conspiracy thesis of the fall of China, a theory "which was to blossom fully into a witch hunt in the era of McCarthyism." [9]

Truman wasted little time appointing General George C. Marshall his special representative to China. Marshall's exact instructions, issued on December 19, were "to persuade the Chinese Government to call a national conference of representatives of the major political elements to bring about the unification of China and, concurrently, to effect a cessation of hostilities, particularly in North China." [10] Marshall was given a twofold mission: politically he was to help formulate a coalition government, and militarily he was to help effect a cease-fire.

Less than a week after Marshall arrived in Chungking, Secretary of State James F. Byrnes met with the British and Russian foreign ministers in Moscow; there it was agreed that the three governments would cooperate in efforts aimed at ending the civil war and unifying China under the Nationalist government. The apparent willingness of the Soviets to cooperate with the Western powers on the China issue, and more specifically to work toward the formulation of a broadly-based, democratic government under the leadership of Chiang, was most encouraging.

Optimism regarding the success of the Marshall mission heightened when it was learned that the General had obtained the Nationalist government's acceptance in principle of a Communist-sponsored truce proposal. On January 10, 1946, an actual cease-fire was in effect, and on the same day a Political Consultative Conference gathered at Chungking. It was quickly decided that a coalition government would be formed through the convening of a National Assembly in May. This government would adopt a constitution and recognize parties of all political persuasions; importantly, during the Consultative Conference both sides agreed to reduce their troop strength.[11] But the outward signs of goodwill and the very promising resolutions regarding the unification of China masked the rigid opposition of powerful, reactionary groups in the Kuomintang.

The crucial test of the truce's effectiveness came in Manchuria, where the internal conflict was enormously complicated by Russia's decision to remove "Japanese" machinery as spoils of war. Chiang

[9] Tang Tsou, *America's Failure in China, 1941–1950* (Chicago: University of Chicago Press, 1963), p. 344.

[10] Truman, *Memoirs*, II, p. 87.

[11] The series of agreements reached at the Political Consultative Conference are reprinted in United States Department of State, *United States Relations with China* (Washington, D.C.: Government Printing Office, 1949), pp. 610–21.

realized, quite rightly, that the flow of machinery from Manchuria to Russia included Chinese as well as Japanese industrial property. American protests most probably had the unfortunate effect of strengthening the Nationalist's anti-Communist stance, a position which was made more rigid by anti-Soviet, government-encouraged student demonstrations in February and March. For their part the Communists had also hardened their position, bolstered as they were by the acquisition of massive amounts of war materiel captured from the Japanese and left behind by the gradually withdrawing Soviet forces. In March of 1946 the Communists boasted a northern army of approximately 300,000 men.[12] Ominously, that same month it was learned that the final Soviet withdrawal from Manchuria would be "delayed."

Thus each combatant in the civil strife was encouraged by the apparent support of one of the two superpowers. The Nationalists believed that the Truman Administration would not permit a Communist takeover of China, while the Chinese Communists enjoyed at least tacit support from the USSR. Although the United States did not attempt to deepen its influence in China, 12,000 American troops remained at the close of 1946.

The Manchurian time bomb exploded on April 14, 1945, when Soviet troops evacuated the capital, Changchun, leaving the Communists and Nationalists to fight for control of the city and for all of Manchuria. This was the beginning of the last round of the Chinese civil war. Nationalist military reversals in the north, and continuing indications of the anti-democratic, repressive nature of the Chungking government, led Truman to warn Chiang sternly of an imminent American reassessment of its position.

> There is a growing feeling . . . that the aspirations of the Chinese people are being thwarted by militarists and a small group of reactionaries, who, failing to comprehend the liberal trend of the times, are obstructing the advancement of the general good of the nation. Such a state of affairs is violently repugnant to the American people.[13]

In July, a month before the President's dramatic letter to Chiang, a Gallup poll concluded that fully half of the American public believed that the nation should adopt a "hands off" policy toward China, and only 13 percent were in favor of continuing aid to Chiang.[14]

With the Chinese situation rapidly deteriorating, Truman re-

[12] Clubb, *Twentieth Century China*, p. 268.
[13] Truman, *Memoirs*, II, p. 104.
[14] Gallup poll figures are in A. T. Steele, *The American People and China* (New York: McGraw-Hill, 1966), p. 31.

called General Marshall in January 1947 and appointed him Secretary of State. The very next day Marshall's report of his year in China was made public. He concluded that internal stability was possible only if the liberals in the government and in the minority parties assumed a stronger role in a reorganized government which remained under Chiang's direction. Years later Truman concluded that the "Marshall mission had been unable to produce results because the government of Chiang Kai-shek did not command the respect and support of the Chinese people. The Generalissimo's attitude and actions were those of an old-fashioned warlord, and, as with the warlords, there was no love for him among the people." [15]

Chiang's woes were more than political and military: they were economic as well. By the opening of 1947 the nation was experiencing a ruinous inflation, a drain on its foreign exchange reserves, and a trade imbalance. The continuing civil strife was an enormous burden on the already weakened economy, for it not only required huge expenditures but also partly paralyzed the internal transportation and production systems. A complete overhaul of the economy to bring it in line with the demands of a government in the throes of a large-scale military operation was imperative. By March the newly appointed American Ambassador to China, John Leighton Stuart, concluded that economic development was impossible while the civil war continued. Stuart's assessment was particularly useful since he was born in China and spoke the language fluently; as President of Yenching University in Peking he had an intimate, firsthand view of the China scene.

This clear recognition of the political, military, and economic deterioration of China led Truman to ask Lieutenant General Albert C. Wedemeyer, Chiang's chief of staff (1945–46), to appraise the situation. His highly controversial report was suppressed until 1949, largely because of the General's recommendation that Manchuria be placed under a United Nations Trusteeship. With the exception of the Manchuria recommendation, Wedemeyer's findings were reasonably consistent with those of other observers. The General urged extensive military and economic aid to China, on the condition that China pledge to

> make effective use of her own resources in a program for economic reconstruction . . . give continuing evidence that the urgently required political and military reforms are being implemented . . . accept American advisors . . . to assist China in utilizing United States aid in the manner for which it is intended.[16]

[15] Full text in *United States Relations with China*, pp. 686–89; also see Truman, *Memoirs*, II, p. 111.

[16] *United States Relations with China*, p. 774. For the full text, see pp. 764–814. Much

The suppression of the Wedemeyer report fanned the discontent of the China Lobby, a loose coalition of highly vocal individuals and organizations who in the late 1940s rigorously resisted efforts to reach an accommodation with the Chinese Communists. This pressure group included Chiang's American admirers, former military officers, ex-missionaries, several Republican Congressmen, influential publishers, and a number of militantly anti-Communist organizations. It is often charged that the lobby was supported financially by the Nationalist Chinese government.[17] The pressure group's pleas met partial success in April of 1948 with the passage of the Foreign Assistance Act extending $338 million in economic aid and $125 million in unspecified, but presumably military, assistance. Given the Nationalist government's urgent request for $3 billion in November 1947, news of the Assistance Act was not kindly received by Chiang. It is important to recognize, nevertheless, that between 1945 and 1949, American economic and military aid to China amounted to over $2 billion.[18]

Throughout 1948 the American public was deeply divided over China and the Truman Administration was inundated with advice regarding an appropriate response to the crisis. A large-scale military aid program was urged by a variety of prominent individuals, including former Ambassador to the Soviet Union, William C. Bullitt, and Generals Claire L. Chennault, MacArthur, and Wedemeyer. In early spring, as the Nationalist defensive crumbled under impressive Communist victories, a limited foreign aid bill was passed reducing economic assistance to China. Nationalist defeats in Manchuria, the steady movement of Communist troops southward, repressive governmental measures to control demonstrations and strikes, and a runaway inflation boded ill for Chiang's future. (The cost of living in June 1948, for example, rose 110 percent.[19]) In October the Secretary of State reminded Ambassador Stuart that "underlying our recent relations with China have been the fundamental considerations that the United States must not become directly involved in the Chinese civil war and that the United States must not assume responsibility for

---

information is contained in Albert C. Wedemeyer, *Wedemeyer Reports!* (New York: Holt, Rinehart & Winston, 1958).

[17] For a denial of the existence of an organized "China Lobby," see Joseph Keeley, *The China Lobby Man: The Story of Alfred Kohlberg* (New Rochelle, N.Y.: Arlington House, 1969), pp. 113–33.

[18] This figure is based upon a March 21, 1949, State Department report, "Summary of United States Government Economic, Financial, and Military Aid Authorized for China Since 1937," reprinted in the Congressional Quarterly Service, *China and United States Far East Policy, 1945–1967* (Washington, D.C.: Congressional Quarterly, 1967), p. 256.

[19] *Ibid.,* p. 45.

underwriting the Chinese Government militarily and economically."
In this October policy review Marshall also explained that the China
Aid program of April had precluded the use of American combat
troops or American personnel in command of Chinese troops.[20]
Tsinan, the capital of Shantung and a vital industrial and railroad
center, had fallen to the Communists a month earlier, and throughout
the latter part of 1948 city after city was wrested from Nationalist
control.

Inevitably, the China tangle was affected by Truman's 1948 bid
for a full term as President. Chiang could not have been comforted by
the news that the Republican challenge had been turned back since
for years conservative Republicans had been urging a "hard line"
toward Asian communism. Chiang's worst fears were realized two
days after Truman's election when the President informed Congress
that, given the many difficulties experienced by the United States in
its attempt to aid the Nationalists, the Administration would exercise
great caution in extending further assistance to China. In what must
certainly be viewed as a desperate effort to bypass the President by
appealing directly to the American people, Mme. Chiang Kai-shek
arrived in Washington a month after Truman's triumph to plead for
the long-sought $3 billion in aid. Despite the warm reception accorded
her by China Lobby enthusiasts, Mme. Chiang's mission was a grim
failure. The position of the Chiangs was made more precarious by the
outcome of the 1948 Congressional races, which resulted in the return
of a Democratic-dominated Congress. The demise of the Republican
Eightieth Congress removed much of the pressure to placate the
Generalissimo.

The final act of the great contest for China was quickly played.
With the Communists near victory by the opening of 1949, Mao
Tse-tung refused to negotiate with Chiang's government; on the
twenty-first of January Chiang retired as President of his beleaguered
nation. Ten days later Peking fell to the Communists. As the drive
south gained momentum in the early spring, the Yangtze River was
crossed and Nanking, Hankow, and Shanghai fell. The People's
Republic of China was proclaimed at Peking on September 21, 1949,
and Mao Tse-tung was elected Chairman. The government's formal
inauguration followed a week later and the very next day the Soviet
Union extended diplomatic recognition. By late fall, Canton and
Chungking were lost. The Nationalist government went into exile on
the island of Formosa on December 8; the humiliated and bitter
Chiang quickly joined his loyal band.

[20] *United States Relations with China*, pp. 280–81.

McCARTHYISM

Few events in the history of recent American foreign policy have attracted more Monday-morning quarterbacking than has the Fall of China. Demands for an accounting led the State Department to issue its now infamous one-thousand page "White Paper" on China in August of 1949. In a prefatory "Letter of Transmittal" to President Truman, Secretary of State Dean Acheson assessed and defended American policy.

> The unfortunate but inescapable fact is that the ominous result of the civil war in China was beyond the control of the government of the United States. Nothing that this country did or could have done within the reasonable limits of its capabilities could have changed that result; nothing that was left undone by this country has contributed to it. It was the product of internal Chinese forces, forces which this country tried to influence but could not. A decision was arrived at within China, if only a decision by default.[21]

The China bloc of orthodox Republicans was outraged; the group, headed by Senators Styles H. Bridges and William F. Knowland, labeled the White Paper "a 1,054 page whitewash of a wishful, do-nothing policy which has succeeded only in placing Asia in danger of Soviet conquest." [22] Republican indignation soared to even greater heights when it was learned that Acheson, in secret guidance papers to United States missions abroad, instructed that the importance of Formosa was to be minimized. "[The island] has no special military significance. . . . [L]oss of the island is widely anticipated and the manner in which civil and military conditions there have deteriorated under the Nationalists adds weight to the expectation." [23] The demands of the Korean War, however, led the Administration to change its policy toward Formosa considerably. The positioning of the Seventh Fleet in the Formosa Straits shortly after the outbreak of the war provided military protection to Formosa—protection that the Republicans, ironically, bitterly resented because it prevented Chiang from attacking the mainland!

At the same time, the GOP fought long, hard, and successfully to prevent the granting of diplomatic recognition to Red China. Ignoring

[21] *Ibid.*, p. xvi. The "White Paper" is discussed briefly in Dean Acheson, *Present at the Creation* (New York: Norton, 1969), pp. 302–7.

[22] Quoted in H. Bradford Westerfield, *Foreign Policy and Party Politics: Pearl Harbor to Korea* (New Haven, Conn.: Yale University Press, 1955), p. 356.

[23] *New York Times*, 4 Jan. 1950, p. 14.

the principle of *de facto* recognition and unrealistically assuming that Chiang could be returned to the mainland, the GOP's China bloc viewed the recognition of the mainland government as the height of perfidy. The British and Indian decisions in December 1949 to recognize the Chinese Communist government only reinforced the China Lobby's determination to support Chiang.

While insisting that the Truman Administration champion the Nationalist cause, dissident Republicans and far-Right journalists were also formulating a theory on the Fall of China and the disaster in the Far East. Rejecting the thesis of the White Paper that monumental social, economic, and political upheavals *within* China accounted for the Communist victory, these individuals charged that pro-Communist elements in the Roosevelt and Truman Administrations had worked for Chiang's defeat. A purge was soon demanded to rid the federal government and especially the State Department of these traitorous figures. (Acheson characterized the onslaught as "the attack of the primitives." [24]) It was this issue which led to the uneasy alliance between Senator Robert A. Taft of Ohio, a leading Asialationist, and Senator Joseph R. McCarthy of Wisconsin. In Wheeling, West Virginia, McCarthy delivered an address on February 9, 1950, which gave his name to an era.

> The reason why we find ourselves in a position of impotency [in international affairs] is . . . because of the traitorous actions of those who have been treated so well by this Nation. . . . The bright young men who are born with silver spoons in their mouths are the ones who have been worst. . . . In my opinion the State Department, which is one of the most important government departments, is thoroughly infested with Communists.[25]

Adding force and appeal to McCarthy's charges were two events which contributed greatly to the growing "Red menace" hysteria. The first was Truman's announcement on September 23, 1949, that within recent weeks the Soviet Union had exploded an atomic device. Those seeking to prove widespread treasonable activity within the government were aided by the conviction of Alger Hiss, once a high-ranking member of the State Department. Hiss, who was found guilty of perjury, was charged with having passed government secrets to communist agents; he soon came to personify New Deal intellectualism and postwar internationalism.[26]

---

[24] Gaddis Smith, *Dean Acheson* (New York: Cooper Square, 1972), p. 163.

[25] Quoted in Eric Goldman, *The Crucial Decade—And After* (New York: Random House, 1960), p. 142.

[26] For a particularly hostile view, see Anthony Kubek, *How the Far East Was Lost: American Policy and the Creation of Communist China, 1941–1949* (Chicago: Henry Regnery, 1963).

Although it is most doubtful that a majority of Americans ever accepted such explanations of the Fall of China, Washington's China policy had obviously failed. Acheson argued that the "Fall" was due to forces beyond the nation's control; McCarthy charged that China might have been saved had it not been for pro-communist plots hatched within the State Department. In all of this, one is tempted to turn to John K. Fairbank's final estimate:

> If one assumed that American aid was a determining factor in China's domestic affairs, that the Nationalists could have lost their military superiority only through treachery, that American policy-makers had been anti-Chiang and therefore pro-Communist, and that Communist conspiracy could be detected through a man's associations (a series of *untrue* non sequiturs accepted by many during the McCarthy era)—then it became a public duty (and a rich opportunity) to investigate. . . . Very little if any Communism, espionage, or treachery was uncovered but everyone was intimidated. . . . My own impression is that the American people responded to the cold war and the Chinese Communist victory more fearfully than creatively.[27]

Without minimizing the intrinsic importance of the detonation of the first Soviet nuclear bomb and the demise of Nationalist China, it is important to consider why McCarthyist seeds fell on such fertile ground in the late 1940s. Why did Americans in such numbers come to believe that their most basic values and the very future of their nation were imperiled by communism? While attacks on the loyalty of State officials were not substantiated, official denials of such charges failed at first to convince millions. A recent "revisionist" study theorizes that the enthusiastic, if short-lived, reception to the Senator can be traced to the "Cold War consensus" which had been nourished by the Truman Administration between 1945 and 1948. In his *The Truman Doctrine and the Origins of McCarthyism*, Richard M. Freeland postulates that Administrative campaigns to win public and Congressional support for the Truman Doctrine and the Marshall Plan "implanted the idea in the public mind that the United States was imminently threatened by a massive, ideologically based assault upon everything Americans valued." It was within this "emotional and conceptual context" that the public reacted to Soviet nuclear status, Red China, the Hiss conviction, and the Korean War.[28] It is quite possible that the atmosphere of fear created by Truman's hard line toward the Soviets did in fact nourish McCarthy's demagogy.

[27] Fairbank, *The United States and China*, pp. 272–74.
[28] Richard M. Freeland, *The Truman Doctrine and the Origins of McCarthyism: Foreign Policy, Domestic Politics and Internal Security 1946–1948* (New York: Knopf, 1972), p. 11.

JAPANESE RECONSTRUCTION

The attacks by McCarthy and his ilk against American Far Eastern policy caused many to lose sight of an outstanding accomplishment: the restoration and reconstruction of Japan. In a span of seven short years the United States moved swiftly and effectively to transform the defeated nation into a vital counterweight to the growing power of communism in Asia. At first, it had been assumed that the Republic of China would occupy a position of leadership in postwar Asia by replacing Japan (slated for second-class status, at best). But the growing crisis in China and the early realization that hopes for continued Allied unity after the war were visionary led to a basic shift in America's policies toward Japan. The lessons of Eastern Europe, and particularly the difficulties encountered in attempting to effect the quadripartite division of Germany, caused the Truman Administration to abandon any consideration of a joint occupation and restoration effort. Truman held the high cards. Just as Russia's would-be allies were frustrated in Eastern Europe because of Soviet military dominance there, so too were Moscow's hopes for a role in Japan shattered by the overwhelming American military control of that nation. Even the 11-member Far Eastern Commission, which technically had the authority to initiate or review basic policies relative to Japan, was powerless without American support. The Allied Council in Tokyo, representative of the United States, Great Britain, China, and the Soviet Union, was merely an advisory body whose assistance was rarely sought by the United States.

To General Douglas MacArthur, so long associated with war and its destruction, fell the task of the peaceful restoration of Japan and its 80 million people. Appointed the Supreme Commander for the Allied Powers by President Truman, MacArthur's temperament and strength of character proved ideal for an occupation leader. In his role as benevolent dictator the General was to emerge as one of the greatest and most beloved of Japanese heroes. Former United States Ambassador to Japan Edwin O. Reischauer has attempted to explain MacArthur's enormous professional and personal triumph.

> His strength of will rivaled that of the strongest Japanese hero; his dignity and the firmness of his authority were all that they could hope for in their leaders; his austerity was only matched by his capacity for hard work; his insistence on strict obedience and . . . on unwavering personal loyalty . . . were qualities which the Japanese . . . understood and admired. . . . MacArthur provided the Japanese with the

leadership and also the hope they so desperately needed in their hour of confusion and despair.[29]

The demilitarization of Japan's home islands was a major early objective of the Truman Administration. During the initial phase of the occupation all arsenals and military weapons factories were closed; naval bases were destroyed; more than two million soldiers were demobilized; and the Army and Navy Ministries were abolished. The process of demilitarization was greatly complicated by the following stipulation in the July 26, 1945, Potsdam Declaration: "There must be eliminated for all time the authority and influence of those who have deceived and misled the people of Japan into embarking on world conquest, for we insist that a new order of peace, security and justice will be impossible until irresponsible militarism is driven from the world." [30] In practical terms this meant a purge of the Japanese leadership, including the trials of hundreds of Japanese soldiers and officers accused of committing war atrocities. Stiff penalties, including long prison terms and even death, were meted out to those convicted.

More complicated was the American decision to try two score top military and civilian leaders in Tokyo, including ex-Premier General Hideki Tojo. These trials became extremely complex because the prosecution attempted to prove that the individuals involved were personally responsible for Japan's militaristic and aggressive course of action and therefore were subject to individual punishment. There had been serious consideration of including the Japanese emperor in these trials, but it was determined that his role had been more symbolic than real. At the conclusion of the trials (December 1948) seven of the 25 defendants, including Tojo, were hanged; the remainder, save two, were given life imprisonment. A related phenomenon was the purge edicts issued against 200,000 Japanese citizens. These edicts were directed toward those who had been active exponents of militant nationalism and aggression, or who were expected to have been supportive of such views because of their official positions (e.g., military officers and conservative political party leaders). Individuals identified by these definitions were forbidden to hold public office.

This initial stage in the reconstruction was followed by far more

[29] Edwin O. Reischauer, *The United States and Japan*, rev. ed. (New York: Viking, 1965), p. 224. For an almost worshipful account of MacArthur's years in Japan, see Courtney Whitney, *MacArthur: His Rendezvous with History* (New York: Knopf, 1956), Part II.

[30] The Potsdam Declaration reprinted in Department of State *Bulletin*, Vol. XIII, pp. 137–38.

productive efforts toward basic political and economic reform. The drive for political change became more clearly focused with the drafting of a new Japanese constitution, based upon the British and American systems and only minimally reflective of Japanese tradition. The Emperor's function was severely circumscribed, for he was to be "the symbol of the State and of the unity of the people, deriving his position from the will of the people with whom resides sovereign power." [31] The basic governmental structure was to be parliamentary, except for an American-styled Supreme Court with the power of legislative review; the Cabinet was to be responsible to the lower house of the Diet. The inclusion of an exceedingly comprehensive bill of rights became one of the most admired American political accomplishments in Japan. Importantly, Chapter II, Article 9 of the Constitution pledged the renunciation of war "as a sovereign right of the nation and the threat or use of force as means of settling international disputes." To accomplish this aim, "land, sea and air forces, as well as other war potential, will never be maintained." Further, the "right of belligerency of the state will not be recognized." [32] Such restrictions have undergone fundamental modification, however, in the years since ratification.

One of the more interesting aspects of MacArthur's efforts to reorient Japanese society was his attempt both to end the influence of Shinto militarism on the political life of Japan and to sponsor the propagation of Christianity. While his efforts on behalf of Christianity were largely unsuccessful, the General steadfastly insisted upon the importance of Christian doctrine to the "democratization" goal of the occupation. The Foreign Missions Conference of North America was assured that through its teaching "of the immutable principles of Christianity [it had] infused knowledge and understanding of the democratic concept [and an] appreciation of the basic tenets which govern our own free way of life." [33] A "Western" ideology long opposed to communism's "materialism," Christianity had an added attraction for MacArthur, for he viewed it as a spiritual force in opposition to Moscow's atheistic philosophy.

The Japanese economic miracle of the past decade or so has become one of the most widely admired phenomena of the postwar era. Immediately after the war Japan was faced with ruined cities, a destroyed industrial machine, declining agricultural production, and a critical shortage of raw materials. Mass starvation seemed the likely

---

[31] The constitution is reprinted in Reischauer, *The United States and Japan*, pp. 349–62.

[32] *Ibid.*, p. 351.

[33] Quoted in Lawrence S. Wittner, "MacArthur and the Missionaries: God and Man in Occupied Japan," *Pacific Historical Review* (Feb. 1971), p. 82.

consequence, and so the United States sent nearly a half a billion dollars a year to prevent such a catastrophe. Despite some early, and partially successful, American attempts to improve the Japanese economic picture by balancing the budget, controlling inflation, and eliminating the black market, it was the Korean War which provided the spark for the economic revival. With the United States once again deeply engaged in the Far East after June 1950, vast amounts of war supplies and services were purchased from the Japanese. Thus provided with capital, foreign markets, and exchange currency, capital investment soared. By the opening of the 1960s this economic resurgence, together with a series of agreements resolving Japan's reparations disputes, accounted for the fantastic economic boom which was to follow.

LIMITED WAR IN KOREA

The origins of the Korean War are closely associated with Korea's attempts to isolate herself from the aggressive designs of Japan, China, and Russia.[34] Strategically located on a peninsula in Northeast Asia, Korea was seen by all three as a gateway to Manchuria and as a source of year-round harbors. Victories in the Sino-Japanese War (1895) and the Russo-Japanese War (1904–05) resulted in Tokyo's ascendancy over the Hermit Kingdom; in 1910 Japan formally annexed the territory, renaming her colony Chosen. Within ten years of the takeover militant Korean nationalists engineered an unsuccessful effort to rescue their nation from foreign control and, once defeated, these insurgents fled to China where they established the Korean Provisional Government under the direction of Syngman Rhee. The very next year the Korean Communist Party was established by exiled Koreans living in Russia, and the Soviets actively cooperated by providing political and military training. By 1935 members of the Korean Communist Party had established themselves in the Northeastern portion of Chosen, working for the eventual removal of the imperialists.

Continuing Japanese control of Korea after the outbreak of the Second World War necessitated an Allied agreement on the eventual disposition of the region. At the 1943 Cairo Conference the United States, England, and China pledged that Korea would again become an independent nation: "The aforesaid three great powers, mindful of

[34] The author wishes to express his gratitude to the University of Pennsylvania Press for its permission to utilize material from his *The Korean War and American Politics* (Philadelphia: University of Pennsylvania Press, 1968).

the enslavement of the people of Korea, are determined that in due course Korea shall become free and independent." [35] While the 1945 Yalta Conference did not result in any formal agreement on Korea, Roosevelt and Stalin did discuss the concept of a trusteeship to help prepare the nation for self-rule. At Potsdam, however, the Soviets endorsed the Cairo Declaration as it related to Korean independence.

Only days after Russian entry into the Far Eastern phase of the war Soviet troops crossed into northeastern Korea, leading the United States to suggest that a line be drawn at the thirty-eighth parallel so as to facilitate the surrender of Japanese troops. Russia was to accept Japanese forces north of the line, while the United States was to be responsible for troops south of the demarcation. The thirty-eighth parallel had no justification beyond the immediate necessity of accepting the surrender of Japanese troops; the border was a temporary expedient, having no relation to natural boundaries, economics, or the history of the country. However, beneath the surface lurked the realization that in the absence of such a barrier the Soviet Union might easily have extended its influence throughout Korea.

Very serious problems arose as it became apparent that Moscow was regarding the line as a permanent political division. Between 1945 and 1947 the United States attempted to fulfill the Cairo and Potsdam pledges by seeking Russian acceptance of the removal of the boundary. Frustrated, the United States sought the aid of the United Nations, which in 1947 established the United Nations Temporary Commission on Korea. The commission was to sponsor a free, nationwide election and thus provide the basis for an independent government. Since Russia would not agree to supervised elections in the Soviet "zone," the United Nations limited its activities to what had emerged as South Korea. Elections were held in May of 1948 and at the end of the month the Korean Assembly was convened; in July Syngman Rhee was elected the republic's first president. Rhee had close personal ties with the United States—he had received a master's degree from Harvard and a doctorate in international relations from Princeton.

There were some intriguing parallels between Rhee's South Korea and Chiang's Nationalist China. Both nations were ruled by dictatorial, elitist, corrupt regimes; both governments were highly unstable; and both persecuted political dissidents, particularly communists, in a most ruthless manner. The internal disintegration of these regimes was slowed by American assistance. Chiang and Rhee

---

[35] The Cairo Declaration is reprinted in Leland M. Goodrich, *Korea: A Study of U.S. Policy in the United Nations* (New York: Council on Foreign Relations, 1956), p. 214.

were hardly averse to using such assistance to entrench their own positions rather than to support meaningful reform.

While the United States and the United Nations sought a political solution to the Korean impasse, Russia insisted that the Korean elections were illegal. In retaliation, the Democratic People's Republic of Korea, a Russian-dominated state in the North, was established with Kim Il Sung at its head. A member of the communist underground which had fought the Japanese, Sung had fled to Russia in 1938 and returned to Korea in 1945 as a major in the Russian occupational army.

With the formation of these two hostile governments, the United States and the Soviet Union began to remove their troops. Under guidelines set forth by the General Assembly, the United States withdrew all its forces with the exception of 500 American advisors who remained in South Korea after June of 1949 to train an army for the Republic of Korea. While the USSR claimed that it had completely removed all military personnel, some men were retained to develop the North Korean army. The period between the withdrawal of most American and Soviet troops and the invasion of South Korea was an uneasy time on the peninsula. North Korea harassed the republic to the south with a series of border disturbances, raids, and propaganda campaigns. So bitter was the rivalry that a United Nations Commission on Korea warned on September 8, 1949 of the danger of a "barbarous civil war." [36]

Rhee was hardly inactive. His determination to march north was well known and was made credible by his ambitious, if unfulfilled, military plans. Although the United States provided South Korea with military assistance and $110 million for economic rehabilitation, the Administration was so apprehensive of Rhee's designs on the North that it withheld such potentially offensive material as tanks, planes, and heavy guns. The Soviets showed no such reticence; at the time of the invasion the North Koreans were the dominant military power. However, revisionist historians Joyce and Gabriel Kolko have concluded from official American accounts that the expansion of the North Korean defensive army began after January 1950—that is, after Rhee's plans for unquestioned military superiority on the peninsula had become a threat.

> Although the North Korean military build-up prior to June has always been interpreted as proof of aggressive intent, in fact it was more a response to the military imbalance of power that Rhee and the United States had created during 1949 and 1950, the aggressive declarations of Seoul, and the possibility of further military growth in the south.

[36] *New York Times*, 9 Sept. 1949, p. 1.

According to this thesis, as late as April 1950, the North Korean "military build-up was designed mainly to restore military equilibrium in the region." It was only when the communists became convinced that Rhee's dictatorial government would not disintegrate and therefore constituted an imminent threat that the North decided upon a military solution.[37] The Kolkos do not explain how, six months after the massive buildup began, the North was able to achieve such an impressive margin of military superiority.

Related to the issue of South Korea's military preparedness is a consideration of the degree of responsibility the United States must bear for the attack on South Korea. Often mentioned is the precipitous American withdrawal of troops from the area and the failure to provide a military establishment which could match the one sponsored by the Russians in the northern sector of the peninsula. In September of 1947 the Joint Chiefs of Staff decided to remove American forces from Korea because of two military considerations: the area was not of sufficient military importance to warrant American continuance; given America's general manpower shortage the troops stationed in Korea could be more strategically deployed elsewhere. The position of the Joint Chiefs of Staff, together with the Russian announcement of the withdrawal of troops from North Korea, led to Truman's decision in the spring of 1949 that American forces should leave. There is, nevertheless, much merit in the charge that the Administration was overly complacent regarding South Korean security. In response to an appeal by the American Federation of Labor to maintain a minimum of 5,000 troops as a symbol of "America's determination to safeguard Korean national independence," the Administration gave assurances of the symbolic importance of the 500-man advisory group. This force, plus military equipment and economic aid (the latter was still under consideration) "should go a long way toward establishment of the new Republic on a sound base and deter overt moves on the part of neighboring powers." [38]

The Republican party, which was so critical of America's lack of military preparedness in Korea, was largely responsible for that condition. The economy-minded, Republican-dominated Eightieth Congress had sharply cut defense spending in 1947 and 1948; the army was the chief victim of the austerity program, and at the time of the North Korean invasion there were only one and one-third divisions in the United States. Truman has bitterly noted that the

---

[37] Kolko, *The Limits of Power*, pp. 573–74.

[38] Quotations from Smith, *Dean Acheson*, p. 175. Also see John W. Spanier, *The Truman-MacArthur Controversy and the Korean War* (New York: Norton, 1965), pp. 17–18, and Robert E. Osgood, *Limited War: The Challenge to American Strategy* (Chicago: University of Chicago Press, 1957), pp. 167–68.

Congress took four months to approve his request for $150 million in economic aid to Korea in fiscal 1949. When he requested an additional $60 million in the 1950–51 budget he was turned down by the House, with most of the negative votes cast by members of the Republican party.[39] The funds were approved only with the passage of the combined Korea-China aid bill.

Administration critics have often pointed to Secretary of State Acheson's now infamous "defense perimeter" speech as a major factor encouraging the North Koreans to attack. The Secretary, in an address to the National Press Club in January of 1950, had stated that in the Pacific the protective arm of the United States extended from the Aleutians to Japan, through Okinawa to the Philippines. The areas not included within this perimeter, such as Korea and Formosa, must depend upon the United Nations and their own provisions for defense: "the initial reliance must be on the people attacked to resist it and then upon the commitments of the entire civilized world under the Charter of the United Nations." [40] Acheson's critics notwithstanding, it should be remembered that the Secretary did not necessarily rule out American intervention on behalf of those nations outside the perimeter, particularly under the aegis of the United Nations. Furthermore, it is naive to assume either that the Russians were unaware of American military weakness in the Korean area, or that the West would under all circumstances accept a communist offensive against an Asian nation. The January 26, 1950, mutual defense pact signed by Washington and Seoul was a significant, and prophetic, indication of American intentions.

At four o'clock in the morning of June 25, 1950 (Far Eastern time), the Communists of North Korea attacked the Republic to the south. In the absence of specific documentation, any conclusion regarding the motivation for the invasion must be tentative and conjectural. It is, nevertheless, logical to assume that given the pervasive Soviet involvement in the political and military affairs of North Korea, Kim Il Sung's government did not itself initiate the attack. From the very outset of the war Secretary of State Acheson was certain that the Soviets had conceived the offensive as part of a "grand design" to affect adversely Western influence and to undermine the European balance of power. Should America choose not to take a firm stand, its position among its Allies and the uncommitted nations

[39] For a study of the Republican party's response to the Korean War, see Caridi, *The Korean War and American Politics*. Also Caridi, "The G.O.P. and Korea," *Pacific Historical Review*, Nov. 1968.

[40] Dean Acheson, "Crisis in Asia—An Examination of U.S. Policy," Department of State *Bulletin*, XXII (Jan. 23, 1950), p. 116.

would be weakened. Conversely, Acheson theorized that an overreaction would most probably bring Russia into the war, bog down American power in Asia, and thus render Europe—the most important battleground—vulnerable.[41]

Soviet strategy in Korea would appear to have been closely linked to American designs for postwar Japan, for the apparent willingness of the United States by 1949 to ignore Russian objections and to conclude a separate peace treaty with Japan signaled a new role in Asia for both Tokyo and Washington. Japan would not for long remain a demilitarized state, and the United States, through air, land, and naval bases in Japan, would increase its impact in the Pacific. The Soviet Union realized that a North Korean victory would go far toward reversing the growing American influence in Asia. The military superiority of the North, and the absence of a firm commitment by the United States to protect Rhee, presaged well for a quick victory. Relatedly, although the extent of Chinese Communist participation in the attack plan remains in doubt, research undertaken by the RAND Corporation indicates that while Communist China knew of the Soviet strategy, it was not directly involved in its formulation.[42]

There exists some evidence that the North Korean attack was more limited in scope and intent than is usually assumed. It has been noted, for example, that in attacking during the monsoon season the North Koreans weakened the potential effectiveness of their air power and tank force. The assault may have been directed toward Seoul only, for it has been estimated that perhaps one-half of Pyongyang's troops and a quarter of its tanks were utilized: "both the manner in which [the North Koreans] deployed their troops, and the expected resistance of the defenders, suggest that [they] had embarked on a limited war to capture the Seoul region and shake loose Rhee's government." [43] Such an interpretation is not, however, widely shared and most accounts accept the theory of an all-out Communist assault to unify the peninsula.

President Truman was spending the weekend with his family in Independence, Missouri, when news reached him of the invasion; he has written that while flying back to Washington he

> felt certain that if South Korea was allowed to fall Communist leaders would be emboldened to override nations closer to our own shores. If the Communists were permitted to force their way into the Republic of Korea without opposition from the free world, no small nation would

[41] Smith, *Dean Acheson*, p. 189.

[42] This analysis is in a study prepared for the United States Air Force by the RAND Corporation. Allen S. Whiting, *China Crosses the Yalu: The Decision to Enter the Korean War* (New York: Macmillan, 1960), pp. 34–46.

[43] Kolko, *The Limits of Power*, p. 578.

have the courage to resist threats and aggression by stronger Communist neighbors. If this was allowed to go unchallenged it would mean a third world war, just as similar incidents had brought on the second world war.[44]

This conviction (it was not yet known as the "domino theory") was shared by the political leadership of both parties in the war's first phase.

The Security Council met Sunday afternoon, June 25, at the request of the United States. The Russian delegate was absent from this session because of a Soviet protest against the Council's refusal to seat Red China. With a Russian veto precluded, the Council unanimously passed a formal resolution calling for: (1) the immediate cessation of hostilities; (2) the withdrawal of the North Korean army to the thirty-eighth parallel; and (3) the cooperation of all United Nations members in carrying out these demands.

The very next day Truman decided to move beyond the Security Council's resolution by providing air and sea cover for South Korean forces, by utilizing General MacArthur's naval and air forces to attack North Korea's positions south of the thirty-eighth parallel, and by sending the Seventh Fleet into the Formosa Straits to prevent an attack on Chiang's island stronghold. While the announcement of official United States policy was made at 12:30 P.M., June 27, it was not until later that same day that the Security Council requested member nations to "furnish such assistance to the Republic of Korea as may be necessary to repel the armed attack and to restore the international peace and security in the area." [45] The Russians were again absent for this crucial vote, which was witnessed by 1,200 of the more than 6,000 persons who attempted to attend the historic session. Moscow's cumbersome decision-making process seems to have prevented Soviet delegate Jacob Malik from attending the meeting and vetoing the resolution for military assistance to Rhee. At a luncheon earlier that afternoon, United Nations Secretary General Trygve Lie told Malik that it was in the interest of his government to participate in the afternoon meeting. Malik's "No, I will not go there" caused the American representative to experience inexpressible relief. It was, nevertheless, the intention of Secretary Lie to bring the matter before the full General Assembly in the event of a Soviet veto.[46]

[44] Truman, *Memoirs*, II, p. 379. The most complete account of the decision-making process that led to American intervention in the war is to be found in Glenn D. Paige, *The Korean Decision* (New York: Free Press, 1968).

[45] Bartlett, *The Record of American Diplomacy*, p. 769. For a "revisionist" account of the role of the United States in actions taken by the Security Council, see I. F. Stone, *The Hidden History of the Korean War*, 2nd ed. (New York: Monthly Review Press, 1969), pp. 75–81.

[46] The theory regarding Malik's absence from the June 27 meeting from Paige, *The Korean Decision*, pp. 202–3. The Malik quotation from Trygve Lie, *In the Cause of Peace* (New York: Macmillan, 1954), p. 333.

The extent and nature of the newly mandated United Nations "assistance" proved to be one of the most hotly debated issues of the war. Within a week of the Security Council's resolution MacArthur informed Truman that the Communist advance could only be halted with the use of American ground troops. The President responded to this plea on June 30 by escalating the war through the introduction of such forces, by permitting American planes to attack North Korea, and by imposing a naval blockade. Never without critics, Truman and Acheson have been charged with deliberately widening the war for purely political purposes. A "moderate" crisis, it is suggested, would have been of great value "in getting numerous global projects [particularly European and nuclear armament] out of an indifferent and hostile Congress." [47] It would have also served to defuse political opponents charging that the Administration was "soft" on Asian communism.

By the end of the first week of July the United Nations declared that all forces repelling the invasion would be placed under a unified command; that the United States would name the commander (Truman immediately chose MacArthur); and that the United Nations' banner would be flown beside the various national flags.[48] The United States was now faced with a grim dilemma: how to contain the North Koreans while, at the same time, avoiding an all-out, possibly nuclear, war.

The solution was a "limited war," defined by Henry A. Kissinger as a war "fought for specific political objectives which, by their very existence, tend to establish a relationship between the force employed and the goal to be attained. It reflects and attempts to *affect* the opponents's will, not to *crush* it, to make the conditions to be imposed seem more attractive than continued resistance, to strive for specific goals and not for complete annihilation." [49] All wars have significant political implications. But a "limited war" is a highly political phenomenon. It is particularly frustrating because the military is restrained by the political concerns of the home government to an even greater extent than in "conventional" warfare.

In the main, it would seem reasonable to conclude that the United States decided to conduct a limited operation for three reasons: (1) it did not want to provoke Russia into beginning a third world war; (2) it was afraid that if it extended itself in Korea the free

---

[47] Kolko, *The Limits of Power*, p. 580.

[48] *New York Times*, 8 July 1950, p. 1.

[49] Henry A. Kissinger, *Nuclear Weapons and Foreign Policy* (New York: Harper & Row, 1957), pp. 140–41.

world would be vulnerable to attack elsewhere—particularly Europe; and (3) its allies were extremely hesitant to expand the war.

UNIFICATION BY FORCE

By late summer, 1950, the North Koreans seemed close to their goal of unification. The advantage gained by the surprise attack, the clear superiority of the Communist forces over those of South Korea, and the delay in organizing the counteroffensive led to the retreat of United Nations forces to the southern tip of the Korean peninsula. It was feared that one more effective thrust by the enemy would push the defenders into the sea. But just at this critical juncture General MacArthur staged a brilliant amphibious landing behind enemy lines at Inchon, a port city near the western end of the thirty-eighth parallel. The success of MacArthur's surprise attack of September 15 led to a spectacularly swift march north. Part of the United Nations force crossed the Han River as early as September 20, and after intense fighting from the fifteenth to the twenty-seventh of September, Seoul was recaptured. On October 1 the initial wave of South Korean troops crossed the thirty-eighth parallel to pursue the retreating North Koreans.

In less than 15 days the nature of the Korean War had changed, for as a result of the General's great victory the United Nations altered (at least temporarily) its war aims. Once satisfied with achieving the pre-war status quo, the organization now sought the reunification of Korea. The decision to cross the parallel greatly increased the possibility of Red China's entry into the war. Yet the temptation to exploit a great victory, plus the desire to accomplish the long-standing United Nations' goal of unifying Korea, caused the policymakers to underestimate China's reaction to the movement of American troops toward its border.

The United States must bear considerable, if not primary, responsibility for this shift in United Nations policy since the Administration unilaterally decided to attempt the military unification of Korea. Truman candidly admits in his *Memoirs* that he had given his approval to the Joint Chiefs of Staff to send MacArthur new instructions on September 27 informing him that his military objective was " 'the destruction of the North Korean Armed Forces.' " To attain this objective, MacArthur was authorized to conduct military operations north of the thirty-eighth parallel unless Soviet or Chinese Communist forces entered the war, or threatened to do so.[50] Two

---

[50]Truman, *Memoirs*, II, p. 411.

weeks later, on October 7, a formal General Assembly resolution gave the Commander indirect authorization to cross the parallel and unify the country. This resolution was very much the product of American thinking, and the actual phrasing had been chosen, for the most part, by Acheson with the approval of the President.[51] As passed, the resolution authorized "all constituent acts be taken, including the holding of elections, under the auspices of the United Nations for the establishment of a unified, independent and democratic government in the sovereign state of Korea." [52]

In *Mandate for Change*, Eisenhower defended the Korean armistice on the grounds that it was in accordance with the *original* aims of the United Nations. Very much aware that the goals of the international organization had temporarily changed, Eisenhower reminded his readers that "Our nation and the United Nations went into Korea for one reason only, to repel aggression and restore the borders of the Republic of Korea—not to reunite Korea by force." [53] Yet for a time the reunification of Korea by force was precisely the policy Truman had decided to follow. The Administration's optimism was infectious; spurred on by the new aims of the General Assembly, United Nations forces moved closer and closer to the Chinese border. By the middle of October, Pyongyang, the capital of North Korea, was captured. But as the Allies moved north, the Communist Chinese filtered south. At the end of October came the first signs of direct Chinese intervention: a captured Chinese prisoner on the twenty-sixth; 16 captured Chinese on the thirtieth; and evidence on the thirty-first that a whole regiment had crossed the Yalu River by train two weeks earlier. MIG-15's were encountered on the first day of November, and in the early days of that month there were signs of Chinese intervention everywhere.[54] MacArthur sounded the alarm in a November 6 letter to the Joint Chiefs of Staff: "Men and material in large force are pouring across all bridges over the Yalu from Manchuria. This movement . . . threatens the ultimate destruction of the forces under my command." [55]

One of the most hotly debated issues of the war involved MacArthur's decision to pursue the unification attempt despite a clear warning early in November of Chinese intervention. The United Nations continued its offensive, and one is left to ask: why did Truman

[51] Richard E. Neustadt, *Presidential Power: The Politics of Leadership* (New York: John Wiley, 1960), p. 124.

[52] *New York Times*, 8 Oct. 1950, pp. 1, 6; text, 5 Oct. 1950, p. 10.

[53] Eisenhower, *Mandate for Change*, p. 241.

[54] For an account of this buildup, see Richard H. Rovere and Arthur M. Schlesinger, Jr., *The MacArthur Controversy and American Foreign Policy* (New York: Farrar, Straus & Giroux, 1965), p. 137.

[55] Quoted in Truman, *Memoirs*, II, p. 427.

permit MacArthur to continue north?; why did the General not heed the seemingly obvious warnings of the Chinese? Richard Neustadt's *Presidential Power* contains a fairly extensive analysis of the first question, and his conclusion is, in part, that Truman did not take the initiative in halting the General's advance because at the urging of his advisers he had "tied himself to unification." [56] MacArthur had done better than most had expected in the Inchon campaign and the Administration sought a similar triumph at the Yalu. Also, official Washington was unwilling to have it said that it was the timidity of the Democratic party, rather than aggression from Peking, which halted the Far East Commander. One must also consider that since Inchon the General's political stock had been on the rise while the Democrats' prestige, particularly after the November midterm elections, was falling rapidly. MacArthur could count upon much Congressional support at a time when the Congress was growing increasingly skeptical of the President's handling of the war.

Predictably, revisionist historians have offered dissenting critiques of the decision to unify Korea by moving to the Yalu. William Appleman Williams sees the decision as a naked attempt to realize a turn-of-the-century objective: the elimination from Korea of Russian and Japanese influence. Tokyo had been removed by World War II, and a more moderate confrontation would complete the exit of elements hostile to American political and economic interests in the area. American policymakers, according to Williams, were certain that an expanded war would not lead to mainland China's intervention. They based their strategy on the conviction that China and Russia were "natural enemies" and in a crisis China would align itself with the United States.[57] Joyce and Gabriel Kolko have concluded that a continuation of the crisis was required to achieve Truman's European objectives. The President, in the late summer and early fall, had unsuccessfully attempted to win Congressional approval of a widely expanded military program for the defense of Europe and other areas of strategic importance. A quick ending of the Korean War would have provided an obvious temptation to utilize military cutbacks as an issue in the 1950 Congressional elections. "Truman did not want war in Korea, but he did not want peace too quickly either. . . . In this context, MacArthur was to remain the master of the situation." [58]

The self-styled liberal journalist turned muckraker, I. F. Stone, had reached the same conclusion 20 years prior to the publication of

[56] Neustadt, *Presidential Power*, pp. 143–47.
[57] Williams, *The Tragedy of American Diplomacy*, rev. ed., pp. 301–2.
[58] Kolko, *The Limits of Power*, p. 598.

the Kolko study. In his *The Hidden History of the Korean War,* Stone argued that the Red scare and the Korean War provided the Truman Administration with powerful propaganda to win public and Congressional approval of relief and reconstruction efforts abroad and rearmament at home. "Those who would not be moved by pity or moral obligation to alleviate suffering abroad could be frightened into appropriations by fear of Communism. Powerful domestic interests ready to combat enlarged expenditure for social purposes could be led to acquiesce readily . . . if it took the profitable form of an armament boom." Hence, according to Stone, Truman was utilizing the containment of communism issue to control the opposition party. The journalist further charged that since Truman wanted something less than war but more than peace, he was in a poor position to restrain the single-minded MacArthur. The "crossing of the 38th Parallel, the demand for 'unconditional surrender,' and the provocative advance to the Chinese and Russian borders must be read in light of Truman's fear of peace." [59]

There is not much debate over General MacArthur's motivation for wishing to pursue the enemy still further north. In 1964 he published his memoirs and in them the General explained: "The danger was that by meeting naked force with appeasement we would not only perpetrate military disaster in Korea, but would enable Communism to make its bid for most of Asia." [60] It is now clear that for a variety of reasons the decision to move north after the Inchon success impelled China to enter the war. These reasons include: the desire to preserve North Korea as a political, rather than a territorial, entity; the hope of dissuading Japan from signing its impending peace treaty with the United States; Mao's awareness that his prestige in Asia was at stake; and Red China's desire to keep an ideological enemy, the United States, from further encroachments upon Asian territory.[61]

The massive infusion of Chinese Communist troops south of the Yalu, in MacArthur's view, had created "an entirely new war against an entirely new power . . . under entirely new conditions." [62] The bitter controversy between the Commander and the President which developed after the Chinese intervention was the product of their widely divergent solutions to the crisis; to an equally large extent, it was the product of MacArthur's decision to publicly attack Truman's

---

[59] Stone, *The Hidden History of the Korean War,* pp. 106–7.

[60] Douglas MacArthur, *Reminiscences* (New York: McGraw-Hill, 1964), p. 370.

[61] Whiting, *China Crosses the Yalu,* pp. 151–62.

[62] Quoted in Truman, *Memoirs,* II, p. 447. The best study of the controversy is Spanier, *The Truman-MacArthur Controversy.*

foreign policy. Briefly put, MacArthur insisted that the Administration, through the Joint Chiefs of Staff, had placed intolerable burdens upon him in his direction of the war. To secure victory, he proposed that the United States blockade the Chinese coast; that China's industrial centers, supply bases, and communications network be bombed from the air; that Chiang Kai-shek's offer to send his Nationalist troops to Korea be accepted; and that the possibility of a counterinvasion by Chiang against the mainland of China at least be considered.[63] The President, his advisors, and the Joint Chiefs of Staff argued that such a course would threaten a third world war. America's allies concurred with this assessment, and the General was left with the support of some of the more conservative members of the Republican party.

MacArthur had responded to the pressures of fighting the Korean War by rejecting the very concept of limited war and by calling for total victory against the enemy. The Administration (somewhat self-righteously in light of its unfortunate decision to move to the Yalu after the General's success at Inchon) insisted that the United States had entered the Korean conflict to protect and preserve the political and territorial sovereignty of the Republic of Korea against attacks from the Communist North. Had MacArthur limited his disagreement to communications with the Joint Chiefs he probably would not have been dismissed by the President. Unfortunately, on a number of occasions in March 1951, he boldly and publicly challenged the President's policy; such a challenge was not only a personal embarrassment to the Commander in Chief, it was also a threat to the entire concept of civilian authority over the military.

In late March, just as the United Nations and President Truman were seeking to arrange a cease-fire, MacArthur issued a statement of his own in which he threatened to attack Red China and thereby achieve the political objectives of the United Nations. Truman, vowing that he would not tolerate the General's insubordination any longer, decided to oust him. But before this could be accomplished, Joseph Martin, the Republican Minority Leader in the House, released a letter from MacArthur challenging the entire concept of limited war: "if we lose this war to Communism in Asia the fall of Europe is inevitable, win it and Europe most probably would avoid war and yet preserve freedom . . . we must win. There is no substitute for victory."[64] Such challenges to civilian authority could not go

---

[63] See Dec. 30, 1950 letter from MacArthur to the Joint Chiefs of Staff, reprinted in MacArthur, *Reminiscences*, p. 379.

[64] Quoted in Truman, *Memoirs*, II, p. 505. It is discussed in Trumbull Higgins, *Korea and the Fall of MacArthur: A Précis in Limited War* (New York: Oxford University Press, 1960).

unanswered and so after meeting with Secretary of State Acheson, General Marshall, General Omar Bradley, and Ambassador Averell Harriman, the President called a press conference on April 11 and revealed his decision to relieve MacArthur of his command.

The return of the almost mythical MacArthur after a nearly 14-year absence aroused a popular response that had rarely, if ever, been witnessed in the United States. The General was mobbed by a huge, demonstrative crowd on his arrival in San Francisco; many of the demonstrators carried signs reading "MacArthur for President." Two days later the General addressed the Congress and attacked the Administration's handling of the war. "War's very object is victory— not prolonged indecision. In war, indeed, there can be no substitute for victory." [65] MacArthur insisted that those who sought to appease Red China were blinding themselves to the clear lesson of history that appeasement can only result in bloodier warfare. The effect of the speech was sensational; Representative Dewey Short of Missouri exclaimed: "We heard God speak here today, God in the flesh, the voice of God." [66] Popular enthusiasm for the General waned very slowly, and pollster Louis Harris found that in 1952 Eisenhower and MacArthur were the two most admired living Americans.[67]

THE REPUBLICAN PEACE

The hero's speech to the Congress was followed by the so-called MacArthur Hearings (the General testified for a scant three days) which began on May 3 and ended a month and a half later. The psychological appeal of the MacArthur program was that it served as a welcome relief from the subtleties of limited war. His warmest supporters were those Republicans who shared the conviction that for all intents and purposes the United States was already at war with Red China; these individuals were unwilling to take seriously the Administration's warning of possible Russian intervention. Secretary of Defense Marshall was the chief spokesman of the Administration's fear that Soviet troops might invade Western Europe once the United States was heavily engaged in the Far East. Acheson took a similar position.[68] In perhaps the most quoted observation of the hearings,

---

[65] MacArthur, *Reminiscences*, p. 404.

[66] See David Rees, *Korea: The Limited War* (New York: St. Martin's, 1964), p. 227.

[67] Louis Harris, *Is There a Republican Majority?* (New York: Harper & Row, 1954), p. 56.

[68] For the Marshall and Acheson testimony, see United States Congress, *Military Situation in the Far East, Hearings Before the Joint Senate Committee on Armed Services and Foreign Relations,* 82nd Cong., 1st Sess. (Washington, D.C.: Government Printing Office, 1951), pp. 325, 1718.

General Bradley declared that MacArthur's Red China/Korea strategy "would involve us in the wrong war, at the wrong place, at the
wrong time, and with the wrong enemy." [69] But after more than two
million words of testimony, the Republicans issued a Minority Report
endorsing the philosophy of the former Commander and charging
that, by contrast, the Truman Administration had no plan to win.

By July the hearings had faded into history and MacArthur had
retired to New York's Waldorf Towers. But American and South
Korean troops remained stalemated just north of the thirty-eighth
parallel. As a result of Communist overtures late in June, truce talks
began at Kaesong on July 10 (after several months of fruitless
negotiation, they were moved to Panmunjom, a site midway between
the two battle positions). The talks remained deadlocked over the
prisoners-of-war issue throughout the fall, and so a frustrating peace
conference, plus mounting casualties in a bloody stalemated war,
provided the grim backdrop for the 1952 Presidential election.

The Republicans gained an insurmountable advantage in the
contest by their selection of General Dwight D. Eisenhower, the
enormously popular World War II hero. Having defeated Senator
Robert Taft's bid for the nomination and neatly side-stepped MacArthur's formula for victory, Eisenhower was highly successful in his
"crusade" to convince the American public that he was uniquely
qualified to bring the war to an honorable conclusion. In their party
platform the Republicans charged that after abandoning South Korea
and announcing that that hapless land remained outside the American "defense perimeter," the United States refused to fight in a
manner which would achieve its objectives. John Foster Dulles, who
wrote the foreign policy plank, charged that the Democrats offered no
hope of victory. MacArthur, of course, delivered the keynote address,
in which he warned against entering wars without the will to win.

To Democratic candidate Adlai E. Stevenson fell the politically
impossible task of defeating a folk hero while the Democrats were
engaged in a seemingly fruitless land war in Asia. Waging a low-keyed
campaign against great odds, Stevenson supported the Truman-Acheson policy in Korea; his intelligence and his sincerity won him the
warm regard of millions of Americans. As the campaign progressed
Eisenhower leaned more and more heavily on his record as a
successful general to assure the public that only he could unravel the
Korean knot. This aspect of the campaign climaxed in Detroit on
October 24 when the General pledged an honorable solution to the
war. "That job requires a personal trip to Korea. . . . I shall make
that trip. . . . I shall go to Korea." [70]

While Eisenhower sought votes on the strength of his appeal as

[69] *Ibid.*, p. 732.
[70] *New York Times*, 25 Oct. 1952, p. 8.

the candidate best able to end the war, he took a distinctly moderate position. He rejected both the isolationism of former President Herbert Hoover (who was much criticized for his "Fortress America" position) and the militancy of Senator Taft, who was advocating reliance upon retaliatory air striking power. Eisenhower also rejected MacArthur's "there is no substitute for victory" approach. Equally important, while many in his party had been insisting that Korea must be unified if the peace was to be honorable, Eisenhower never once supported this view. The Republican candidate ignored the pitfall of unification and wisely avoided any reference to the exact nature of his "honorable settlement."

The American people registered an impressive victory for the General, who won 55 percent of the total votes cast; the electoral count was 442–89. It is important not to overemphasize the Korean War as an issue in the 1952 election. Eisenhower the man, the crusader in Europe, was a powerful positive force.[71] And too, the election was influenced by many issues—charges of corruption and communism in government, McCarthyism, inflation, taxation, social-ism, and Korea.

As President, Eisenhower achieved peace in Korea by treading a tortuous route between his desire to terminate rather than to expand the war and his belief that unless the Communists were threatened with the use of force they would never agree to a settlement satisfactory to the United Nations Command. As a first step, the new President ordered that the Seventh Fleet no longer be employed to "shield" Communist China from Chiang's forces on Formosa. The obvious implication in this announcement, despite Eisenhower's disavowal of aggressive intent, was that the Administration would not shrink from threatening the Communists with an extension of the war. The "unleashing" of Chiang was at this point clearly a symbolic gesture, but it left open the possibility of increased military aid to Formosa should there be a decision to attack the mainland.

Yet the war continued stalemated. The President's next move was far more dramatic. In May of 1953 the Administration informed India's Prime Minister Jawaharlal Nehru and others of its intention to expand the war through the use of atomic weapons if the negotiations were not brought to a successful conclusion. This decision very significantly influenced the termination of the war. The apparent unwillingness of the Communists in the spring and early summer of 1953 to risk an expanded conflict made the settlement possible.[72]

[71] See Angus Campbell *et al., The Voter Decides* (Evanston, Ill.: Row, Peterson, 1954), pp. 56–58.

[72] Eisenhower's decision to threaten the use of atomic weapons is discussed in Eisenhower,

There can be little doubt that the Administration transmitted to the United Nations Command its intention to use atomic weapons. General Mark Clark, Commander in Chief of the United Nations forces, was informed that if the Panmunjom truce talks remained stalemated he was to "prosecute the war along lines we had not taken to make the Communists wish they had accepted our terms." This new concept very much appealed to the commanding general, who has written that these orders "sounded more like the American way of doing business." [73]

The threat of atomic warfare was not the only element influencing the armistice. The at least partial settlement of the prisoners of war issue in April 1953 was an important factor leading to the final settlement. In his study of the Panmunjom talks, William Vatcher has offered several reasons for the changed attitude of the Chinese Communists on the prisoner issue: the fear that the Administration would allow the forces of Nationalist China to fight in Korea; the inability of the communists to obtain further propaganda from the conference; the economic strain of the Korean War on the Chinese economy; the fear that China's increased prestige might be lost in an expanded war; and the death of Stalin in March.[74]

Finally, at 10:00 A.M., July 27 (Korean time) the Senior United Nations Command Delegate and the Senior Communist Delegate signed 18 copies of the armistice agreement without saying a word to one another. The armistice had come about in part because Eisenhower, willing to accept a settlement which reflected the basic aims of the recently discredited Truman Administration, did not seek to unify Korea by force. The General also wisely decided not to attempt to utilize the Korean War to settle other pressing problems of the Far East. Had Truman signed such an armistice, he would have been denounced by the GOP and by the general public. Yet while Eisenhower suffered the attacks of several conservative members of his party who had hoped for a clear-cut victory, he won the sincere gratitude of the American people.

The armistice did not result in the unification of the embattled peninsular nation. By July 30, 1953, both sides had withdrawn to positions on either side of a demilitarized zone which ran just north of the thirty-eighth parallel; these positions are still occupied by

---

Mandate for Change, pp. 229–32. Also in Sherman Adams, *Firsthand Report* (New York: Harper & Row 1961), p. 48, and C. Turner Joy, *How Communists Negotiate* (New York: Macmillan, 1955), pp. 161–62.

[73] Both quotations in Mark W. Clark, *From the Danube to the Yalu* (New York: Harper & Row, 1954), p. 257.

[74] William Vatcher, *Panmunjom* (New York: Praeger, 1958), pp. 177–78.

communist and anti-communist forces. At Geneva, from April 26 to July 15, 1954, the Big Four considered Korean unification but could not agree on a formula. The Allies insisted that elections be supervised by the United Nations, while the communists would agree only to a joint commission consisting of equal representatives of North and South Korea. On this issue the conference deadlocked. In 1958 the North Korean and Communist Chinese governments sent notes to those countries which had contributed to the United Nations Command, claiming that Chinese troops had been withdrawn from the peninsula and insisting that the United Nations withdraw from Korea as well. Consideration of the unification of the country, it was announced, depended upon such a withdrawal. Yet in 1972, after extensive and largely private preliminary negotiations, there appeared some hopeful signs that a negotiated settlement of outstanding problems might eventually lead to a peaceful unification.

The Korean War was uncommonly grim. It was fought on difficult terrain by soldiers often demoralized by an inconclusive struggle and flagging home support. Even when news of the armistice reached the battlefield there was no repetition of the joyful celebrations which followed the conclusion of the Second World War. General Matthew B. Ridgway has written in his history of the war that when informed of the armistice his men "just grinned at each other or flopped wearily on the ground." [75] At home the news was greeted with sighs of relief, not unmixed with a bitter sense of frustration—despite the death of more than 23,000 Americans and the expenditure of nearly $20 billion, the war had ended where it had begun. But there were important lessons learned about the nature of limited war and the objectives of the great powers. Perhaps most important of all, the war had accomplished its most fundamental objective: the North Koreans had been contained without engulfing the world in a nuclear holocaust.

The armistice deeply disturbed a nation accustomed to thinking of itself as preeminent. The resultant bitterness took the form of an increasingly rigid Asian policy. Although the Korean War greatly enhanced Peking's standing in Asia, mainland China was stubbornly rejected as the legitimate government of the Chinese people. Instead, the United States made commitments to Formosa which greatly exaggerated the island's strategic value. The war did convince American policymakers of the tremendous potential importance of

[75] Matthew B. Ridgway, *The Korean War* (New York: Doubleday, 1967), p. 225.

Japan in the struggle to contain Asian communism. It so sensitized the public to the danger of Asian communism, however, that the American leadership was all but relieved of the responsibility of distinguishing between those threats which were of legitimate concern and those which were not.

Seven

THE FRUITS
OF REALIGNMENT

The most important consequence of the Second World War was the collapse of the established power structure and the emergence of two very delicately balanced superpowers, the United States and the Soviet Union. The older structure had included Germany, Japan, and Italy (the Axis nations), and France, England, the Soviet Union, and the United States (the Allies); of these seven, five had been either conquered or fundamentally weakened by the political, economic, and social consequences of the war. Early in the post-war period the leaders of several neutral nations and declining powers—especially, General Charles de Gaulle of France—optimistically anticipated that a loose coalition of the world's lesser states would provide a meaningful counterweight to the two giants. Yet the world has continued to be dominated by the attitudes and policies of the superpowers.[1] The United Nations, regional defense pacts, and the like have not been without influence, but neither have they greatly affected the fundamental realignment which was the major consequence of World War II.

[1] For a discussion of the "Third World" concept of de Gaulle and others, see Steel, *Pax Americana*, Chap. V.

The standoff resolution of the Korean War has been offered as evidence that by the mid-1950s the United States and the Soviet Union were still quite evenly matched; the balance of fear which had so regrettably become the world's legacy was clearly preferable to the return of open warfare. Although deeply engaged in Asia during the Korean conflict, Washington expended billions of dollars to contain Soviet expansion in Europe. The economic integration of Western Europe was a major American goal in the 1950s. The creation of the Jewish state of Israel in the midst of openly hostile Arab neighbors greatly heightened the instability of the Middle East. Egypt's capture of the Suez Canal, coupled with Anglo-French and Soviet willingness to capitalize on the instability of the area, created a situation which remains a continuing threat to the existing order. The emergence of a number of African nations from colonial status precipitated a series of conflicts on that continent, and the determination of these nations to end their colonial status at a time when many seemed incapable of achieving internal stability posed a cruel dilemma for American policymakers. Finally, in Guatemala, Cuba, and the Dominican Republic the United States was forced to choose between security considerations and the right of other nations to determine their own destinies under governments of their own choosing.

DULLES THE COLD WARRIOR: SOPHISTICATION AND EVANGELISM

American diplomacy in the first full decade after the close of the Second World War was inevitably dominated by President Dwight D. Eisenhower and his Secretary of State, John Foster Dulles. Long sought by both parties, Eisenhower finally agreed to make his bid for the Presidency in 1952 as a Republican because of his conviction that the national consensus had been lost on domestic, and more importantly, foreign policy. Trained in the military and imbued with its ethos, the new President placed a high premium on national unity and the maintenance of the status quo.[2] The diplomatic milieu of the 1950s was profoundly influenced by the Administration's perception of a world threatened by two monolithic blocs, each competing for predominance. Every diplomatic issue was seen as influencing this competition, and an abiding distrust was displayed toward those nations which hoped to remain neutral. In his second term, however,

[2] A perceptive analysis is David B. Capitanchik, *The Eisenhower Presidency and American Foreign Policy* (London: Routledge and Kegan Paul, 1969).

Eisenhower did pay increasing attention to the possibility of a rapprochement with the Soviet Union.

If the President's hope for an accommodation with Moscow increased during his tenure in office, his Secretary of State continued to favor a more stark and suspicious outlook. The grandson of Benjamin Harrison's Secretary of State and the nephew of Woodrow Wilson's, Dulles has often been regarded as the most thoroughly prepared of the nation's diplomatic stewards; he is also often viewed as the Secretary who most ambitiously and single-mindedly sought his appointment. There can be no doubt as to his preparation: he served the administrations of Wilson, Franklin Roosevelt, and Truman, and worked with all five Secretaries of State from Cordell Hull to Dean Acheson. Dulles' key role in the negotiations leading to the Japanese peace treaty won him international acclaim. In the early postwar period he was clearly the chief policy formulator for the GOP.

Yet there were very serious drawbacks, as well as assets, to his appointment. Critics have condemned him for his self-righteousness, inflexibility, and "colossal self-esteem."[3] A journalist who closely observed the Eisenhower Administration's more prominent players has characterized Dulles as a mixture of "sophistication and evangelism, of great knowledge and a weakness for glib slogans, of shrewdness and windy idealism, of harsh realism and the most naive wishful thinking."[4] Dulles was, to be sure, preoccupied with his conceptions of personal freedom, Christianity, democracy, and capitalism. This forthright defense of basic national values won for the Secretary the sincere admiration of millions of Americans; but in his single-mindedness of purpose and in his rigidity he was, as the Italian Ambassador to Paris observed, both the "conscience" and the "straightjacket" of American foreign policy.[5]

From the late 1940s, Dulles often viewed Soviet diplomatic objectives in terms of zones—Inner, Middle, and Outer. The Inner Zone was the Soviet Union itself, much expanded as a result of Hitler's concessions during the Nazi-Soviet détente (a portion of Finland, all of Estonia, Latvia, Lithuania, and large sections of Poland and Rumania). The Middle Zone, gained partly through conquest and partly through negotiation at Tehran and Yalta,

[3] See, for instance, Herman Finer, *Dulles Over Suez: The Theory and Practice of His Diplomacy* (Chicago: Quadrangle, 1964), p. x. This work is particularly critical of the Secretary's handling of the crisis.

[4] Marquis Childs, *Eisenhower: Captive Hero—A Critical Study of the General and the President* (New York: Harcourt Brace Jovanovich, 1958), p. 190.

[5] Statement by Pietro Quaroni, quoted in Roscoe Drummond and Gaston Coblentz, *Duel at the Brink: John Foster Dulles' Command of American Power* (Garden City, N.Y.: Doubleday, 1960), pp. 18–19.

comprised Eastern Europe and that portion of the Far East under Russian control. The rest of the world, the Outer Zone, was in Dulles' view targeted for Soviet expansion and domination through propaganda, infiltration, and fifth-column movements.[6] The expansionist, revolutionary, and dictatorial nature of Soviet ideology was constantly emphasized. The Secretary's diplomatic posture, basically defensive and negative, was reflective of his belief that the Soviet Union always took the initiative.

Dulles' tendency to see himself as a soldier in ceaseless battle against communist ideology took on certain messianic overtones; a fervently religious man, he had served as an officer of the National Council of Churches and was a prominent and active Protestant layman. His official pronouncements had at times the air of sanctimonious preaching:

> Jesus said that the nations of the world had failed because they put material things first. He pleaded with men to seek first the Kingdom of God. . . . It behooves us to keep this in mind today when America is engaged in a bitter struggle with an atheistic communist system centered on materialism.[7]

In sum, unlike Eisenhower, who tended toward a more conciliatory world view, the Secretary of State saw Russia as an implacable foe whose imminent threat to American security must be thwarted by such deterrents as the Strategic Air Command and nuclear bombs. While Eisenhower was willing to go to considerable lengths to seek negotiated settlements, Dulles all too often reacted as if a gain for the Soviet Union was automatically a loss for the United States. Hence his initial opposition to the 1955 Geneva Summit Meeting; his insistence in 1954 that a rapprochement with the Soviet Union was impossible until Moscow renounced its Leninist doctrines; and his willingness to intervene in Indochina after the fall of Dienbienphu.[8]

Eisenhower's alleged deference to his Secretary in the field of foreign affairs has often been assumed, but the evidence does not support such a view. It is a fact that the President gave Dulles perhaps a freer rein to run the State Department than was accorded any of his predecessors; and too, during the Eisenhower Administration it was

[6] See Louis Gerson, *John Foster Dulles* (New York: Cooper Square, 1967), pp. 45–46.

[7] Quoted in Andrew H. Berding, *Dulles on Diplomacy* (Princeton, N.J.: Princeton University Press, 1965), p. 102. Also John Foster Dulles, "Freedom's New Task," in Conrad Cherry, ed., *God's New Israel: Religious Interpretations of American Destiny* (Englewood Cliffs, N.J.: Prentice-Hall, 1971), pp. 320–27.

[8] Eisenhower, *Mandate for Change*, p. 602; Drummond and Coblentz, *Duel at the Brink*, pp. 115–25; Matthew B. Ridgway, *Soldier: The Memoirs of Matthew B. Ridgway* (New York: Harper & Row, 1956), pp. 277–78; and Capitanchik, *The Eisenhower Presidency*, pp. 45–48.

tacitly assumed that the Secretary of State was the ranking member of the Cabinet. Dulles had the expertise, and in general he set the tone and was responsible for the execution of policy. But the reason his mandate was so broad was that he followed the President's policy directives. Thus Eisenhower explains in his memoirs that it was possible to delegate to Dulles an unusual degree of flexibility as his representative, "well knowing that he would not in the slightest degree operate outside the limits previously agreed between us." [9]

Dulles' penchant for a hard and uncompromising line toward the Soviets, together with the neurotic anxiety created by Senator Joseph McCarthy and the "Red Scare" of the early 1950s, conspired to produce an ugly rift between the Secretary and his own department in the early months of the new Administration. In fairness to Dulles, it is important to recall that by 1953 McCarthy had already catapulted to national prominence as Chairman of the Senate's Permanent Sub-committee on Investigations and was conducting a reign of fear over government employees. The loyalty issue had been a highly emotional one in the Presidential race, and shortly after taking office Eisenhower ordered his Cabinet to "Get along with Congress" [10]—the initiated knew to read "McCarthy" for "Congress."

The State Department was a particular target of the purge following accusations that a high-ranking official, Alger Hiss, was in league with Red agents. The Wisconsin Senator showed no signs after the 1953 inauguration of tempering his scathing attacks in deference to a new President from his own party. Since millions of Americans had become highly suspicious of the State Department's alleged harboring of communists and their sympathizers, Dulles issued a memorandum during his first day in office which rocked the State Department to its foundations. Characterizing his staff as the "front-line defenders of the vital interests of the United States which are being attacked by a political warfare which is as hostile in its purpose and as dangerous in its capabilities as any open war," he heavy-handedly attempted to impress upon Department personnel their special responsibility. "It requires of us competence, discipline and positive loyalty to the policies that our President and the Congress may prescribe. Less than that is not tolerable at this time." The staff was assured that they were not being called upon to "practice intellectual

[9] Dwight D. Eisenhower, *Waging Peace, 1956–61* (Garden City, N.Y.: Doubleday, 1965), p. 365. Also see Drummond and Coblentz, *Duel at the Brink*, pp. 20–36. For the view that Dulles' influence over the President was very considerable, see Sherman Adams, *Firsthand Report: The Story of the Eisenhower Administration* (New York: Harper & Row, 1961), p. 87.

[10] Quoted in Deane and David Heller, *John Foster Dulles: Soldier for Peace* (New York: Holt, Rinehart & Winston, 1960), p. 156.

dishonesty or to distort [their] reporting to please superiors." But this was little comfort to those who were also informed that to uphold this responsibility it would be necessary, from time to time, to "adjust" personnel because "national welfare must be given priority over individual concerns." [11] This message, plus Eisenhower's order that every government employee must submit to an FBI loyalty check, caused a storm of protest in liberal circles and in the liberal press. But the President and Secretary stood firm. While State Department morale sank to a frustrating low, public confidence appeared to rise.

The department's morale deteriorated even further when it was learned that an avid supporter of Senator McCarthy, Robert Walter "Scotty" McLeod, had been appointed director of personnel security; within seven months the number of department employees dropped from 42,154 to 20,321. Nearly 16,000 of those discharged were transferred to other agencies, but 5,000 were terminated. Of the total, 306 United States citizens and 178 aliens were dismissed because of the new security regulations, even though there was no indication of active disloyalty.[12] Dulles' personal decision to retire a number of prominent career diplomats, including John Carter Vincent, John Paton Davies, George F. Kennan, and Paul Nitze, further incensed liberals and State Department personnel.

EXPERIMENTS IN EUROPEAN INTEGRATION

With the Soviet Union and its satellites massed at the eastern portion of the continent of Europe it is not surprising that a continuing and essential concern of American foreign policy was European security. NATO had been formalized at the close of the 1940s, in large part to establish a unified force to counter further Russian aggression; that this deterrent was to rely heavily upon American military assistance was soon evidenced by the passage, in September of 1949, of the Mutual Defense Assistance Act authorizing $1 billion for military aid to the NATO nations. This measure, along with the billions to be expended for European recovery under the Marshall Plan, was a clear indication of the broad American commitment to that continent. A key objective of American policy was the economic unification of Europe, and that issue, bound as it was to political unification, and the unification of Germany in particular, proved to be a most vexatious

---

[11] Dulles quoted in Heller, *John Foster Dulles*, pp. 157–58. Also useful for Dulles' early months in office is John Robinson Beal, *John Foster Dulles: A Biography* (New York: Harper & Row, 1957), pp. 138–52.

[12] See Gerson, *John Foster Dulles*, p. 111.

one. At the root of the problem was the existence in Europe of what one historian has described as an "attachment to the status quo" on the question of the unification of Germany.[13] That is, just as Russia conducted much of her diplomacy in Eastern Europe almost as a conditioned response to her past experiences with Germany, so too did many in Western Europe look upon the creation of a German state as a potential threat to European stability. To the exhausted nations of Europe there appeared to be a distinct advantage in Russia's counterbalancing this potential threat—so long, of course, as the expansionist designs of the Soviet Union stopped at Eastern Europe. The great unwillingness of England to join in a supranational agreement which would in any way threaten her sovereignty or her long-standing ties with the Commonwealth nations and with the United States constituted a further complication.

The outlines of a solution to the unification and economic integration issue emerged with the formulation of the Council of Europe in May of 1949. This group, comprising Great Britain, France, Italy, Ireland, Belgium, the Netherlands, Luxembourg, Norway, Sweden, and Denmark (and later joined by West Germany, Iceland, Greece, Turkey, Austria, and Cyprus), had been established to foster greater political, economic, and social cooperation; to help contain communism; to restore Germany to her proper place in European affairs; and, ideally, to become a third force in international affairs. The need for cooperation was clear, but the method of achieving it was not. Should it be achieved through the establishment of an overriding federal structure with supranational powers and representative of its several members? Or was the Council's goal to be achieved through the "functionalist" faction's plan for the establishment of specific supranational authorities to aid in the coordination of distinct activities? The latter tack was eventually taken, and this alternative was given a powerful boost when in May of 1950 Robert Schuman, France's Foreign Minister, proposed a multinational organization—the European Coal and Steel Community—to coordinate the efforts of participating nations in creating a common market for their coal, iron, and steel products. Workers, capital, and goods involved in coal, iron, and steel production would eventually move freely across boundaries. Despite Britain's refusal to join, the Schuman Plan was ratified by France, Italy, West Germany, and the three Benelux countries in April of 1951; by mid-1954 almost all duties on the three commodities had been abolished, and a transportation network was established.

[13] Norman A. Graebner, *Cold War Diplomacy, 1945–1960* (Princeton: Princeton University Press, 1962), p. 72.

The Schuman Plan was a major factor in the economic resurgence of Europe and was also important in providing a model of a supranational authority for the European defense alliance. Given American designs to integrate West Germany into Western Europe's common defense system, several nations, and particularly France, were fearful of Germany's rising, Phoenix-like, to disturb the delicate equilibrium. This serious concern led the French to initiate a new plan for the defense of Europe; the outbreak of the Korean War and Europe's growing fear that the communists, now on the offensive, would soon turn their attention to Western Europe were the direct causes of the French initiative. And too, with the United States caught off guard and deeply involved in the Far East, it was obvious that the continent would have to assume a greater share of responsibility for its own defense. It was the firm view of Washington that any meaningful counterforce would have to include the West Germans, 50,000,000 strong and clearly showing signs of a resurgence. Europe was thus left to choose between possible Russian attack while the United States was preoccupied in Korea and the potential long-range consequences of a rearmed Germany.

These alternatives were not pleasing, but France's Premier, René Pleven, saw a solution modeled after the Schuman Plan. Hence Pleven proposed on October 24, 1950, that a European Defense Community force of six nations be included within the NATO defense structure. Such a plan would satisfy American insistence that Germany be included in the general European defense plan, while neutralizing the threat of a rearmed German national army. The plan was also attractive in terms of the economic condition of Europe in the early 1950s. While the danger of Russian attack was generally acknowledged (more conservative Europeans argued that the very mobilization of Europe would provide the catalyst for a Soviet Offensive), it was widely doubted that the West European economy could withstand the strain of mobilization. The average yearly income in the United States approximated $1,800, compared with only $600 for Western Europe. The diversion of perhaps 20 percent of its national income for rearmament would not cause severe hardship in the United States but an equivalent investment by the European nations would lead to a serious diminution of the very necessities of life.[14] So the incentives for a multinational force were both economic and political.

Despite the origin of the European Defense Community formula,

[14] These figures from William G. Carleton, *The Revolution in American Foreign Policy* (New York: Random House, 1963), p. 180. A related work of interest on this general topic is James L. Clayton, ed., *The Economic Impact of the Cold War* (New York: Harcourt Brace Jovanovich, 1970).

it was destined to be sidelined by France's fear of a revitalized Germany and of the economic burdens of an ambitious defense plan.[15] The chances of success for the scheme were greatly diminished when it was decided in May of 1952 that the Bonn Convention ending the occupation of Germany would go into effect with the ratification of the EDC.

The following month Winston Churchill sponsored a nine-power foreign ministers' conference in London to explore alternative methods of both rearming West Germany and including that nation in NATO. The result of this historic meeting was the signing of a series of agreements, including a provision for a committee to arrange the final details of the termination of the German occupation. West Germany was invited to enter NATO and to contribute 12 divisions and an air force of 1,000 planes. Additional provisions included: expansion of the power of the Supreme Allied Commander in Europe to prevent the independent deployment of German forces; limitation of the size of a continental European nation's contribution to the NATO force; and prohibition of German manufacture of missiles or atomic, biological, or chemical weapons.[16] The new defense structure, known as the Western European Union, was greatly strengthened by a British pledge to maintain four divisions and a tactical air force on the continent of Europe for as long as a majority of the WEU desired. This was an excellent plan under the circumstances, but it did not achieve the EDC's goal of a supranational force. Instead, the national armies of each of the signatory powers were linked by a series of alliance—including, of course, the NATO agreement. This was undoubtedly as much as France and some of the other nations were willing to risk at the time.

These agreements were formalized in October of 1954, with the signing of the Western European Union treaty in Paris. A most significant step taken at this same time was the implementation of the so-called Bonn Convention of May 26, 1952, ending Allied occupation of West Germany. That convention gave the Federal Republic full authority over its internal and external affairs, except as provided, while the three powers retained certain rights relating to the stationing of armed forces in Germany, the protection of their troops, security, Berlin, and German unification.[17] A separate protocol inviting West Germany to join NATO was also framed.

The formation of the Western European Union was warmly

---

[15] For details, see Eisenhower, *Mandate for Change*, pp. 476–91.

[16] Summarized in *Ibid.*, pp. 489–90.

[17] The Bonn Convention printed in *Congressional Record*, 82nd Cong., 2nd sess., Part 7, pp. 8665–66.

received in Washington, largely because it satisfied the Eisenhower Administration's desire for a more "economic" foreign policy. The great cost of World War II, the billions expended for NATO and the Marshall Plan, and the general level of foreign aid ($3.5 billion to West Germany alone between 1945 and 1955)[18] convinced many that an intolerable burden had been placed on the national economy. The issue had been an important one during the 1952 campaign, for Eisenhower had warned of economic disaster resulting from the Democrats' huge military spending program.

> We must achieve both security and solvency. In fact, the foundation of military strength is economic strength. A bankrupt America is more the Soviet goal than an America conquered on the field of battle. . . . [O]ur defense program need not and must not push us steadily toward economic collapse. . . . The cost of security today amounts to 75 percent of our enormous national budget.[19]

Determined to avoid the ominous consequences of Democratic fiscal irresponsibility, the economically minded Administration set out to develop what it termed a "New Look" in the nation's defense posture. The President defined this "New Look" as a reallocation of resources among the various combat forces of the United States (e.g., nuclear strike force, overseas force, reserve force) and "the placing of greater emphasis than formerly on the deterrent and destructive power of improved nuclear weapons, better means of delivery, and effective air-defense units." [20] Importantly, as part of this new design Eisenhower attempted to set aside the Truman Administration's strategy of planning for a number of limited brush-fire wars once a nuclear stalemate had been achieved. Such a policy had required the maintenance of large numbers of ground forces, which the new President rejected as timid, defensive, and economically ruinous. The serious strain of the Korean War, and the frustration which was the legacy of that war, convinced the General of the futility of fighting wars on terms laid down by the nation's enemies. The role of the army was to be deemphasized, and reliance was to be placed upon the striking power of the nuclear force. The retaliatory power of the air force was to act as a "deterrent" to Soviet ambitions. "The Communists would have to be made to realize that should they be guilty of major aggression, we would strike with means of our own choosing at the head of the Communist power." [21] There was, however, too little

---

[18] Eisenhower, *Mandate for Change*, p. 477.
[19] *New York Times*, 26 Sept. 1952, p. 12.
[20] Eisenhower, *Mandate for Change*, p. 540.
[21] *Ibid.*, p. 544. For a critique of the Eisenhower-Dulles policy, see Dean Acheson,

consideration in the Eisenhower circle of the tremendous risks of such a policy. Atomic bombs might very well replace ground forces in a blueprint for defense—but only if a nation were willing to accept the consequences of a nuclear holocaust. The Korean War was expensive and frustrating, but as a limited war it did not threaten the planet's existence (except, at times, in the ruminations of General MacArthur).

The Administration's defense budget for fiscal 1954 was nearly $7 billion below Truman's estimate, and actual expenditures for the 1954 fiscal year were nearly $3.5 billion lower than the previous period. The rate of reduction was dramatic. The Truman Administration had requested $61.7 billion for fiscal 1952, and $52.4 billion for fiscal 1953. By contrast, Eisenhower's first defense budget was $34.5 billion.[22]

The anticipated benefits from the conclusion of the German occupation and the beginning of German integration into the economic and military structure of Europe were somewhat offset by increased Soviet militancy. German rearmament and the end of the occupation by the Western Big Three, Moscow charged, were violations of all Big-Four agreements regarding the final disposition of Germany. In retaliation, the USSR threatened the permanent partition of that nation. The nonaggression pacts which Russia had signed with England and France during the war were broken in May of 1955, but this constituted a mere formality in light of the tension between Russia and her wartime allies by the mid-1950s. In direct response to the formation of the Western European Union, Moscow concluded the Warsaw Pact on May 14, 1955. The signatory powers—the Soviet Union, Poland, Czechoslovakia, East Germany, Hungary, Rumania, Bulgaria, and Albania—were pledged to act in consort against the "aggressive" designs of the NATO nations. Ironically, the Warsaw Pact's military alliance included a combined command structure which appeared to be an almost exact duplication of the NATO plan.

Despite its frustration over the growing cooperation among Western European states and its sponsorship of the retaliatory Warsaw Pact, the Soviet Union was at least partially conciliatory. The day after the Warsaw Pact was signed, Moscow announced agreement on a treaty formally ending the occupation of Austria. This treaty stipulated that Austria was to be neutral—it could not participate in any military alliance directed against one of the victorious nations of

---

" 'Instant Retaliation': The Debate Continued," reprinted in Robert A. Divine, ed., *American Foreign Policy Since 1945* (Chicago: Quadrangle, 1969), pp. 93–100.

[22] Figures from Arthur S. Link, *American Epoch: A History of the United States Since the 1890's*, 2nd ed. (New York: Knopf, 1965), p. 789.

World War II. Foreign military bases were not to be installed on Austrian soil.

On the same day (May 15) Eisenhower's invitation for a July Big-Four Summit meeting at Geneva was accepted. That conference was attended by the world's most powerful figures: President Eisenhower, Prime Minister Anthony Eden (Winston Churchill's successor), French Minister Edgar Faure, and Russian Premier Nikolai Bulganin (the Russian delegation, predictably, included Party Secretary Nikita Khrushchev); the foreign ministers of each nation were also present, along with a dazzling array of dignitaries. The "Spirit of Geneva" was epitomized by a public exchange between Eisenhower and Bulganin in which the American President declared: "The United States will never take part in an aggressive war," and the Russian Premier replied, "We believe that statement." [23]

This "Spirit of Geneva" notwithstanding, the concrete achievements of the conference were few. The West had proposed that the reunification of Germany be accomplished by free elections, and the Russians gave their conditional approval to the concept. But when the foreign ministers met to resolve the practical details of this accord, the initial agreement was quickly repudiated. The other major question, disarmament, also failed to inspire any lasting solutions since the West insisted upon inspection as a basic condition to any disarmament agreement; the Soviets would have nothing to do with such a proviso. Perhaps the most dramatic proposal set forth at Geneva was the Open Skies formula designed by Special Assistant to the President, Nelson Rockefeller, and his staff. Under this scheme the East and West were to exchange "blueprints" of their military establishments and permit mutual aerial inspections of their territory. The offer proved most useful as propaganda to offset Soviet warnings of American aggressiveness and the threat of surprise attack. But the likelihood of Russian acceptance of such an arrangement was slim, and few were surprised when it was quickly dismissed. In turn, the Russian proposition that NATO be dismantled and American troops be withdrawn from Europe was flatly rejected.

Such reversals, and the continuing pessimism in Washington regarding meaningful cooperation between East and West, led to an increased determination to bolster the Free World's military and economic posture. With the failure of the Big-Four Foreign Ministers Conference in Geneva, the atmosphere darkened. Moscow took the offensive by sending Bulganin and Khrushchev on globe-trotting

[23] Quoted in Hollis W. Barber, *The United States in World Affairs, 1955* (New York: Council on Foreign Relations, 1957), p. 64.

expeditions to increase Russian economic influence in Asia, Africa, and Latin America. Their appeal to the peoples of largely undeveloped areas of the world fell on willing ears, especially when these emissaries played to growing anti-colonial sentiment. The Eisenhower Administration was divided in its response to this challenge; Rockefeller and other more liberal internationalists argued for greatly increased mutual assistance through economic aid. The more conservative faction of the party, which believed that little more could or should be done in this direction, won only a partial victory when the President, modifying the Rockefeller recommendation for dramatic aid increases, requested early in 1956 a near doubling of the existing aid levels. That the liberal wing of the GOP was deeply dissatisfied with this solution was perhaps best expressed in Rockefeller's resignation.

Tariff reductions were another, if more indirect, method of aiding the economic recovery of the Free World. A bipartisan Commission on Foreign Economic Policy had been established to advise the President, and in January of 1954 it reported that the most effective method of ensuring recovery was not through outright grants but rather by stimulating international trade. Lower tariffs would enable foreign nations to purchase more American goods because of their increased sales to the United States. Eisenhower therefore recommended specific tariff reductions of up to 15 percent and also endorsed a plan for lowering taxes on incomes derived from overseas investments. In his message to the Congress the President summarized the new economic assistance program: "Aid—which we wish to curtail; Investment—which we wish to encourage; Convertibility [of currency]—which we wish to facilitate; and Trade—which we wish to expand." [24]

Perhaps the most dramatic and far-reaching accomplishment of the postwar drive for European economic recovery and stability was the formation in 1957 of the Common Market (more formally, the European Economic Community). The Market greatly extended the economic integration which had been envisioned in the European Coal and Steel Community, and in fact its charter membership was the same: France, Italy, West Germany, and the three Benelux nations. As was the case in other supranational associations, the Six of the Market hoped not only to advance the prosperity of their individual nations but also to create a powerful economic and political force which would rival the United States and the Soviet Union. The most essential objective of the Common Market was the elimination of

[24] Quoted in Eisenhower, *Mandate for Change*, p. 358.

import and export duties and industrial quotas among the member nations. This was to be accomplished gradually and in three stages, so that by 1970 all tariffs would be removed. The group also viewed as one of its goals the elimination of barriers to the free flow of capital and labor across their national boundaries (it will be recalled that in the European Coal and Steel Community agreement these tariff barriers were also to be lowered, but for specific commodities only). The sweep of the proposal was apparent in its inclusion of agricultural as well as industrial goods.

Great Britain chose to disassociate itself from the Common Market. Although this policy was to be regretted by the middle of the 1960s, London's reasons at the time seemed sound. Her special arrangements with members of the Commonwealth would have been endangered by a scheme which obligated her to accept the products of Market members on an open basis. The major disadvantage of disassociation was that British goods would be unable to compete with Market goods within the six nations of the organization, a factor which further threatened the already greatly weakened British economy.[25] By the opening of the 1970s the disadvantages of nonmembership seemed to outweigh the benefits; under the skillful direction of Prime Minister Edward Heath's Conservative government Great Britain, however reluctantly, joined her Western European sisters.

"LIBERATION" AND EASTERN EUROPE

In the aftermath of the 1955 Summit Conference at Geneva, the Soviet Union redoubled its efforts to win converts among the oppressed and backward nations, while the United States and Western Europe strengthened their determination to upgrade the political, military, and economic structures of the Free World. The "Spirit of Geneva" had provided only an exceedingly short interlude between the postwar realignment and the cold and hot wars which were the consequence of that realignment.

The expansive diplomacy of the Soviet Union during the decade following the war was somewhat offset by sharp dissension within the Communist bloc. In 1948 Yugoslavia's Marshal Tito displayed an extraordinary degree of self-confidence by refusing to commit his

[25] For studies of the Common Market, see J. F. Deniau, *The Common Market* (New York: Praeger, 1960); J. W. Nystrom and Peter Malof, *The Common Market* (Princeton, N.J.: Princeton University Press, 1962); and Emile Benoit, *Europe at Sixes and Sevens: The Common Market, The Free Trade Association, and the United States* (New York: Columbia University Press, 1961).

nation to a blind following of Stalinist Russia. Tito thereby won for his country an enviable degree of sovereignty, and although Yugoslavia continued as a communist state, its orientation was increasingly allied with the so-called "Third World" nations (such as Nasser's Egypt and Nehru's India). Reacting to an obvious opportunity to gain some small influence in Eastern Europe, Washington dispatched American military and economic aid to Yugoslavia despite the severe criticism of right-of-center members of the Congress, a conservative-minded faction of the public, and various pressure groups. This strategy, based on the theory that by bolstering Tito's regime Yugoslavia could retain its independent stance within the erstwhile communist monolith, was reasonably successful. In 1954 the Balkan Pact was signed by Tito's government, Turkey, and Greece. This alliance of two NATO members with a communist nation was a most encouraging development, but one which did not prove to be a model for the future.

Yugoslavia's partial liberation from satellite status was an early indication of strain within the Soviet bloc, a strain which dominated headlines in 1956. In the period immediately following Stalin's death in 1953, Moscow was faced with insurrectionary activity in Czechoslovakia, East Berlin, and East Germany. Confronted with the alternatives of stiffened repression or a measured relaxation of control, the new Russian leaders chose the latter, perhaps theorizing that a tight lid would ensure a dramatic explosion. The new policy was at first demonstrated by easing the economic burden borne by the Eastern European states. When in February of 1956 Khrushchev denounced Stalinism at the Twentieth Party Congress, the way was cleared for a far more liberal attitude toward individual expression.

The denunciation of Stalinism was difficult to keep in bounds, and the movement soon went far beyond the intention of Khrushchev's "revisionism." Testing the relaxation of strict party restraints, nationalist communist forces in Eastern Europe challenged Stalinist leaders, threatening to depose the Old Guard.[26] There followed an inevitable conflict between new-line nationalists and a Moscow leadership determined to regulate—and diminish—the rate and extent of change.

Poland was a clear case in point. Wladyslaw Gomulka, a Communist nationalist with considerable following, had been released from prison in 1954. He resumed his public career when the Polish Communist Party Congress was convened in October of 1956. The very morning of the meeting, Khrushchev and other leaders appeared in Warsaw to bully and browbeat Gomulka out of the leadership

---

[26] Louis J. Halle, *The Cold War as History* (New York: Harper & Row, 1967), Chap. 31.

position. These verbal attacks behind closed doors were accompanied by the ominous movement of Russian troops and the stationing of Soviet warships in the Baltic near the harbors of several Polish cities. Such a display of force, together with harsh verbal attacks, had been successful in the political subjugation of Rumania and Czechoslovakia. But Gomulka, to the astonishment of Khrushchev and his group, stood his ground and appeared ready to rely on the armed workers of Warsaw to maintain some semblance of independence. Faced with the threat of an escalated conflict, Khrushchev withdrew, pledging his support to the Gomulka government.

The Polish rebellion, and Gomulka's good sense in not forcing sweeping reforms, led to a considerable easing of Moscow-imposed restrictions in that country. Greater freedom of expression was tolerated, the power of the police was restricted, Russian military authority was greatly diminished, and, perhaps most symbolic, Poland was reasonably free to establish meaningful contacts with the West.

The degree of independence and sovereignty achieved by the limited revolution in Poland proved a tempting model for the rest of Eastern Europe. The shock waves from the October nineteenth revolution were almost immediately felt in Hungary, whose Soviet-directed leadership was despised by both the intellectuals and the general populace. In July of 1956, Moscow replaced the much hated Matyas Rakosi with Erno Gero, who in a few short months was viewed as the personification of Soviet repression. Only four days after the Polish revolt, university students and Budapest workers joined in a spontaneous anti-communist demonstration. This group, soon fired upon by the secret police, was quickly joined by citizens from the surrounding countryside. Within one day a full-scale revolt was underway, a massive statue of Stalin was destroyed, and Hungarian flags were displayed with the much resented Communist emblem removed. The faltering Hungarian Communist regime attempted to placate the dissidents by installing the moderate (and former Prime Minister) Imre Nagy at the head of the government. Russian military assistance was also sought. There followed incredible pitched battles between Russian tanks and Hungarian insurgents armed, at times, simply with stones. The Hungarian Revolution was as heroic and spontaneous as it was leaderless and, so far as the objective of complete independence was concerned, doomed.

Under the circumstances, however, a good deal was accomplished. Nagy, enjoying considerable public support, had replaced Gero; Russian tanks and troops, it was announced on October 30, were to be withdrawn from Budapest and then from all of Hungary. Moscow pledged its support of the Nagy government, and there were strong hints at the end of October that the Soviet bloc, shaken to its foundations by the events in Poland and Hungary, would soon enjoy a much altered relationship with the USSR. Faced with threats of Hungarian withdrawal from the Warsaw Pact and other agreements, the Soviet leadership seemingly compromised at the end of the month by announcing a plan which would grant "commonwealth status" to Hungary.[27]

When this compromise statement failed to quell the revolt (which was not surprising since the Hungarian people doubted that such a "commonwealth" would actually be established), Moscow decided that the time had come for massive retaliation. The threat of a growing revolt throughout Eastern Europe, the November 1 renunciation of the Warsaw Pact by the Nagy government, the triumphant entrance of the anti-communist Roman Catholic Cardinal Joseph Mindszenty into Budapest, and the formal declaration of Hungary's neutral status among nations were all beyond the point of tolerance. Two hundred thousand troops, accompanied by 5,000 tanks, were sent into Budapest to pound the joyous and by now reckless Hungarians to submission. The "official" Russian explanation for the retaliation was that the rebellion had been generated by aristocratic and middle-class elements who were attempting to subjugate the people to their own form of Fascist dictatorship. Rhetoric aside, the even partial defection of Yugoslavia and Poland would have constituted a serious setback to long-range Russian strategy of utilizing Eastern Europe as a buffer against the hostile nations to the West (particularly Germany). To allow Hungary its freedom might very well have destroyed the fabric of the Iron Curtain.

Despite the extent of the Russian force, the Hungarians continued to fight heroically through most of November and December. But without heavy weapons, and with their leadership in flight, effective resistance was impossible. With the return of Russian troops and tanks, Nagy sought asylum in the Yugoslav embassy, only to be kidnapped and later executed in 1958; his government was replaced by the pro-Soviet regime of Janos Kadar. The fighting, strikes, and passive resistance continued; but by the close of 1956 Hungary was securely within Moscow's orbit once again.

Much criticism has been leveled at the Eisenhower Administration for its role in "encouraging" such revolutions in Eastern Europe, and particularly for its unwillingness to come to the assistance of the

[27] For a portion of this "Declaration by the Soviet Government on the Principles of Development and Further Strengthening of Friendship and Cooperation between the Soviet Union and Other Socialist States," see Eisenhower, *Waging Peace*, pp. 78–79.

Hungarian people. It is charged, for example, that the Republican party's announced policy of support and encouragement of the liberation of satellite nations had led many in Hungary to believe that once they had taken up arms the United States would come to their assistance.[28] Others have concluded that American propaganda, especially through Radio Free Europe and Voice of America, irresponsibly encouraged nationalist leaders in the satellite states to fight for unrealistic goals; such efforts only brought harsh Soviet reprisals and the reinstatement of Moscow-directed governments.[29]

"Liberation" had been a popular concept among Republicans in the early 1950s. For example, Dulles had insisted in his "A Policy of Boldness" article for *Life* that "liberation from the yoke of Moscow will not occur for a very long time, and courage in neighboring lands will not be sustained, *unless the United States makes it publicly known that it wants and expects liberation to occur.*" [30] It is, however, important to consider that almost from the beginning Eisenhower had strong reservations about such an assumption, and when the concept of "liberation" was adopted in the 1952 Republican Platform the General was careful to stress "by peaceful means." [31] One should not, therefore, be surprised to learn that upon hearing of the Soviet assault on Hungary and the formation of a new puppet government, Eisenhower immediately wrote to Bulganin: "I urge in the name of humanity and in the cause of peace that the Soviet Union take action to withdraw Soviet forces from Hungary immediately." [32] No threat of force was contained in this letter, and Eisenhower has very frankly explained his reasons for excluding the possibility of American intervention: Hungary was not accessible by sea or through the territory of America's allies; Britain and France, deeply engaged in the Suez crisis, would never have joined an expeditionary force; it was "unimaginable" that the major nations of Europe would immediately ally themselves with the United States in an intervention effort; and, finally, unilateral intervention "into Hungary through hostile or neutral territory would have involved us in a general war." [33]

In assessing the reaction of both the United States and the United Nations to the Hungarian Revolt, it is necessary to consider the enormous complications presented by the Suez crisis, and espe-

[28] Denna F. Fleming, *The Cold War and Its Origins, 1917–1960* (New York: Doubleday, 1961), II, pp. 806–14.

[29] David Horowitz, *The Free World Colossus* (New York: Hill & Wang, 1971), Chap. 16.

[30] John Foster Dulles, "A Policy of Boldness," *Life*, May 19, 1952, p. 146.

[31] See Gerson, *John Foster Dulles*, p. 88.

[32] Quoted in Eisenhower, *Waging Peace*, p. 87.

[33] *Ibid.*, p. 89.

cially by the division in Western ranks caused by Washington's unwillingness to side with the British and French in that conflict.[34] The very preoccupation of the major Western powers with the Middle East, which permitted the Soviets to act with impunity, effectively tied the hands of the Western Big Three. It is doubtful, nevertheless, that in the absence of the Suez crisis the United States, England, and France would have been willing to spark a general war by open intervention in Hungary. The Eisenhower Administration's error was in espousing Dulles' vague liberation concept. The Secretary had seen containment as immoral and had consistently urged a collapse of communism from within. Hungarians understandably calculated that the United States would come to their aid; after years of encouragement, liberation through peaceful evolution had a rather hollow ring. Cabell Phillips of the *New York Times* asked the critical question: "How do we maintain our integrity with the other captive nations when, by our propaganda and diplomacy, we have constantly fanned the flames of freedom?" [35] The Eisenhower-Dulles liberation campaign was not the primary cause of the Hungarian Revolt. That largely spontaneous movement was a reaction to severe Soviet repression. However, in the absence of American propaganda pointing to support of captive peoples, the movement for change might well have been more tempered and ultimately more successful.

The tragedy of Hungary, the threat of further Soviet repression in Poland, and the desire for German unification sent a number of diplomats on both sides of the Atlantic scurrying for relief from the ongoing crisis in Europe. For a while, and only to some, "disengagement" appeared to be a reasonable solution. It was theorized that the USSR could not be expected to compromise unless the West offered a major concession of its own. The most generous concession possible was the removal of armed forces from Central Europe. Under most schemes, provision would have been made for the neutralization of Eastern Europe and all of Germany; the withdrawal of foreign troops from Germany, Poland, and Hungary; the dissolution of the 1955 Warsaw Pact; and the withdrawal of West Germany from NATO. There were of course variations, including the reunification of Germany as a precondition.

In the United States, this plan was most closely identified with former Ambassador George F. Kennan and a group of his supporters. But Secretary of State Dulles was adamantly opposed to the scheme and subscribed to the characterization provided by Belgium's Paul-

[34] See below, pp. 295–303.
[35] Quoted in Fleming, *The Cold War and Its Origins, 1917–1960*, pp. 812–13. Also, Horowitz, *The Free World Colossus,* pp. 280–81.

Henri Spaak: that disengagement, a dirty word, could not even be translated into a decent language like French. "If I had to choose between a neutralized Germany and Germany in the Soviet bloc," Dulles insisted, "it might be almost better to have it in that bloc. . . . disengagement is absolutely not acceptable." [36]

This reaction was not unexpected, and the risk to both power blocs was too great for any such settlement to have a realistic expectation of success.[37] The Soviets' concern over security and boundaries, together with what was viewed as their determination to spread communism westward, rendered the plan unacceptable. For the West, the threat disengagement posed to the survival of the Western Alliance, and therefore to the security of Europe, was an insuperable obstacle.

Given the demise of disengagement, the continued partition of Germany, and the existence of a divided Berlin deep within Soviet-controlled East Germany, it is not surprising that Berlin continued to be a major Cold War focal point. In June of 1953 riots by workers against Russian control of East Berlin had sparked demonstrations in several East German cities. Soviet reprisals were swift, and the at best lightly armed workers were soon subdued by the force of Russian tanks and troops. As was to be the case in Poland and Hungary, the United States, while sympathetic to the resistance groups, did not come to their aid.

The second and far more extensive threat to the status quo in Berlin occurred in November 1958, when Khrushchev abruptly announced that his government would soon sign a peace treaty with East Germany terminating the rights of the Allies in West Berlin. Under the conditions of World War II agreements the former capital had been divided into four sectors, but the United States, Britain, and France soon agreed to administer their sectors as one entity. The lifeline to the city was a 110-mile corridor through East German territory, and the two million Berliners were protected by 4,000 American and 7,000 British and French troops. It was the intention of the Western Allies to work for the unification of Germany, but this goal was constantly frustrated by a clear Russian design to keep Germany divided and weak. Once again, given the Russian experience with German invaders, it was not at all surprising to find Moscow utterly at odds with the Western objective.

In his statement of November 1958, Khrushchev called for the withdrawal of Allied troops from West Berlin, the creation of a

---

[36] Quoted in Gerson, *John Foster Dulles*, pp. 307–8.

[37] An analysis is in Hugh Seton-Watson, *Neither War Nor Peace: The Struggle for Power in the Post-War World* (New York: Praeger, 1960), pp. 346–50.

so-called free city, and the renegotiation of access rights to West Berlin. In return, the Russians pledged to end their military occupation of East Berlin and to permit the United Nations, or token forces from either the big powers or several of the lesser powers, to guarantee the free status of the city. Should the Western Allies fail to endorse his proposal, Khrushchev threatened to give East Germany control of all routes to Berlin, thereby forcing the Allies to recognize the puppet state in order to retain free access to the city. The Western states in turn continued to insist that the final disposition of both Berlin and Germany would have to be settled by a carefully supervised national referendum, and that once reunited, Berlin would again become the capital of all of Germany.

This then was the setting for the November 27, 1958, note threatening that the four-power arrangement in Berlin either would be voluntarily terminated within six months, or Soviet control of East Berlin would be given to East Germany. In mid-December Secretary of State Dulles flew to Paris to confer with the foreign ministers of Britain, France, and West Germany, as well as with the North Atlantic Council. At these meetings it was determined that negotiations would not be conducted under the threat of force.

Throughout the early months of 1959 Khruschev skillfully side-stepped his six-month ultimatum. At the same time the Russian leader made it increasingly clear that he desired a Big-Four summit conference on the German question. At the insistence of Eisenhower the foreign ministers of the United States, the Soviet Union, England, and France met as a precondition to American endorsement of summit talks, but the resultant conference failed to reveal any meaningful shift in the positions of each side. (The United States was represented by its new Secretary of State, Christian A. Herter; Dulles had waged an unsuccessful battle against intestinal cancer, resigned his post in April of 1959, and died the following month.)

Despite Eisenhower's position that he would not agree to a summit meeting without some meaningful preliminary accord at the foreign minister's level, he was so concerned over the crisis that he invited Khrushchev to visit the United States. The expressed purpose of the visit was not to discuss Berlin, but rather, in the words of the President, "to melt a little of the ice" of the Cold War.[38] Perhaps the most important result of Khrushchev's September trip was his announced willingness to suspend the time limit on the Berlin issue; there the matter stood for nearly two years.

[38] Richard P. Stebbins, *The United States in World Affairs, 1959* (New York: Council on Foreign Relations, 1960), p. 30.

In the interim Eisenhower concluded his second term and the Republicans lost the White House to John F. Kennedy. During the summer of 1961 the new President met with Khrushchev, who reaffirmed his position on Berlin and established a new deadline, the end of the year, for the implementation of the Soviet solution to the Berlin question. Ominously, East Berliners were flowing in increasing numbers into West Berlin, a most serious setback to Soviet propaganda efforts. The solution to this exodus was decided upon in August of 1961, when Khrushchev met with Walter Ulbricht, Communist leader of East Germany. Barbed wire and the East German army were used to close the border, and this division was soon made permanent with the construction of a cement barrier known as the "Berlin Wall." [39] The divided city and nation remained at this tragic impasse until a series of initiatives early in the 1970s provided some hope for a more creative resolution of the partition.

REDUCING THE FEAR OF GLOBAL CATACLYSM

It would be a mistake to assume from such an account of Cold War tensions in the 1950s that the two superpowers had not turned at least some of their attention to peaceful concerns, such as the very vexing problem of disarmament and nuclear arms limitation. In a moving passage in his memoirs, Eisenhower writes of his dedication to the task of the controlled reduction of armaments:

> Atomic and hydrogen bombs and long-range ballistic missiles, preposterously destructive, have so enormously increased mutual apprehensions that effective measures toward universal disarmament are essential in achieving a world of security—at least of reducing the fear of global cataclysm and the practical extinction of civilization.

But despite this commitment, the President admits that his accomplishments were negligible, largely because of "the adamant insistence of the Communists on maintaining a closed society." [40] One of the very few concrete accomplishments of the Eisenhower Administration in this regard was the Atoms-for-Peace plan, which provided for the contribution of uranium and fissionable materials to an International

[39] There are a number of useful works on the subject of German partition, including Gerald Freund, *Germany Between Two Worlds* (New York: Harcourt Brace Jovanovich, 1961); N. J. G. Pounds, *Divided Germany and Berlin* (Princeton, N.J.: Princeton University Press, 1962); and Edgar McInnis, Richard Hiscocks, and Robert Spencer, *The Shaping of Post-War Germany* (New York: Praeger, 1960).

[40] Eisenhower, *Waging Peace*, pp. 467–68.

Atomic Energy Agency which would utilize them for peaceful purposes. The proposal was made in 1953, but was not implemented until July 1957.

At the Geneva Summit Conference, Eisenhower had unveiled his Open Skies formula for mutual aerial inspection of the military installations of each nation. This useful concept was eventually rejected by the Soviet Union on the grounds that the plan called for the surveillance of American territory but not of American military installations on foreign soil. The demise of the Open Skies proposal and the dramatic events of 1956 caused a temporary lull in efforts toward arms control, but in 1957 there were growing signs that the Russians, perhaps alarmed by the rapid strides being made by Great Britain in the development of atomic weapons, were ready to assume a more conciliatory posture. And so Harold E. Stassen, Special Assistant to the President, met privately in London with Soviet representatives to outline a broad disarmament scheme. This plan prohibited all nations—except the United States, the Soviet Union, and Great Britain—from manufacturing or using nuclear weapons; enjoined the three powers from utilizing their nuclear weapons except under specified circumstances; and stipulated that after July of 1959 production of fissionable material be limited exclusively to non-weapon uses. An inspection system consisting of some aerial inspection and fixed control posts was included in the formula. After much debate Moscow rejected the proposal.

By the beginning of 1958 the Soviet Union offered an alternative to disarmament by proposing that further nuclear weapons testing be suspended. In August the President announced limited American acceptance of the plan—for one year's duration—if both sides agreed to enter into negotiations leading to the control of future tests. Several hundred conference sessions were held without any substantive agreement.[41] The unwillingness of the Soviet Union to permit meaningful inspection, while insisting that the United States withdraw from Europe and other parts of the world, doomed the entire project.

Frustrated, Eisenhower chose to rely upon aerial surveillance of strategic installations within the Soviet Union. In 1956 authorization was given for the use of specially designed U-2 planes capable of operating within the Soviet Union at extremely high altitudes and, hopefully, above the range of Russian anti-aircraft devices. Despite the range of such aircraft, a plane piloted by Francis Gary Powers was

[41] See Joseph L. Nogee, *Soviet Policy Towards International Control of Atomic Energy* (Notre Dame, Ind.: University of Notre Dame Press, 1961), and Bernhard G. Bechhoefer, *Post-War Negotiations for Arms Control* (Washington, D.C.: Brookings Institution, 1961). Also John W. Spanier and Joseph L. Nogee, *The Politics of Disarmament* (New York: Praeger, 1962).

downed 1,200 miles inside the Soviet Union on May 1, 1960. Six days after the Powers incident electrified the nation, the State Department announced that no aircraft had been authorized to violate Soviet air space.[42] The apparent strategy behind this lie was Dulles' judgment that Khrushchev would be unwilling to admit to such a deep penetration of Russian territory,[43] a theory which was shattered when, on May 5, Khrushchev announced to the Supreme Soviet that the pilot, and equipment, had been recovered from the American plane.

It was at that point that Eisenhower reversed his strategy and admitted that Powers had been spying; the President insisted that he was personally responsible for authorizing such flights, which he considered essential. It seems not to have occurred to Eisenhower that to take such a tack was to needlessly challenge the Russians. Totally aware of the full range of propaganda opportunities presented by the American handling of the incident, Khrushchev first attempted to have the United Nations' Security Council condemn the United States for aggression, and when this measure failed by a vote of seven to two, he announced that he would visit the world forum. But the Soviet leader then overplayed his hand, and before a packed session affronted the shocked delegates by boasting of Soviet missile production, attempting to shout down Prime Minister Macmillan, and referring to the United Nations as a "spittoon." In one of the most publicized gestures of recent history he removed his shoe and hammered away at the rostrum to drive home his message. Even if one were to assume that the United Nations had by this time been reduced to a debating society, there were still certain amenities which were not to be ignored without a considerable loss of following.

SUEZ AND THE EISENHOWER DOCTRINE

The Soviet Union's preoccupation in the immediate postwar period with securing its Western border through the absorption of a number of East European nations did not cause Moscow to curtail its very active involvement in the rest of the world. The Middle East's strategic position and natural resources, for example, insured Russian interest. By 1955, under the leadership of Secretary of State Dulles, a regional alliance of Middle Eastern states had been formed, resembling the NATO arrangement; this Baghdad Pact included Turkey,

---

[42] The May 7, 1960, statement in Council on Foreign Relations, *Documents on American Foreign Relations, 1960* (New York: Council on Foreign Relations, 1960), pp. 114–15.

[43] See Eisenhower, *Waging Peace*, p. 547. The U-2 incident is recounted in David Wise and Thomas B. Ross, *The U-2 Affair* (New York: Praeger, 1962).

Iran, Pakistan, Iraq, and Great Britain. American sponsorship of such an arrangement was strongly motivated by a desire to protect the region's vast oil deposits, controlled by the West, from Moscow. The refusal of the United States to become a party to the alliance caused several Middle Eastern states to refrain from membership, but it is quite likely that the American position was based on a desire to placate Israel and Egypt. Both refused to join a security pact with the West.[44] In 1959, following the withdrawal of Iraq, the Baghdad Pact was renamed the Central Treaty Organization (CENTO).

The most important source of continuing turbulence in the Middle East has been the existence of Israel among hostile Arab neighbors. The Jewish state's great success in attracting immigrants and in establishing a solid military and economic foundation for its stable government has increased Arab determination to forcibly liquidate the nation. The United Nations attempted to ease tensions in the late 1940s, but as these efforts went unheeded, the United States, Great Britain, and France issued a tripartite declaration in May 1950, insuring the existing boundary between Israel and the Arab states. The declaration failed in its attempt to put an end to border raids, and these incidents became more serious with Nasser's decision to place greater emphasis on the Soviet Union as a source of arms and war materiel.

The issue which kindled the Middle East to flash point was, ironically, water. Nasser had conceived of the Aswan Dam project as the key to the economic resurgence of his nation, and indeed the project constituted a grand design for the irrigation and hydro-electrification of Egypt. Located on the Nile River 800 miles south of Cairo, the dam was to be one of the largest in the world, storing and controlling enough water to increase Egypt's usable land by fully one-third. It was a huge undertaking, one which greatly appealed to Nasser's ambition and sense of grandeur. The project was certainly immense: it would take 12 to 15 years to complete, at a cost of more than $1.5 billion borrowed from the United States, Great Britain, and the World Bank. When in December of 1955 the United States and Great Britain announced a modest preliminary grant of $70 million, Nasser refused to discuss details and instead began negotiating with the Soviets. Such a move was consistent with his strategy of playing one superpower off against the other. Then suddenly in July of the following year he sent an emissary to Washington to present Dulles with the alternative of guaranteeing the full cost of the Aswan Dam or seeing the project's financing placed in the hands of the Russians.

[44] Gerson, *John Foster Dulles*, pp. 258–59.

Refusing to be blackmailed, the Secretary of State replied that it was no longer feasible for the United States to participate in the project, and so Egypt would have to consider the offer of December 1955 (an offer to which Egypt had never responded) withdrawn.

In defending what many considered to be a precipitous action, Dulles explained that Congress, and particularly the Senate Appropriations Committee, was opposed to aiding Egypt under current circumstances; in addition, it is obvious that Egyptian "flirtations" with the Soviet Union had jeopardized American participation in the project.[45] But several students of Dulles' Suez diplomacy have been highly critical, charging that the Secretary's heavy-handedness was unwarranted. The real motivation, it is suggested, for the tirade against Nasser and the loan refusal was the outrage of a man of "monumental self-righteousness . . . at being jilted by a nonentity like Nasser who preferred all the Soviet black iniquities to all the shining moral achievements and potentialities of the West and of Dulles." [46] But there were also a number of specific pressures on the Secretary which made a weakening of Nasser's position in the Middle East particularly attractive. The Colonel's May 1956 decision to withdraw diplomatic recognition from Chiang Kai-shek in favor of Communist China was, for example, a particular irritant. Closer to home, Southern congressmen were asking why the United States was willing to underwrite a project which would greatly expand Egyptian cotton production and jeopardize the competitive position of American cotton. Perhaps most important of all, Nasser had refused to reverse a September 1955 decision to buy war materiel from Czechoslovakia. Dulles' response was to refuse the loan, theorizing that he would weaken Nasser politically at a time when Soviet assistance was not forthcoming.[47]

Although Dulles was quite sure that Nasser had been prepared for the American rejection, the Egyptian leader was furious. On July 26 he announced the nationalization of the Suez Canal, including all of the assets and property of the Universal Maritime Suez Canal Company (the canal represented approximately one-half of the company's total assets). The ostensible reason for the nationalization was to utilize the canal company's assets to finance the dam; Russian aid on terms acceptable to Nasser was apparently not forthcoming either.

[45] Eisenhower, *Waging Peace*, p. 33. A formal statement by Dulles explaining American withdrawal from the Aswan Dam project is reprinted in Bartlett, *The Record of American Diplomacy*, pp. 833–34.

[46] Finer, *Dulles Over Suez*, p. 51.

[47] Walter La Feber, *America, Russia, and the Cold War, 1945–1966* (New York: John Wiley, 1967), pp. 188–91.

Great Britain and France were the two Western nations most directly affected by the action—British nationals held about 45 percent of the Canal Company stock, and French citizens owned more than 50 percent. Provision was made for payment to stockholders, at the current market rate. Basically, it was the contention of London and Paris that in seizing the waterway Egypt had threatened the Convention of 1888 calling for joint protection of the canal; threatened the efficient operation of the canal and thereby seriously damaged the commerce of both nations; and threatened the status quo in the Mediterranean by an attempt to further Egyptian hegemony over that area.[48] The Eisenhower Administration believed that since the canal was situated entirely within Egyptian territory and therefore under Egyptian sovereignty, Nasser could legally nationalize it, provided its former owners were compensated for the expropriated property. Nasser had made such provision. (One cannot help but wonder what the Administration's position might have been had Americans held a considerable portion of the Canal Company's stock.) As to the actual operation of the water highway, in July it was deemed too early to judge whether the Egyptians could keep it going. Eisenhower made it abundantly clear to British Prime Minister Anthony Eden that in his view Nasser's action did not warrant the use of military force.

Suddenly, and without informing the United States, England and France referred the Suez issue to the United Nations. While the Security Council met in mid-October 1956, Britain, France, and (ominously) Israel conferred secretly in Paris. A Russian veto of the Council's resolution urging that the canal remain open for the world's commerce concluded one phase of the deliberations.

The object of the Paris meetings became stunningly clear on the evening of October 29 when Israel overran the Sinai Peninsula and positioned its troops within striking range of the canal. By design, England and France then demanded that both sides withdraw from the waterway. Their refusal led to the October 31 attack of Egyptian airfields, followed by an Anglo-French invasion of Egypt. Nasser promptly closed the canal by sending some 30 ships to its bottom; oil pipelines belonging to the British were blown up by Syrian saboteurs. French Premier Guy Mollet stated the obvious when, after the crisis, he admitted that the American government was not informed of the strategy because of "our fear that if we had consulted it, it would have prevented us from acting." [49] In his own account of the Suez crisis Eden has written:

[48] Eisenhower, *Waging Peace*, pp. 38–39.
[49] Quoted in *Ibid.*, p. 77.

The Government determined that our essential interests in this area must be safeguarded, if necessary by military action, and that the needful preparations must be made. Failure to keep the canal international would inevitably lead to the loss one by one of all our interests and assets in the Middle East, and even if Her Majesty's Government had to act alone they could not stop short of using force to protect their position.[50]

Despite the depth of his commitment to England and France, Eisenhower was outraged by their precipitous action and their refusal to utilize the United Nations. The *New York Times* reported intense negotiations between the furious Eisenhower and representatives of Washington's major allies. Eisenhower was highly sensitive to the political ramifications of the intervention; with the 1956 Presidential election only days away, the potential adverse affect of the decision on his reelection was most unwelcome.[51]

Upon learning of Israel's surprise attack the United States immediately sponsored a Security Council resolution calling for a cease-fire—Israel was to withdraw its armed forces at once behind the established armistice lines. But Great Britain and France exercised their veto power to defeat this initiative. The Administration once again turned to the United Nations after the joint Anglo-French intervention, but this time Secretary of State Dulles issued a dramatic personal appeal to the General Assembly. The absence of veto privilege in the General Assembly led to the passage of the cease-fire resolution by a vote of 64 to 5, with 6 abstentions.

Although the war continued in defiance of the Assembly's resolution, it did not result in the quick Anglo-French victory which London and Paris had anticipated. The British Parliament was deeply divided on the venture, and Eden was soon under attack by his own Conservative party, the opposition Labour party, and members of the Commonwealth nations. And too, in deciding upon joint intervention without first consulting Eisenhower, the British and French risked American censure. International opposition to the offensive was quickly mobilized. The day following the invasion Eisenhower told the nation: "There can be no peace without law. And there can be no law if we work to invoke one code of international conduct for those who oppose, and another for our friends." [52]

The Soviet Union, doubtlessly delighted over the swing in public

[50] Anthony Eden, *Full Circle* (Boston: Houghton Mifflin, 1960), pp. 474–75. The then Israeli Chief of Staff, Moshe Dayan, has written his own account in Moshe Dayan, *Diary of the Sinai Campaign* (New York: Harper & Row, 1966).

[51] For example, the *New York Times*, 3 Nov. 1956.

[52] Quoted in Carol A. Fisher and Fred Krinsky, *Middle East in Crisis: A Historical and Documentary Review* (Syracuse, N.Y.: Syracuse University Press, 1959), p. 170.

attention away from the Hungarian Revolt, warned of retaliation against the British, French, and Israelis if they did not withdraw from Egyptian territory. The Russians had joined the United States in both the Security Council and General Assembly resolutions regarding Suez and soon reinforced their position by threatening to send troops to Egypt. The crisis presented an ideal opportunity for Moscow to widen the breach between the United States and its two principal allies, and so on November 5 Premier Nikolai Bulganin wrote to Eisenhower, proposing that the United States and Russia join forces, invade Egypt and end the war! The Administration rejected the plan as "unthinkable," while Eden unburdened himself by sharply attacking the "hypocrisy of the Soviet Union's coming as a peacemaker into the Middle East while its hands were still stained with Hungarian blood." [53]

The combined pressures of world opinion, General Assembly opposition, Russian threats, and the American government's disfavor caused the British and French to back down and withdraw. Israel, with little alternative, quickly followed suit. The cease-fire, policed by the United Nations Emergency Force, went into effect on November 6, and British and French troops were removed by the end of the year; Israel pulled back to the armistice line by March of the following year. The debacle seriously undermined Britain's already weakened economy and further eroded the self-confidence of both England and France. The commanding influence of Washington and Moscow was humiliatingly underscored.

In dealing with the Suez crisis the United States wisely withheld support of British and French policies which were reflective of an earlier period of colonialism. To condemn the Soviet Union for its violations of Polish and Hungarian sovereignty in October of 1956, and then to support Anglo-French violations of Egyptian sovereignty the following month, would have caused America to lose considerable ground among the emergent nations of Asia and Africa. The fabric of the United Nations would have been seriously weakened had Washington, in concert with London and Paris, decided to ignore the established peace-keeping mechanisms by invading Egypt. The NATO pact was of course very seriously strained, but Eisenhower's determination to regard the split over Suez as simply a family feud went far in restoring the badly shaken alliance.[54]England and France had come out of the affair very poorly indeed, but Nasser emerged—in the Middle East at least—with his stature increased.

[53] Eisenhower, *Waging Peace*, p. 90.
[54] See Lionel Gelber, *America in Britain's Place* (New York: Praeger, 1961).

The Suez crisis left London and Paris with little influence in the Middle East, thereby providing still another possibility for tension between the two superpowers as each vied to fill that power vacuum. This realization led Eisenhower and Dulles to formulate a plan to assist any independent Arab nation in the Middle East against communist aggression. The result was the Eisenhower Doctrine,[55] authorizing the Chief Executive, as Commander in Chief, to deploy the armed forces of the United States to protect threatened Arab nations from overthrow if such nations requested American aid. The President's proposal, in addition to the provision for the utilization of armed force, called for assistance to Middle Eastern nations in developing their economies. The United States also pledged its cooperation in the implementation of regional programs of military assistance. An initial expenditure of $200 million for economic development and military aid was offered.

The measure's progress through the Senate was tortuous. Some Senators believed that the power granted the President to use armed force was beyond constitutional limitations, while others argued that to attempt to strengthen the Arab nations unilaterally would weaken the United Nations and the Western European alliance. Supporters of Israel, and those members of the Senate who had been deeply alarmed by Nasser's role in the Suez crisis, were most reluctant to aid the Arab nations. But after two months of often bitter debate the measure passed the Senate by a vote of 72 to 19, with the provision that by concurrent resolution the two houses could terminate the agreement; following House approval, it was signed in March 1957. The doctrine was an extension of the containment theory of the late 1940s, compounded by a desire to act unilaterally in the Middle East. It was dangerous to the extent that Washington's commitment to the region remained undefined. Rather than attempt neutralization through stabilization agreements with the Soviet Union, the United States opted to extend the Truman Doctrine to one of the globe's most volatile areas. It is little wonder that revisionist historian D. E. Fleming has charged that the Eisenhower Doctrine "constituted a major intensification of the Cold War. . . . [It was] a plan for ordering the affairs of the vast Middle East region through secret diplomacy, secret use of money, power politics, and unilateral action." [56]

While the Eisenhower Doctrine attempted to shield the Arab

[55] For the text Bartlett, *The Record of American Diplomacy*, pp. 842–46. Some of the details of the Administration's battle to have the doctrine approved by the Senate are offered in Sherman Adams, *Firsthand Report*, pp. 271–93.

[56] Fleming, *The Cold War and Its Origins*, II, pp. 844, 833.

nations of the Middle East from communist penetration, it could not effectively control the growing instability of the area which had resulted from Nasser's drive for Arab nationalism. In 1958 Nasser linked Egypt and Syria in the United Arab Republic, which was soon allied to the sheikdom of Yemen. Fired by a dream of Arab unity, he then set out on a vigorous campaign to topple several of the existing Middle Eastern governments so as to replace the leadership of each with men more receptive to his concept of Arab unity under the direction of the United Arab Republic.

Even before the formal creation of the UAR, both Egypt and Syria had attempted to overthrow the monarchy of King Hussein of Jordan. In July of 1958 a bloody revolution erupted in Iraq which resulted in the death of both the Premier, Nuri as Said, and King Faisal. Lebanon was soon caught in the struggle between the UAR and the opposition Arab bloc of Jordan and Iraq (which had concluded a rival pact of their own known as the Arab Union). When a civil war broke out in Lebanon between the supporters of the UAR and those seeking closer ties with the Arab Union, the half Christian, half Moslem Lebanese army could not restore order. The continuing turmoil led Lebanese President Camille Chamoun to appeal for American troops under the terms of the Eisenhower Doctrine. While communists were not directly involved in the civil war, Chamoun convinced Eisenhower that his country was the victim of "indirect aggression," and that communists might very well capitalize on the growing chaos. Responding to the Lebanese call, Eisenhower sent three Marine battalions into Beirut, and eventually over 14,000 American troops were involved in the intervention. The British, meanwhile, flew troops to Jordan to strengthen Hussein's shaky monarchy. Attempts by the Administration to obtain Security Council authorization for an international peace-keeping force failed when the Russians vetoed the American resolution.

The Soviets then threatened to retaliate for the Anglo-American moves in the Middle East by conducting maneuvers near Turkey. An alarmed Dulles flew to London to meet with the member nations of the Baghdad Pact; he obtained a commitment to extend increased military aid and to negotiate a collective security agreement with Lebanon. By the time the General Assembly met, General Fuad Chehab, acceptable to both factions in Lebanon, was elected president. In the end it was the Arab nations themselves, prodded by the United States and the Soviet Union, who sponsored a resolution pledging noninterference in one another's affairs. Under the terms of the resolution Secretary-General Dag Hammarskjöld was to arrange for the orderly withdrawal of Western troops from both Jordan and Lebanon; by the end of October 1958 all American troops had left. Yet important issues were left unanswered. How long would the Soviets permit the United States to act unilaterally in the Middle East? Should Washington have squandered the credit it had gained with the Arabs by its role in the Suez crisis? Could America continue to be the "austere opponent of all political change, on a planet that was alive with revolutionary change of several kinds"? [57] To what lengths would successive administrations go to protect a Middle Eastern oil cartel whose annual profits were in the billions? It was, after all, the enormous inequality of income distribution in the Middle East, the desperate gulf between the extraordinarily wealthy and the hungry, which caused much of the instability and provided the impetus for change.

BRINKMANSHIP AND FORMOSA

Capitalizing on American preoccupation with the Middle East, and with Lebanon in particular, the Chinese Communists in 1958 launched a major drive to gain possession of two tiny groups of islands off the mainland, Quemoy and Matsu. These two island clusters, approximately 120 miles from Nationalist-controlled Formosa, remained in the hands of Chiang Kai-shek after Mao Tse-tung's 1949 victory. In January of 1955 Congress had authorized the President

> to employ the Armed Forces of the United States as he deems necessary for the specific purpose of securing and protecting Formosa and the Pescadores against armed attack, this authority to include the securing and protection of such related positions and territories of that area now in friendly hands and the taking of such other measures as he judges to be required or appropriate in assuring the defense of Formosa and the Pescadores.[58]

It was this Formosa Resolution of 1955 which played such a prominent part in the so-called brinkmanship controversy. That is to say, in 1956 James Shepley, chief of Time-Life's Washington Bureau, published an article entitled "How Dulles Averted War." In it, Shepley not only recounted Dulles' opposition to the Truman-Acheson policy of containment but also reviewed the Secretary's theory of preventing aggression by threatening "massive retaliatory power."

[57] *Ibid.,* p. 923.
[58] The text reprinted in Eisenhower, *Mandate for Change,* Appendix "N," p. 716.

Shepley then offered three case studies of this theory—Korea, Indochina, and Formosa. Dulles was quoted as saying:

> You have to take chances for peace, just as you must take chances in war. Some say that we were brought to the verge of war. Of course we were brought to the verge of war. The ability to get to the verge without getting into the war is the necessary art. . . . If you try to run away from it, if you are scared to go to the brink, you are lost. We've had to look it square in the face—on the question of enlarging the Korean war, on the question of getting into the Indochina war, on the question of Formosa. We walked to the brink and we looked it in the face.[59]

That the Formosa Resolution—explicit as it was—constituted "brinkmanship" is doubtful, but many of Dulles' critics wondered if he had not foolishly risked war over a few tiny islands which were of very questionable strategic importance.

Since it had never been made clear whether or not Quemoy and Matsu were included under the resolution's protective umbrella as "related positions," their fate remained precarious. Against the advice of the United States, Chiang Kai-shek bolstered his troop strength on the islands so that by the summer of 1958 a third of his total ground force, some hundred thousand men, was stationed at Quemoy and Matsu. Eisenhower took the position that despite the provocative nature of Chiang Kai-shek's action, "an attack on the offshore islands would justify our military participation only if, I, as President, should judge the attack to be a preliminary to an assault on Formosa."[60] These concerns became far more pressing when in August of 1958 the Chinese Communists began massive shellings of the offshore islands; while the military and civilian population suffered some casualties, the island's main fortifications remained essentially intact. Although the Administration had not considered itself necessarily responsible for the defense of Quemoy-Matsu under the so-called Formosa Resolution of January 1955, the President did order the Seventh Fleet to convoy Nationalist Chinese supply ships to the beleaguered islands. In addition, Dulles flew to Taiwan in an attempt to convince Chiang to modify his over-all position toward Communist China and to accept a proposal which would lead to the neutralization of Quemoy and Matsu. But the Secretary obviously made little headway with the Generalissimo, who responded to Dulles' appeals by reaffirming his determination to return to mainland China.[61] The only concrete achievement of Dulles' October mission was Chiang's decision to reduce his troop strength on Quemoy.

---

[59] James Shepley, "How Dulles Averted War," *Life*, Jan. 16, 1956, p. 78.
[60] Eisenhower, *Waging Peace*, p. 294.
[61] Gerson, *John Foster Dulles*, pp. 210–12.

The Administration and the public both seemed to lose interest in the islands after Dulles' return; but at the height of the 1960 Nixon-Kennedy duel for the presidency, Vice-President Nixon strongly urged the protection of the islands and every other inch of territory in the free world. Kennedy, instead, refused to anchor Asian policy on those tiny Pacific dots. Interestingly, when in 1962 the Chinese Communists appeared to be on the verge of still another attempt to wrest the islands from the Nationalists, President Kennedy declared that basic American policy had not changed since the enunciation of the Formosa Resolution.

AMERICAN COUNTERINSURGENCY

In the postwar period, a host of nations in Asia, the Middle East, and Africa accelerated their struggles against colonialism. This fierce drive for self-determination often occurred in critical areas of the globe, and it appeared to successive American administrations that the outcome of these upheavals would almost certainly affect the world power balance. The United States actively sought the inclusion of emerging nations into the Western bloc; Moscow was assured that it would pay dearly for any attempt to absorb such regions into its sphere of influence. Such a policy, however, involved the commitment of very considerable amounts of American aid and expertise; all too often American efforts were niggardly and directed toward the maintenance of the status quo.

American reaction to post-World War II anti-colonial revolutions was complicated by a number of factors: the necessity, at times, to sharply dissent from colonialist policies of European allies; Washington's determination to exercise considerable influence over the outcome of the struggles; and the understandable tendency of latter-day revolutionaries to identify with, and employ the rhetoric of, eighteenth-century Americans such as Washington and Jefferson. The tradition, and perhaps the myth, of the American Revolution often served as an inspiration to colonial powers. The United States was respected in some quarters for its more recent policies toward Hawaii, Puerto Rico, and the Philippines. And too, American pressure on the English and Dutch to liberate India and Indonesia respectively was often admired.

While American policymakers frequently sympathized with Third World aspirations and lent technical and economic assistance, these friendly overtures were almost always tempered by considerations of national security. That is, the quest for allies in the global

balance of power often led the United States to render military
support to the very same colonial powers which were the targets of
Third World independence movements.[62] Racism at home, and the
tendency to support British and French colonialism in areas where a
communist menace loomed, have led to harsh censure. Even President
John F. Kennedy, long viewed as a liberal intellectual sympathetic to
the aspirations of Third World peoples, has been vigorously attacked
as a "cold warrior" and counterrevolutionary because of the obsessive
anti-communist bias of his diplomacy. In his *Cold War and Counterrevolution*, Richard J. Walton indicts the New Frontier President:

> It did not seem to occur to Kennedy or his advisors that there might be
> circumstances when a people, through revolution, might validly choose
> communism as offering the best path to economic and social development.
> Freedom of choice or diversity—Kennedy's admirers constantly
> cite his devotion to diversity—did not extend that far.[63]

The obsession with communism's containment in the post-1945
era tragically affected the nation's ability to respond intelligently and
compassionately to the needs of scores of emerging nations. An
excessive concern over security and the effects of the McCarthy witch
hunt too often caused American leaders to cling to anti-communist
regimes which proved to be as repressive and anti-democratic as the
European colonizers had been. Native insurgent efforts to replace such
regimes with reform governments were often regarded in Washington
as communist-inspired and therefore dangerous to American security.
Reform efforts then fell victim to Washington's support of the social
and economic status quo (under the guise of containment).[64] Aside
from the immorality and insensitivity of such an approach, the results
were often in complete variance with American goals; nationalist
leaders, frustrated by Washington's penchant for supporting feudal
regimes, understandably turned to the communists, whose sensitivity
to class struggle was often far more acute.

Theories purporting to explain why the United States has
adopted seemingly self-defeating policies toward revolution in the
Third World fall into several categories. There is, first of all, the
"security for its own sake" concept. This is the view, widely held by
official Washington, that the security and vital interests of the United

---

[62] See Seyom Brown, *The Faces of Power: Constancy and Change in United States Foreign Policy
from Truman to Johnson* (New York: Columbia University Press, 1968), p. 24.

[63] Richard J. Walton, *Cold War and Counterrevolution: The Foreign Policy of John F. Kennedy*
(New York: Viking, 1972), p. 207.

[64] This thesis is developed in John W. Spanier, *American Foreign Policy Since World War II*,
4th rev. ed. (New York: Praeger, 1971), Chap. VII.

States are directly threatened by Third World insurgency movements sponsored or supported by communists. The insignificance of the struggle and the remoteness of the locale often do not alter Washington's determination to react against this "global communist challenge." Louise FitzSimons has defined this counterinsurgency philosophy: "Despite the inherent weaknesses and severe social and economic dislocations that frequently exist in underdeveloped areas, nations can be 'built,' if only enough Americans are willing to put their energies and efforts to the task." [65]

A provocative alternative to this thesis has been offered by Richard J. Barnet, founder and co-director of the Institute for Policies Studies. Barnet suggests that the basic ideological clash in the world is not between the United States and the Soviet Union, since both adhere to the goal of an abundant consumer economy; rather the clash is between revolutionaries and "National-Security Managers" (White House, State Department, Pentagon, and CIA personnel). This official elite, deeply affected by the World War II experience and memories of Hitler's aggression, has associated the instability caused by anti-colonial insurgencies with the threat posed by the policies of the Axis powers. Insurgents must be controlled, the managers insist, because if they are not their disruptions will directly affect the United States. This belief was vividly expressed by President Johnson in 1966, when he told American troops in Vietnam: "There are 3 billion people in the world and we have only 200 million of them. We are outnumbered 15 to 1. If might did make right, they would sweep over the United States and take what we have. We have what they want." [66]

If one sets this view in tandem with the conviction that the Kremlin and Peking are continually probing for weak spots in the world power structure, then the determination of National-Security Managers to prevent revolution and anti-colonial activity from creating such instability becomes understandable. There is also an ideological consideration, for convinced of the inherent evil of the communist movement, these individuals find justification in "rescuing" unstable regimes from insurrections which might lead to a Soviet takeover.

Such attitudes have led to the characterization of National-Security Managers as "imperial peacekeepers" obsessed with the maintenance of America's "preeminent economic and political position." [67]

[65] Louise FitzSimons, *The Kennedy Doctrine* (New York: Random House, 1972), p. 177.
[66] Quoted in Richard J. Barnet, *Intervention and Revolution: The United States and the Third World* (New York: World Publishing, 1968), p. 25.
[67] *Ibid.,* pp. 29–31.

Barnet charges them with equating Third World insurgency with German and Japanese aggression simply because they too were violent challenges to the status quo. But the policy-makers are not consistent since they tend not to oppose violence which is employed to maintain the established order (France in Indochina). Also, the number of dictatorships which have been the beneficiaries of American largess in the post-1945 era further strains the credibility of the national security thesis. Military takeovers by elements aligning themselves with United States' policies—such as Argentina in 1955, South Korea in 1961, Indonesia in 1966, and Ghana in 1966—have certainly not been thwarted by Washington. Finally, Barnet charges that it is a "psychotic fantasy" [68] to insist that revolutionaries in Latin America, Asia, and Africa will band together and threaten the security of the United States.

A quite different thesis regarding the prevailing American stance toward Third World revolutionary activity is offered by adherents of the theory of economic causation. In his *The Roots of American Foreign Policy*, Gabriel Kolko has charged that Washington's determination to ensure a continuing supply of raw materials, plus a market for its exports, has molded its response to the Third World:

> The dominant interest of the United States is in world economic stability, and anything that undermines that condition presents a danger to its present hegemony. Countering, neutralizing and containing the disturbing political and social trends thus becomes the most imperative objective of its foreign policy.[69]

Evidence for American dependence upon raw materials furnished by so-called developing nations is not difficult to find; in 1965 they produced 37 percent of the world's iron ore output, 65 percent of the oil, and 69 percent of the bauxite (for aluminum).[70]

On another level, it is charged by Kolko that American overseas loan, investment, and tariff policies have made the United States "the bastion of the *ancien régime*, of stagnation and continued poverty for the Third World." Thus even modest reform movements are opposed for their implied threat to the existing order. In this view, the United States was in Vietnam not because its major interests were specifically threatened, but rather because it wished to provide a lesson to Third World nations of what they will encounter if they seek to control their own destinies. Massive American intervention has been most significant as an

---

[68] *Ibid.,* pp. 273. Also, pp. 257–85.

[69] Gabriel Kolko, *The Roots of American Foreign Policy: An Analysis of Power and Purpose* (Boston: Beacon Press, 1969), p. 55.

[70] *Ibid.,* p. 52.

example of America's determination to hold the line as a matter of principle against revolutionary movements. . . . All the various American leaders believe in global stability which they are committed to defend against revolution that may threaten the existing distribution of economic power in the world.[71]

POWER PLAY IN THE CONGO

The realignment of power following the Second World War was a profound phenomenon because it affected virtually every sector of the globe; a direct result of the power shift was the awakening of the continent of Africa. The appearance on the world scene of scores of emergent nations—many with artificial boundaries, if measured in terms of geographical unity or racial homogeneity—made for staggering problems. A huge, brooding continent, Africa was deeply affected by the post-1945 decline of the colonial powers; its intellectuals, many of whom had studied in the capitals of the imperialist states which had captured their peoples, soon were in the vanguard of those determined to create a new role for Africans. Reconstruction, the distractions of the Cold War, and European political, social, and economic reform had enabled these new African leaders to enjoy a period of self-direction unknown for more than a century.[72] The aggressive Arab nationalism personified by Egypt's restless Colonel Nasser provided a model for many, but the expectations of those active in the growing African nationalist movements were only very minimally fulfilled. In the absence of political stability, foreign investment, population control, and widespread industrialization, Africa experienced a slow, often dispiriting, and in many instances fruitless struggle for modernization. Too often the insistence that the former imperialists depart at once has worked against the success of emerging nations. The admission of dozens of these newly liberated states into the United Nations, and their extreme visibility as a voting bloc in the Assembly, have proven a very poor index of their actual power and importance. Nevertheless, as the crisis in the Congo soon made apparent, the continent of Africa has been viewed by the two superpowers as a major diplomatic battlefield. Relatedly, one of the cruelest dilemmas for the United States in the postwar period involves

[71] *Ibid.*, pp. 78, 85–86.
[72] See Chester Bowles, *Africa's Challenge to America* (Berkeley, Calif.: University of California Press, 1966), and G. W. Shepherd, Jr., *The Politics of African Nationalism* (New York: Praeger, 1962). Also Rupert Emerson, *From Empire to Nation* (Cambridge, Mass.: Harvard University Press, 1960).

the conflict between Washington's responsibility to its European allies (some of whom were still playing the role of nineteenth-century imperialists in Africa) and America's sympathy for those African states attempting to win their independence.

In the years before the Second World War the United States had relatively few diplomatic contacts with Africa, although from 1853 on, consular posts were established in Liberia, the Congo, Ethiopia, Nigeria, Kenya, Morocco, South Africa, and Zanzibar. But it was only with the outbreak of World War II that Washington took a political interest in these areas. The level of military activity on the continent during the war, and the over-all importance of the continent in the war effort, made such a development inevitable. In 1937 the State Department transferred responsibility for African affairs from the Division of European Affairs to the Near Eastern Division. But because of extensive European colonial involvement in the continent, almost all substantive decisions were still made by the Division of European Affairs. Only in the midst of the war, in 1943, was a separate African Section created within the Near Eastern Division. By 1956 the post of Deputy Assistant Secretary for African Affairs was established, and two years later the Bureau of African Affairs—for all of Africa except Egypt—was formed under the direction of an Assistant Secretary for African Affairs.[73]

The conflict between the demands of the emergent African nations for more active American support for their independence struggles and the corresponding hostility of the colonial powers when such encouragement was suggested led to the October 1953 "decision" to forego a comprehensive policy and to deal with specific colonial issues. Not only was this unsatisfactory to African nationalists, it also played into the hands of the Soviet Union, which was not burdened with allies having a stake in the maintenance of the colonial system. Russian support of Africa's rigorous anti-colonialism, together with Soviet economic assistance, greatly enhanced Moscow's position on that continent.

The complex struggle for control of colonized Africa was most clearly evidenced in the Congo crisis. The Belgian Congo, like almost every other area of Africa, had been seared by the fiery nationalism which swept the continent in the postwar era. In January 1959 the growing tension between Belgian authorities and impatient Congolese erupted in a riot in Leopoldville, resulting in the killing of many natives. The resident whites and Belgian authorities, terrified by the

---

[73] This development is outlined in G. Mennen Williams, "Diplomatic Rapport between Africa and the United States," Department of State *Bulletin*, L (May 4, 1964), pp. 698–703.

thought of a racial civil war, supported a policy calling for the almost immediate independence of that colony. It was announced that on June 30, 1960, the Congo would be granted its freedom. Such a decision, probably inevitable, proved tragic: the abruptness of the transfer and the Congolese people's lack of preparation to assume control of their own affairs boded ill for success.

Untrained for these new responsibilities, the Congolese were also deeply divided by bitter political infighting over a basic ideological issue involving the very structure of the emergent government. Two of the nation's most prominent political figures, President Joseph Kasa-vubu and Prime Minister Patrice Lumumba, personified the opposing theories. It was Kasavubu's view that given the Congo's hundreds of tribes and more than 400 dialects it was both appropriate and inevitable that a federal government be established with a loose central structure. The mercurial leftist Lumumba argued for a strong centralized government which would pursue a neutralist position. The intense rivalry of these two major political figures, and the extreme emotionalism of their respective campaigns, greatly added to the general deterioration of order in the Congo. Within a week of the nation's independence renewed tribal warfare, accompanied by barbaric atrocities which terrified both the whites and native groups, reduced the region to chaos. Accounts of attacks by Congolese soldiers on white women and children electrified world public opinion, which extended its sympathy to the fleeing Belgian settlers. The internal chaos and the exodus of Belgian technicians led to a collapse of all public services.

Ominously, in the face of this disaster the mineral rich province of Katanga seceded from the Congo and established its own govern-ment under the direction of Moise Tshombe at Elizabethville. The secession was encouraged by powerful European and American mining interests, particularly the Société Générale, Belgium's most powerful industrial-financial conglomerate. The considerable number of British stockholders in the Société Générale added substance to the charge that the secession of Katanga was not only of use to the former colonists but had indeed been plotted by them.[74] It is certainly true that Belgian technicians, civil servants, and administrators who fled from the Congo often made their services available to Katanga, and that Katanga's military force was considerably strengthened by the presence of Belgian, French, and Rhodesian mercenaries.

Faced with the near collapse of his country and with the realization that Belgian troops would return to restore order, Prime

[74] La Feber, *America, Russia, and the Cold War,* p. 241.

Minister Lumumba desperately appealed to the United Nations Security Council. The result was a July 1960 resolution to provide the country with sufficient military aid to restore order; the United Nations called upon Belgium to withdraw all troops from the Congo, including Katanga. Prime Minister Lumumba also issued an appeal for Soviet assistance, and by September Soviet technicians were visible in Leopoldville, as was Soviet military assistance to Lumumba's army. Greatly alarmed by his Prime Minister's interjection of the Soviet Union into the already chaotic situation, Kasavubu fired Lumumba, closed the Soviet and Czechoslovakian embassies, and voiced his strong preference for a United Nations directed solution. These swift actions dealt a death blow to the main thrust of Soviet ambition in the Congo, leading Khrushchev to order the use of Russia's veto in all future Security Council actions. A bitter personal attack on Secretary-General Dag Hammarskjöld was launched, since Chairman Khrushchev was fully aware that the 20,000 troops sent by the United Nations greatly reduced the justification for any further Soviet intervention in Congolese affairs.

By the time Kennedy took office in January of 1961, Colonel Joseph Mobutu had seized control of the Congolese government, thereby averting still another bloody round of the civil war between Lumumba and Kasavubu supporters. The Mobutu government leaned strongly toward the West and permitted the orderly return of many Belgian nationals who wished to resume their official positions. At the United Nations, after a bitter fight between rival Congolese delegations representing Kasavubu and Lumumba, the United States threw its support behind the followers of Kasavubu, and that delegation was finally seated. In the meantime, Lumumba, whose followers were organizing a revolt against the central government, was captured, mysteriously turned over to Tshombe, and executed. Thus the new American President was faced with a continuing crisis in Africa, one which was heightened by Russian demands for the withdrawal of United Nations troops from the Congo. According to Special Assistant to the President, Arthur Schlesinger, Jr., it was Kennedy's view that "unless the United Nations filled the vacuum in the Congo, there would be no alternative but a direct Soviet-American confrontation." [75] The avoidance of such a conflict depended in large measure upon the restoration of the Kasavubu-Mobutu government's authority over all of the Congo. In another sense, it was necessary for the Kennedy Administration to support Kasavubu

[75] Arthur M. Schlesinger, Jr., *A Thousand Days: John F. Kennedy in the White House* (Boston: Houghton Mifflin, 1965), p. 575.

against Tshombe to prove to the rest of the world that the United States was not seeking a return of the colonialists via Katanga. The election in July 1961 of a new Congolese government headed by Prime Minister Cyrille Adoula precipitated another round in the conflict between Katanga and the United Nation forces. When Hammarskjöld flew to the Congo to mediate a cease-fire, he was killed in a plane crash.

Ironically, the growing bitterness between the United States and the Soviet Union over the Congo question, coupled with the extreme frustration experienced by the United Nations in its attempt to ease the crisis, led to a solution along lines originally suggested by Lumumba. That is to say, with the strong support of the Kennedy Administration the United Nations reversed its original policy of utilizing its forces for peace-keeping and self-defense; instead, the United Nations contingent took the offensive by actively supporting the central government against Tshombe's mercenaries.

The shift in policy unleashed a storm of criticism from Moscow, which threatened direct intervention. Tshombe's resistance was of very short duration, and by the opening of 1963 the Katanga secession was crushed. Apparently Kennedy had been absolutely convinced that failure by the United Nations to unite the Congo would have led Leopoldville to turn to the Soviet Union to achieve its goal of unification; such assistance would have been forthcoming at the probable expense of the Congo's sovereignty. According to Schlesinger, Kennedy had "already decided to lend American fighter planes to the UN force if they were requested; and this suggests that he was ready, if necessary, to go very far down the military road to secure a unified Congo." [76]

It is precisely this attitude which has caused much debate over American involvement in the Congo and elsewhere in the Third World. Schlesinger defends Kennedy's support for the United Nations' counterinsurgency activity by asserting that such action preserved the Congo as a national entity, gave the United Nations a great moral victory, greatly lessened the possibility of a Soviet-American military confrontation in Africa, and, "above all," won for the President the confidence of the new African states.[77] But the Presidential Assistant's account omits a number of considerations which have not escaped less partial observers. For example, in his *The Faces of Power,* Seyom Brown observes that the American goal in the Congo was to avoid direct involvement while excluding the Soviets. To this end, Washington

[76] *Ibid.,* p. 578.
[77] *Ibid.,* p. 579.

utilized the United Nations to forestall the introduction of Soviet military assistance and even encouraged the Secretariat to assume supranational functions to ensure domestic order. In so doing, the United States dispensed with its

> formal legalistic position in favor of the sovereignty of nations and the inability of the United Nations to act on domestic matters, particularly to take sides in favor of certain contending political factions within a nation. The balance of power was at stake, and we knew where our interests lay.[78]

The revisionist David Horowitz has gone beyond Brown by charging that the United States Central Intelligence Agency actually engineered the coup d'état against Lumumba, utilizing the Secretariat of the United Nations to further its policy of global containment. It is Horowitz's contention that the Katanga secession was instigated by Belgium, and that in its unification offensive the United Nations "returned political control of the Congo to agents of the Belgian-British and United States mining interests of the same Katanga province." [79] Hence America's Congo policy is seen as part of that anti-revolutionary doctrine which in the postwar period was applied to Guatemala, Lebanon, Cuba, the Dominican Republic, and Vietnam.

Despite the success of American anti-Soviet strategies in the Congo, the tension between Washington's European allies and their African colonies continued. When in the winter of 1960 an Afro-Asian bloc of 43 nations sponsored a resolution calling upon the United Nations to act at once to put an end to the colonial status of all peoples, the United States abstained. In the words of Resolution 1514, the General Assembly

> Solemnly proclaims the necessity of bringing to a speedy and unconditional end colonialism in all its forms and manifestations; And to this end Declares that: . . . Immediate steps shall be taken . . . to transfer all powers to the peoples of those territories, without any conditions or reservations, in accordance with their freely expressed will and desire, without any distinction as to race, creed or colour, in order to enable them to enjoy complete independence and freedom.[80]

This resolution was adopted on December 14, 1960, by a vote of 89 to 0, with nine members, including the United States, abstaining.

[78] Brown, *The Faces of Power*, p. 237.

[79] Horowitz, *The Free World Colossus*, p. 425. Also Conor Cruise O'Brien, "The Congo: A Balance Sheet," *New Left Review*, 31, May-June 1965.

[80] Resolution 1514 is reprinted in its entirety in Bartlett, *The Record of American Diplomacy*, pp. 854–55.

In explaining the American position, Ambassador James J. Wadsworth, Deputy United Nations Delegate, voiced the Administration's concern that the sponsors had all but disregarded the necessity of preparing for an orderly and effective transition of power. And too, as the United States read the document, the insistence that all armed action against dependent peoples cease appeared to disregard the—at times—legitimate necessity to resort to arms to maintain order.[81] While some of the objections to Resolution 1514 were obviously sound, the abstention was viewed by many in the Afro-Asian bloc as an endorsement of continued colonialism. It was not until the Kennedy Administration's vigorous campaign for the restoration of complete sovereignty for the entire Congo that some of these suspicions were allayed.

GUATEMALA TESTS THE GOOD NEIGHBOR POLICY

Still another continent, South America, was of deep concern to the United States during the two postwar decades. The great number of underdeveloped nations in Latin America at once invites comparison with Africa, but there are a number of substantive differences between the continents. Whereas America's role in Africa had been minimal before the Second World War, there had been continuing, if sporadic, involvement in Latin American affairs for more than a century. The existence of the Monroe Doctrine, and its application by James Polk, Secretary of State William Seward, and Theodore Roosevelt, ensured continued contacts, if not harmonious ones. The Good Neighbor Policy had, by 1960, officially defined United States-Latin American relations for a generation. In the years following World War II, billions of dollars of investment capital flowed into Latin American countries, but these funds were grossly inadequate to even begin to meet the needs of these nations since they were not designed to effect basic social or economic reforms. Even given the limited nature of American financial resources, the emphasis placed on Western European recovery after 1945 led to Washington's near abandonment of Latin America. Only with the formulation of the Alliance for Progress during the Kennedy years was a reasonably responsible beginning made to provide capital for public services—housing, schools, hospitals, and transportation.

Certain parallels between Africa and South America emerge, for both continents were torn by the "rising expectations" of their various

---

[81] Wadsworth's statement, in part, appears in *Ibid.,* pp. 855–57.

national groups. While in Africa the nationalists were attempting to rid their homelands of European imperialists, in South America traditional conservative oligarchies were the principal targets. And while there were some examples of limited economic success—particularly in Colombia and Venezuela—the great majority of Latin American countries shared Africa's almost hopeless frustration in attempting to both industrialize and achieve broad social reform. While the successes of Colombia and Venezuela were encouraging, Cuba, Haiti, the Dominican Republic, Guatemala, Chile, Ecuador, Paraguay, and Bolivia were among the many nations whose levels of industrialization and social reform were very discouraging. Throughout the 1950s these and other Latin American countries, beleaguered by poverty, overpopulation, corruption, economic instability, and oligarchic governments, smoldered while the United States rushed to the aid of Europe or intervened militarily in Asia. Given American priorities, they enjoyed a most unenviable position.

It was concern over a communist takeover of the Central American state of Guatemala which convinced the Eisenhower Administration of the crisis to the south. Unfortunately, the major solution was found not in programs for the alleviation of Latin America's most crushing economic and social problems, but rather in a self-serving military effort against an alleged communist threat. Toward the end of the Second World War, Guatemala's military dictatorship had been overthrown, and after a half dozen years of leftist agitation, control of the government rested with Jacobo Arbenz Guzmán, a military officer with strong communist leanings. In the early 1950s American relations with the Arbenz government were cordial, if somewhat cool, but in February of 1953 it was announced that 225,000 acres of land belonging to the United Fruit Company was to be expropriated under a new agrarian reform law. In the resultant settlement, United Fruit was awarded $600,000 in long-term, nonnegotiable agrarian bonds. (In criticizing this "woefully inadequate compensation" in his memoirs, Eisenhower does not question the propriety of United Fruit's owning hundreds of thousands of acres of land in a foreign country.)[82] Shortly thereafter Guatemala withdrew from the Organization of Central American States on the grounds that its neighbors were openly hostile to the Arbenz government. At the end of 1953 Eisenhower appointed a new ambassador, John E. Peurifoy, who had served in Greece during the attempted communist takeover of that country; within a month Peurifoy concluded that Arbenz "thought like a Communist and

[82] Eisenhower, *Mandate for Change,* p. 505.

talked like a Communist, and if not actually one, would do until one came along. . . . unless the Communist influences in Guatemala were counteracted, Guatemala would within six months fall completely under Communist control." [83]

In an attempt to mobilize hemispheric opinion against Arbenz, a draft resolution of a "Declaration of Solidarity for the Preservation of the Political Integrity of the American States against International Communist Intervention" was sponsored by the Administration at a March 1954 meeting of the Organization of American States in Caracas, Venezuela. The document condemned "The activities of the international communist movement as constituting intervention in American affairs." Since the right of any American state to freely adopt a communistic system was not seriously considered, it was resolved:

> That the domination or control of the political institutions of any American State by the international communist movement, extending to this Hemisphere the political system of an extracontinental power, would constitute a threat to the sovereignty and political independence of the American States.[84]

Guatemala voted against the resolution, which passed by a vote of 17–1, with Argentina and Mexico abstaining.

Scarcely two months later it was learned that the Swedish freighter *Alfhem* had delivered 2,000 tons of Czechoslovak-made arms to the Arbenz government. Nicaragua and Honduras declared themselves to be threatened by the alleged Communist regime in Guatemala, and the United States airlifted war materiel to them to counter the Czech shipment. While the United States was considering further action against Guatemala—including an arms quarantine— Arbenz proclaimed a dictatorship in early June. Shortly thereafter he ordered a bloody purge of his political enemies.

Within weeks an exiled Guatemalan army colonel, Carlos Castillo Armas, formed an expeditionary force in Honduras and invaded Guatemala. When the loss of two of the three bombers Castillo was using threatened to bring his offensive to a halt, Eisenhower, overruling the objection that American intervention would lead to charges of a resumption of turn-of-the-century policies, ordered arms shipped to the insurgents. Castillo's success was insured. In disregarding the United Nations and the OAS, the United States by its unilateral intervention lent considerable plausibility to the

[83] Quoted in *Ibid.*, p. 506.
[84] Reprinted in Bartlett, *The Record of American Diplomacy*, p. 860.

charge that it had sponsored Castillo's campaign in the first place. It was assumed after Castillo took power in July that his regime was under the direction of the United States.[85] The unwillingness to distinguish between Moscow- or Peking-directed communism and its more indigenous varieties accounted at least in part for much of the criticism which followed the Guatemala episode. The tendency to regard *any* instance of communism in the Western Hemisphere as a *direct* threat to American security was most questionable. The United States had not as yet achieved that very delicate balance between protecting its own security and recognizing the legitimate right of Western Hemispheric nations to self-determination.

But there is an even more basic question: the extent to which communism had actually gained a foothold in Guatemala before Eisenhower and Castillo came to the rescue. The official position of the American government was outlined in a State Department "White Paper," [86] but these findings have been bitterly challenged. For example, David Horowitz has pointed out in *The Free World Colossus* that in May of 1954, 3,000 to 4,000 of the 3,000,000 inhabitants of the country were members of the Communist party and the average age of those on the Central Committee was 26. Only four of the 56 Congress seats were held by party members; not one of the Cabinet personnel was affiliated with the party. The army and police were not controlled by the Communists, Horowitz charged, although a number of important government bureaucracies were.[87]

The role of labor, and the extent of communist penetration in the Guatemalan labor movement, is of course a major test. In a study of this critical issue a political analyst for the State Department has concluded that the Communists had far less influence than is usually assumed. The Communists had gained important key positions in the Guatemalan political struggle, but they "had not found sufficient time to build a broad base or sink their roots deeply. . . . when the showdown came in June 1954 only a proportionally small number of workers were ready or willing to act." [88] In the absence of communist

---

[85] See Philip B. Taylor, Jr., "The Guatemalan Affair: A Critique of United States Foreign Policy," *American Political Science Review*, Vol. L (Sept. 1956), and John Gillen and K. H. Silver, "Ambiguities in Guatemala," *Foreign Affairs*, Vol. XXXIV (Apr. 1956). The incident is also considered in a very brief manner in Gerson, *John Foster Dulles*, pp. 313–14.

[86] Department of State, White Paper, *Intervention of International Communism in Guatemala*, 1954.

[87] D. Horowitz, *The Free World Colossus*, p. 163.

[88] Ronald M. Schneider, *Communism in Guatemala* (New York: Praeger, 1958), pp. 317–18. Also see John D. Martz, *Communist Infiltration in Guatemala* (New York: Vantage, 1956); and Philip B. Taylor, Jr., "The Guatemalan Affair: A Critique of United States Foreign Policy," *The American Political Science Review*, L, No. 3 (Sept. 1956). The last work is particularly useful for the U.N. debate.

control of the army or of rank and file labor, it is doubtful that the danger of a communist takeover of Guatemala was as imminent—or as probable—as Eisenhower and Dulles assumed.

It is not surprising that Vice President Richard Nixon's good-will tour of eight South American countries in April of 1958 was greeted by unmistakable expressions of Yankeephobia in every country he visited. By the time the Vice-President reached Caracas these attacks had become so intense that he was forced to cancel the remainder of his trip and return to Washington (the picture of Nixon trapped in his limousine by an ugly Venezuelan mob will long be remembered). The need for a revision of priorities was so evident after the Nixon trip that in May 1959, Eisenhower proposed the formation of an Inter-American Development Bank to provide economic assistance to its members. In addition, the United States supported the so-called Act of Bogotá, which was endorsed by 21 hemispheric states on September 13, 1960.[89] This blueprint for economic cooperation called for the improvement of conditions of rural living and land use; of housing and community facilities; of educational systems and training facilities; and of public health. The mobilization of domestic resources, as well as general economic development, was also stressed.

CASTRO, KHRUSHCHEV, AND KENNEDY

The greatest test of America's policy of nonintervention in the internal affairs of another hemispheric nation occurred during Fidel Castro's takeover of Cuba. At the time Castro's revolutionaries became active Cuba was under the reign of one of Latin America's most tyrannical dictators, Fulgencio Batista. While still in his early twenties Castro, the son of a landowner and himself a lawyer, had assembled a band of followers dedicated to the overthrow of the government. These revolutionaries had attempted, on July 26, 1953, to overrun the Moncado barracks in Santiago de Cuba, but were beaten back; for the next three years Castro continued his struggle both on the island and from his exile in Mexico. Castro had been given a 15-year prison term for his anti-Batista activities but was released under a general government amnesty. By the end of 1956 he was again organizing, and in December he launched an attack from his Mexican base on Cuba's Oriente province; despite the intensity of the Batista-directed defensive, the bearded revolutionary and some few of his followers succeeded in reaching the Sierra Maestra. Castro led an effective

---

[89] For the text, see Department of State *Bulletin*, Vol. XLIII (Oct. 3, 1960), pp. 533–40.

guerrilla campaign from these hills until his victory early in 1959. Press censorship, Batista-inspired reports of Castro's death, and brutal reprisals against those suspected of guerrilla activity failed to prevent the revolutionary's swiftly gaining the stature of a national hero.

The growing strength of the movement placed considerable strain on the Eisenhower Administration, especially since it was obvious that millions of American dollars in military aid to Batista were being used to defeat Castro, and not for hemispheric defense. In March of 1958 an embargo was ordered against further shipments of arms to Cuba, and in a November news conference Eisenhower announced that the United States would pursue a policy of nonintervention, unless the lives of Americans in Cuba were endangered. But by this time Allen Dulles' Central Intelligence Agency had become convinced that American interests would not be served by a Castro victory. "Communists and other extreme radicals appear to have penetrated the Castro movement," the CIA reported to the President. "If Castro takes over, they will probably participate in the government." [90] Rejecting the CIA's recommendation that the United States back Batista, Eisenhower hoped for the emergence of a third alternative, which was not forthcoming.

The conflict over Castro's reputed adherence to a Marxist-Leninist line prior to 1960 will rage for a very long time. There were those in the Department of State, particularly the American Ambassador to Cuba, Earl Smith, who were convinced of Castro's early communist leanings. But others more sympathetic to Castro have argued that his greatest support came from the middle class—doctors, lawyers, teachers, and others disillusioned and disgusted by the dictatorship— and that it was the support of this group which made his victory possible.[91] Once successful, the revolutionary did embrace a Marxist position, for he had concluded that he would be unable to fulfill his pledge of restoring democracy to Cuba. He also adopted a decidedly anti-American line. The promised early elections were postponed, and by March of 1959 Allen Dulles reported to Eisenhower:

> [T]he Castro regime is moving toward a complete dictatorship. Communists are now operating openly and legally in Cuba. And although Castro's government is *not* Communist-dominated, Communists have worked their way into the labor unions, the armed forces, and other organizations.[92]

[90] Quoted in Eisenhower, *Waging Peace*, p. 521.
[91] See Earl Smith, *The Fourth Floor: An Account of the Castro Communist Revolution* (New York: Random House, 1962). Perhaps the strongest statement of the opposing view is contained in Theodore Draper, *Castro's Revolution: Myths and Realities* (New York: Praeger, 1962).
[92] Quoted in Eisenhower, *Waging Peace*, p. 523. Italics his.

Having concluded that the regime constituted a communist penetration of the Western Hemisphere, the Eisenhower Administration was faced with a grave dilemma. To take strong action against Castro, whose government was viewed as a menace to American security, would most assuredly alienate millions of Latin Americans who were Castro's enthusiastic supporters. At the same time the American public had grown increasingly critical of Havana as reports of mass trials and executions of Castro's political enemies were revealed. And too, the nationalization of many American companies, and the expropriation of foreign-owned land, did not increase Castro's popularity in the United States; neither did the announced sale of more than a million and a half tons of Cuban sugar to the USSR.[93]

Alarmed by Havana's threat to the anti-communist tradition of the Western Hemisphere, Eisenhower embarked on a good-will tour of South America in February of 1960. The trip itself was unexceptional, but within days of his return the President personally ordered the CIA to organize and train Cuban exiles in Guatemala and other parts of Central America for a future invasion of Cuba. It is little wonder that by early in 1961 diplomatic relations were broken. The activities of the Central Intelligence Agency were the direct result of the Eisenhower Administration's decision to actively support an invasion of Cuba. In his memoirs Eisenhower is very candid about the invasion plans, and notes that at least one serious difficulty was the inability of the exiles to settle upon a leader who was both anti-Castro and anti-Batista.[94]

Among its many other legacies to the Kennedy Administration, the outgoing government left its commitment to support CIA-trained Cuban exiles in their expected offensive against Castro. It is tempting to conclude that the extent of the Eisenhower Administration's commitment to these exiles made it impossible for Kennedy to reverse the policy. Such an argument, however, is very unconvincing in light of the evidence. Admittedly, given an American electoral system which permits a two-month delay between the election and inauguration of a president, the CIA had been free to develop its new design for an amphibious invasion of the island. Yet the new President clearly had the opportunity to withdraw American support from the planned offensive, had he desired to do so. The very intensity of early Cabinet meetings indicates that the decision was far from final and that Kennedy might well have reversed the course set by the previous Administration.

[93] Nicolas Rivero, *Castro's Cuba: An American Dilemma* (Washington, D.C.: Robert B. Luce, 1962).

[94] Eisenhower, *Waging Peace*, pp. 613–14. Also Richard M. Nixon, *Six Crises* (Garden City, N.Y.: Doubleday, 1962), pp. 352–55.

One is then left to question why the decision was made to support the invasion. The major reason was a failure to keep in perspective the threat posed by Castro's introduction of communism to the Western Hemisphere. The fear that Cuba would move into the Soviet orbit, and at the behest of Russia instigate a series of revolutions in Latin America, preyed upon the President's imagination. More importantly, Kennedy and his advisors (with the exception of some, such as J. William Fulbright, Chairman of the Senate Foreign Relations Committee, Arthur M. Schlesinger, Jr., Special Assistant to the President, and Adolf Berle, head of the Latin American task force) overestimated the threat presented by Havana. As Fulbright unsuccessfully argued, the United States could afford to tolerate the Castro regime, especially if through the Organization of American States and the Alliance for Progress it could be contained. To attempt to use armed force, Fulbright argued, would violate Washington's pledges of noninterference in the internal affairs of Latin American nations, would violate the charter of the OAS, would place a great strain on the United Nations, and, finally, would ignore America's traditional support of the self-determination of nations. Through all of this, Fulbright accomplished something which eluded Kennedy and most of his advisors—that is, a sense of proportion. In his memorandum to the President opposing the invasion, Fulbright wrote: "The Castro regime is a thorn in the flesh; but it is not a dagger in the heart." [95] That was the central point, and failure to recognize this was one of Kennedy's most serious blunders. Like his predecessors, the new President was trapped by a Cold War, Communism vs. the Free World, frame of reference.

There were, of course, other reasons for the decision. The so-called "disposal problem" was much discussed, for what was the Administration to do with the nearly 1,500 men (mostly in Guatemala) who had been trained and equipped by the CIA? Should they be left in Guatemala to foment trouble elsewhere in Latin America; should they be moved to the United States, where they would grow restive and troublesome?[96] In evaluating the President's decision, Schlesinger excuses much since Kennedy had been in office only a short time and did not have a clear impression of the competence of his advisors. Moreover, senior career officers in the Foreign Service, the Director of the Central Intelligence Agency, the Joint Chiefs of Staff, and the Secretaries of State and Defense supported the adventure. Schlesinger also points to a very personal factor which was surely of great importance:

[95] Quoted in Schlesinger, Jr., *A Thousand Days*, p. 251.
[96] See Karl E. Meyer and Tad Szulc, *The Cuban Invasion* (New York: Praeger, 1962).

[T]he enormous confidence in his [Kennedy's] own luck. Everything had broken right for him since 1956. He had won the nomination and the election against all the odds in the book. Everyone around him thought he had the Midas touch and could not lose. Despite himself, even this dispassionate and skeptical man may have been affected by the soaring euphoria of the new day.[97]

The failure of the Bay of Pigs invasion is quickly told. The April 1961 White Paper on Cuba which denounced Castro's government as a threat to the security of the Western Hemisphere was followed by the April 17 invasion of 1,200 anti-Castro Cubans. This expeditionary force, trained and equipped by the United States, arrived at the Bay of Pigs in American ships. It had been expected that the invasion on the southern coast would encourage the island's presumably suffering millions to rise up and overthrow the Castro regime. These expectations were cruelly dashed when the anticipated uprising did not occur; within three days the invaders were either killed or captured by Castro's still-loyal militia.

The whole affair was a total disaster, a great embarrassment to the United States and a useful (and utilized) piece of propaganda for the Soviet Union. The new President's reputed Midas touch was very seriously tarnished, despite his courageous admission that responsibility for the debacle must rest on his shoulders: "Victory has one hundred fathers but defeat is an orphan." [98] The Cubans rightfully brought the matter to the United Nations on the very day of the invasion, charging that the United States had violated two fundamental principles of the inter-American system: political sovereignty and economic security. Among the many tragedies of the affair was the way in which the Kennedy Administration handled the crisis in the United Nations. The United States Ambassador to the United Nations, Adlai Stevenson, had been incompletely briefed on American participation in the invasion and was later to tell Pierre Salinger that the entire incident had been the most "humiliating experience" of his many years in government.[99] Unaware of the depth of American involvement in the adventure, Stevenson replied to Cuban charges by asserting that the United States had committed no aggression against Cuba—nor had it launched an offensive from Florida. Ambassador Stevenson's uninformed protest notwithstanding, the New Frontier had erred in embracing the Eisenhower Administration's invasion scheme, in retaining Allen Dulles as head of the CIA, in losing control

[97] Schlesinger, Jr., *A Thousand Days,* p. 259.
[98] Pierre Salinger, *With Kennedy* (Garden City, N.Y.: Doubleday, 1966), p. 154.
[99] *Ibid.*, p. 147.

of the adventure and, most of all, in overestimating and overreacting to the threat posed by Castro.

The painful acknowledgment that Castro would be a long-term fixture in Latin American affairs, coupled with the dictator's May 1, 1961, announcement that Cuba had been transformed into a socialist state, reinforced Kennedy's belief in the necessity of strengthening the social and economic structures of the other Latin American governments. The Administration's major thrust in this direction, the Alliance for Progress, had been considered as early as March of 1961. Following the Bay of Pigs fiasco, an August meeting of economic leaders was scheduled at Punte del Este, Uruguay, where the charter of the Alliance was formalized. Signed by all Latin American republics with the exception of Cuba, the Alliance pledged a minimum of $20 billion in aid for economic development throughout the Sixties. The United States alone would contribute half of this amount, and the balance would be made available by a variety of international agencies, European powers, and private sources.

Cuba's exclusion from the Alliance and Castro's sensational December 1961 speech in which he announced his conversion to a Marxist-Leninist philosophy moved the island nation closer to the Soviet Union and, correspondingly, increased the fears of those in power in the United States.[100] This polarization continued the following year, for in January of 1962 Castro signed a far-reaching trade agreement with the Soviet Union. It was also announced that the Cuban army had grown to 250,000. Fears and rumors that the hemispheric Marxist had dispatched agents to other Latin American nations to plot their overthrow led to Cuba's expulsion from the Organization of American States.

A major crisis loomed in the spring and summer as evidence mounted that Russian-built missiles were being installed on the island. At first, U-2 surveillance flights revealed the construction of so-called surface-to-air missile sites, but their importance was discounted because of their relatively short range. But in mid-October these U-2 photos disclosed construction of sites for medium-range missiles capable of traveling approximately 1,000 miles. The threat to the United States was now apparent, and the Administration's anxiety was increased when intermediate-range missiles (over 2,000 miles) were sighted. The Russians had never before stationed such strategic war materiel beyond their own borders, and even though the United

---

[100] For the view that America's failure to deal effectively with Cuba's revolutionary nationalism led to Castro's conversion, see William Appleman Williams, *The United States, Cuba, and Castro: An Essay in the Dynamics of Revolution and the Dissolution of Empire* (New York: Monthly Review Press, 1962).

States had missile installations in Turkey, none had been placed in East Europe.

The challenge to American security was obvious, and in the President's view the introduction of such weapons in Cuba was a deliberate attempt to unsettle the balance of power. From the very first he established his objective: to force Soviet capitulation, by military means if necessary. Robert Kennedy recalls in his *Thirteen Days* that only a small minority of the Executive Committee of the National Security Council believed that the missiles did not alter the existing balance of power and so retaliatory action was not necessary. On the first day of the crisis most of the President's closest advisors favored an air strike against the sites.[101] During those 13 most eventful days of the Kennedy Administration, several alternatives were discussed: an air strike; an invasion of Cuba; and a naval quarantine (blockade) of Cuba to prevent Russia from delivering additional materiel or preparing additional sites. Apparently only military solutions were seriously considered, for when United Nations Ambassador Adlai Stevenson suggested that political solutions be explored, his concept was "instantly rejected" by the President.[102] After meeting with the National Security Council on the nineteenth the President concluded that a blockade was the most appropriate answer to the Soviet threat, particularly since it would constitute a far more flexible arrangement than either an invasion or an air strike.

It was agreed that the President would address the nation on October 22 to underscore the gravity of the crisis and to outline the quarantine strategy. At the same time, the Organization of American States and Washington's principal allies were briefed on the American position. The United States also readied itself militarily by placing its missile crews on maximum alert and by moving troops to the Southeast, particularly Florida and Georgia. One hundred and eighty ships were deployed in the Caribbean and the B-52 bomber force, carrying atomic weapons, was ordered into the air. The Congress was briefed hours before the President's nationwide speech, but many Congressional leaders, including Senator Fulbright, believed the blockade to be a weak, ineffective response.

On the evening of October 22, Kennedy addressed the nation and sharply attacked Russian duplicity. Soviet Foreign Minister Andrei Gromyko was a particular target since he had told the President that Soviet assistance to Cuba had been " 'pursued solely for the purpose of contributing to the defense capabilities of Cuba. . . .

[101] Robert F. Kennedy, *Thirteen Days* (New York: Norton, 1969), p. 31.
[102] FitzSimons, *The Kennedy Doctrine*, pp. 128, 156: Brown, *The Faces of Power*, p. 262.

training by Soviet specialists of Cuban nationals in handling defensive armaments was by no means offensive.' " The President's outrage was clear:

> [T]his secret, swift, and extraordinary build-up of Communist missiles —in an area well known to have a special and historical relationship to the United States and the Nations of the Western Hemisphere, in violation of Soviet assurances, and in defiance of American and hemispheric policy—this sudden, clandestine decision to station strategic weapons for the first time outside of Soviet soil—is a deliberately provocative and unjustified change in the status quo which cannot be accepted by this country if our courage and our commitments are ever to be trusted again by either friend or foe.

The *initial* American response was then outlined: "a strict quarantine on all offensive military equipment under shipment to Cuba"; "close surveillance of Cuba and its military build-up"; "the policy . . . to regard any nuclear missile launched from Cuba against any nation in the Western Hemisphere as an attack by the Soviet Union on the United States requiring a full retaliatory response upon the Soviet Union." As Alexander George has demonstrated in his study of "coercive diplomacy," the blockade device was important in signifying to the Soviets that Kennedy was determined to take extraordinary measures to remove the missiles from the island—measures which, potentially, could go far beyond the imposition of a naval blockade.[103]

Kennedy used the October 22 broadcast to announce that a meeting of the OAS and an emergency meeting of the Security Council would be called that very evening. When the OAS met the following day, it unanimously agreed to support the American initiative and, under its own auspices, called for the withdrawal of all missiles and other offensive weapons from Cuba.

Despite the President's message and the ongoing American preparation for war, Russian freighters carrying missiles for Cuba continued toward their destination while navy planes kept them under constant surveillance. The ships kept on course, but as they approached the quarantine line the day after Kennedy's warning, many stopped, and the following day several turned round and headed back to Russia. This immediate success left the central question of the removal of missiles from Cuba itself unresolved. While Stevenson and his Russian counterpart exchanged angry charges in the United Nations Security Council, Acting Secretary General of the United

---

[103] The text of the President's speech in Kennedy, *Thirteen Days*, pp. 163–71. Alexander George essay in George *et al.*, *The Limits of Coercive Diplomacy: Laos, Cuba, Vietnam* (Boston: Little, Brown, 1971), pp. 126–36.

Nations, U Thant, proposed that the United States voluntarily suspend its quarantine for two or three weeks in exchange for Russia's suspension of all arms shipments to Cuba. Meanwhile Stevenson, as part of his presentation, created a sensation in the United Nations by showing Security Council members aerial photographs of the nuclear installations. When Russian Ambassador V. A. Zorin denied the authenticity of these photographs, Stevenson once again called upon the Soviets to agree to on-the-spot inspection.

As the Security Council debate raged and Thant, Kennedy, and Khrushchev exchanged personal notes, the missile site construction continued. A military response to the threat once again gained popularity among the President's advisors. It was apparently Robert Kennedy who saw a way out of the growing crisis. On October 26 Khrushchev sent a letter to the President in which he offered to remove Russian missiles from Cuba if the United States ended the quarantine and gave assurances that it would not invade Cuba. But the following day the Soviet leader addressed a second letter to Kennedy, raising the ante by offering to remove the missiles if in exchange the United States dismantled its own missiles in Turkey. Since the President found this second offer unacceptable, Robert Kennedy suggested that his brother respond only to the first note. Hence the deadlock was effectively broken when on October 27, Kennedy, in response to Khrushchev's first note, agreed to remove the quarantine and give assurances against a Cuban invasion if Russia, under United Nations observation and supervision, removed the missiles systems from Cuba and pledged not to introduce such weapons in Cuba in the future.[104] In a personal note to the President dated October 28, Chairman Khrushchev agreed to halt Soviet construction of the missile sites, to dismantle offensive weapons, and to return them to the Soviet Union—all steps to be taken under the scrutiny of the United Nations.

By the close of 1962 the quarantine had been lifted with the removal of the Russian missiles and other offensive weapons; most Russian technicians had also left by the end of the year. At about the same time, Castro released a thousand Cuban prisoners captured during the Bay of Pigs invasion; they were ransomed by the United States for $50 million in medicine and drugs.

Kennedy's success and skill in handling the threat posed by Soviet missiles understandably muted criticism of the enormous risks which he took to insure American hegemony over the hemisphere. More recently, however, the President's policies have been sharply

[104] See Henry M. Pachter, *Collision Course* (New York: Praeger, 1963), pp. 63–68.

attacked for failing to seriously consider a diplomatic solution[105]—the removal of the missiles in exchange for American concessions to Moscow. The Administration might have secretly confronted Khrushchev with evidence of missile deployment, giving the Soviets a private, face-saving opportunity to reverse their position without a public confrontation. Such action, it is argued, would have lessened the risk of nuclear war, although at a price. Richard J. Walton, for example, insists that while "political realities" forced Kennedy to demand the removal from Cuba of the missiles,

> he could have done it diplomatically. It is difficult to escape the conclusion that . . . he deliberately built up the crisis, possibly to influence the [1962 Congressional] elections, possibly to force the showdown with Khrushchev that he had long thought might be necessary. . . . without sufficient reason [he] consciously risked nuclear catastrophe.[106]

Summarizing her objections to the course of action taken by the Administration in October, Louise FitzSimons concludes that Kennedy chanced nuclear war because of his past "preoccupation" with Cuba and because of his fear that American prestige would suffer if Khrushchev were not confronted directly. The President permitted "vestiges of cold-war thinking to freeze his policy and prevent any flexibility in dealing with the Soviet Union." FitzSimons concurs with I. F. Stone's earlier estimate of Kennedy's deep concern that in the absence of a vigorous response the Democrats would be soundly defeated in the November 1962 Congressional elections.[107] Such a conclusion is, however, weakened by the presumption that the American public and its elected officials would have supported a settlement which included important concessions to the Soviets. Two mid-October Gallup polls are cited to demonstrate that Americans were opposed to a military offensive against Cuba: only one in four surveyed approved of such a move and a majority feared an invasion would bring war with Russia.[108] But these polls are not a particularly accurate measure since they were taken *before* the October 22 public revelation of the extent of missiles buildup. Relatedly, in late September the Senate (86 to 1) and the House (384 to 7) resolved to support American efforts to prevent "the creation or use of an

---

[105] For Adlai Stevenson's reservations regarding the military solution, see Elie Abel, *The Missile Crisis* (Philadelphia: Lippincott, 1966), p. 49.

[106] Walton, *Cold War and Counterrevolution*, pp. 141, 103–4.

[107] FitzSimons, *The Kennedy Doctrine*, p. 169. Stone's seminal essay was published as "The Brink" in the Apr. 14, 1966, issue of *New York Review of Books.* It is reprinted in Robert A. Divine, ed., *The Cuban Missile Crisis* (Chicago: Quadrangle, 1971), pp. 155–65.

[108] FitzSimons, *The Kennedy Doctrine*, pp. 138–39.

externally supported military capability endangering the security of the United States." [109]

Kennedy's critics minimize the consideration that concessions to the Soviets might well have spawned further provocations. Also, the largely unspecified nature of the proposed concessions is troublesome. Would a negotiated withdrawal have depended upon a limitation of missile sites in Italy and Turkey? Or greater Soviet control over Berlin? Yet the central issue remains: did the presence of Soviet offensive missiles in Cuba warrant so great a risk? Did not the nation have the right to expect its President to have more fully explored the possibility of a negotiated settlement?

With increasing signs of a possible détente following Khrushchev's capitulation, the President expressed his hopes for a meaningful accommodation with the Soviets during a June 1963 speech at Washington's American University. He urged the nation to

> deal with the world as it is, and not as it might have been had the history of the last eighteen years been different. . . . We must conduct our affairs in such a way that it becomes in the Communists' interest to agree on a genuine peace . . . let each nation choose its own future, so long as that choice does not interfere with the choices of others. . . . For, in the final analysis, our most basic common link is the fact that we all inhabit this small planet. We all breathe the same air. We all cherish our children's future. And we are all mortal. . . . The United States, as the world knows, will never start a war.[110]

Five months later Kennedy was assassinated in Dallas and the direction of the nation's diplomacy became the responsibility of Lyndon B. Johnson.

THE DOMINICAN CRISIS

The foreign relations of Kennedy's successor were also strained by an attempt at hemispheric counterinsurgency: the Dominican Republic intervention. After a 32-year reign, General Rafael Trujillo, the island nation's dictator, was assassinated in May of 1961. There followed 18 months of political confusion but in December 1962, the liberal intellectual Juan Bosch was elected president after pledging land reform, cooperatives, a new industrial base, and a variety of public works. A new constitution was formulated in 1963, embodying several

---

[109] Debate and votes in *Congressional Record*, Sept. 20, 1962, p. 20058 (Senate) and Sept. 26, 1962, pp. 20910–11 (House).
[110] The text of the American University speech in the *New York Times*, 11 June 1963, p. 16.

of Bosch's commitments to agrarian and industrial reform. The new charter alienated domestic and foreign business interests by prohibiting land holdings beyond a certain size and by restricting the ownership of Dominican land by foreigners. By circumscribing some of the prerogatives of the island's Roman Catholic establishment (for example, by legalizing divorce and by deemphasizing parochial education), the constitution provided additional difficulties for Bosch.

An anti-Bosch alliance was quickly forged of foreign and domestic business interests and the Roman Catholic establishment. At its head was General Elias Wessin y Wessin, a Catholic who successfully engineered Bosch's ouster in seven months. The Kennedy Administration, which had been receptive to Bosch, refused diplomatic recognition to Wessin's government and curtailed assistance programs to the republic. After Kennedy's assassination the Johnson Administration eased some of the restrictions against economic aid, anticipating that the new dictatorship would at least insure internal stability.

This strategy failed, and in April of 1965 some young army officers who favored Bosch's return engineered a coup against the government; the nation was again engulfed in civil war. On the twenty-eighth, four days after the outbreak of violence, the United States embassy in Santo Domingo was informed that the safety of United States citizens and other foreign nationals could no longer be guaranteed. It was at this point that Johnson took the first step toward intervention by sending 400 marines to the embattled area to safeguard the safety of thousands of Americans there. Within four days, 1,500 men attached to the Eighty-second Airborne Division followed, together with several marine detachments. Immediately, questions were raised as to the size of a force appropriate to a rescue mission.

To the extent that the President was indeed involved in a rescue operation, his action was legitimate, for such efforts are a President's constitutional responsibility. However, it became almost immediately apparent that another, more far-reaching objective concerned the Administration. Johnson and his staff had become convinced that an organized communist effort had gained control of the revolution; they were thus prepared to support with force the conservative regime in power. More than 6,000 additional American troops were quickly dispatched to the island (eventually more than 20,000 were sent) to the consternation of Latin Americans and domestic liberals. But the President stood firm, assuring a May 2 television audience that communist leaders, many Cuban trained, had taken control of the Dominican revolution. The next day his position was starkly stated:

"We don't expect to sit here on our rocking chairs with our hands folded and let the Communists set up any government in the Western Hemisphere." In an analysis of the intervention for *Commentary,* Theodore Draper shrewdly observed that the Johnson Administration first defended its action on the grounds that communists had taken over the revolution but later claimed credit for having prevented such an eventuality.[111]

Journalist Philip Geyelin concluded in his study of Johnson's foreign policy that the President "at a remarkably early stage" had decided "to slam the door to outright rebel victory." [112] A *New York Times* correspondent who covered the civil war, Tad Szulc, supports this view, observing that United States embassy officials in Santo Domingo were convinced even before the shooting began that Bosch's return would mean "Communism in the Dominican Republic in six months." The embassy was committed, Szulc reports, to the idea that American troops must be introduced if General Wessin was to defeat a pro-Bosch rebellion. Given this apparent bias, it is not surprising that the "seed of the idea of a major intervention . . . came into being at the embassy little more than 24 hours after the rebellion had erupted." [113]

The problem, of course, was verification of the communist infiltration charge, and that proved most difficult. Geyelin reports, for example, that an official State Department summary of communist activity on the island was quite candid about the problem: "much of the information concerning the first few days," the report admits, "was obtained only after the landing of U.S. forces on April 28." [114] Senator J. William Fulbright, Chairman of the Foreign Relations Committee, has written that the communists in the Dominican Republic "did not participate in planning the revolution . . . but . . . they very rapidly began to try to take advantage of it and to seize control of it. The evidence does not establish that the communists at any time actually had control of the revolution." [115] Degree of influence and outright control was a meaningful distinction which seems to have escaped the Administration. And if one accepts Szulc's contention that American Ambassador to the Dominican Republic W. Tapley Bennett had "little, if any," contacts with opposition groups such as Bosch's

[111] Theodore Draper, "The Dominican Crisis: A Case Study in American Policy," *Commentary,* Dec. 1965, p. 53. Johnson's television address quoted in Richard P. Stebbins, *The United States and World Affairs,* 1965 (New York: Council on Foreign Relations, 1966), p. 87.

[112] Philip Geyelin, *Lyndon B. Johnson and the World* (New York: Praeger, 1966), p. 245.

[113] Tad Szulc, *Dominican Diary* (New York: Dell Publishing Co., 1965), pp. 29–30. Also, Draper, "The Dominican Crisis," p. 39.

[114] Quoted in Geyelin, *Lyndon B. Johnson,* p. 247.

[115] J. William Fulbright, *The Arrogance of Power* (New York: Random House, 1966), p. 90.

Dominican Revolutionary Party, it is difficult to determine the embassy's basis for its conclusions.[116] The embassy staff had confined its contacts to influential business leaders, land owners, and loyalists in the military apparatus.

The outcry against intervention was seriously compounded by charges that the Johnson Administration had blatantly violated the Charter of the Organization of American States. That compact enjoined any nation from interfering in the internal affairs of a member state for any reason whatsoever. Not only did the United States ignore OAS agreements, it failed even to consult the organization prior to the landing of American troops; and once the deed was accomplished, the Administration persuaded the OAS to sponsor an Inter-American Peace Force to guarantee stability on the island. This move enabled the President to withdraw most American troops and yet retain an anti-revolutionary posture. Eventually, in June of 1966, the rightist Joacquín Balaguer defeated Bosch for the presidency. Given the vagaries of Latin American politics, it is perhaps not too surprising to learn that both Balaguer and Bosch had opposed the government in the 1965 civil war and that Balaguer had spoken out against American intervention.

Secretary of State Dean Rusk stated in May of 1965 that American military intervention had been ordered to enable the Dominicans to establish "a broadly based provisional government which can accept responsibility for the affairs of that country pending elections and pending full return to the democratic and constitutional processes." [117] This condition was achieved, but the actual influence of American arms remains in doubt. What is clear is that the United States demonstrated its willingness to utilize force to achieve its political aims in the hemisphere; such a lesson could not have been lost on Latin Americans.

The Cold War, as it was understood in the decade following the Second World War, has undergone a significant change. This is not to imply that the rhetoric of each side has altered, for the Soviet Union, having worked through its anti-Stalinist phase, gives every sign of a continuing dedication to the spread of communism. Conversely, the United States appears just as determined to forestall Soviet designs by its willingness to utilize force to protect and to spread the capitalistic/democratic system. In Africa, Asia, and South America, the United

---

[116] Szulc, *Dominican Diary*, p. 30.

[117] Quoted in Brown, *The Faces of Power*, p. 362. For Bosch's personal assessment, see his *Pentagonism: A Substitute for Imperialism* (New York: Grove Press, 1968), esp. Chap. 7.

States has been an active counterrevolutionary force, ready to employ its economic and military might to contain insurgency movements. The unfortunate tendency to regard any area of the globe as being of strategic interest to the United States has not been discredited by the events of the past 20 years. There has been, nevertheless, a discernible shift in strategy. Since the Korean War there has been a growing tendency for the two superpowers to regard the world in terms of modern spheres-of-influence in which the hegemony exercised by one has the tacit approval of the other. Hence the decision of the United States not to interfere in the satellite uprisings in Eastern Europe and the Soviet retreat in Cuba. This process has not as yet been stabilized, and so areas of tension remain. In both the Middle East and in Southeast Asia, the two powers have pursued policies which are reminiscent of the more frosty days of the Cold War.

Eight

VIETNAM AND
THE INDOCHINA WAR

In the postwar period the United States intervened militarily and politically in the internal affairs of a number of Third World nations under the very questionable assumption that the spread of communism or the disruption of the status quo automatically constituted a clear threat to American security. The assumptions of Dean Acheson and John Foster Dulles about revolution and communism persisted long after they ceased to be useful, and Eisenhower, Kennedy, Johnson, and Nixon all played the role of "cold warrior." When creative statesmanship was required to respond to the inevitable revolutionary struggles in Latin America and Asia, American policymakers tragically failed to distinguish responsibly between threats to American security and legitimate challenges to authority in the Third World. Vietnam, and indeed all of Indochina, has become the most celebrated example of Washington's intervention in essentially nationalistic struggles. It has been difficult to perceive how the outcome of the Indochina War could have affected American security to a degree commensurate with the nation's massive involvement in that blighted Southeast Asian peninsula.

The United States has paid dearly for its intervention. One of the many deeply disturbing consequences of the Asian war has been its effect upon the American nation for, in challenging Washington's policies, elected officials, students, the media, and the public at large have come to question the basic premises on which the nation has operated.

In this chapter, American involvement in Vietnam will be examined beginning 1954, when the French wisely, but belatedly, relinquished their colonial holdings in Southeast Asia. Since the signing of the 1954 Geneva Agreements ending the French phase of the Indochinese War, the United States sought to control the seemingly relentless force of nationalism in Vietnam by attempting to affect the outcome of a civil war which had been raging between communist and anti-communist elements in Indochina for at least a generation. As a result, the war was ruthlessly expanded, the Vietnamese were subjected to a nightmarish existence, and the communist "threat" was at least temporarily neutralized. At the same time, the American nation experienced its most profound polarization of the twentieth century. In 1966, the Chairman of the Senate Foreign Relations Committee, J. William Fulbright, astutely warned:

> America is showing some signs of that fatal presumption, that overextension of power and mission, which has brought ruin to great nations in the past. The process has hardly begun, but the war which we are now fighting can only accelerate it. If the war goes on and expands, if that fatal process continues to accelerate until America becomes what she is not now and never has been, a seeker after unlimited power and empire, the leader of a global counter-revolution, then Vietnam will have had a mighty and tragic fallout indeed.[1]

ORIGINS OF THE FIRST INDOCHINA WAR

During the second half of the nineteenth century the French gradually gained control of Vietnam, Laos, and Cambodia by the traditional route of military victories and treaties favorable to the would-be colonial power. In exchange for wide commercial privileges and extraterritoriality,[2] the internal and external security of Vietnam was guaranteed by the French; modernization efforts and military assistance were also pledged. The Vietnamese people (with very few exceptions) remained disenfranchised and, inevitably, economic exploitation followed. By the opening of the twentieth century, paved

[1] Fulbright, *The Arrogance of Power*, p. 138.
[2] For an explanation of such rights, see Fulbright, Chapter I, p. 35.

roads, railroads, and the telephone and telegraph were introduced along with huge rubber and cotton plantations. The expropriation of peasant land and the exploitation of human life, together with oppressive taxation and French assumption of former royal monopolies on salt, opium, and alcohol, greatly embittered the Vietnamese. Scattered resistance and revolutionary groups were quickly formed, but rigid French repression kept them sternly in check until the 1930s. Of all the disorganized underground organizations, the Communist party emerged as the most successful revolutionary force in Vietnam, in large measure because of the effectiveness of Nguyen Ai Quoc (alias Ho Chi Minh).

With the Fall of France in June of 1940, Paris' authority in Indochina was directly challenged by the Japanese goal of hegemony over Southeast Asia. To prevent the loss of the colony, the French puppet government at Vichy permitted the Japanese to utilize French bases in Indochina to attack British and Dutch holdings in Asia; the Japanese, in turn, demanded the withdrawal of neither French troops nor French administrative personnel. This strategy succeeded until March of 1945 when Japan, reacting to what appeared to be growing French resistance, forcibly removed the French military and administrative establishment from Vietnam. Elsewhere in Southeast Asia, Japan had encouraged nationalist movements, but in Vietnam limited political and administrative authority was vested in a group of pro-French intellectuals and bureaucrats who at best represented a minority of the Vietnamese. Thus Japanese policies after the removal of the French greatly intensified the bitter rivalry within the Vietnamese nationalist movement.

Japanese destruction of French colonial authority, followed within a few months by the defeat of the Japanese themselves, set the stage for a protracted struggle for control of Vietnam and indeed of all Indochina. In the spring of 1941, the Central Committee of the Indochina Communist Party had founded the Vietnam Independence League (popularly known as the Vietminh), a political organization destined to play a central role in the nationalist struggle. The league had been an active and important factor in the resistance movement against Japanese occupation, and so the Vietminh's leader, Ho Chi Minh, expected in return French recognition of the newly proclaimed Democratic Republic of Vietnam.[3] Paris, however, hoped to reassert its colonial authority in Southeast Asia and had absolutely no intention of abandoning Indochina.

[3] See John T. McAlister, Jr. *Viet Nam: The Origins of Revolution* (New York: Knopf, 1969). The "Declaration of Independence of the Democratic Republic of Vietnam," is reprinted in Marvin E. Gettleman, ed., *Vietnam* (Greenwich, Conn.: Fawcett, 1965), pp. 57–59.

It was difficult for France's allies to counter these colonialist designs since London was then actively seeking the restoration of at least part of the British empire. The July 1945 Potsdam Agreement stipulated that Tokyo's surrender was to be followed by the occupation of Vietnam by British and Chinese troops: the British to occupy the area up to the sixteenth parallel, and the Chinese to hold the northern portion of the country (above the sixteenth parallel). Two months later, British forces in southern Vietnam aided France in wresting control of Saigon from the Vietminh. By December, the cooperative British had permitted France to increase its troop strength below the sixteenth parallel to 50,000. Meanwhile, the Chinese (whose troops in northern Vietnam numbered about 180,000) announced formal recognition of Ho Chi Minh's government in Hanoi.

By March of 1946 British and Chinese forces had been withdrawn from Vietnam, leaving the French to confront Ho Chi Minh. Faced with the certain knowledge that France's allies would not support the continuance of his government, Ho agreed to permit limited French occupation of the northern portion of Vietnam. His decision was influenced, doubtlessly, by the virtual destruction of the Vietnamese economy, which had led to severe hardship, and even starvation, in the North. Paris, in return, recognized the Democratic Republic of Vietnam "as a free state, having its Government, its Parliament, its army, and its finances, and forming part of the Indochinese Federation and the French Union." [4] But it was almost immediately apparent that the French did not intend to honor this agreement, which also called for the unification of Vietnam. Thus on June 1, 1946—less than three months after the armistice was signed—a puppet government was established in the South.

Stung by this action and now certain that the French would not comply with the terms of the armistice, Ho's Vietminh began to consolidate its military and political efforts. The crucial stage was reached by the fall of 1946 when France, in violation of earlier agreements, established its own customs control at Haiphong. Demonstrations against these encroachments led to a French naval bombardment of Haiphong on November 23; it is estimated that between 6,000 and 20,000 Vietnamese were killed in this raid. Tragically, not even the election of a Socialist French government under the leadership of Leon Blum (long a supporter of a liberalized colonial policy) could stay the seemingly relentless course of events. As the Vietminh retaliated with attacks against the French in Hanoi, Paris attempted to strengthen its hold on the South and refused even to negotiate with

[4] Gettleman, *Vietnam*, p. 61.

Ho. The French had a clear economic motive in refusing to relinquish South Vietnam since 60 percent of their Indochina holdings were centered in that region.[5]

By mid-December the eight-year war which was to engage France to the point of exhaustion had commenced. Despite some early military victories, Paris quickly discovered the frustrations of guerrilla warfare against a determined nationalist offensive. The Vietnamese War was for France an eight-year ordeal which emptied its treasury, divided its people, and slaughtered its young men.[6] While Paris' motivation in attempting to control the southern portion of Vietnam originally may have been economic, it is impossible to explain its willingness to fight a protracted war simply on economic grounds— particularly when one considers that by 1954 the war had cost France many times the value of all of its Indochinese investments. The nation was clearly loath to surrender its economic base in Southeast Asia, but national pride (deeply wounded by Hitler's long occupation) was surely an additional factor. And, it was reasoned the French colonies of Algeria, Morocco, and Tunisia might very well profit by the example set by Indochinese independence.

Faced with determined Vietminh opposition to a compromise settlement which favored the French, Paris was forced to seek allies. The United States soon proved a willing partner. With the victory of the Chinese Communists in 1949 and the resultant flight of Chiang Kai-shek to the island of Formosa, the deeply alarmed American government was much inclined to regard France's struggle in Indochina as part of a larger battle against Asian communism. Hence President Harry Truman has confided: "It was our policy to strengthen the weak spots in the defense of the free world. . . . our increased aid to Indo-China and the Philippines and our move for the defense of Formosa by the Seventh Fleet were designed to reinforce areas exposed to Communist pressure." [7] The implementation of just such a policy was announced by Secretary of State Dean Acheson in Paris on May 8, 1950.

> The United States Government, convinced that neither national independence nor democratic evolution exists in any area dominated

[5] George McTurnam Kahin and John W. Lewis, *The United States and Vietnam*, rev. ed. (New York: Dell Publishing Co., 1969), p. 26.

[6] According to Bernard Fall, over 75,000 Frenchmen were killed in Indochina between 1946 and 1954. Bernard B. Fall, *Street Without Joy*, 4th ed. (Harrisburg, Pa.: The Stackpole Company, 1967), Appendix II, p. 385. Perhaps the best studies of guerrilla warfare are Douglas Pike, *Viet Cong: The Organization and Techniques of the National Liberation Front* (Cambridge, Mass.: M.I.T. Press, 1966), and Douglas Pike, *War, Peace and the Viet Cong* (Cambridge, Mass.: M.I.T. Press, 1969). Also useful is Frank E. Armbruster *et al., Can We Win in Vietnam?* (New York: Praeger, 1968), pp. 92–128.

[7] Truman, *Memoirs*, II, p. 393.

by Soviet imperialism, considers the situation to be such as to warrant its according economic aid and military equipment to the associated states of Indochina and to France in order to assist them in restoring stability and permitting these states to pursue their peaceful and democratic development.[8]

The ideological underpinning of American economic, political, and, ultimately, military efforts to thwart the nationalist ambitions of millions of Vietnamese was conveniently provided by Truman and Acheson.

AMERICA TAKES OVER

By the time General Dwight D. Eisenhower was elected Chief Executive, the French were stalled in a quagmire of their own creation: yet their faltering crusade was even then supported by massive doses of American financial aid. Eisenhower himself has acknowledged that upon taking office his "main task was to convince the world that the Southeast Asian war was an aggressive move by the Communists to subjugate that entire area." This conclusion was reached despite a report by the State Department that France retained paramount authority over military affairs, trade and exchange, and internal security. France's virtual stranglehold over the economic life of the Associated States (of Indochina) was documented. The widespread resentment of large elements of the native population was also reported.[9]

The Administration's unfortunate, and now infamous, perspective on the Indochinese War was explained by the President at an April 7, 1954, press conference: "You have a row of dominoes set up . . . you knock over the first one, and what will happen to the last one is that it will go over very quickly." [10] This "domino theory" was deceptively, extraordinarily, naive. Yet the day before Eisenhower's press conference it was announced that United States aid for the following fiscal year would amount to $1.33 billion, more than 75 percent of what the war cost France. Ominously, in August of 1954 the Administration had also seriously considered but finally rejected a plan sponsored by Secretary of State John Foster Dulles for committing American troops to Indochina.[11] The force was to be sent as part

[8] Department of State *Bulletin*, May 12, 1950, p. 821.

[9] See Eisenhower, *Mandate for Change*, p. 217.

[10] Quoted in Arthur M. Schlesinger, Jr., *The Bitter Heritage* (Greenwich, Conn.: Fawcett World Library, 1967), p. 25.

[11] For the monetary commitment, see Kahin and Lewis, *The United States and Vietnam*,

of a larger allied contingent composed of troops from England, Australia, New Zealand, and, hopefully, the Philippines and Thailand. The French were to continue to assume full responsibility for the prosecution of the war and, as a condition of American involvement, Paris was to guarantee the future independence of Vietnam, Laos, and Cambodia.

Even with American financial aid, the colonialists by mid-1953 had lost control of most of Vietnam north of Saigon. But in September a last-ditch effort was attempted, and forces under the direction of General Henri Navarre, Commander in Chief of the French Union Army in Indochina, prepared an offensive designed to regain key military positions and thereby to strengthen France's hand at the negotiating table. More than 500,000 soldiers (less than one-fifth were French) participated in the "Navarre Plan," but this latest offensive resulted in still another shattering loss of territory to the Vietminh. The most dramatic, and certainly the most important, military confrontation of the entire war, the Battle of Dienbienphu, was part of this offensive. In the spring of 1954 Navarre hoped to lure the Vietminh into attacking the heavily armed but exposed fortress of Dienbienphu.[12] Assuming his position to be impregnable, Navarre anticipated the slaughter of the lightly armed Vietminh as they attempted to storm his position. While the Vietminh were indeed tempted by the exposed fortress, they were not nearly as defenseless as Navarre had expected. The General's stunning defeat ended the much heralded French offensive and left the government at Paris to face a protracted, humiliating series of talks to extricate itself from a bloody colonial war.

Even before the Battle of Dienbienphu had begun, the diplomatic stage had been set for a negotiated settlement. A Geneva Conference of the Big Four's foreign ministers had been planned early in 1954, and Communist China was invited for the purpose of discussing Korea and Indochina. The defeat at Dienbienphu and the election of Prime Minister Pierre Mendes-France, who had pledged to resign if a peace settlement were not reached by mid-July, meant that the Vietminh and its Chinese and Russian supporters would hold the high cards at the conference. In the opening round of talks the Democratic Republic of Vietnam proposed that France recognize the independence of Vietnam, Laos, and Cambodia; that all foreign

---

p. 32, and Schlesinger, Jr., *The Bitter Heritage*, p. 24. The troop plan is discussed in Adams, *Firsthand Report*, pp. 120–23, and Eisenhower, *Mandate for Change*, Chap. XIV.

[12] Most accounts of the war consider the fall of Dienbienphu, but it is studied in detail in Bernard B. Fall, *Hell in a Very Small Place: The Siege of Dien Bien Phu* (New York: Vintage Books, Random House, 1966).

troops be withdrawn from the three nations; that free elections be held; and that a cease-fire be arranged. The State of Vietnam (representing the French-dominated South) countered with a plan for the unification of the country under former Emperor Bao Dai and elections supervised by the United Nations. This proposal was highly unrealistic, given the extent of Vietminh control over most of the Vietnamese countryside. The absence of a precise line of demarcation, and the fact that approximately half of what emerged as South Vietnam was in the hands of the Vietminh in the spring of 1954, further complicated the settlement.

These difficulties notwithstanding, three separate cease-fire agreements covering Vietnam, Cambodia, and Laos were reached on July 20. The Vietnam settlement stipulated that the Democratic Republic of Vietnam was to receive full control of the area north of the seventeenth parallel. A demilitarized zone on each side of that parallel was provided. Additionally, Article 14, dealing with political and administrative measures in the two regrouping zones, specified:

> Pending the general elections which will bring about the unification of Vietnam, the conduct of civil administration in each regrouping zone shall be in the hands of the party whose forces are to be regrouped there in virtue of the present Agreement.[13]

There followed an attempt to render explicit several of the cease-fire accord's implicit agreements. The British delegate, Anthony Eden, proposed that a "Final Declaration of the Geneva Conference" (July 21, 1954) be endorsed by the conference's participants: the Kingdom of Cambodia, the Democratic Republic of Vietnam, the State of Vietnam, the Kingdom of Laos, France, the People's Republic of China, Russia, Great Britain, and the United States. Such a final agreement was particularly desirable since the formal cease-fire was signed only by France and the Democratic Republic of Vietnam. Further need for an accord was evident when the American delegate to the Conference, Secretary of State John Foster Dulles, proved reluctant to acknowledge the loss of Indochina. The Final Declaration is most important in understanding the two key purposes of the cease-fire since it clearly established that the "military demarcation line [for Vietnam] is provisional and should not in any way be interpreted as constituting a political or territorial boundary." This concept was essential to the agreement, for the Vietminh, in military control of over half of what emerged as South Vietnam (south of the

---

[13] The "Agreement on the Cessation of Hostilities in Vietnam" is reprinted in Gettleman, *Vietnam*, pp. 137–50.

seventeenth parallel) would never have endorsed any settlement that implied a permanent division of Vietnam. A military demarcation line, not a frontier, had been established; one country with two zones had resulted. Furthermore, given its wide support in all of Vietnam, the Vietminh had understandably sought to move its struggle for national independence from the military to the political arena. It was for this reason that Article 7 of the Final Declaration provided for general elections by secret ballot in July, under the supervision of an international commission composed of representatives of the member states of the International Supervisory Commission, Canada, India, and Poland.

At the final meeting of the Geneva Conference, United States delegate General Bedell Smith announced that his government was not prepared to join in the declaration as submitted. Smith gave assurances that the United States would "refrain from the threat or the use of force to disturb [the Agreements]," but that it would "view any renewal of the aggression in violation of the aforesaid Agreements with grave concern as seriously threatening international peace and security." [14] The basic reason for this decision is not difficult to discern. The United States was deeply disturbed by the conference's implicit recognition that much, if not all, of the area of Vietnam would fall to the communists. It is obvious from Eisenhower's memoirs that his major regret was not that the French had wasted so much blood and treasure in an indefensible attempt to retain a colony, but apparent that the attempt was unsuccessful. This is obvious despite the President's assertion of America's "tradition of anti-colonialism." [15] Dulles pointedly observed that the United States could not be a party to the agreement because American public opinion would not tolerate the subjection of millions of Vietnamese to communist rule.[16] By the late 1960s, the issue had become the unwillingness of significant numbers of Americans to condone the loss of tens of thousands of lives in an attempt to keep South Vietnam free from communism.

In assessing American policies after the 1954 Geneva accord, the legal implications of the American refusal to endorse the Final Declaration should be considered. In his detailed study of the Geneva Conference, Robert F. Randle concludes that the United States was, after all, free to withhold its consent from the declaration and the

[14] *Ibid.*, pp. 152, 156.

[15] For a discussion of the American position, see Eisenhower, *Mandate for Change*, pp. 447–52; Eden, *Full Circle*, pp. 132–33; Robert F. Randle, *Geneva, 1954: The Settlement of the Indochinese War* (Princeton, N.J.: Princeton University Press, 1969), pp. 415–19; and Adams, *Firsthand Report*, p. 125.

[16] Dulles' position in Robert Shaplen, *The Lost Revolution* (New York: Harper & Row, 1965), pp. 94–96.

cease-fire agreement. Washington's decision did not violate any international obligation of the United States, such as the United Nations Charter.[17] But the United States has been sharply criticized for its subsequent distortion of the pledge made by Under Secretary of State Bedell Smith at the Conference. The Eisenhower Administration had agreed to refrain from the threat or the use of force to disturb the Geneva Agreements, and had agreed to seek Vietnamese unity through United Nations supervised elections. It had also pledged to refrain from endorsing agreements which interfered with the self-determination of peoples. Washington's understanding, however, specifically provided for the exercise of certain prerogatives under Article 51 of the United Nations Charter:

> Nothing in the present Charter shall impair the inherent right of individual or collective self-defense if an armed attack occurs against a member of the United Nations, until the Security Council has taken measures necessary to maintain international peace and security.[18]

Furthermore, Smith underscored his government's determination to "view any renewal of the aggression in violation of the aforesaid Agreements with grave concern and as seriously threatening international peace and security." [19] Thus in any evaluation of the legality of American involvement in Vietnam it is necessary to consider that the United States did *not* endorse Article 4 of the Final Declaration, and so did *not* pledge to withhold troops, military personnel, or arms from Vietnam; additionally, it did *not* pledge to refrain from establishing bases south of the seventeenth parallel (Article 5 of the Final Declaration). American violation of the *spirit* of the conference is quite another matter.

It was hardly a coincidence that following the 1954 Geneva Agreement, Secretary of State Dulles invited representatives of Britain, France, Australia, New Zealand, the Philippines, Thailand, and Pakistan to meet with him in Manila to discuss plans for the containment of Asian communism. India, Burma, Ceylon, and Indonesia had also been invited to attend, but preferring their neutralist positions, they refused; as a result, only three Asian nations participated in the formulation of the South East Asian Treaty Organization (SEATO). This so-called Manila Pact of September 8, 1954, has often been compared with the NATO agreement, but it is actually far less binding on its members. In essence, the signatory

---

[17] Randle, *Geneva*, p. 417.
[18] For the full text of Article 51, see Bartlett, *The Record of American Diplomacy*, p. 685.
[19] See Bartlett, p. 342.

powers pledged that each would recognize "that aggression by means of armed attack in the treaty area against any of the Parties or against any State or territory which the Parties by unanimous agreement may hereafter designate, would endanger its own peace and safety." It was further understood that in the event of such attack, each participant would "act to meet the common danger in accordance with its constitutional processes." [20] Nowhere did the Manila agreement stipulate that the United States or any other power was bound to come to the aid of a nation threatened by communist takeover. Moreover, unlike NATO, this pact did not establish a common armed force.

The SEATO accord was strategically important to the United States because it provided the opportunity to operate under the umbrella of a collective security agreement when and if it decided to intervene in Vietnam. In fact, under the terms of the "Protocol to the Southeast Asia Collective Defense Treaty" the State of Vietnam (later South Vietnam) was specifically placed under the jurisdiction of the SEATO pact. The stage was thus set for an accelerated American involvement in Vietnam; Eisenhower concluded that "The dilemma of finding a moral, legal, and practical basis for helping our friends of the region need not face us again." [21] The SEATO pact only barely masked the Eisenhower Administration's intention to violate the spirit, if not the letter, of the Geneva Agreement.

The United States moved a step closer to intervention when Eisenhower accepted the widely shared belief that an election in Vietnam would result in 80 percent of the populace voting for Ho Chi Minh rather than Bao Dai.[22] This assumption strongly influenced his decision to discourage such elections and to sponsor a separate state in South Vietnam under the direction of Ngo Dinh Diem. A Roman Catholic with strong ties to the French colonial period, Diem had been appointed Prime Minister by Bao Dai during the Geneva talks, but an intense political rivalry soon developed between the two leaders; Eisenhower strongly supported Diem. Given the level of American aid to the State of Vietnam, such backing by the President was highly significant. Throughout the winter and early spring of 1955 Diem steadily increased his control over South Vietnam, winning an important victory when Bao Dai, under American pressure, dismissed his Commander in Chief (and Diem's principal rival), General Nguyen Van Hinh. By October Diem had won a landslide victory in a

[20] The text of the SEATO pact in Bartlett, ed., *The Record of American Diplomacy*, pp. 792–93.

[21] Eisenhower, *Mandate for Change*, p. 452.

[22] *Ibid.*, p. 449.

rigged election for Chief of State, and on October 16, 1955, he established the Republic of Vietnam and named himself President. The extent to which the United States was willing to underwrite the new regime can be easily measured. In 1955 alone, Vietnam received $325 million in economic aid; by the time Eisenhower left office, $1.5 billion in such aid had been provided along with an additional $800 million in military assistance.[23] And while there were some indications that this aid was strengthening the economy, basic social reforms, particularly the long-range goal of land reform, were of little interest to the authoritarian, upper-class Diem. The result was a growing disenchantment, followed by armed resistance in the countryside. By 1958 there were significant numbers of South Vietnamese guerrillas— popularly, Viet Cong—who attested to the weak supportive structure of the Diem regime.

The United States was the only foreign military power in all of Vietnam after the final French troop withdrawal in April 1956. American military presence in the Republic of Vietnam took the form of the Military Assistance Advisory Group, which had come into being before the Geneva talks. The entire cost of training, equipping, and operating the South Vietnamese army was borne by the United States, which channeled all military assistance directly through President Diem.

Given the extensive American involvement in the economic, political, and military life of the Diem regime, it is not surprising that in 1955 South Vietnam's head of state steadfastly refused to cooperate with Ho Chi Minh's call for the elections provided for in the Geneva settlement. Diem, supported by the Eisenhower Administration, took the position that his newly formed republic had not participated in the Geneva talks, had endorsed neither the cease-fire agreement nor the Final Declaration, and so was not bound to abide by provisions for a national election. From the very beginning both Saigon and Washington insisted that such elections could be held only if Ho Chi Minh accepted certain preconditions, even though the Geneva agreements stipulated that the International Supervisory Commission was to ensure that the elections represented the free expression of national will. England and France warned the United States in February of 1955 that since Diem refused to hold elections they would not cooperate as SEATO powers if Ho's forces attacked South Vietnam. America's two principal allies gave the Eisenhower Administration notice concerning their very fundamental disagreement with United States policy in Vietnam.

[23] See table on the cumulative economic assistance to the Vietnamese government in Kahin and Lewis, *The United States and Vietnam*, p. 73.

So even before the close of Eisenhower's second term there were many indications that American policymakers were treading treacherous waters. Despite Diem's stranglehold on the government there were obvious signs of internal discontent—Buddhists, peasants, urban intellectuals, and others were restive, and the Viet Cong resistance movement, which in 1960 had been formally organized as the National Liberation Front, was increasingly active. The United States was sending vast sums to the republic, but little was done to effect basic social reforms which were so fervently desired by millions of peasants. By channeling its defense assistance directly through President Diem the Eisenhower Administration encouraged and strengthened the repressive tendencies of the Saigon government. Elections which had been sanctioned at Geneva were actively discouraged while a separate South Vietnamese government was supported, in direct violation of the letter and the spirit of those agreements. Finally, America's two major allies, England and France, were warning the Administration that they would not cooperate with such policies.

KENNEDY'S LEGACY

American participation in Vietnam by 1960 might be measured against the standard set by Eisenhower himself in an October 23, 1954, letter to Diem offering American economic aid and supporting his attempt to unseat Bao Dai.

> The purpose of this offer is to assist . . . in developing and maintaining a strong, viable state, capable of resisting attempted subversion or aggression through military means. . . . the United States expects that this aid will be met by performance on the part of the Government of Vietnam in undertaking needed reforms.

The President also expressed the hope that the government of South Vietnam would be "so responsive to the nationalist aspirations of its people, so enlightened in purpose and effective in performance, that it will be respected both at home and abroad and discourage any who might wish to impose a foreign ideology on your free people." [24] The discrepancy between these goals and Diem's performance should have discouraged even the most ardent exponent of America's Vietnamese policy.

The Eisenhower Administration left office at a critical juncture.

[24] The text of Eisenhower's letter in Department of State *Bulletin*, Nov. 15, 1954, pp. 735–36.

As in the case of the Bay of Pigs, it is inviting to rationalize the new President's handling of the growing crisis by observing that by the time he had moved into the White House the nation had already become committed to a particular policy. But just as Kennedy might have extricated the United States from the Cuban invasion scheme, so too might he have disengaged the nation from Vietnam. A very astute observer of American foreign policy, Hans J. Morgenthau, has advanced the theory that Kennedy, like Presidents before and after him, had committed a fundamental error in judgment regarding the nature of the Vietnamese struggle:

> [W]e have been unable to judge Vietnamese Communism on its own national merits, as an indigenous phenomenon resulting from the peculiar circumstances of time and place. Instead, Vietnamese Communism has appeared to us as a special instance of a general phenomenon which is not by accident the same regardless of time and place; for it has been created by a world-wide conspiracy whose headquarters are assumed to be in Moscow or Peking or both, and whose aim is to Communize the world.[25]

President Kennedy shared the belief that Vietnam was an episode in America's unending struggle to protect the Free World from communist domination; he therefore assumed that the outcome of the Vietnamese War would have worldwide significance.

The new Administration, like the preceding one, often proclaimed its dedication to the goal of self-determination. However, in an analysis of the New Frontier's foreign policy published nearly a decade after Kennedy's death, Richard J. Walton has indicted the young President for his "crucial misconception" about the war in Vietnam. "He recognized the irresistible force of nationalism, yet he believed it could be exploited from outside to defeat communism. He believed that the United States could manipulate the strong emotions of a downtrodden people so as to enlist them in America's crusade, not theirs." [26] Kennedy's failure was his inability to see that nationalism was more crucial to the struggle than was communism.

While very marked differences soon developed between Eisenhower's and Kennedy's approaches to the Vietnamese War, the basic suppositions remained constant. The permanent division of the nation was assumed and, consequently, military activity by Ho Chi Minh's forces or by the Viet Cong was viewed not as a continuation of the civil strife, but rather as part of a larger communist threat to the Free

---

[25] Hans J. Morgenthau, *A New Foreign Policy for the United States* (New York: Praeger, 1969), p. 148.
[26] Walton, *Cold War and Counterrevolution*, p. 163.

World. As a Senator, Kennedy had expressed the conviction that no amount of American military assistance in Indochina could conquer " 'an enemy of the people' which has the sympathy and covert support of the people. . . . For the United States to intervene unilaterally and to send troops into the most difficult terrain in the world, with the Chinese able to pour in unlimited manpower, would mean that we would face a situation which would be far more difficult than . . . we encountered in Korea." [27] But this earlier, realistic assessment fell victim to the Administration's anti-communist crusade. In his history of the New Frontier, Theodore C. Sorensen, Special Counsel to Kennedy, reveals the strategy of the White House. In 1961 South Vietnam was too weak to stand alone; to attempt to neutralize Vietnam in 1961, at a time when the communists had an upper hand in both the South and the North, "would have left the South Vietnamese defenseless against *externally supported Communist domination.*" Sorensen also reports that given Red China's goal of driving all remnants of Western power and influence from Asia, "free world security also had a stake in our staying [in South Vietnam]." Summing up what he terms the "Kennedy Southeast Asia policy," Sorensen reports:

> [It] respected the neutrality of all who wished to be neutral. But it also insisted that other nations similarly respect that neutrality, withdraw their troops and abide by negotiated settlements and boundaries, thus leaving each neutral free to choose and fulfill its own future within the framework of its own culture and traditions.[28]

Thus seven years after the Geneva talks Vietnam remained divided, communist strength in the South steadily increased, over a billion and a half dollars in American aid failed to "secure" the Diem regime, and a new President faced a growing crisis. A major turning point in the American response occurred in October of 1961 when the President sent General Maxwell Taylor and Professor Walt W. Rostow, Deputy Assistant Secretary for National Security Affairs, to study the feasibility of utilizing American troops to train and advise Diem's faltering forces. In particular, the team had been sent to test Vice President Lyndon B. Johnson's conclusion after his May 1961 visit to East Asia that a major American commitment was needed to save South Vietnam from communism. Johnson had clearly stated, however, that he was not advocating outright American defense of

---

[27] Schlesinger, Jr., *A Thousand Days*, p. 322.
[28] Theodore C. Sorensen, *Kennedy* (New York: Harper & Row, 1965), p. 649. Emphasis added.

South Vietnam: "American combat troop involvement is not only not required, it is not desirable." [29]

Taylor and Rostow's formula for containing the communist advance went beyond the suggestions of the Vice President. That is, it was proposed that the United States concentrate on a military solution by sending American troops to undertake special functions such as airlifts and air reconnaissance flights; it was also envisioned that these forces would function as technical advisors to Vietnamese officers, and that an American military task force of perhaps 10,000 men might conduct operations on a limited scale. Such a contingent would boost the morale of the South Vietnamese government while demonstrating Washington's determination to forestall a communist victory. But at the very time the Taylor-Rostow report was submitted, the CIA issued a National Intelligence Estimate predicting that Hanoi had the capability of matching an American escalation of hostilities.[30] Apparently this judgment was not taken seriously by the White House.

Two key Cabinet members, Secretary of State Dean Rusk and Secretary of Defense Robert McNamara, warmly endorsed the introduction of support troops (for helicopters, reconnaissance aircraft, and intelligence units), but opposed "larger organized units with actual or potential direct military mission." [31] While determined not to convert the Vietnamese struggle into a French-styled "white man's war," the President had taken a very long stride down the path of direct involvement. There were, of course, gnawing doubts over continued American support to Diem's government, but Washington decided to back Diem in the strongest possible terms hoping gradually to move him toward basic social, political, and economic reforms. The increased instability in the South, the alarming rate of communist infiltration, and the growing communist control of South Vietnamese hamlets (aided in large measure by thousands of Viet Cong assassinations and kidnapings of local supporters of the Saigon regime) convinced Kennedy that a meaningful alternative to the Taylor-Rostow strategy was not forthcoming. By 1963 over 15,000 American military "advisors" were in South Vietnam.[32]

Although the Viet Cong were at first put on the defensive by the introduction of helicopters and other tools of modern warfare, their guerrilla tactics soon overcame much of the effect of American

[29] Quoted in Schlesinger, Jr., *The Bitter Heritage*, p. 38.
[30] FitzSimons, *The Kennedy Doctrine*, p. 197.
[31] Quoted in *Ibid.*, p. 199.
[32] Statistic from Roger Hilsman, *To Move a Nation* (Garden City, N.Y.: Doubleday, 1967), p. 422. For a summary account of Diem's stewardship by the early 1960s, see The Committee of Concerned Asian Scholars, *The Indochina Story: A Fully Documented Account* (New York: Pantheon Books, 1970), pp. 24–41.

technology. Washington was further disheartened by the resistance of the Diem family to American insistence upon basic reform. Religious persecution, political repression, and Diem's insensitivity and remoteness from his people complicated and handicapped the war effort. The Diem regime's attempt to paper over the realities of its despotic hold on South Vietnam soon alienated American reporters in Vietnam, who persisted in criticizing the war effort and most particularly the attempts by American officials in Vietnam to present an optimistic picture of the struggle. The enormous impact which American public opinion was to have on the prosecution of the war was greatly assisted by these early journalistic critiques of American policy. Official expressions of optimism by Secretary of State Dean Rusk and Secretary of Defense Robert McNamara only further alienated those newspapermen who were disposed to see the United States floundering in a quagmire.[33]

The growing reaction to the Diem regime's political repression— Buddhist monks died on Saigon streets of self-immolation to protest these policies—and the disturbing arbitrariness of Diem's dictatorial government led to the November 1963 coup. High-ranking Vietnamese generals murdered Diem and his totalitarian-minded younger brother, Ngo Dinh Nhu, and assumed power. The Diem family's fall from power was followed by detailed, shocking accounts of murders, tortures, and other atrocities committed by the deposed police state. Militarily, the coup brought to light the truth about the war's progress. The government had long insisted that the Viet Cong were being compressed into progressively smaller areas of Vietnam, that significant numbers of hamlets were being brought under Saigon's protection, and that the rate of attacks on Viet Cong strongholds had been effectively increased. The generals who assumed power revealed that Viet Cong influence was spreading and had not been contained, that there was little truth in the government's statistics regarding the number of hamlets which had been brought under control, and that the number of government-instigated attacks had been greatly inflated. As one of the Vietnamese generals told an American friend, "Your Secretary of Defense loves statistics. We Vietnamese can give him all he wants. If you want them to go up, they will go up. If you want them to go down, they will go down." [34]

The much more accurate assessment of the military situation which was made possible by Diem's ouster failed to resolve the fundamental military dilemma faced by the United States: How could

[33] See, for example, David Halberstam, *The Making of a Quagmire* (New York: Random House, 1965) and Shaplen, *The Lost Revolution.*
[34] The incident is recounted in Hilsman, *To Move a Nation,* p. 523.

a technically advanced superpower, committed to a limited war, cope with guerrilla warfare? Given the Vietnamese peasant's experience with colonial rule, despotic home-rule, and social and economic injustice, could the United States hope to succeed? To make matters even worse, the Korean War had demonstrated that the American public had little sensitivity to the nonmilitary aspects of limited warfare.

Three weeks after Diem's murder, Kennedy was assassinated in Dallas. Inevitably, predictions of the direction of American policy had Kennedy lived have occupied many commentators. That the President had not been single-minded in his attitude toward the war was, of course, to be expected. He had visited Vietnam as a Congressman in 1951 and had returned deeply convinced of the folly of French policies. He had criticized both the French and the American military establishments on the Senate floor in 1954 for their "predictions of confidence which have lulled the American people." [35] The discrepancy between the optimistic predictions of his Secretaries of State and Defense, and the pessimistic, cynical reports from journalists on the scene was, of course, apparent to the President. One must also consider that there were respected men in his party and in his Administration, such as Ambassador W. Averell Harriman and Roger Hilsman, director of Intelligence and Research at the State Department and later Assistant Secretary for Far Eastern Affairs, who were becoming increasingly outspoken in their opposition to the war.

Yet only months before his death Kennedy told a press conference that the nation's goal in Vietnam was "a stable government there, carrying on a struggle to maintain its national independence. We believe strongly in that. . . . In my opinion, for us to withdraw from that effort would mean a collapse not only in South Vietnam but Southeast Asia. *So we are going to stay there.*" [36] Sorensen has assessed the President's attitude in November 1963 as follows:

> The struggle could well be, he thought, this nation's severest test of endurance and patience. . . . Yet at least he had a major counterguerrilla effort under way, with a comparatively small commitment of American manpower. He was simply going to weather it out, a nasty, untidy mess *to which there was no other acceptable solution.* Talk of abandoning so unstable an ally and so costly a commitment "only makes it easy for the Communists," said the President. "I think we should stay." [37]

[35] Quoted in Sorensen, *Kennedy*, p. 660.

[36] Quoted in Schlesinger, Jr., *A Thousand Days*, p. 989. Emphasis added.

[37] Sorensen, *Kennedy*, pp. 660–61. Emphasis added. This conclusion is shared by Walton, *Cold War and Counterrevolution*, pp. 200–201. In *The Faces of Power*, Seyom Brown argues that such speculation is fruitless; see p. 326.

MASSIVE ESCALATION/DOMESTIC DISSENSION

The fall of the Diem government, followed by strong evidence in Saigon that the optimism generated by the American military establishment had been unwarranted, forced the Joint Chiefs of Staff to reconsider their response to the Vietnamese War. Kennedy's successor, Lyndon B. Johnson, agreed to support of an escalated policy, including the bombing of North Vietnam. Counterpressures were present, particularly in the form of a scheme put forth at various times by United Nations Secretary General U Thant and Cambodian Chief of State Norodom Sihanouk for the neutralization of Vietnam. But scarcely a month after taking office, Johnson informed Saigon's new chief, General Duong Van Minh:

> The United States government shares the view . . . that single "neutralization" of South Vietnam is unacceptable. As long as the Communist regime in North Vietnam persists in its aggressive policy, neutralization would only be another name for a Communist take-over.[38]

Harriman, Hilsman, and Presidential Assistant Michael V. Forrestal vigorously opposed the growing clamor for the bombing of infiltration routes on the grounds that such an escalation would undoubtedly lead the other side to step up its efforts, and might even cause Hanoi to send northerners south of the seventeenth parallel (it was believed up to this time that those who slipped through the Ho Chi Minh Trail were southerners returning home to join the resistance). Actually, bombing of the infiltration routes was but one part of a larger scheme which included raids inside South Vietnam. Such a plan had been proposed despite the very real differences between guerrilla and "traditional" warfare, and despite the consideration that such bombings would almost certainly alienate the very populace whose cooperation had long been considered essential to the anti-communist effort.

Many of those who favored a large-scale bombing campaign included in their proposals the destruction of industrial plants and power installations in North Vietnam; still others advocated attacks

---

[38] The *New York Times*, 2 Jan. 1964, p. 7. For a defense of the Johnson policy, see Eugene V. Rostow, *Law, Power and the Pursuit of Peace* (Lincoln, Neb.: University of Nebraska Press, 1968), pp. 59–73.

north of the seventeenth parallel, limited to military installations and communications routes. In either case the risk of direct North Vietnamese and/or Communist Chinese intervention below the seventeenth parallel was considerable. On the back burners simmered the question of increasing the number of American troops in Vietnam, and of redefining their function.

These very grave issues were complicated by the 1964 Presidential campaign and Johnson's effort to win a term in the White House on his own account. In selecting a candidate the Republican party disregarded its liberal wing and enthusiastically embraced the conservative junior Senator from Arizona, Barry Goldwater. To some extent the hawkish position taken by Goldwater (escalation, bombing, and defoliation) moved Johnson toward a somewhat harder line in an attempt to short-circuit the traditional Republican charge that Democratic administrations tended to be "soft" on communism. Some, however, have argued that Johnson had been planning a measured escalation months before Goldwater's nomination.[39] In his public position during the campaign, Johnson disclaimed any intention of sending "American boys to do the fighting for Asian boys." [40]

Shortly after the two national parties had completed their nominating rituals, an incident occurred, which provided the Johnson Administration with an opportunity to escalate substantially the war in Vietnam. On August 2, North Vietnamese torpedo boats attacked the *Maddox*, an American destroyer engaged in a routine patrol of the Gulf of Tonkin. Washington protested the attack while warning North Vietnam of possible reprisals. But two days later Hanoi launched an assault against the *Maddox* and the *C. Turner Joy*, another destroyer in the gulf. Neither action had resulted in American casualties or damage to the ships, but they did offer the President a tempting opportunity to move the nation one notch closer to total involvement in the war. Politically, Johnson might have tempered his response to the Tonkin Gulf episode so as to further his image as a prudent statesman; but to have done so would have risked Goldwater's charge that the White House had failed to react to a stepped-up enemy offensive. And so retaliatory air strikes against Hanoi's torpedo boat installations were ordered and executed.

The matter did not rest there since the alleged communist provocation, about which so little was known, provided the Administration with an irresistible opportunity to obtain from Congress a "blank check" for future military escalation in Vietnam. This was

[39] See David Schoenbrun, *Vietnam* (New York: Atheneum, 1968), p. 50.
[40] This aspect of the Johnson-Goldwater contest is discussed in Geyelin, *Lyndon B. Johnson and the World*, pp. 193–202.

accomplished the day following the second Tonkin attack, when the President sent a message to Congress which argued, in part, that the world's hostile powers must be made to understand that despite the Presidential campaign, America was not divided in its response to aggression. Two days later the so-called "Gulf of Tonkin Resolution" was passed, authorizing the President "to take all necessary measures to repel any armed attack against the forces of the United States and to prevent further aggression." [41] This Congressional authorization, which was soon to cause liberal legislators acute embarrassment, passed the House by a vote of 466–0 and the Senate by a 88–2 margin; only Ernest Gruening of Alaska and Wayne Morse of Oregon voted against the measure. The politically astute Johnson had placed himself in an enviable position. During the three months prior to the November election he was able to present Goldwater in a decidedly unfavorable light by picturing the Senator's Vietnam program as dangerously aggressive; at the same time he had obtained prior Congressional approval for actions resembling his Republican opponent's formula. The gamble was that Hanoi would stay its hand until the election so that the President would not have to draw upon his curiously open-ended authorization.

There has been so much argument over the Gulf of Tonkin Resolution because it was eventually used to justify direct, massive American intervention in the war. For one thing, Hanoi vigorously denied that the second attack (against the *Maddox* and the *C. Turner Joy*) had ever occurred. Secondly, Senator Fulbright and others have come to doubt seriously that an attack actually took place,[42] charging that the Administration, and Secretary of Defense McNamara in particular, deliberately misinformed the Congress as to the nature and extent of the Gulf of Tonkin incident. Finally, one may argue that the Tonkin Resolution had never been meant to give the President a free hand. At least one student of Johnson's foreign policy has insisted that to understand the extent of the Congress' mandate one must consider the legislative history of the resolution. During the debate, Senator Gaylord Nelson of Wisconsin had attempted to amend the resolution to state specifically that the Senate was against an "extension of the present conflict" and in favor of a continuation of the fundamentally advisory role of the United States. As a Democrat and Chairman of the Senate Foreign Relations Committee, Fulbright was in a good

[41] Quoted in *Ibid.*, p. 191.

[42] See Schoenbrun, *Vietnam*, p. 52. Johnson's honesty is challenged in Joseph C. Goulden, *Truth Is the First Casualty: The Gulf of Tonkin Affair—Illusion and Reality* (Chicago: Rand McNally, 1969). For the President's defense, see Lyndon B. Johnson, *The Vantage Point: Perspectives of the Presidency, 1963–1969* (New York: Holt, Rinehart & Winston, 1971), pp. 112–19.

position to interpret the Administration's understanding of the measure, and he assured Nelson that "the joint resolution is quite consistent with our existing mission and our understanding of what we have been doing in South Vietnam for the last ten years." [43]

It was not until February of 1965 that Johnson, newly elected for a full four-year term, had the opportunity to draw upon the Tonkin Resolution. With still another Saigon government near collapse and threatening to assume dictatorial powers, the Chief Executive rejected attempts by Ho Chi Minh and United Nations Secretary General U Thant to negotiate a conclusion to the hostilities. Throughout the 1964–65 winter the President and his staff studied maps of North Vietnam, identifying potential targets should a decision be reached to accede to the growing demands of the military to bomb Saigon's enemy. Then on February 7, 1965, the United States Air Force barracks at Pleiku were attacked by a Viet Cong raiding party. In the mortar fire and hand grenade attack eight Americans were killed and 126 wounded. The President ordered the immediate implementation of Rolling Thunder, a secret code name for the bombing of North Vietnam. A decisive, tragic corner had been turned. The February decision would ultimately cost Johnson the Presidency, alienate the liberal wing of his party, torpedo his Great Society legislation, and involve the United States in a grisly land war in Asia.

Critics of war by Executive fiat quickly emerged. Mavericks like Gruening and Morse were soon joined by a host of liberal, mostly Democratic, Senators who questioned the President's goals and urged him to seek a negotiated peace; in this early stage of disenchantment, however, few were calling for outright cessation of the bombings.[44] The publicity accorded these men, and the tough, cynical reports from Vietnam-based American journalists, were responsible for the growing public resistance to the Administration's war policies. Increasingly, this chorus of dissent attacked not only the progress of the war and the escalation, but also the very philosophy behind American involvement. Selective bombing of North Vietnam had been part of the Maxwell Taylor-Walt Rostow report to Kennedy in 1961. This report theorized that such raids would convince the North Vietnamese that by supporting the southern insurgents they would incur heavy penalties. While the Kennedy Administration had rejected the concept, the intervening years witnessed a major American ground troop commitment; as the stakes increased, Washington's determina-

---

[43] This question is discussed in Geyelin, *Lyndon B. Johnson and the World*, p. 192.

[44] The dissent was led by the following Senators: George McGovern (South Dakota); Frank Church (Idaho); J. William Fulbright (Arkansas); Eugene McCarthy (Minnesota); Gaylord Nelson (Wisconsin); Stephen Young (Ohio); and Joseph Clark (Pennsylvania).

tion deepened. In agreeing to test the effect of bombing North Vietnam, Johnson sought to influence Hanoi by applying the "equalization of pain" [45]—in kind retribution for the suffering inflicted on the South by Vietcong aggression. It was a lesson of American power and a warning of what was to come. Yet the official justification stressed the need to terminate the flow of troops and materiel to the South.

It was in the State Department's "White Paper" of February 1965 that the Administration set forth its operating assumptions on Vietnam. The "Conclusion" section of that report closely reflected the official view that the war in Vietnam was not a local, civil action, but rather a clear example of calculated communist aggression:

> The record is conclusive. It establishes beyond question that North Vietnam is carrying out a carefully conceived plan of aggression against the South. . . . This aggression violates the United Nations Charter. It is directly contrary to the Geneva Accords of 1954 and of 1962 to which North Vietnam is a party. It shatters the peace of Southeast Asia. . . . The people of South Vietnam have chosen to resist this threat. At their request, the United States has taken its place beside them in their defensive struggle.[46]

At the Johns Hopkins University in April, Johnson emphasized his support for the fundamental underpinnings of the "White Paper." "Let no one think for a moment," he warned, "that retreat from Vietnam would bring an end to conflict. The battle would be renewed in one country and then in another. The central lesson of our time is that the appetite of aggression is never satisfied. To withdraw from one battlefield means only to prepare for the next. We must say in Southeast Asia, as we did in Europe, in the words of the Bible: 'Hitherto shalt thou come, but no further.' " [47] The temptation to draw simplistic parallels with Munich was irresistible.

With its decision to launch unretaliatory bombing raids against North Vietnam the Johnson Administration sowed the seeds of its own destruction. In the years which followed hundreds of thousands of American ground forces were introduced into Southeast Asia, and tens of thousands returned home dead. Yet military victory eluded the President, and many of the nation's top policy-makers believed that hopes for such a victory were illusory. The combined strength of the

[45] Brown, *The Faces of Power*, p. 334.

[46] The White Paper is reprinted in Gettleman, ed., *Vietnam*, pp. 284–316. The section quoted is found on pp. 313–14.

[47] Quoted in *Ibid.*, p. 325. For a discussion of this aspect of the President's thinking, see Eric F. Goldman, *The Tragedy of Lyndon Johnson* (New York: Knopf, 1969), Chap. XIV.

American armed forces and the South Vietnamese military was unable to quell the civil war. Similarly, American expectation of reducing Viet Cong guerrilla strength to a level which would render it manageable by Saigon was bitterly frustrated. At the urging of the Joint Chiefs of Staff and, in particular, General William Westmoreland, Johnson's Vietnam military commander, additional forces and additional funds were poured into that unfortunate country. But victory remained somewhere down a long, dark tunnel despite assurances of a glimmering light at the end. Relatedly, the attempt to force a settlement which would exclude participation by the Viet Cong's National Liberation Front proved impossible.

By the opening of 1968 the Administration was under intense pressure to unwind its commitment to South Vietnam. With the communists' successful "Tet offensive" in February of 1968 it became apparent that the massive infusion of American men and materiel into South Vietnam had failed. All of the air strikes, napalm, artillery, naval bombardments, tanks, rifles, and men had failed to stem the National Liberation Front. Viet Cong were on the offensive in the imperial city of Hue and in a wide range of lesser cities; Saigon itself was rocked by a series of spectacular attacks. Well over a thousand American soldiers died during the month-long Tet offensive, and by the end of February few could argue with the *Wall Street Journal's* conclusion that "the American people should be getting ready to accept, if they haven't already, the prospect that the whole Vietnam effort may be doomed, that it may be falling apart beneath our feet." [48]

A major, long overdue, reappraisal of America's role in Vietnam followed the Tet offensive. Newspaper accounts of Pentagon requests for American manpower levels of upwards of 700,000 greatly alarmed a significant segment of the public; the Congress, too, had grown restive under the relentless pressure from Westmoreland and his supporters for a large-scale call-up of reserves. This mood was not quieted by the realization that the expanded role in Vietnam had aggravated many of America's economic problems. A significant number of Americans had become convinced that the United States should never have introduced its own troops into the conflict, and the public's reservations, if not outright hostility, toward the war were encouraged by liberal Congressmen, intellectuals, and much of the press. Protests and acts of civil disobedience, some involving impressive numbers of citizens, grew more common. By the end of February the

[48] Quoted in Townsend Hoopes, *The Limits of Intervention* (New York: McKay, 1969), p. 147.

new Secretary of Defense, Clark Clifford, had come to the conclusion that a military victory in Vietnam was impossible.[49] On March 22 it was announced that Westmoreland would be recalled from Vietnam to become Army Chief of Staff.

Nine days later the President delivered his long-awaited address to the American people on Vietnam. He was seeking, he assured them, some basis for beginning peace talks. As a first, unilateral step, he announced a cessation of all air and naval bombings, except in the area immediately north of the Demilitarized Zone. A program for the Vietnamization of the war was outlined. Here was cause to hope that the seemingly endless, open-ended American escalation of the war had come to a halt by the President's implicit repudiation of military victory.

The speech was also significant for its disclosure of one of the best kept of all political secrets. Johnson informed his stunned national audience that he would not seek a second full term. Asserting that "the unity of our people" represents the nation's "ultimate strength," the President admitted:

> There is division in the American house now. . . . holding the trust that is mine, as President of all the people, I cannot disregard the peril to the progress of the American people. . . . With American sons in the fields far away, with America's future under challenge right here at home . . . I do not believe that I should devote an hour or a day of my time to any personal partisan causes. . . . Accordingly, I shall not seek, and I will not accept, the nomination of my party for another term as your President.[50]

It was surely not a coincidence that Johnson's renunciation of future public office had closely followed the Tet offensive.

With Johnson withdrawn from the race, the Democratic party was convulsed by a bitter rivalry for the nomination, a rivalry dominated by the issue of Vietnam. Senator Eugene McCarthy's candidacy—which preceded, and to some extent most probably helped precipitate, the President's decision not to run—was followed by the candidacy of New York's Senator Robert F. Kennedy, Senator George McGovern of South Dakota, and Vice President Hubert H. Humphrey. In the end, the assassination of Robert Kennedy, the political ineffectiveness of McCarthy, and the still powerful influence of Lyndon Johnson resulted in the nomination of Humphrey as the Democratic standard-bearer.

[49] See *Ibid.*, p. 204.
[50] Johnson, *The Vantage Point*, p. 435. For a most interesting account of Johnson's decision to withdraw, see Theodore H. White, *The Making of the President, 1968* (New York: Atheneum, 1969), pp. 96–125.

Long before the Democratic hopefuls had entered the race, former Vice President Richard M. Nixon had doggedly persevered against great odds, overcome his twin defeats of 1960 and 1962 (when he lost the Presidency and the California governorship, respectively), and emerged to collect the highest honor that could be bestowed by the Republican party. James Reston of the *New York Times* analyzed the mood in March 1968:

> Washington is now the symbol of the helplessness of the present day. . . . Yet the political opposition offers no alternative that commands the confidence of a majority of the people. The main crisis is not Vietnam itself, or in the cities, but the feeling that the political system for dealing with these things has broken down.[51]

Yet in turmoil and confusion the nation, or perhaps those who were in a position to decide for the nation, saw fit to nominate two politicians whose roots ran deep into the very political establishment which so many had thought would be repudiated.

After some preliminary skirmishes the Republican party's Vietnam plank was endorsed unanimously by the GOP Convention. Pledging a negotiated end to the war rather than further escalation, the platform charged "it is time to realize that not every international conflict is susceptible of solution by American ground forces. . . . We pledge . . . a positive program that will offer a fair and equitable settlement to all, based on the principle of self-determination, our national interests and the cause of long-range world peace." [52] This, clearly, was not the type of peace plank that the war's bitterest foes would have endorsed since the Republicans merely pledged to pursue a policy that would lead to a negotiated peace. While an all-out military victory had been disavowed, there was nothing in the GOP's position to prevent Richard Nixon, if elected, from continuing the military phase of the war.

The tragic escalation of the war during Johnson's tenure, the emergence of several charismatic peace candidates, and the close identification of the murdered Robert Kennedy with the antiwar movement, convinced many that the Democrats were headed for a stormy confrontation when they convened at Chicago. Few were prepared for the violent, bloody affair which took place in the nation's "second city." With the presentation of the "war plank," the emotions fired by McCarthy's trek through the snows of New Hampshire, the

[51] Quoted in White, *The Making of the President, 1968*, p. 95. For another perspective, see Richard H. Rovere, *Waist Deep in the Big Muddy: Personal Reflections on 1968* (Boston: Little, Brown, 1968).

[52] The Platform Committee's draft in the *New York Times*, 5 Aug. 1968, pp. 25–26.

President's renunciation of his candidacy, and Kennedy's assassination converged, sometimes hysterically, in that floor fight. The majority plank, sponsored by forces loyal to Vice President Humphrey, rejected "as unacceptable a unilateral withdrawal. . . . We strongly support the Paris talks and applaud the initiative of President Johnson which brought North Vietnam to the peace table." This majority report also stipulated that the United States "Stop all bombing of North Vietnam, [but only] when this action would not endanger the lives of our troops . . . This action should take into account the response from Hanoi." [53]

The minority plank was sponsored by Senator McCarthy and Richard Goodwin, a close aide of Senator Kennedy and a former speech writer for President Johnson. The McCarthy-Goodwin proposal contained three basic tenets: (1) "an unconditional end to all bombings in North Vietnam"; (2) "mutual withdrawal of all United States forces and all North Vietnamese troops from South Vietnam . . . over a relatively short period of time"; (3) "encourage our South Vietnamese allies to negotiate a political reconciliation with the National Liberation Front looking toward a government which is broadly representative of these and all elements in South Vietnamese society." [54] Thus the choice before the convention was a clear one: renounce America's tragic commitment to South Vietnam and withdraw, or continue the war at any cost until an acceptable peace is reached. Three days after its presentation the "peace plank" was defeated while several delegations—including those from California and New York—sang "We Shall Overcome" and the smell of tear gas wafted through the shafts of the Hilton's air-conditioning system. Millions of Americans who had for years been watching the bloody battlefields of Vietnam on television must have experienced a shock of recognition when battered and bloody delegates, Hippies, Yippies, peace advocates, and policemen appeared on the screen. The violence of Vietnam had come to roost where it belonged—at the heart of the American political process, which had proven incapable of handling the Southeast Asian crisis with intelligence and restraint.

VIETNAMIZATION AND THE NIXON ARMISTICE

To survive politically, Richard Nixon, the first Republican in the White House in over a decade, would have to deescalate the war

[53] The *New York Times*, 27 Aug. 1968, p. 26.
[54] Quoted in White, *The Making of the President, 1968*, p. 276.

bequeathed to him by the Democrats. At the time the new Chief Executive took office troop levels, rising for the past five years, had reached 550,000; American combat deaths had averaged 278 weekly in 1968; monthly draft calls were at the 30,000 level; 33,000 tactical air sorties were being flown monthly in Indochina; the South Vietnamese economy was nearly ruined by an annual inflation rate of between 35 and 40 percent; and only about 40 percent of the rural population was under government control.[55] While Nixon's critics grew more hostile and called for immediate disengagement, the peace talks, so recently begun, were mired in innumerable difficulties, both petty and fundamental. Worse, the Johnson Administration had apparently left no plan for the withdrawal of American troops engaged in a war which was costing the United States over $20 billion annually.

As perceived by Nixon and his advisors, the Administration had five possible courses of action. Three of these were discounted: further escalation (which would risk a widening of the war and which would further alienate the war-weary public); a continuation of the status quo; and "precipitate disengagement." The last of these alternatives was ruled out on the grounds that it would eventually lead to recriminations at home and "contempt" abroad.[56] The two alternatives which won a favorable reaction involved redoubled efforts at a publicly and privately negotiated settlement, and Vietnamization. The latter policy has been defined by the President as "the process of progressively turning over defense responsibilities to the South Vietnamese and thereby reducing U.S. involvement." [57] The new strategy was shrewdly geared toward moderating public hostility by sharply reducing American casualties; at the same time, it appeared to encourage Hanoi's expectation that the withdrawal of American troops would mark the collapse of Saigon's resistance.

The war in South Vietnam was scaled down dramatically in the new Administration's shift from "maximum pressure," to "protective reaction," to Vietnamization. President Nixon was able to cite some impressive statistics supporting Vietnamization: American troop strength by May 1972 was announced at 69,000; monthly combat deaths in 1971 averaged 26 per week, while monthly draft calls averaged 7,500; and the cost of the war dropped more than 50

[55] Richard M. Nixon, *U.S. Foreign Policy for the 1970's—The Emerging Structure of Peace: A Report to the Congress* (Feb. 9, 1972) (Washington, D.C.: U.S. Govt. Printing Office, 1972), pp. 110–11.

[56] *Ibid.*, p. 111. See Rowland Evans, Jr., and Robert D. Novak, *Nixon in the White House: The Frustration of Power* (New York: Randon House, 1971), p. 78.

[57] Nixon, *U.S. Foreign Policy for the 1970's*, p. 111.

percent. According to statistics supplied by the Administration, the South Vietnamese army's strength in 1972 was 1.1 million, an increase of 300,000 over 1968; the Administration claimed that by 1972 approximately 73 percent of the rural population was under Saigon's control; the inflation rate dropped almost two-thirds, to 15 percent per year; and long-range economic reform through land redistribution was underway.[58]

Such glowing official statistics leave two fundamental questions regarding the success of Vietnamization unanswered. First, government reports do not reflect meaningfully the degree to which the accomplishments of the program were offset by the escalation of American air involvement in Cambodia and Laos. As the ground war in Vietnam wound down, the air war in Indochina dramatically intensified.[59] Also, the success of Vietnamization must be measured in more than military terms. That is to say, the President defined his strategy as including "in its broadest sense . . . establishing security and winning allegiance in the countryside; developing responsive political institutions; managing a war-torn economy and steering it toward longer range development." [60] Success, then, meant more than troop withdrawals and reduced draft calls.

If one takes, for example, the test of political stability as it related to the Saigon government, a number of inconsistencies at once become apparent. Washington has boasted of the effectiveness of the South Vietnamese constitution and the steadily broadening base of political participation.[61] Yet in the 1971 Presidential election incumbent Thieu's candidacy was uncontested. The Nixon Administration claimed that the "interplay of personalities and circumstances in South Vietnam simply failed to produce a contest." Yet after insisting for so long that the United States was in Indochina to ensure "freedom of choice," the President concluded in his February 1972 report to the Congress that "South Vietnam's political development contrasts favorably . . . with North Vietnam, where there are no true elections at all." [62]

It is little wonder that Robert Shaplen, who covered the war for *The New Yorker* for more than a decade, bitterly attacked official GOP conclusions regarding South Vietnam's political evolution. Writing a year before Saigon's Presidential elections, Shaplen supported those

[58] *Ibid.*, p. 112.

[59] Perhaps the most virulent statement of this view is Noam Chomsky, *At War with Asia* (New York: Random House, 1970).

[60] Nixon, *U.S. Foreign Policy for the 1970's*, p. 122.

[61] *Ibid.*, p. 126.

[62] *Ibid.*, pp. 126–27.

who warned that Thieu was moving toward what his aides politely described as a "clear-sighted dictatorship." [63] The avowed reason for this rule by fiat was the urgency of the economic crisis, but it was obvious that once given such license all matters of state could be handled in a like manner. Hence, moderate but constant troop withdrawals did not quiet the criticism of determined Congressional, campus, and media spokesmen who attacked the political and economic failures of Vietnamization. Worse, Thieu often proved a most uncooperative partner. While Nixon ignored demands that he disavow the General's regime, the Vietnamese head of state doggedly resisted compromises involving a broadening of his government's base and publicly refused Administration pleas to enter into a coalition government via free elections.

Such rigidity undermined the central goal of Vietnamization, to prevent the downfall of the Saigon government and its reversion to communist control. But the General's stubborn resistance to an accommodation was far from the only factor prolonging the struggle. The Nixon Administration charged that as American troops withdrew from South Vietnam, communist activity increased markedly in Laos and Cambodia. This led to a major American escalation of the war and particularly the April 1970 order of United States troops into Cambodia to neutralize enemy "sanctuaries." [64] Although the President defended this highly divisive action on the grounds that it would speed the withdrawal of American troops from Indochina, Congressional critics threatened to deprive the Executive branch of funds to prosecute the expanded war. On the nation's campuses, thousands of students were involved in demonstrations against the "incursion"; in the most widely publicized of these war protests, four young students were shot to death by National Guard troops. The soul-searching which followed these violent protests and bloody reprisals caused many to wonder if the Administration had done any better, after all, than its predecessor. The cost of the Vietnam war must be measured in terms of its economic drain, its impact on the Western alliance, and its domestic political repercussions.

Those most hostile toward the President insisted that troop withdrawals under the guise of Vietnamization were merely transparent attempts to divert the public's attention from an intensified effort to gain control over all of Indochina via a highly technological, but no less brutal, air war. It has been urged, for example, that the

[63] Robert Shaplen, *The Road from War* (New York: Harper & Row, 1970), p. 351.

[64] Nixon, *U.S. Foreign Policy for the 1970's*, p. 132. For a perceptive analysis of the Cambodian intervention, see Chester L. Cooper, *The Lost Crusade: America in Vietnam* (New York: Dodd, Mead, 1970), pp. 434–41. Also, Evans and Novak, *Nixon in the White House*, pp. 246–56.

President's stated reasons for the Cambodian invasion were "plainly absurd" [65] since American military sources in Saigon denied any knowledge of an increased communist threat. This view has been supported by a 1970 staff report issued by the Senate Foreign Relations Committee which concluded that the communists were moving toward a defensive posture in Cambodia, and that in fact they were withdrawing from the South Vietnamese border.[66]

In the face of such evidence, many have supported the view that Washington's objectives in Indochina were other than those publicly expressed. It has been argued that the Cambodian incursion and the expanded Indochinese war were part of a broad effort "to support reactionary, even feudalistic elements, and to suppress an emerging peasant-based movement of national independence." [67] Unable to overcome postwar, anti-communist obsessions, the United States has constantly pursued counterrevolutionary policies in Indochina and the Third World by supporting reactionary governments.

It is doubtful that historians will credit Vietnamization with a major role in ending American involvement in the Vietnam phase of the Indochina War. One respected critic has observed that the strategy was "comprised of one part hokum, one part wishful thinking, and one part genuine policy." [68] Such a conclusion is understandable even if one only considers the military defense of Vietnam itself. Poor leadership, inept coordination, and low morale made it exceedingly difficult for United States servicemen to abandon command positions. The underlying cynicism of Vietnamization has not gone unnoticed; since the American public objected primarily to the killing of its sons, why not provide guns and money to Asians and lead them into slaughter to achieve Washington's goals? [69]

Yet an armistice in Vietnam was achieved. After more than four years of intensive public and private negotiations the Nixon Administration accomplished the first phase of America's disengagement from the Indochina War. The most dramatic, and fruitful, of these efforts toward a negotiated settlement was conducted by Presidential Advisor Henry A. Kissinger, a former Harvard professor highly critical of President Kennedy's conception that America should serve as the world's defender of freedom. Such assumptions, Kissinger believed,

[65] Chomsky, *At War with Asia*, p. 164.
[66] *Ibid.*, p. 165.
[67] *Ibid.*, p. 155. Also see his *American Power and the New Mandarins* (Pantheon, 1969).
[68] Cooper, *The Lost Crusade*, p. 436.
[69] For this analysis, see Shaplen, *The Road from War*, p. 318. Also, Hans J. Morgenthau, *Truth and Power: Essays of a Decade, 1960–1970* (New York: Praeger, 1970), p. 430.

had produced the legacy of Vietnam. At the same time, he supported President Nixon's position that "precipitate withdrawal" was unacceptable. It was the Administration's view that immediate disengagement would seriously weaken the nation's ability to deal with its allies and with its Cold War enemies. Two years after assuming his White House post, Kissinger told a group of editors: "If the United States utterly fails in something that it has undertaken with so much effort, it is bound to affect the judgment of other countries as to the degree to which the United States can be significant in their areas." [70]

It is clear that the Nixon Administration was able to extricate the nation from its land war in Vietnam because the Soviet Union and China were willing to cooperate in that effort. Both nations had become convinced by 1972 that there was more to be gained by establishing closer ties with the United States than by continuing to encourage and support Hanoi in its quest for a military solution to the Vietnamese civil war. Wider travel opportunities, cultural exchanges, and expanded trade were in the offing. The mutual benefits to the three powers of expanded trade in nonstrategic goods proved particularly tempting. China had much to gain from the possibility of diplomatic recognition, admission to the United Nations, and settlement of its claim to Formosa. It also could not ignore the consideration that closer ties with the United States would strengthen its hand against its neighbor and ideological enemy, the Soviet Union.

Moscow, in turn, saw a number of advantages: the promise of a solution to the Berlin problem; progress toward a reduction of strategic arms; and a mutual reduction of troops from Europe (a reciprocal agreement to limit NATO and Warsaw Pact forces was a distinct possibility).[71] The Nixon Administration's diplomatic feat was a particularly delicate one because it attempted to benefit from the mutual suspicions of China and Russia while strengthening relations with both. And while the detente will probably not affect the bipolar world structure and may not even be sustained, pragmatically it was an ingenious piece of diplomacy. One of its practical consequences was the Vietnam armistice.

Nixon's jockeying for position with the Peking and Moscow leadership, and his insistence upon "peace with honor," frustrated the demands of those who sought the quickest possible disengagement from a defenseless war. But on January 23, 1973, after dozens of rumors had flourished and expired in the world's capitals, an armistice

---

[70] Quoted in the *New York Times*, 24 Jan. 1972, p. 18. Also see David Landau, *Kissinger: The Uses of Power* (Boston: Houghton Mifflin, 1972), pp. 157–59.

[71] For background, see Evans and Novak, *Nixon in the White House*, pp. 402–10.

was announced in Paris. The agreement stipulated: a cease-fire; withdrawal of American combat troops within 60 days of the signing; release of all American prisoners of war within 60 days of the signing; and truce supervision by an international force consisting of troops from Canada, Hungary, Indonesia, and Poland. Both the United States and North Vietnam agreed to respect "the South Vietnamese people's right to self-determination." The vagueness of this aspect of the truce was underscored by the document's failure to establish a date for a national election in South Vietnam; pending such an eventuality, it was understood that President Thieu would remain in office.[72] The central political problem, whether to divide or unify Vietnam, had eluded resolution on the battlefield and at the peace table.

The armistice did not settle the political division of Vietnam, and neither did it resolve the intense internal conflict in Laos and Cambodia. The accord only stipulated that the sovereignty and neutrality of both countries would be respected; that foreign countries "shall put an end to all military activities in Cambodia and Laos" (date unspecified); and that the internal affairs of the two nations "shall be settled by the people of each of these countries without foreign interference."[73] Kissinger made clear at a January 24 news conference that America expected "within a short period" a formal cease-fire in Laos, accompanied by the withdrawal of foreign troops. The situation in Cambodia, however, was far more ambiguous given the number of factions vying for control.[74] Seven months after signing the armistice, the United States continued its air war in Cambodia and insisted that it would do so until communist forces there ceased military operations and accepted a cease-fire. This position led to charges that the Administration had intensified its military role in Indochina so as to ensure its hegemony over the area.[75]

The lingering air war over Indochina and the realization that the fragile Paris accord could be easily shattered by either side led to fears that total military disengagement would continue to elude Washington. Through its anti-communist offensive, the United States has emerged as the most powerful force in Southeast Asia; but it has paid dearly for the broad influence and authority gained in the region in the past decade. Forty-six thousand Americans have been killed

[72] Text of the accord reprinted in the *New York Times*, 25 Jan. 1973, pp. 15–17.

[73] The *New York Times*, 25 Jan. 1973, p. 16.

[74] For background, see The Committee of Concerned Asian Scholars, *The Indochina Story*, pp. 53–61. Kissinger news conference text in the *New York Times*, 25 Jan. 1973, p. 20.

[75] See, for example, I. F. Stone, "Toward a Third Indochina War," *The New York Review*, Mar. 8, 1973, pp. 16–20. The Nixon Administration position on bombing Cambodia reported in the *New York Times*, 28 Mar. 1973, pp. 1, 10.

and nearly a half-million wounded, 150,000 seriously so. By contrast, the South Vietnamese lost 184,000 and the combined death toll of North Vietnamese and Vietcong has been estimated at 925,000.[76] During the peak period of American involvement, the war effort cost $20 billion annually. Such massive spending, without compensatory tax increases, resulted in a ruinous inflation. Internationally, the war was the direct cause of a huge deficit in the United States balance of payments; the devaluation of the dollar and the destruction of the existing world monetary system resulted.[77] And the price of America's counterrevolutionary effort will continue to rise. Billions more will be expended to support the American military presence in Southeast Asia, and additional billions will be needed to sustain friendly governments in Indochina, Thailand, and the Philippines.

NEW DIRECTIONS?

Vietnam and the Indochina War must be viewed in tandem with America's attitude toward its role in world affairs. The rising number of critics charging that Washington has pursued a basically counter-revolutionary policy in the post-World War II period cannot be ignored; neither can the evidence. It is useful to consider that in December of 1965 both the United States and the USSR voted in favor of the United Nations General Assembly's "Declaration of the Inadmissibility of Intervention in the Domestic Affairs of States and the Protection of their Independence and Sovereignty." This policy asserts:

> [N]o state has the right to intervene, directly or indirectly, for any reason whatever, in the internal or external affairs of any other state . . . no state shall organize, assist, ferment, finance, incite or tolerate subversive, terrorist or armed activities directed toward the violent overthrow of another state, or interfere in civil strife in another state.[78]

Yet each superpower continues to justify intervention. The Soviet Union has used its resources to support nations attempting to throw off colonial or neocolonial rule; yet it has stifled the demands of its European satellites for a greater measure of autonomy. The United States, in arguing that its intervention is justified to ensure the

---

[76] Figures from United States Defense Department; South Vietnamese command; and North Vietnamese and Vietcong estimates. The *New York Times*, 25 Jan. 1973, p. 21.

[77] Figures from Edwin L. Dale, Jr., "What Vietnam Did to the American Economy," the *New York Times*, 28 Jan. 1973, Sec. 3, pp. 1–2.

[78] Quoted in Morgenthau, *A New Foreign Policy for the United States*, p. 111.

political status quo against outside violence, has in Vietnam and elsewhere opposed the legitimate revolutionary activities of peoples long repressed by feudal and dictatorial elements within their borders.

While accusing the Soviet Union of a fixed determination to forcibly convert "free" nations to its ideological position, the United States has in the twentieth century intervened in Latin America and in Asia for reasons which rarely involved national security. In the postwar period intervention has become, if anything, a more volatile issue because of the accelerating rate of decolonization in the Third World and because of the concern that this process will affect the balance between the two superpowers. More specifically, since Moscow and Washington have, more often than not, been unwilling to risk a head-on clash, they have chosen Third World nations for their ideological and military battlefields.

Signs of a new American orientation toward the Third World are difficult to discern. The rhetoric, but not the requisite operational evidence is there. Two examples from recent official pronouncements may illustrate the deficiency. During his first year in office President Nixon issued a broad restatement of Washington's objectives in Latin America, in which he acknowledged:

> For years we in the United States have pursued the illusion that alone we could remake continents. Conscious of our wealth and technology, seized by the force of our good intentions, driven by our habitual impatience . . . we have sometimes imagined that we knew what was best for everybody else and that we could and should make it happen. Well, experience has taught us better.[79]

Three years later, in a major foreign policy review, the President was once again careful to pay homage to the nonintervention tradition:

> In our view, the hemisphere community is big enough, mature enough and tolerant enough to accept a diversity of national approaches to human goals. We therefore deal realistically with governments as they are—right and left. We have strong preferences and hopes to see free democratic processes prevail, but we cannot impose our political structure on other nations.[80]

Yet Washington has remained stubbornly inflexible in its approach toward the Castro regime in Cuba. The fear that Castro's revolution might spread has dominated Latin American policy. Military and economic assistance has been lavished on regimes which have ignored the legitimate demands of their citizens.

[79] Text in the *New York Times*, 1 Nov. 1969, p. 14.
[80] Nixon, *U.S. Foreign Policy for the 1970's*, p. 96.

It is true that the blatant use of force represented by the Dominican Republic incursion has been avoided, but the Nixon Administration has not escaped charges of hemispheric interference. For example, there are disturbing indications that Washington may have encouraged attempts to keep the Marxist Salvadore Allende Gossens from winning the 1970 Chilean presidential election.[81] In a dramatically emotional speech to the United Nations General Assembly in December 1972, Allende charged that American corporations, banking interests, and governmental agencies were guilty of "serious aggression" against Chile:

> From the very day of our election triumph . . . we have felt the effects of large-scale external pressure against us, which tried to prevent the inauguration of a Government freely elected by the people and which has tried to bring it down ever since. It has . . . tried to cut us off from the world, to strangle our economy and to paralyze trade in our principal export, copper, and to deprive us of access to sources of international financing.[82]

If allegations regarding United States interference in Chile in the present decade are based on fact, additional evidence will exist that America's counterrevolutionary position has become more sophisticated.

The most sweeping statement of Washington's determination to assume a lower profile and to limit its far-flung peace-keeping commitments is the Guam, or Nixon, Doctrine of July 1969. At an informal background briefing and press conference on the island of Guam, the President informed his Asian hosts that the United States would modify its commitment to that part of the world.

> "But so far as our role is concerned, we must avoid the kind of policy that will make countries in Asia so dependent upon us that we are dragged into conflicts such as the one we have in Vietnam. . . . the United States is going to encourage, and has a right to expect, that [Asian security] will be increasingly handled by, and the responsibility for it taken by, the Asian nations themselves." [83]

Asians have joined Congressional and media critics in wondering what this new doctrine would mean in practice.

[81] The *New York Times*, 23 Mar. 1972, p. 16; 24 Mar. 1972, p. 1; 25 Mar. 1972, p. 1; 21 Mar. 1973, p. 1; 22 Mar. 1973, p. 1; and 29 Mar. 1973, p. 1.

[82] Allende speech reported in *Ibid.*, 5 Dec. 1972, p. 1. Also see Anthony Sampson, *The Sovereign State of ITT* (New York: Stein & Day, 1973), esp. chap. XI.

[83] Richard Wilson, ed., *Setting the Course—The First Year: Major Policy Statements by President Richard Nixon* (New York: Funk & Wagnalls, 1970), p. 304.

The new thrust seems to have been designed to meet repeated criticisms of the unrealistic sweep of Washington's anti-communist commitments. Kissinger has observed that at the core of the Nixon Doctrine is the recognition that "The United States alone cannot make itself responsible for every part of the world at every moment of time against every danger and to capitalize every opportunity." [84] Yet there is little evidence that the promised reduction in America's conventional forces around the world has led to a parallel reduction in political commitments. Since the doctrine's promulgation, the Vietnam War was widened with the Cambodian invasion of April 1970 and the mining of North Vietnam's harbors in May 1972. The air war over Indochina continued long after the signing of the Vietnamese armistice, and American involvement in the Mediterranean and the Middle East would appear to have been deepened since 1970.[85]

THE SEARCH FOR CAUSES

Since the Kennedy Administration escalated America's commitment to Vietnam, a weary and often skeptical national audience has been offered a variety of rationales for the intervention. Most official accounts have been characterized by a lack of sophistication and clarity. If the purpose of our presence has been to contain Red China, it has long been obvious that Peking has been "contained" by its monumental domestic problems and by its continuing rift with the USSR over the Sino-Soviet border, ideology, and expansion in Asia. If, as the 1966 Honolulu Declaration and Manila Communique insisted, the reason for the American presence was to uplift the lot of the Vietnamese people, the virtual destruction of that nation shatters such a thesis. As for the "domino" concept, it is reasonable to conclude that unless Asian nations deal successfully with their enormous social, political, and most especially economic problems, they will fall to the communists regardless of the fate of Vietnam.

Perhaps the most persistent reason given for American intervention has been to offer the Vietnamese a meaningful measure of choice in the conduct of their affairs. Nixon offered this rationale as *the* fundamental American goal when, on September 18, 1969, he told the United Nations General Assembly:

> In good conscience we cannot . . . accept a settlement that would arbitrarily dictate the political future of South Vietnam and deny to the

[84] Landau, *Kissinger*, p. 112.
[85] Evans and Novak, *Nixon in the White House*, p. 267. For criticism of the doctrine, see Morgenthau, *Truth and Power*, Chap. 39.

people of South Vietnam the basic right to determine their own future
free of outside interference. . . . To secure this right—and to secure this
principle—is our one limited but fundamental objective.[86]

The difficulty with such an objective is that freedom of choice in the
form of democratic elections may be irrelevant to the Vietnamese
experience. Also, the Thieu government has hardly been responsive to
such ideals. An influential group of Asian scholars has concluded that
despite the publicity given to South Vietnamese elections by American presidents and Vietnamese military men, these elections have
been "largely peripheral to the lives and struggle of the great majority
of Vietnamese. What makes them important is the way they have
been staged and used by a small clique of power-hungry men in
Saigon as well as by the U.S. government to deny peace and social
progress to Vietnam." [87]

New Left historian Gabriel Kolko observed a month after the
signing of the Vietnamese peace accord that the way Americans
"define the causes of the Indochina debacle will determine whether
they shall be intellectually prepared to anticipate future crises.
Conventional wisdom still attributes America's role in Vietnam to
accidents or bureaucratic myopia, thereby slighting the real meaning
of the consistency of American interventions in the Third World in
suppressing radical forces and preserving semicolonial societies." [88]
The Indochina tragedy was compounded by the eventual realization
of lost opportunities to cooperate creatively with other powers. The
war, after all, retarded for at least a decade America's "opening" to
China and the Soviet Union. At the same time it critically strained
Washington's relations with its economic and ideological partners. If
Americans permit themselves to be manipulated by ideological
abstractions and simplistic anti-communist campaigns, if they do not
insist upon careful, sophisticated definitions of threats to their survival
before being led into battle, then other Vietnams will be inevitable.

[86] Wilson, ed., *Setting the Course*, p. 310.
[87] The Committee of Concerned Asian Scholars, *The Indochina Story*, p. 150.
[88] Gabriel Kolko, "A War from Time to Time," the *New York Times*, 6 Mar. 1973, p. 41.

INDEX